This is a full rate Telegram, Cablegram or Radiogram unless otherwise indicated by signal in the check or in the address.

DL	DAY LETTER
NL	NIGHT LETTER
NM	NIGHT MESSAGE
LCO	DEFERRED CABLE
NLT	NIGHT CABLE LETTER
	RADIOGRAM

P9-APV-855

WESTERN UNION

CLASS OF SERVICE

This is a full-rate Telegram or Cablegram unless its deferred character is indicated by a suitable symbol above or preceding the address.

R. B. WHITE
PRESIDENT

NEWCOMB CARLTON
CHAIRMAN OF THE BOARD

J. C. WILLEVER
FIRST VICE-PRESIDENT

SYMBOLS

DL=Day Letter
NL=Night Letter
LC=Deferred Cable
NLT=Cable Night Letter
Ship Radiogram

The filing time shown in the date line on telegrams and day letters is STANDARD TIME at point of origin. Time of receipt is STANDARD TIME at point of destination

SB144 35 NL=TDS VANNUYS CALIF 26

HAROLD OBER=

40 EAST 49 ST NYK=

DEC 27 1938

METRO NOT RENEWING TO MY GREAT PLEASURE BUT WILL FINISH
CURIE THERES LOTS OF OTHER WORK OFFERED STOP HOWEVER PLEASE
SAY NOTHING WHATEVER TO PERKINS OR TO SCOTTIE WHO WOULD NOT
UNDERSTAND STOP AM WRITING=

SCOTT.

AND THIRTY TODAY

SIGNS

DL = Day Letter
NM = Night Message
NL = Night Letter
LC = Deferred Cable
NLT = Cable Night Letter
Ship Radiogram

1220-S

shown on all messages, is STANDARD TIME.

1934 FEB 21 PM 2 53

MINUTES IN TRANSIT
FULL-RATE DAY LETTER

TIDE ME OVER THE
ON WITHOUT
E PROMINENT
ZATION OTHERWISE
TO THE PICTURES
BE DECIDED
MORROW AND WANT
OULD LIKE TO PLAY

WESTERN UNION

CLASS OF SERVICE

This is a full-rate Telegram or Cablegram unless its deferred character is indicated by a suitable symbol above or preceding the address.

R. B. WHITE
PRESIDENT

NEWCOMB CARLTON
CHAIRMAN OF THE BOARD

J. C. WILLEVER
FIRST VICE-PRESIDENT

1201

SYMBOLS

DL=Day Letter
NL=Night Letter
LC=Deferred Cable
NLT=Cable Night Letter
Ship Radiogram

The filing time shown in the date line on telegrams and day letters is STANDARD TIME at point of origin. Time of receipt is STANDARD TIME at point of destination

SA47 77 NL=TDS VANNUYS CALIF 13

HAROLD OBER=

40 EAST 49 ST NYK=

STILL FLABBERGASTED AT YOUR ABRUPT CHANGE IN POLICY AFTER 20
YEARS ESPECIALLY WITH STORY IN YOUR HANDS STOP MY COMMERCIAL
VALUE CANT HAVE SUNK FROM 60 THOUSAND TO NOTHING BECAUSE OF
A SLOW HEALING LUNG CAVITY STOP AFTER 30 PICTURE OFFERS
DURING THE MONTHS I WAS IN BED SWANSON NOW PROMISES NOTHING
FOR ANOTHER WEEK STOP CANT YOU ARRANGE A FEW HUNDRED ADVANCE
FROM A MAGAZINE SO I CAN EAT TODAY AND TOMORROW STOP WONT
YOU WIRE=

SCOTT.

THE COMPANY WILL APPRECIATE SUGGESTIONS FROM ITS PATRONS CONCERNING ITS SERVICE

Form 1201 S

SIGNS

DL = Day Letter
NM = Night Message
NL = Night Letter
LCO = Deferred Cable
CLT = Cable Letter
WLT = Week-End Letter

1201-S

VICE-PRESIDENT

se shown on all messages, is STANDARD TIME.

1928 MAR 18 PM 9 16

MAR 19 1928

NEWYORK TOMORROW
RED FIFTY DOLLARS
COUNT ON ABOUT
DAY OR HAD I BETTER
L TRY TO GET IT TO
USUAL

WESTERN UNION

CLASS OF SERVICE

This is a full-rate Telegram or Cablegram unless its deferred character is indicated by a suitable symbol above or preceding the address.

R. B. WHITE
PRESIDENT

NEWCOMB CARLTON
CHAIRMAN OF THE BOARD

J. C. WILL
FIRST VICE-PRESIDENT

(48)

SYMBOLS

DL = Day Letter
NM = Night Message
NL = Night Letter
LC = Deferred Cable
NLT = Cable Night Letter
Ship Radiogram

The filing time shown in the date line on telegrams and day letters is STANDARD TIME at point of origin. Time of receipt is STANDARD TIME at point of destination.

Received at 41 East 46th St., New York

NBM13 57 DL=BALTIMORE MD 28 843A

1935 DEC 28 AM 9 50

HAROLD OBER=

40 EAST 49 ST=

HAVE TRIED LIFE ON SUBSISTANCE LEVEL AND IT DOESNT WORK
STOP I THOUGHT IF I COULD HAVE THIS MONEY I COULD HOLD MY
HEAD UP AND GO ON STOP WHAT YOU SUGGEST POSTPONES BY HALF A
YEAR THE LIQUIDATION WE BOTH WANT STOP PLEASE CARRY ME OVER
THE SECOND GWEN STORY AND GIVE ME TWENTY SEVEN HUNDRED=

FITZGERALD.

AS EVER,
SCOTT FITZ–

ALSO BY MATTHEW J. BRUCCOLI

The Composition of Tender Is the Night:
    A Study of the Manuscripts
Checklist of F. Scott Fitzgerald *(compiler)*
Profile of F. Scott Fitzgerald *(compiler)*
F. Scott Fitzgerald in His Own Time:
    A Miscellany *(editor, with Jackson Bryer)*
Ernest Hemingway, Cub Reporter:
    Kansas City Star Stories *(editor)*
Ernest Hemingway's Apprenticeship:
    Oak Park 1916–1917 *(editor)*
The Fitzgerald/Hemingway Annual *(editor)*

AS EVER,

J. B. LIPPINCOTT
COMPANY
Philadelphia and New York

Letters Between
F. Scott Fitzgerald
and His Literary Agent
Harold Ober
1919-1940

SCOTT FITZ–

Edited by
MATTHEW J. BRUCCOLI

With the Assistance of
JENNIFER McCABE ATKINSON

Foreword by
SCOTTIE FITZGERALD SMITH

Letters from F. Scott Fitzgerald which have been published in *The Letters of F. Scott Fitzgerald*, edited by Andrew Turnbull (copyright © 1963 by Frances Scott Fitzgerald Lanahan), are reprinted with the permission of Charles Scribner's Sons.

Copyright © 1972 by S. J. Lanahan, Trustee; Anne Reid Ober; and Matthew J. Bruccoli

All rights reserved
First edition

Printed in the United States of America

U.S. Library of Congress Cataloging in Publication Data

Fitzgerald, Francis Scott Key, 1896–1940.
  As ever, Scott Fitz—.

  I. Ober, Harold, 1881–1959. II. Bruccoli, Matthew Joseph, birth date, ed. III. Title.
PS3511.I9Z554   813'.5'2 [B]   71–156367
ISBN–0–397–00732–9

To Alexander Clark
Curator of Manuscripts, Princeton University Library:
friend, counselor, scholar

and
Anne Ober
who preserved these letters

Contents

A section of illustrations will be found following page 170.

Foreword

Harold Ober, born circa 1881, was a rare and precious human being. I should know, because I lived with him for four years during World War II; shared his anguish every morning as we turned on the radio, hoping neither of his two sons (nor my husband) was involved in some new parachute landing in Europe or Pacific island invasion; walked with him through the woods every morning from his enchanting house to the Scarsdale railroad station; learned everything I know about music from him—Rachmaninoff, Shostakovich, and Prokofiev were his favorite composers at the time, though his wife, Anne, tells me that later he preferred Gustav Mahler to them all; and played terrible tennis with him on the court belonging to our neighbors, Bob Haas of Random House and his wife Merle, our closest family friends. Though I didn't know it at the time, it was Bob who had lent "Gramps," as I called him for some long-forgotten reason, the money to see my father through during the depression years.

Though he had been a fine tennis player (he was good at all sports except golf, which he was too impatient to enjoy), he then played a wicked "veteran's game," lobbing balls high into the air to catch his younger opponents off-base at the net. He played with the same intensity of purpose with which he often disappeared into his darkroom at night, after he was tired of reading manuscripts, to develop his near-professional pictures. Of all his many hobbies (he was a skilled carpenter), his pet, his dream, his love was his garden. Later, after I had left, he grew prize gladiolas, but during the years when I helped him occasionally, it was succulent vegetables of every variety. His garden was his great escape from the woes of frustrated authors—for all his authors, not just my father, brought their personal problems to him—and from the war. He often pretended he was going out to work in the garden when he was, in fact, found stretched out, sound asleep in the sun, on his favorite deck chair behind the asparagus.

I certainly didn't know, back when I was fourteen or fifteen and Daddy decided to dump me on the Obers for a summer month—Hollywood being no fit place for a growing girl in his opinion—that Harold Ober was the most celebrated literary agent of his time. Actually, he hated the term "agent," smacking as it does of contracts and money. He preferred the term "author's representative." Corey Ford, one of his favorite authors, goes one step further in his book *The Time of Laughter*: "A seventh [of the great editors he had known] would be Harold Ober, whose infallible judgment and taste and rigid integrity made him the greatest editor of them all."

My reluctance to be sent to Dromore Road, when all the teen-age action was in Baltimore where my friends were, was matched only by the reluctance of the Ober boys—Richard, my own age, now the most responsible of government officials and owner of a small farm of his own in the country outside Washington, D.C., and Nathaniel, two years younger, now a superintendent of schools in Minneapolis—to accept this "instant sister" who had been thrust upon them. It was more through luck than cunning that I was eventually able to win a certain grudging acceptance of my presence. There was a movie house in White Plains that their father refused to go to, and in the next block was a Schrafft's which served "dusty sundaes," a concoction made of vanilla ice cream, chocolate sauce, and powdered malt. Wanting to give Scott's daughter a good time, Gramps —I still called him Mr. Ober then—made the supreme sacrifice of taking us to the movies at least once a week, and watching us make pigs of ourselves afterward. I'll never forget Dick's pained expression when Nat said to me, the night I was leaving, as he rocked back and forth on the hind legs of the dining-room chair (a habit which drove his mother crazy): "Well, we sure don't much like having you here, but I'll say this for you: Father's a lot nicer to us when you're around." The battle was clearly won, and from then on I was a full-fledged member of the household.

Hospitable as the Obers always were to me—and that very first summer I became hooked on the apple trees, the shaggy Briard dogs, and the New-England-in-Westchester-County atmosphere that captivated everyone lucky enough to be invited—it wasn't until I was graduated from Vassar, partly thanks to Gramps who advanced me most of the tuition money after Daddy died, that I really got to know Harold Ober as a friend rather a parent-substitute. Most evenings during the war, we used to catch the 6:07 from Grand Central Station together, and I can still hear that sonorous litany: "One Hundred and Twenty-FIFTH Street, Mount Ver-NON,

Brooooonx-ville, Fleet-WOOD, TUCK-ahoe, Crrrrrest-WOOD, Scaaaaaars-DALE." He refused to look out the window as we passed the slums of Harlem and the Bronx because, as he said, "I don't like prying into their private lives." The plain fact is that he was a terrible ostrich and didn't want to think about those miserable souls in their crowded, ugly tenements. He would bury himself in the *World-Telegram*, the *Sun*, and the *Post* until he came to Westbrook Pegler's column, which he would read aloud, eyebrows bristling with fury. We hated Westbrook Pegler because he attacked our hero, President Roosevelt, and made fun of Eleanor Roosevelt, whom we extravagantly admired. Gramps never tolerated any of those Eleanor jokes which were so popular at the time. He was a liberal Democrat to the core, and remained so, inflexibly, until he died in 1959.

Back at the house, if it was summer ("Auntie," as I called her and still do, generally met us at the station, the walk home being largely uphill), we would hurry out of our city clothes and down to the garden to pick the supper tomatoes, cucumbers, beans, corn, strawberries, or whatever was abundantly luxuriating in the garden. For this was no ordinary garden: my mother called it "the garden of the Three Bears." It was a work of art, so perfect in detail you half expected to see Mr. McGregor come chasing out with a rake after Peter Rabbit. Walter Edmonds, author of *Drums Along the Mohawk* and a great personal friend, feels it was symbolic of him: "Everything about it was impeccable, for he would never let a weed grow larger than a hair. In the same way, he made me write and rewrite, for he always strove for perfection."

After dinner, if it was winter, we'd sit in front of the roaring fire in the book-lined living room, with the music on (sometimes records, sometimes WQXR if we wanted to follow the news every hour, as for instance when Dick's 17th Airborne Division landed in Germany during the Battle of the Bulge). That was when Gramps read his manuscripts, for he found it impossible to concentrate with all the interruptions in the office. If he liked what he was reading, he was so cheerful he'd even get himself an extra piece of the delicious chocolate cake that Minnie Trent, the housekeeper, always kept in the pantry for him. Often, if he didn't like the book or story (for he detested bad writing and always claimed it gave him the ulcer from which he suffered intermittently for twenty years), the bushy eyebrows would form two arches of disapproval, and he would cough and go down to inspect the recalcitrant furnace or occupy himself in the darkroom. Occasionally, if he had doubts, he'd ask Auntie or me to read something for him. "I think this is trash," I remember him saying about a lady novelist's pretentious effort, "but she's disguised it so cleverly I'm not sure."

Anne Ober, always loyal, always devoted, and provider with the aforementioned Minnie of the most delicious meals I have ever feasted upon—shrimp curry was the *specialité de la maison* until Gramps developed his ulcer—had been an editor herself when they met, having quit her job on the magazine *Suburban Life* to go to Paris with the Red Cross during World War I. After being turned down by the Army for some slight physical defect, Harold Ober was sent to Paris by the War Department to decide whether dogs should be used by our armed forces, for he was by then a well-known dog fancier, owner of champions, and judge, especially of Airedales. He was thirty-six, a confirmed bachelor, living a virtually hermitic life in what was then the woods of Scarsdale and riding his horse to the station every morning, which his Japanese manservant would lead back. Auntie loves to tell the story of how this Japanese gentleman hid all his dishes because Harold gave them to his dogs to lick after he had finished dinner, and therefore the man no longer considered them fit for human use.

Having decided that dogs, though being successfully used by the French Army, were not practical for ours, HO signed on with the Red Cross in Paris and stayed until after the Armistice in 1918, when he and Anne made the return trip home on the *Baltic* together. "He spent the entire trip home reciting all the reasons why it would be bad for me to marry him," she recalls. "All about the hardships I would have to endure in the country, and so on." By the time the ship landed, he had her practically convinced, but married they were the following fall in the Cathedral of St. John the Divine in New York. It is characteristic that they began their honeymoon at the Forest Hills tennis matches, then picked up an ailing Airedale in Tarrytown and proceeded to his native town of New Ipswich, New Hampshire, where the Auberts, as the family was then called (later changed to Obear, then Ober), had moved some two centuries before. Anne remembers passing the small ancestral farmhouse where they were to spend their honeymoon three times before she grew suspicious that nobody who had grown up in New Ipswich could possibly be that lost. It was typical of Gramps to be scared that she might be disappointed. He hated imposing himself on people, just as he hated being imposed upon by any but those he loved.

He was his own man at any time, in any place, and under any

circumstances; no compromises to be contemplated. He never felt quite comfortable in the Madison Avenue two-martinis-before-lunch atmosphere, and his shy New England manner seemed strangely out of place on those few occasions when he felt he must attend the literary cocktail parties he so detested. As one of his closest friends, Randolph Compton of Scarsdale, puts it, "He was perhaps the most upright, forthright person I have ever known, with an infinite capacity for friendship and an infinite appreciation of values." Yet he was never stuffy, except about the social scene in New York or Scarsdale; nothing could get him to a party, though I do think Auntie once succeeded in getting him to the wedding reception of the daughter of a friend. As I remember—perhaps I am flattering myself—he took one sip of champagne and never left my side during the entire reception. He hated mobs of people; he preferred sitting under his apple trees with cozy friends like the Comptons or Horton and "Vio" Heath, two of his favorites.

Asked for an anecdote about him, the Heaths wrote: "Harold was simply the opposite of the type of person who builds a personal legend of anecdotal material. He was too gentle, too sensitive, too self-effacing. He did not lead crusades, make wisecracks, get drunk, or go in for brawls and vendettas . . . but he was lots of *fun*!" Horton Heath also recalls that Gramps used to run up the nine flights of stairs to his office on 49th Street, to the consternation of everybody else in the building. He was something of a health addict, and Merle Haas remembers his running around her meadow with Nat, then a chubby twelve-year-old, before breakfast. After skiing with the Comptons in Vermont when he was over sixty-five, he returned to the Harmon, New York, station in a cast and on crutches to greet Auntie with the remark, "What an old fool you married!"

He was personally fond of many of his authors, of whom Daddy was undoubtedly the most demanding. Catherine Drinker Bowen, Paul Gallico, and Philip Wylie are among those who used to be part of our bucolic life in Scarsdale. Walter Edmonds told this story as one of a group of recollections of him published in *Esquire* (under the title "The Saint"): "I learned indirectly that Harold had been a varsity oar, just as his son, Dick, was to become one in his turn at Harvard. For many years their crimson-bladed varsity oars lay across two beams in the living room of the red house in Scarsdale which had been built round the frame of an old barn . . . when Nat made the junior varsity, Harold and Dick fashioned a half-sized oar and slung it on a wire cradle between their own."

I want to guard against making him seem perfect, however; he was too disagreeable at the bridge table ever to qualify for that encomium. Whenever their friends Mabel Baldwin or Helen Noyes would appear for the week-end bridge game, I would run for cover, unless I was drafted as the figurative, and usually literal, dummy. "It was the only time he was horrible," says Auntie. He taught her to play bridge but, according to their friends, pupil outdistanced teacher and Gramps found Auntie's supremacy intolerable. I can remember one argument about who should have bid three no-trump instead of four spades that went on for two days. There, in a nut-shell, was the dichotomy: the man of the soil and the outdoors, who should have been a farmer, a musician, or a teacher, yet whose competitive instinct was so strong that he was able to build a business which still bears his name and has tentacles all over the world.

I adored Harold Ober. I wish I could climb on the 6:07 with him again and say, "Hi, Gramps!" I don't know whether he did more for my father or for me, but as I think of him in his New England heaven, surrounded by rocks and rills, fresh tomatoes, and Briard dogs, wearing a threadbare tweed jacket and peering at the world from under those expressive, bushy, pepper-and-salt eyebrows, I remember him not only with love but as one of those rare people in this world of whom it can be truly said that he was a man of TOTAL integrity.

SCOTTIE FITZGERALD SMITH

August, 1971

Introduction

Perhaps the three most valuable attributes of an agent are his emotional detachment from a very emotional profession, his ability to organize the bargaining power of his clients, and his management of the businsss side of a writer's career.

—Raymond Chandler, "Ten Percent of Your Life"

The terms of professional writing are these: that it provides a living for the author, like any other job; that it is a main and prolonged, rather than intermittent or sporadic, resource for the writer; that it is produced with the hope of extended sale in the open market, like any article of commerce; and that it is written with reference to buyers' tastes and reading habits. The problem of the professional writer is not identical with that of the literary artist; but when a literary artist is also a professional writer, he cannot solve the problems of the one function without reference to the other.

—William Charvat, *The Profession of Authorship in America, 1800–1870*

Harold Ober was a conventional man who nevertheless had an extremely unconventional relationship with F. Scott Fitzgerald. But all relationships with Fitzgerald were unconventional. Ober always preferred to call himself an "author's representative," which helps to explain why he departed from the business rules of an "agent" to serve as Fitzgerald's representative in the largest sense. Ober did not take an agent's 10 per cent and run; he became involved with his authors, most of all with Fitzgerald.

Harold Ober became emotionally involved with F. Scott Fitzgerald, especially after 1931, when the Fitzgerald dream of success became a nightmare. He lent him money when there was only a fifty-fifty chance that it would be repaid; and he assumed responsibility for Fitzgerald's teen-age daughter, Scottie. When in 1939

Ober refused at last to begin a new cycle of debt, the resulting break was painful to both men. Perhaps Fitzgerald—on paper—understood their relationship better than did Ober. In his 1938 story, "Financing Finnegan," Fitzgerald described the response of Finnegan's (Fitzgerald's) publisher (Maxwell Perkins) and agent (Ober) to the writer's appeals for money: "The two men had entered into a silent conspiracy to cheer each other up about Finnegan. Their investment in him, in his future, had reached a sum so considerable that Finnegan belonged to them. They could not bear to hear a word against him—even from themselves." This story was published in *Esquire* while Fitzgerald was still paying off his debts out of his Hollywood earnings. Since Fitzgerald always dealt directly with Arnold Gingrich of *Esquire*, Ober did not receive a commission on the $250 sale, a matter of small financial, but great emotional, import between them.

Harold Ober did a superb job of marketing Fitzgerald's stories, which were, of course, the author's main source of income before Hollywood. Between 1919 and 1929, Fitzgerald's *Saturday Evening Post* story price went from $400 to $4,000. But during the Depression, when the magazines no longer paid big money, Fitzgerald began interposing himself between the editors and his agent and thereby weakened Ober's power to place stories. The only context in which Fitzgerald's behavior can be understood is his desperate frustration at having to pay his wife's hospital bills and his daughter's tuition out of sums he would have considered tip money a few years before.

Although Fitzgerald was hampered by his inability to handle money, it is utterly typical of him to have kept a detailed ledger for his 1919–1936 earnings.* His total earnings before he went to Hollywood were $394,928 (after commissions), of which $225,784 came from stories. The sixty-four *Post* stories brought $193,300—of which Ober received 10 per cent.

Fitzgerald's book earnings through 1936 were $66,588 (including advances and serial payments).† Ober received no commission on the book royalties, for Fitzgerald dealt directly with Scribners. He

---

*All the figures in the editorial notes are based on Fitzgerald's arithmetic.

†This is what the books made through 1931: *This Side of Paradise*, $14,372; *The Beautiful and Damned*, $15,994; *The Great Gatsby*, $6,889; *Flappers and Philosophers*, $3,813; *Tales of the Jazz Age*, $3,416; *All the Sad Young Men*, $4,012; *The Vegetable*, $1,242. After 1931 Fitzgerald stopped itemizing his book royalties because the yearly totals were so small.

had already contracted for *This Side of Paradise* before coming to the Paul Revere Reynolds agency, which was primarily an agency for dealing with magazines; Reynolds had very little interest in handling books.

Ober, despite himself, became Fitzgerald's banker and accountant. He met almost all of Fitzgerald's endless requests for advances and somehow kept the family going during the terrible years of 1932–1937. But he was never able to keep Fitzgerald solvent. Even in 1930 and 1931 when Fitzgerald's income from stories was $25,000 and $31,500 respectively, Ober was advancing money against unwritten stories.

Their relationship was a mixture of business and the personal—as can happen between doctors and patients. The nature of Fitzgerald's literary relationship with Ober is in certain ways obscure. Their letters rarely discuss purely literary matters, apart from the marketability of Fitzgerald's magazine work; but Ober did not handle the novels. Clearly, Ober valued Fitzgerald's talent, but he nowhere indicated that he regarded Fitzgerald as one of the major American writers. The highest praise Ober gave Fitzgerald came on 19 May 1931: "I believe, and others who are much more competent judges than I, believe that you ought to go further than any American writer and I think now is the time for you to get down to hard work and finish the novel." However, this praise must be considered in terms of Ober's obvious desire to encourage Fitzgerald to write *Tender Is the Night*. If I am right about Ober's estimation of Fitzgerald's stature—an estimation in which he was not alone (before 1945 almost nobody considered him a great writer)—his dedication to his friend Scott is the more moving. There is always a mixture of motives in helping one whose greatness is unquestioned; but Ober's goodness to Fitzgerald was not for the sake of posterity. It was a matter of humanity, of New England conscience. Like Nick Carraway with Gatsby, Ober was drawn into a relationship with a man whose life style he disapproved of. Ober saved Fitzgerald as best he could simply because there was nobody else around to do it.

Harold Ober was a Yankee from New Hampshire. He was born at Lake Winnipesaukee in 1881 and died in 1959 at the age of seventy-eight. A member of the class of 1905 at Harvard, he worked his way through college as a tutor and made the varsity crew. "I left Harvard with the idea of becoming an author. After two years in England and France I came to New York in 1907 and took a job with a literary agency, where I became so involved in the lives of authors that I abandoned all idea of myself becoming one," he wrote in his Harvard 50th Anniversary Class Report. He went to France with the Red Cross in 1917 and became a partner in the Reynolds firm in 1919. Just before the Crash in 1929, he opened his own literary agency, which became Harold Ober Associates in 1949. Although the tradition exists that Fitzgerald's reply to Ober's announcement that he was setting up his own firm was to wire UNRESERVEDLY YOURS, the only surviving wire reads FOLLOWING YOU NATURALLY.

If there is an oversimplified key to Harold Ober's unlikely and brilliant career, it may be the fact that he had wanted to be a writer.[*] There is no evidence that he made a real start as a writer. So he did the next best thing: He took care of writers—most of all, F. Scott Fitzgerald. Catherine Drinker Bowen has described his feelings about Fitzgerald:

Harold worried more about Fitzgerald than any author he ever took care of, and with reason. Yet even when Fitzgerald's drinking had brought him to near ruin, Harold kept on with him, hoping against hope. Once I walked into the office at 40 East 49th Street and found Harold at his desk, reading manuscript and looking depressed, a condition unusual with him. When I asked the reason, he passed me some typed sheets and asked what I could make of them. The pages were interlined, written over in red ink, blotched, almost illegible, and made no sense at all. Harold said that was the way Scott's stories had been coming in lately. He got up and stood with his back to me, looking out the window; I saw him take out his handkerchief and blow his nose. I think it was as though one of his own sons had defected and gone past the point of no return.[†]

Most of the letters in this volume are owned by Mrs. Harold Ober, and are identified by "AO" (for Anne Ober). Unidentified letters belong to Frances Fitzgerald Smith. Most of the remaining letters are in the Princeton University Library: some with the Fitzgerald papers, some with the Scribner archive, and some donated by Harold Ober. All the Princeton Library letters are identified by "PU." There are lacunae in both ends of the correspondence which our research has failed to fill. Many letters have simply disappeared. Ober's end of the correspondence is very thin before 1926, and the years 1931 to 1934 and 1940 are full of holes.

---

[*]Mrs. Ober, however, says: "I never felt Harold was a frustrated writer. . . . His real wish was to study music and he would have liked to be a composer" (Anne Ober to the editor, 30 November 1970).
[†]"Harold Ober, Literary Agent," *Atlantic Monthly*, CCVI (July 1960), 35–40.

It is regrettable that this volume does not include all the surviving Fitzgerald/Ober correspondence. The economics of publishing compelled us to omit some routine business letters and many wires. These omitted wires are simple requests for money by Fitzgerald (SEND 500) and Ober's acknowledgments. But in some ways these financial wires are basic to their relationship. It is impossible to understand Fitzgerald's career without understanding his feelings about money. Nevertheless, something had to be cut; and we were obliged to omit 28 Fitzgerald-to-Ober letters, 109 Ober-to-Fitzgerald letters, 110 Fitzgerald-to-Ober wires, and 155 Ober-to-Fitzgerald wires. Wherever possible, wires that say something in addition to the money requests have been included; e.g., STARTING STORY SEND 500.

Unless otherwise indicated, the letters are ink holographs (i.e., hand-written). Thus, "ALS (pencil)" indicates an autograph letter, signed, written in pencil. "TLS" indicates a typed letter, signed, and "(cc)" indicates a carbon copy.

All the letters and wires are printed in diplomatic (exact) transcriptions. Since it is impossible to duplicate Fitzgerald's holograph letters short of reproducing them in photo-facsimile, some typographical accommodations have been required:

1. Interlineal insertions have been incorporated into the letters, but are always set in italic type—the only use that has been made of italics in the body of the letters. Underlinings in the original letters have been printed as underlinings.

2. Recoverable deleted words are printed within brackets. Obliterated words are indicated by the word "obliterated" within brackets. The only other use made of brackets is to supply Harold Ober's name at the close of carbon-copy letters.

No corrections *of any kind* have been made in the letters and wires. They are all printed here exactly the way they were written. A letter is a personal document and provides an intimate glimpse of the writer as well as insights into his writing habits. It would be a distortion to correct these letters for publication, precisely because they were not written for publication. The chief responsibility of an editor of letters is not to edit, but to preserve the character of the letters. The reader of a letter volume should be confident that he has the letters in the purity of their original form. The only textual emendations we have made relate to holographic problems —it has been necessary to cross a *t* or dot an *i*.

Normally a name is footnoted only the first time it appears. But sometimes the identification is repeated when there has been an extended period since the first note. Fitzgerald frequently neglected to date his letters, but nearly all were stamped with a received date at the Ober office. The chronology for transatlantic letters employs a ten- to fourteen-day interval.

I have many debts. First, this book would not have come into being without the generous participation of Anne Reid Ober. There is no way to acknowledge her help without using the conventional language of appreciation; but she has been special. Ivan Von Auw, Jr., of Harold Ober Associates wrapped the package. Genevieve Young, my editor, is a wonder. Nobody can do serious work on Fitzgerald without the help of Wanda Randall and Alexander Clark of the Princeton University Library.

I also thank H. N. Swanson, Jeanne Bennett, C. Grove Smith, R. L. Samsell, I. S. Skelton, John C. Guilds, Frances Kroll Ring, Catherine Drinker Bowen, William Dozier, Mr. and Mrs. Albert Hackett, Alan Margolies, Roger Mayer, Anne Louise Davis, Constance Smith Whitman, Dorothy Olding, John N. Wheeler, James L. W. West III, Betty Trueblood, Pam Barrett, Richard Taylor, and Arlyn Bruccoli. The English Department of the University of South Carolina provided me with a summer research grant for this project.

MATTHEW J. BRUCCOLI

I
EARLY SUCCESS

1919-1923

After Fitzgerald's discharge from the Army in February 1919, he tried to make a fast success in the New York advertising field in order to marry Zelda Sayre. In June she broke the engagement, and Fitzgerald returned to St. Paul, Minnesota, to revise the novel he had written in the Army.

At the time Fitzgerald first approached Paul Revere Reynolds, he was twenty-three years old, and his first novel, This Side of Paradise, *had just been accepted by Charles Scribner's Sons. In an article for* American Cavalcade *(October 1937) titled "Early Success," Fitzgerald said of these first days: "Then the postman rang and that day I quit work and ran along the streets stopping automobiles to tell friends and acquaintances about it—my novel* This Side of Paradise *was accepted for publication. That week the postman rang and rang, and I paid off my terrible small debts, bought a suit, and woke up every morning with a world of ineffable top-loftiness and promise.*

"While I waited for the novel to appear, the metamorphosis of amateur into professional began to take place—a sort of stitching together of your whole life into a pattern of work so that the end of one job is automatically the beginning of another."

> 599 Summit Ave.
> St. Paul, Minn
> October 28th, 1919

Mr. Paul Revere Reynolds
70 Fifth Avenue
New York City

Dear Sir:

Tho Scribner has accepted my first novel and I have sold several stories to <u>Scribner's Magazine</u> and to <u>The Smart Set</u> I am not having much luck with my manuscripts in general. Mrs. Grace Flandrau* suggested that I send one to you to see if you would undertake the disposal of any of my stuff.

The enclosed manuscript, <u>Nest Feathers</u>,† has never been submitted anywhere. If you feel you can place it anywhere your regular terms will be satisfactory to me.

---

*Grace Hodgson Flandrau of St. Paul was a novelist of the 1920s and 1930s.

†"Head and Shoulders," *The Saturday Evening Post*, 21 February 1920—Fitzgerald's first *Post* story, for which he was paid $400.

I'd liked to ask you also if you object to handling manuscripts typed in single space.

Hoping to hear from you, I am

Very truly yours
F. Scott Fitzgerald.

ALS, 1p. (AO)

599 Summit Ave.
St. Paul, Minn
November 1st 1919.

Mr. Paul Revere Reynolds

Dear Sir:

I am sending you another story[‡] to see if you can undertake to place it also. It was with Scribner for awhile but was returned with the remark that "it is a clever expression of a character and well worth publishing but ect. ect."

Hoping to hear from you

Very Truly Yours
F Scott Fitzgerald

ALS, 1p. (AO)

599 Summit Ave.
St. Paul, Minn
November 4th, 1919

Mr. Paul Revere Reynolds:

Dear Sir:

I am enclosing you a story which in its original form of ten thousand words, though it drew several personal letters was turned down by four magazines.[§] The present version has been cut to seven thousand words, entirely [w] rewritten and greatly improved.

Hoping to hear from you I am

Very Sincerely Yours
F. Scott Fitzgerald

ALS, 1p. (AO)

[‡]A note in the bottom margin, not in Fitzgerald's hand, reads: "A Smile for Sylvo". Published as "The Smilers," *The Smart Set,* June 1920.

[§]A note in the bottom margin, not in Fitzgerald's hand, reads: "Barbara Bobs Her Hair". Later "Bernice Bobs Her Hair," *The Saturday Evening Post,* 1 May 1920.

599 Summit Ave
St. Paul, Nov. 11th

Mr. Paul Revere Reynolds

Dear Sir:

I recieved your letter acknowledging the reciept of my three stories. I'm going to ask you to hold any communication you may have for me as to their fate, for I'm leaving here Saturday and arrive in New York about the 22nd when I'll come in and see you.

Very Sincerely
F. Scott Fitzgerald

ALS, 1p. (AO)

During November 1919 Fitzgerald visited Zelda Sayre in Montgomery, Alabama, and she agreed to marry him.

Dear Mr. Reynolds:

This is the best story I ever wrote.¶ I wrote it with the Saturday Evening Post in mind and, if in your judgement there's a chance there or with the Cosmopolitan, I wish you'd try them because I think its worth at least $250.00.

I shall drop in to see you next week in New York

Sincerly
F. Scott Fitzgerald

November 14th
599 Summit Ave.
St. Paul, Minn.

ALS, 1p. (AO)

At some point in November 1919, Fitzgerald became the special client of Harold Ober, a partner in the Reynolds Agency, who was responsible for the new or young clients.

Dear Mr. Ober—

Do you think this is Post stuff?# Recieved your letter about

¶Possibly "Variety." Published as "Dalyrimple Goes Wrong," *The Smart Set*, February 1920.

#A note in the bottom margin, not in Fitzgerald's hand, reads: "The Ice Palace". Published in *The Saturday Evening Post*, 22 May 1920.

<u>Variet</u>y and have sent it to Smart Set. If you sell any stories I wish you'd wire at my expense.

F. Scott Fitzgerald

599 Summit Ave
St. Paul, Minn
12/10/19

ALS, 1p. (AO)

Dear Mr. Ober:

I've been quite dissapointed not to hear that you've sold the <u>Ice Palace</u>. I had an idea that the Post was going in strongly for local color and atmosphere stories—and I suppose that the 8000 word length is hard to dispose of elsewhere.

This is an odd sort of thing I just finished.*

Sincerly

F. Scott Fitzgerald

599 Summit Ave
St. Paul, Minn.
12/19/19

ALS, 1p. (AO)

599 Summit Ave. St. Paul, Minn

Dear Mr. Ober—

I was talking to Mrs. Flandrau last night and her saying that she'd gotten offers for movie rights to her Post story reminded me of something I wanted to ask you. Is there money in writing movies? Do you sell scenarios?

The day I called you were out + I talked to Mr. Reynolds. I asked him not to offer my stuff to <u>Smart Set</u>. You see they only pay $40.00 so they'd know you'd tried everybody else first and as I'm on rather good terms with Mr. Nathan[†] and intend to send him half a dozen little one act plays a year, I want to keep on terms with them.

About <u>Scribners</u>—its not as important. I know them very well personally—they're bringing out my novel[‡] in Feb. + have bought 2 stories. But Mr Reynolds told me that to get better prices he'd prefer to have controll of everything I write. but as Scribner pays

---

*A note in the bottom margin, not in Fitzgerald's hand, reads: "Myra Meets his Family". Published in *The Saturday Evening Post*, 20 March 1920.

†George Jean Nathan, coeditor of *The Smart Set*.

‡ *This Side of Paradise.*

only $150.00 I cant afford to write much for them. They have seen the two manuscripts you have at present. Anyway I'm not going to send them any more stuff until they've published the things they have now. The two you have—if you can't sell 'em send 'em here + I'll either rewrite them or try Smart Set.

Go ahead + have the soiled manuscripts retyped. I'll fix up "Barbara Bobs her Hair"—and I'm also writing a lot more.

One more question—Is there any market at all for the cynical or pessimistic story except Smart Set or does realism bar a story from any well-paying magazine no matter how cleverly its done?

I gave your adress to a very clever young writer who was in my class at Princeton. His name is Biggs§ + I think perhaps you can get him better luck than he's having by himself.

Sincerely
F Scott Fitzgerald

ALS, 3pp. n.d. (AO)

F. Scott Fitzgerald, Esq.
599 Summit Avenue
St. Paul, Minn.

Dear Mr. Fitzgerald:

I have just received a letter this morning from the Saturday Evening Post saying that they will be will glad to keep "The Ice Palace". They will pay four hundred dollars for it.

Yours sincerely
Harold Ober

TLS, 1p. n.d.—December 1919. Fitzgerald pasted this letter in his scrapbook.

599 Summit Ave.
St. Paul, Minn
Dec 30th, 1919

Dear Mr. Ober:

I'm delighted about the "Ice Palace".

About Myra Meets his Family—I'm afraid its no good and if you agree with me don't hesitate to send it back. Perhaps if you give me an idea what the matter with it is I'll be able to rewrite it. About A Smile for Sylvo I'm sure if none of the wealthy magazines want it I can sell it to Smart Set.

---

§John Biggs, Jr., Fitzgerald's roommate at Princeton, wrote two novels. He was executor of Fitzgerald's estate and is now a judge on the U.S. Court of Appeals.

I'm just finishing up a really excellent story, the best I have done.¶ I will send it along next week.

Best Wishes

F. Scott Fitzgerald

P.S.   Are you one of the Baltimore Obers that went to Princeton?

ALS, 1p. (AO)

Fitzgerald's total earnings for 1919—his first year as a professional writer —were $879.

F. Scott Fitzgerald, Esq.
599 Summit Avenue,
St. Paul, Minn.

Dear Mr. Fitzgerald;

I am wiring you that the Saturday Evening Post is buying your story "Myra Meets His Family" for four hundred dollars ($400.). I am glad to know about the new story you are writing and I think we can manage a little rise in price on the next story.

I thought we could sell "Myra Meets His Family" because it was clever and was full of surprise. I don't *remember* when I have read a story that has kept me guessing right up to the end as this one did.

If we cannot place "A Smile for Sylvo" during the next month, I shall send it back to you and you can sell it to the Smart Set.

Yours sincerely,

Harold Ober

TLS, 1p. n.d.—early January 1920. Fitzgerald pasted this letter in his scrapbook.

Dear Mr. Ober—

You could have knocked me over with a feather [with a feather] when you told me you had sold Myra—I never was so heartily sick of a story before I finished it as I was of that one.

Enclosed is a new version of <u>Barbara</u>, called <u>Bernice Bobs Her Hair</u> to distinguish it from Mary Rineheart's "Bab" stories in the <u>Post</u>. I think I've managed to inject a snappy climax into it. Now this story went to several Magazines this summer—Scribners, Woman's H. Companion + the Post but it was in an entirely differ- ent, <u>absolutely unrecognizable</u> form, <u>single-spaced</u> and none of 'em kept it more than three days except Scribner, who wrote a personal letter on it.

¶Possibly "The Camel's Back," *The Saturday Evening Post,* 24 April 1920.

Is there any money in collections of short stories?

This Post money comes in very handy—my idea is to go south—probably New Orleans and write my second novel. Now my novels, at least my first one, are not like my short stories at all, they are rather cynical and pessimistic—and therefore I doubt if as a whole they'd stand much chance of being published serially in any of the uplift magazines at least until my first novel + these Post stories appear and I get some sort of a reputation.

Now I published three incidents of my first novel in <u>Smart Set</u> last summer + my idea in the new one is [too] to sell such parts as might go as units separately to different magazines, as I write them, because it'll take ten weeks to write it + I don't want to run out of money. There will be one long thing which might make a novellette for the Post called The <u>Diary of a Popular Girl</u>, half a dozen cynical incidents that might do for <u>Smart Set</u> + perhaps a story or two for <u>Scribners</u> or <u>Harpers</u>. How about it—do you think this is a wise plan—or do you think a story like C. G. Norris' <u>Salt</u> or Cabells <u>Jurgen</u> or Driesers <u>Jenny Gerhard</u> would have one chance in a million to be sold serially? I'm asking you for an opinion about this beforehand because it will have an influence on my plans.

Hoping to hear from you I am

Sincerlerly

F. Scott Fitzgerald

P.S.   The excellent story I told you of probably wont be along for two or three weeks.# I'm stuck in the middle of it.

F S F.

599 Summit Ave.
St. Paul, Minn
Jan 8th 1919.*

ALS, 2pp. (AO)

HAVE RECEIVED TELEGRAM FROM A MAN NAMED S WAKE-FIELD ADDRESS PRINCETON HOTEL WEST FORTY FIFTH STREET CARE BARNEY MYERS ASKING ME LOWEST ROYALTY ON MY PLAY PORCELAIN AND PINK IN CURRENT SMART SET PLEASE GET IN TOUCH WITH HIM AND MAKE ARRANGE-MENTS IF YOU THINK BEST
    SCOTT FITZGERALD

Wire to Reynolds office 9 January 1920. St. Paul. (AO)

#Possibly "The Camel's Back."
*i.e., 1920. At the beginning of a new year, Fitzgerald sometimes retained the previous year in dating letters.

Dear Mr. Ober:

Am leaving for New Orleans tonight. Will wire you when I have a permanent adress. Am sending You another story in about ten days.

I wired you today about atelegram I [ce] recieved concerning a <u>Smart Set</u> playlet. Of course if this man is a burlesque king or on the 10–20–30[†] I don't suppose it'd be best. But any arrangement you make will be satisfactory to me.

Better hold all communication with me until I write or wire you from the south. I mean if you think there's anything in the playlet business go ahead with it.

As ever
F Scott Fitzgerald

P.S. Thanks for getting the checks here so quick. I was rather strapped for money.

Jan 9th 1920.
599 Summit Ave
St. Paul, Minn.

ALS, 1p. (AO)

In January 1920 Fitzgerald went to New Orleans to write and to be near Zelda. While living at 2900 Prytania Street in New Orleans, he read the galley proofs for This Side of Paradise.

2900 Prytania Street
New Orleans La.

Dear Mr. Ober:

Here's a "Post Story"[‡] I feel pretty sure. If you sell <u>Bernice</u> please <u>wire</u> me the money as soon as you can because I am very broke. Am sending another story on in two days.

I recieved the proofs and forwarded them to the Saturday Evening Post. Thanks for your letter.

As Ever
F Scott Fitzgerald

P. S. Smart Set have been after me for a Story for some time so if you don't place <u>Sylvo</u> this month do send it to me. I want to keep

---

†A cheap vaudeville circuit.
‡A note in the left margin of the letter, not in Fitzgerald's hand, reads: " 'The Camel's Back' 500 SEP".

inright with Menken + Nathan as they're the most powerful critic
in the country

F——

ALS (ink and pencil), 1p. n.d.—received c. 26 January 1920. (AO)

2900 Prytania Street
New Orleans.
Jan 27th 1920.

Dear Mr. Reynolds

Enclosed is a very odd story.§ If you think the end spoils it clip
it off.¶ I'll leave that to your judgement. Don't look now but when
you come to sit see if you think it takes the pep out of the story.
Personally I like it as it is.

As I havn't heard I presume the Post didn't take <u>Bernice</u> + I'm
quite dissapointed as its too long for almost anyone else. Hope you
recieved the <u>Camel's Back</u>. There'll be another story along in about
a week

Faithfully
F Scott Fitzgerald

ALS, 1p. (AO)

F. Scott Fitzgerald, Esq.
2900 Prytania Street
New Orleans, La.

Dear Mr. Fitzgerald:

We have sold "The Camel's Back for five hundred dollars. We
shall probably get the check next Tuesday and I shall send it on to
you at once.

Yours sincerely
Harold Ober

TLS, 1p. n.d.—c. January/February 1920. Fitzgerald pasted this letter in his scrapbook.

---

§A note in the bottom margin, not in Fitzgerald's hand, reads: "The Proud
Piracy". Published as "The Offshore Pirate," *The Saturday Evening Post*, 29 May 1920.
¶The discarded ending reveals the kidnaping to have occurred in Ardita's dream.

F. Scott Fitzgerald, Esq.,
2900 Prytania Street,
New Orleans, La.

Dear Mr. Fitzgerald:

The Saturday Evening Post has decided to keep "Bernice Bobs Her Hair". The check will probably come in next week. Please don't forget to send in the missing pages.

Yours sincerely,
Harold Ober

TLS, 1p. n.d.—c. January/February 1920. Fitzgerald pasted this letter in his scrapbook.

The Allerton House
143 East 39th St.
Feb 21st

Dear Mr. Ober:

I think you'll see if you read this from the beginning that I've put the required Jazz ending on it and I don't doubt they'll buy it.# I sold "A Smile for Sylvo" to the <u>Smart Set</u>.

The missing pages of Bernice will be here Tuesday + I'll send 'em right down. My letter went to Palm Beach + then all the way back to St. Paul.

On Thursday I'll send you the second of a series of Jellybean stories (small southern town stuff) of which <u>The Ice Palace</u> was the first.

As ever
F Scott Fitzgerald.

P.S. The last line takes Mr. Lorimer* at his word. Its one of the best *lines* I've ever written.†

F.

P.S.(2) I've changed the title—improved it I believe.

ALS, 1p. New York City. (AO)

#Probably "The Offshore Pirate."

*George Horace Lorimer, editor of *The Saturday Evening Post.*

†The last line of "The Offshore Pirate" reads: " 'Perhaps I can guess the other one,' she said; and reaching up on her tiptoes she kissed him softly in the illustration."

F. Scott Fitzgerald, Esq.,
Cottage Club,
Princeton, N. J.

Dear Mr. Fitzgerald:
　I have a letter from Mr. Lorimer this morning saying that AN OFF SHORE PIRATE has safely reached him. He likes the story as you have revised it and is taking it.

> Yours sincerely,
> Harold Ober

TLS, 1p. n.d.—early March 1920. Fitzgerald pasted this letter in his scrapbook.

Dear Mr. Reynolds:
　Glad you sold The Off Shore Pirate. A movie broker who has been bothering me wrote + asked me for your adress. His name is Rosenbaum + I sent him three old scenarios I've been fooling with.
　A magazine store here showed me next weeks <u>Post</u> containing <u>Myra Meets His Family</u>. Do you suppose they've buried <u>The Ice Palace</u> in their files? It was the 2nd story you sold 'em + I'm quite depressed about it.

> As Ever
> F Scott Fitzgerald

ALS, 1p. n.d.—received 12 March 1920. University Cottage Club, Princeton, stationery. (AO)

Dear Mr. Ober:
　I am writing Rosenbaum as you suggest.
　You can get me on the phone here <u>Princeton 98 W.</u> in case there are any movie offers on Myra Meets His Family.

> Sincerely
> F Scott Fitzgerald

ALS, 1p. n.d.—received 22 March 1920. University Cottage Club, Princeton, stationery. (AO)

Fitzgerald's first novel, This Side of Paradise, *was published by Scribners on 26 March 1920.*
　On Saturday, 3 April 1920, F. Scott Fitzgerald and Zelda Sayre were married in the rectory of St. Patrick's Cathedral, New York City. They lived at first in New York hotels, but in May 1920 they rented a house in Westport, Connecticut, in the hope that Fitzgerald could get back to more regular writing habits.

Dear Mr. Ober:
  My adress is
  c/o Mrs. Marchand
    Westport
    Conn.

We have taken a Cottage here for the summer + I expect to do some real work. When those contracts‡ come better send them out here + any checks deposit in the Chatham + Phenix Bank, 33d St.

Sincerely
F Scott Fitzgerald

ALS (pencil), 2pp. n.d.—received 14 May 1920. (AO)

Dear Mr. Ober:
I am very sorry about the telephone message. We moved yesterday [from] *to* our new house. Adress
      c/o M. C. Wakeman
      Compo Road
      Westport, Conn.
      Telephone 64 Ring 4.

Please ring me on the phone as soon as you have the $1000§ for me and I will let you know whether to hold it or deposit it to my account.

I will consider it a favor if you will deduct $5.10 from the check which is 6% interest on $17,00 for 3 weeks. Thanking you for past favors I am

Sincerely
F. Scott Fitzgerald.

ALS, 1p. n.d.—received 28 May 1920. (AO)

---

‡In May 1920 Fitzgerald was negotiating two contracts: a $3,000 contract with Metro Pictures Corporation for an option on his stories, signed on 27 May 1920; and a contract with *Metropolitan Magazine* for six stories at $900 each, made 11/12 May 1920. After *Metropolitan* had declined six stories, Fitzgerald would have the right to write three stories for *The Saturday Evening Post*; but then *Metropolitan* would have an option for six more stories. The following stories were submitted under this arrangement: "Jelly Bean," "His Russet Witch," "Two for a Cent," "Benjamin Button" (declined), and "Winter Dreams." This contract lapsed when *Metropolitan Magazine* went into receivership.
§From Metro as an advance.

Wakeman's
Westport, Conn.
June 2nd, 1920

Dear Mr. Ober:

I've shortened this story# a little and what's more I think I've managed to improve it—but I think it'd spoil it utterly to give it a happy ending. I've also changed the town + the names so it is not a series with <u>The Ice Palace</u>. So if you think the Metropolitan wants it go ahead. It probably needs retyping.

> Sincerely
> F. Scott Fitzgerald.

P.S. I am also leaving "The I. O. U"* This is the plot that Sell† particularly wanted for Harps. Baz and which I promised him. I think it is pretty good.

> FS.F.

ALS (ink and pencil), 1p. (AO)

Westport, Conn
June 10th 1920

Dear Mr. Ober:

I'm glad this contract has in it about using the original name. I don't think "The Chorus Girl's Romance" is half as good a title as "Head + Shoulders."‡

When you get this check will you please deposit in the Chatham + Phenix Bank to my account and call me up at Westport 64, Ring 4?

> Sincerely
> F. Scott Fitzgerald.

P.S. My mistake. I see that they only agree to use the title in their paid publicity—not as title to the picture

> F.

ALS, 1p. (AO)

#Probably "The Jelly Bean," *Metropolitan Magazine,* October 1920.
　*This story was never published. See Jennifer McCabe Atkinson, "Lost and Unpublished Stories by F. Scott Fitzgerald," *Fitzgerald/Hemingway Annual 1971,* 32–63.
　†Henry Blackman Sell, editor of *Harper's Bazaar.*
　‡The picture was titled *The Chorus Girl's Romance.* Starring Viola Dana and directed by William C. Dowlan, it was the first movie made from a Fitzgerald story.

June 23, 1920.

F. Scott Fitzgerald, Esq.
c/o M. C. Wakeman,
Compo Road,
Westport, Conn.

Dear Mr. Fitzgerald:

I have a letter from Mr. Hovey, of The Metropolitan, this morning, accepting THE JELLY-BEAN, and a check for $900.00 should come to me around the first of the month.

Yours very truly,
Paul R. Reynolds

TLS, 1p. Fitzgerald pasted this letter in his scrapbook.

Westport Conn.
July 17th 1920

Dear Mr. Ober:

I am enclosing under a separate cover "The Lees of Happiness"§ an excellent if somewhat somber story for The Chicago Tribune. They won't get it, I imagine for several weeks + probably couldn't print it until mid-August but I want to ask them for personal reasons not to print it until September first.

In my contract with the Metro people I notice that they have sixty days in which to choose the ones they want from my stories already published. The contract was dated May 27th which gives them less than two weeks to decide for or against.

<pre>
The Camel's Back   ⎫
Bernice Bobs Her Hair   ⎭ Sat.Eve Post
        and
The Four Fists   Scribners
</pre>

Now there is at least one of these—The Camel's Back for which you said you had had several feelers at the time of publication but am I to understand that in case they have not notified you by July 26th I should try to sell them elsewhere.

I want to do what you think best. You remember that there was one story for which you got no offers. It was called Myra Meets His Family. So after waiting six weeks you told me to go ahead and see if I could get rid of it. So I took it to a Miss Webster, a movie agent of no particular standing, and she managed to get me $1000 for it from The Fox Film Co. My only instinct on the subject is not to

§*Chicago Sunday Tribune*, 12 December 1920.

waste any of them. That is—I'd rather get $1000 or $1500 than nothing. Will you please let me know at the expiration of that time what I'd better do. I feel perfectly sure that both "The Four Fists" and "The Camel's Back" would make excellent movies and that I could get a good price for them.

If "The I. O. U." comes back from the Post I wish you'd return it to me as I think I can change it so there'll be no trouble Selling it.

I am starting on that novel for the Metropolitan Magazine.# It will probably be done about October 1st so there will probably be no more short stories this summer

Sincerely
F Scott Fitzgerald

ALS, 3pp. (AO)

July 17th, 1920
Westport, Conn

Dear Mr. Ober:

Just to tell you I'm going away for the three weeks tour. Am not sure where but will be back here about August 1st. Do what you think best about anything concerning my stuff that may come up.

Sincerely
F Scott Fitzgerald

ALS (pencil), 1p. (AO)

In July 1920 the Fitzgeralds drove from Westport to Montgomery in what they called "the rolling junk." Fitzgerald wrote an article based on the trip.

DID NOT GO TO PIEDMONT HOTEL ATLANTA AS EXPECTED SO HAVE HAD NO COMMUNICATIONS FROM YOU WILL YOU PLEASE WIRE RESULTS WITH METRO PICTURE CO AND CHICAGO TRIBUNE BY DAYLETTER TO ME AT SIX PLEASANT AVE MONTGOMERY ALA
   SCOTT FITZGERALD

Wire to Reynolds 3 August 1920. Montgomery, Ala. (AO)

Westport, Conn.
Aug 6th, 1920.

Dear Mr. Ober:

I can't seem to stay solvent—but I think if you can advance me $500.00 on the Chicago Tribune I'll be able to survive the summer.

The Beautiful and Damned, for which *Metropolitan Magazine* paid $7,000 in serial rights.

If this is O. K. send it to the Chatham + Phenix Bank, 33d St + 5th Ave.

Hovey* of the Metropolitan wrote me asking for more short stories but I'm embarked [om] on my new novel now and tremendously interested. Despite Heywood Broun[†] the first novel has sold 30,000 copies + is still going strong.

I will follow your about the Metro people + wait, anyway, until Sept.

Sincerly
F Scott Fitzgerald

ALS, 1p. (AO)

Westport, Conn
August 11th 1920

Dear Mr. Reynolds:

Thank you for the advance.

In regard to the Scribner matter. Young Scribner + I were friends at Princeton and so far he has been so good about all my things that I like to keep that personal relation. On my book of short stories[‡] which is to appear this fall they gave me an advance of $500.00 which is really unusually large for a first novel. My idea, Mr. Reynolds, is to live permanently abroad as soon as I can afford it— I hope within a year + of course in that case I should put the book rights directly in your hands.

So I would rather let this matter wait at present. Should I feel that they weren't giving me enough this fall I'd hand over the matter to you.

The novel is going to be a wonder. I'm half thru it.

Sincerely
F Scott Fitzgerald

ALS, 1p. (AO)

Sept 17th, 1920
Westport Conn.

Dear Mr. Ober:

Thank you for your letter of September 15th. I am sending you a copy of "Flappers and Philosophers." I agree with you absolutely

---

*Carl Hovey, editor of the *Metropolitan Magazine*.

†Broun reviewed *This Side of Paradise* unfavorably in the *New York Tribune*.

‡*Flappers and Philosophers*, published by Scribners in August 1920, was Fitzgerald's first collection of short stories.

that it is not wise to sell things at a low price but I do think also that in the last analysis nothing but the inherent quality of an authors work will keep his price way up—and meanwhile one must live. I am perfectly willing to wait just as long as you think there is a likely chance of selling those two movies thru your movie brokerage.

You speak of the dramatic rights of This Side of Paradise. My idea has been to dramatize it myself rather than have someone else do it. Don't you think it'd be easier to dispose of a [printed] *finished* play than of a book?

Sincerely
F. Scott Fitzgerald

P.S.   Does this contract with Metro mean that they could buy the movie rights of my new <u>novel</u> for $3000.00. Surely not!

F. S. F.

ALS, 1p. (AO)

For Harold Ober who chaperoned these debutantes
with best wishes from
F Scott Fitzgerald

Inscription in *Flappers and Philosophers.* (AO)

In October 1920 the Fitzgeralds moved into New York City, where they took an apartment at 38 West 59th Street.

38 W. 59th St.
New York City

Dear Mr. Ober:

Here is the story for the Metrolitan.§ I think its the best thing I ever wrote. I will probably have another for them soon.

Will you forward the enclosed letter to Mr. Hovey with the story?

Sincerely
F Scott Fitzgerald

ALS, 1p. n.d.—received 18 October 1920. (AO)

38 W. 59th St.
New York City

Dear Mr. Ober:

So far as Scribners Magazine + Smart Set are concerned I have the serial rights to those stories but Scribners in the contract to

---

§Probably "His Russet Witch," *Metropolitan Magazine,* February 1921.

Flappers + Philosophers lay claim to half of any profits I may derive from publication of the things in any other form.

I called them on the phone + they said to go ahead + sell them on condition that they wouldn't appear anywhere until the first of the year as it would kill [of] the sale of the book which as gone into a third edition.

Sincerely
F. Scott Fitzgerald.

ALS, 1p. n.d.—received 23 October 1920. (AO)

38 W. 59th St.
New York City
Oct 23d 1920

Dear Mr. Ober:

Recieved the list of stenographers corrections. All are O. K + I am considerably in her debt. I will wait 'till I get the proof from the Metropolitan to make any others

Sincerelly
F Scott Fitzgerald

P.S.   I wrote you about 2nd serial that Scribners says O.K after January first. Before that it would kill book which is in 3d printing

ALS, 1p. (AO)

38 W. 59th St.
New York City

Dear Mr Ober:

Sorry I havn't been clearer but my first letter must have gone astray.

Niether Smart Set nor Scribners Magazine object to my selling 2nd serial rights to those four stories <u>but</u> I have to divide whatever they bring (after your commission is taken out) with Scribners because it is so written in the contract for <u>Flappers and Philosophers</u>.

Sincerely
F Scott Fitzgerald

ALS, 1p. n.d.—received 30 October 1920. (AO)

Nov 24th 1920
<u>38</u> W. 59th St
↑
Note correct adress. You had <u>33</u>

Dear Mr. Ober:

I'm glad you sold Myra.# I guess you are [write] right about having your english office hold the money. Working hard on my novel

Sincerely
F Scott Fitzgerald

ALS, 1p. (AO)

38 W. 59th St.
New York City

Dear Mr Ober:

Thank you for the complement. Just finishing up the novel. Merry Xmas

As Ever
F Scott Fitzgerald

ALS, 1p. n.d.—received 27 December 1920. (AO)

Fitzgerald's total earnings for 1920 were $18,850. He sold ten stories ($3,975). His book royalties were $6,200 from This Side of Paradise *and $500 from* Flappers and Philosophers. *The balance came from the movie sales of his stories and an option on his output.*†

38 W 59th St.
New York City

Dear Mr. Ober:

Novel finished and I am doing a final revision. Ought to be through shortly.

Yours
F. Scott Fitzgerald

ALS, 1p. n.d.—received 13 January 1921. (AO)

#Refers to the English reprinting of "Myra Meets His Family" in *Sovereign.*
†The annual summaries in this volume include only major sources of Fitzgerald's income. For complete listings, see "Fitzgerald's *Ledger,*" *Fitzgerald/Hemingway Annual 1971.*

> 38 W 59th St.
> New York City.
> Jan 25th, 1920*

Dear Mr. Ober:

   This is to acknowledge your very kind advance of $650.00 on a story which I will deliver the beginin[n]g of next week. I certainly appreciate the favor as I have those in the past.

> Sincerely
> F Scott Fitzgerald.

ALS, 1p. (AO)

> 38 W. 59th St.
> New York City
> Feb 2nd 1920

Dear Mr. Ober:

   As I was trying to wade thru a story furious at myself for having to interrupt my novel, a miracle happened and I got some money. So if you don't mind I'm returning your very gracious advance with a week's interest at six per-cent. So I shall go on with the novel which is all at the typists except one chapter. I will surely have it to you within two weeks.

> Sincerely
> F Scott Fitzgerald.

ALS, 1p. (AO)

> 38 W 59th St.
> New York City
> Feb 7th 1920

Dear Mr Ober:

   Thank you for your very nice letter. I think I can manage now until I send you the novel.

> Faithfully and ever in your
>   debt.
> F Scott Fitzgerald

ALS, 1p. (AO)

---

*i.e., 1921.

April 8th 1921
38 W 59th St
New York City

Dear Mr. Reynolds:

The Chi Trib offer sounds allright to me and of course do what you think best.¶ But don't you think that if my second book (which should reach you early [as] next week) goes as well as <u>This Side of Paradise</u> (which sold around seventy five thousand copies) I might be able to get $1500 a story in the future? It seems to me that many writers who have had far less publicity are getting over a thousand. But your judgement is better than mine on the subject so go ahead as you think best

Sincerely
F Scott Fitzgerald

ALS, 1p. (AO)

April 22nd 1921

Dear Mr Ober:

Here is Part I of the novel. Part II reaches you Monday and Part III Tuesday. I wish you'd forward it to the Metropolitan in parts as I'm sailing on May the third for England and I'm anxious to hear about the book as soon as possible.

Should he# not take it, it seems to me that it should be published [somewhere] either in a weekly or as a four part serial—because it seems to me that the psychological time for my next novel to appear in book form is this coming fall. However, we can discuss that later

Sincerely
F Scott Fitzgerald

ALS, 1p. n.p. (AO)

When Zelda became pregnant, the Fitzgeralds set sail for their first trip to Europe on 3 May 1921. They returned to the United States in late July and settled briefly in Montgomery at 6 Pleasant Avenue.

Dear Mr. Ober:

I intended to send you the movie* before I left. I will forward it from London. I certainly appreciate your kindness in making this

---

¶The nature of this offer is unknown.

\# *Metropolitan Magazine* serialized *The Beautiful and Damned* monthly from September 1921 to March 1922, and Carl Hovey cut some 40,000 words out of the 130,000-word typescript.

*This movie has not been identified.

advance and I hope the Metropolitan will reimburse you promptly.

My best address is %American Express Paris. I will write you from London

Sincerely
F Scott Fitzgerald

ALS, 1p. n.d.—received 21 May 1921. R.M.S. *Aquitania* stationery. (AO)

Rome, June 12th, 1921

Dear Mr. Ober:

Our trip has been rather a dissapointment and we have decided to return to America. We're leaving this week for London and hope to find a boat about the 1st of July.

I am going to ask you if you can let us have another thousand dollars, and if you will have it cabled to us % the American Express, London as we'll need it for our passage home.

I have finished the movie and am forwarding it as soon as I can find a big envelope. I hope Metro will take it. The more I see of Italy the more I think of America.

Of course you are familiar with the Tauchnitz and the Conard series of Brittish + American authors. Do you think there's any chance for any of my books getting in to one of those series? Brentanos in Paris told me they sold a lot of This Side of Paradise.

As liver
F. Scott Fitzgerald

ALS, 2pp. (AO)

Dear Mr. Ober:

Thanks immensely for your furthur advance. We are sailing on the 9th of this month + I'll deliver you my movie when I arrive— I hope to God it will manage to square accounts as I am about 2,400 in your debt.

Sincerely
F Scott Fitzgerald

ALS, 1p. n.d.—July 1921. Hotel Cecil, London, stationery. (AO)

In August 1921 the Fitzgeralds moved to St. Paul, Minnesota, for the birth of their baby. Friends found them a place to live at Dellwood, White Bear Lake.

% Mrs. Mackey Thompson
Dellwood, Whitebear,
August 16th, 1921

Dear Mr. Ober:

I am answering five of your letters at once.

(1st) June 28th. I will take up the Tauchnitz matter with Scribner.

(2nd) I am glad you have sold the Off Shore Pirate‡

(3d) The Sovereign Magazine§ hasn't arrived yet.

(4th) About the novel. I have a hunch that is going to be almost as big a success in book form as <u>Main Street</u>. If so it would be foolish to sell it now as a movie, wouldn't it? I should say that it would be scarcely worth while under $10,000 as I think the value of my stuff will increase as it grows older. However I will instruct Scribner to send you the ms. for copying. Will you have a carbon made too as I wish to send it to Collins¶ in England.

(5th) Thank you for depositing the money.

As Ever
F Scott Fitzgerald

ALS, 1p. (AO)

Dellwood, Minn
White Bear Lake
Aug [22nd] *31st* 1921

Dear Mr. Ober:

I have just recieved word from Perkins# that they have <u>The Beautiful and Damned</u> in hand and therefor the best they can do is to send you a galley *proof* early in Oct. I hope this won't be too late to take up the question of spring publication in [Euro] England.

Sincerely
F. Scott Fitzgerald

P. S.   1st Story will reach you Monday <u>absolutely</u>

ALS, 1p. (AO)

Dear Mr. Ober:

I am enclosing the first of the Saturday Evening Post stories—but I am not sure that it is advisable to submit this one to them if you intend to ask for more money than they have ever given me before

---

‡Probably refers to English reprinting in *Sovereign*.
§The July issue included "Myra Meets His Family."
¶William Collins Sons was Fitzgerald's English publisher at this time.
#Maxwell Perkins, Fitzgerald's editor at Charles Scribner's Sons.

—this is not exactly the kind of thing that my commercial value rests on, not that this is too deep for it is certainly not that, but becauseit contains no female characters at all. However, do as you think best. I have got my hand in now and you can expect some more and some much better stuff along next week and for several weeks thereafter.

Perkins tells me that he is sending you a galley proof shortly so you can sound out the English market.

Sincerely
F. Scott Fitzgerald

Dellwood
White bear Lake,Minn.
Sept. 7th 1921

TLS, 1p. (AO)

Dellwood, White Bear Lake, Minn.
Sept 14th 1921

Dear Mr. Ober:

Glad you like the story.* I don't—particularly. But I'm writing a beauty now.

As to the Metropolitan—it seems to me that the contract is certainly null and void if they are not willing to pay cash within the month for short stories whether they intend publishing them in one month or one year. I mean they can't keep buying my stories agreeing to pay when they've finished paying for the serial. Have they been remitting anything lately?

I should suggest <u>The Beautiful + Damned</u> to be offered to Fatty Arbuckle immediately. (joke!)

So I think you're right. Hovey should be willing to let me sell to the <u>Post</u> until he is ready to pay cash for stories.

Sincerely
F Scott Fitzgerald.

ALS, 1p. (AO)

Dellwood, White Bear Lake, Minn.
September 28th, 1921

Dear Mr. Ober—

Your letter rather worries me. Do you suppose the Metropolitan is going on the rocks along with <u>M^cclures</u>, <u>Leslie's</u>, <u>Judge</u>, <u>Film Fun</u>

---

*Possibly "Two for a Cent," *Metropolitan Magazine*, May 1922.

and the rest. That would be worse than tragic for me , to look at it from one point of view—putting off my book until Spring may hurt it tremendously as it is—several of the things this fall scout the same [ideas] *field* and may reap all the corn before my reaper comes along.

As I understand it they have paid you $3000 and you have advanced me [$5500] $5400.00. They should have paid you $5000 by the 1st of October. There is still coming $1800.00[†] to me and $3300 to you. Is this right.

I am finishing a two part story which should be good for the <u>Post</u> and which I will send you on Tuesday.[‡] Meanwhile I am in the traditional poverty-stricken condition with coal high and a baby about due. I hope to God the <u>Post</u> takes that first story[§] though I feel no confidence about it. I don't want want to howl for money as I am apparently already $2700 in your debt due to the Metropolitan—but you may recieve a howl anyday now. I know you are short yourself because of the recent magazine-slump so I will try to ask as little as possible.

Faithfully
F Scott Fitzgerald.

ALS, 1p. (AO)

New Address————599 Summit Ave,
St. Paul, Minn

Dear Mr. Ober:

I'm calling on you before I thot I'd have to, + rather counting on the fact that the S.E.P. has bought that story.

I need as much of $600.00 as you can let me have if you can let me have any—and I'm going to ask you when you get this to deposit whatever it may be in the Chatham + Phenix Bank, 33d St. and to telegraph me how much it was. If the magazine situation has tied you up all around wire me that bad news + I'll see what I can do right away about it somewhere else.

The Usual bother
F Scott Fitzgerald

Oct 3d, 1921

ALS, 1p. (AO)

---

†Ober wrote "$900" beneath this figure and wrote in the bottom margin: "Metropolitan owes us 4000.00".
‡Possibly "The Diamond as Big as the Ritz," *The Smart Set*, June 1922.
§Possibly "Two for a Cent."

599 Summit Ave.
St. Paul, Minn

Dear Mr. Ober:

I did not realize that I had had so much of the money. It sort of shocked me so I'll probably turn out a lot of work quick. The 2 part story should be back from the typist tomorrow.

Thank you very much for the money.

I am not surprised that the <u>Post</u> didn't take that story. There is something the matter with it—a certain thinness. I will try another flapper story.

Sincerely
F Scott Fitzg—

ALS, 1p. n.d.—received 11 October 1921. (AO)

Adress me here. $\begin{cases} 599 \text{ Summit Ave.} \\ \text{St. Paul, Minn} \end{cases}$

Oct 16th, 1921

Dear Mr. Ober:

There's not a decent typist in town so perhaps you'll [have] want to have this done over before you submit it.# Seems to me there's a movie in it. It comes to 20,000 words and can be divided into a two part story—Parts I–VI (inc.) as the 1st + Parts VII–XI (inc) as the 2nd.

This is a wild sort of extravaganza partly on the order of <u>The Off-shore Pirate</u> + partly like <u>The Russet Witch</u>. I think the <u>Post</u> ought to take it.

I shall begin another one tomorrow.

As to the novel. I made so many changes in the galley proof that I would rather send you a page proof to offer to the movies + have written Scribner to that effect. It should be ready shortly.

[It seems to me that the enclosed might make a movie]

Sincerely
F Scott Fitzgerald

ALS, 1p. (AO)

#"The Diamond as Big as the Ritz" (originally titled "The Diamond in the Sky").

599 Summit Ave,
St. Paul, Minn:

Dear Mr. Ober:

Enclosed is another story.* I don't know what's the matter with me—this has run out to [15,000] [*about 18,000*] *15,000–18,000* words —so instead of having <u>five</u> stories out I have <u>three</u>. This one ought to sell—unless its length [was] *is* a disadvantage. I wish you could offer it to the <u>Post</u> because its precisely their stuff—but I don't suppose you can.†

As to the others. I am not very fond of <u>Two for a Penny</u>. It is a fair story with an O. Henry twist but it is niether 1st class nor popular because it has no love interest. My heart wasn't in it so I know it lacks vitality. Perhaps you'd better return it to me + maybe I can fix it up.

As to <u>The Diamond in the Sky</u>. I was sorry the Post refused but I can understand. It might interest Burton Rascoe of M^ccaulls or Harry Sell ‡ + I feel quite sure that as a last rescourse Nathan of <u>Smart Set</u> would take it for a novellette if you had your stenographer write "Chap. II" instead "II" ect. They once gave me two hundred dollars for a novellette that length + they might give $250. now. Also Bridges of Scribners§ [have] *has* been after a story for some time.

I have a little girl as I may have told you.

I may a little later have to call on you for that last $300.00 as I'm getting pretty low. I'll try a 5000 word story next. I ought to be able to do one in a week.

As Ever
F Scott Fitzgerald

ALS, 2pp. n.d.—early November 1921. (AO)

Nov 22nd 1921

Dear Mr Ober—

You're letter came + I'm glad Hovey bought the story.# I shall not mention its history [too] to him.

I regret to say that I'll have to ask you again for money. Could

---

*Probably "The Popular Girl," *The Saturday Evening Post*, 11 and 18 February 1922.
†*Metropolitan Magazine* had first refusal on stories at this time.
‡Sell reported: "I am sorry to tell you that I cannot get through Scott Fitzgerald's 'The Diamond in the Sky.' "
§Robert Bridges, editor-in-chief of *Scribner's Magazine.*
#"Two for a Cent."

you deposit $500 for me right away at my bank? I think that will carry me to the 1st.

I have no doubt that you'll be able to sell <u>The Popular Girl</u> to any market you send it to. I'm half through another one now.

<u>My new adress is</u> for the winter.

> 626 Goodrich Ave.
> St. Paul, Minn.

If you <u>can't</u> deposit that money in the Chatham + Phenix, 33d St. I wish you'd wire me. Only if you <u>can't</u>.

> As Ever
> F Scott Fitzgerald

ALS, 1p. (AO)

> 626 Goodrich Ave.
> St. Paul, Minn
> November 29th 1921

Dear Mr. Ober—

Some time ago I wrote Scribners suggesting that you place my new novel in England. They answered that that would be agreeable to them except for the fact that Collins in asking to publish <u>This Side of Paradise</u> had specified that they should also have an option on my next two novels. They wrote Scribners last month saying that they intended to bring out <u>Flappers and Philosophers</u> this Spring.

I suppose, therefore, that, <u>if you think it worth while</u>,!! the rest of the stories contained in it should be disposed of now—if at all— to any English magazine market that presents itself—for of course they would lose all value to a magazine if not published before the book appears in April or May.

I believe you have disposed of <u>The Off Shore Pirate</u> + <u>Head + Shoulders</u>—also <u>Myra Meets his Family</u> which story however, I [do not] *never have* liked, + do not intend ever republishing in book form. This leaves the following:

<u>From Flappers</u>	
The Ice Palace	(Post)
Bernice Bobs Her Hair	(Post)
⎰Benediction	(Smart Set)
⎱Dalyrimple goes Wrong	(Smart Set)
The Cut Glass Bowl	(Scribners)
The Four Fists	(Scribners)

Now that I think of it, however, <u>The Smart Set</u> is published in England, so these two are dead.

And there are others, of course,—The Camel's back, the one from the Chicago Tribune,* the three from the Metropolitan† + the new Post one‡ but of course about these there's no hurry. The whole thing is probably too small a matter to bother about.

Do you think there is any chance of serializing The Beautiful + Damned in England? When Scribners sends you the page proof for the movies I wish you'd read it. Its a changed book from the serialized version§ as I've almost completely rewritten parts of it since I came home this summer + think now that its a rather excellent novel.

Sincerely
F Scott Fitzg—

ALS, 5pp. (AO)

November 26, 1921.

F. Scott Fitzgerald, Esq.,
626 Goodrich Avenue,
St. Paul, Minn.

Dear Mr. Fitzgerald:

The Saturday Evening Post is taking THE POPULAR GIRL and will pay fifteen hundred dollars ($1500.) for it. They will use it as a one part story.

Sincerely yours,
Harold Ober

TLS, 1p. Fitzgerald pasted this letter in his scrapbook.

626 Goodrich Ave. St. Paul

Dear Mr. Ober:

Am enclosing The Diamond in the Sky cut to 15,000 words from the original 20,000—from 87 pages to 66. I don't feel that I can [cuil] cut it any farther without ruining the story. I think this much cutting has improved it.

If the [comm] better priced markets won't have it I suggest Scribners or even Smart Set tho I doubt if they'd pay more than $200. or $250. or possibly $300 for it as a novellette.

---

*"The Lees of Happiness."
†"The Jelly Bean," "His Russet Witch," and "Two for a Cent."
‡Probably "The Popular Girl."
§Other correspondence relating to the serialization of *The Beautiful and Damned* seems to be missing.

Thank you for depositing the money for me. I am concieving a play which is to make my fortune¶

Sincerely
F Scott Fitzgerald

ALS (pencil), 1p. n.d.—probably November/December 1921. (AO)

Dear Mr. Ober:

Thanks for the $500.00 . I'm delighted that you got such a good price for <u>The Popular Girl</u>. Will send on the funniest story ever written this week#

As Ever
F Scott Fitzgerald

626 Goodrich Ave. St. Paul, Minn

ALS, 1p. n.d.—received 1 December 1921. (AO)

626 Goodrich Ave.
St. Paul, Minn.

Dear Mr. Ober:

Thank you very much for your telegram + letter + for depositing the money. The play will be finished shortly.

The baby is called Frances Scott Patricia Fredricka Fitzgerald. It can choose its name from among these when it is older. At present it is two (months).

Sincerely
F Scott Fitz

ALS, 1p. n.d.—December 1921. (AO)

626 Goodrich Ave
St. Paul, Minn.

Dear Mr. Ober:

My play won't be finished until about the 10th of January + I'm getting sort of low again. Does Hovey still owe about $500 on that last short story?* If he's still paying slow let me know and I'll put my play aside for a week + tear off another Post story.

My play is the funniest ever written + will make a fortune. I'd

---

¶ *Gabriel's Trombone*, which became *The Vegetable.*
# Possibly "The Curious Case of Benjamin Button," *Collier's*, 27 May 1922.
* "Two for a Cent."

suggest offering it to Miller (of Frohmans)[†] first, as they heard of it in a round about way + wrote me. Harris[‡] was also interested about a year ago—do you remember?

As Ever

F Scott Fitzgerald

ALS, 1p. n.d.—received 27 December 1921. (AO)

626 Goodrich Ave.

St. Paul, Minn

Dear Mr. Ober—

My play will be done by the 1st of Jan. I will have three copies as you suggest. On Jan 1st I'll finish a short story in a day or so of which I have the 1st draft + send it on after the play.

If possible I would like to extort another $500.00 from you. This will really be the last time as my novel appears March 1st + the play is going to make me rich. If O. K. will you deposit?

The Eternal Beggar

F Scott Fitzgerald

ALS, 1p. n.d.—late December 1921. (AO)

Fitzgerald's total earnings for 1921 were $19,065. He sold only one story. Other major sources of income were This Side of Paradise, *which brought in $5,636.68, and* Flappers and Philosophers, *which made $2,730. The serial rights for* The Beautiful and Damned *sold for $7,000.*

January 24th, 1921[§]

626 Goodrich

Dear Mr Ober:

Under a separate cover I enclose a short story[¶] which I began a long time ago and decided to take two days off to finish up. It is a wierd thing and I suppose the <u>Metropolitan</u> would be most likely to take it—but I really feel that unless they pay faster I never want to sign another contract with them. I don't know what I should have done without your generosity in advancing me money but its been

---

†Gilbert Miller, an independent theatrical producer who was associated with Daniel Frohman's producing agency.

‡The play was offered to producer William Harris, Jr., but was produced by Sam H. Harris.

§i.e., 1922.

¶"The Curious Case of Benjamin Button."

terribly embarrassing asking you for it when I know you havn't yet recieved it yourself.

The play should be done by the middle of February. If the <u>Diamond in the Sky</u> is still unsold I wish you'd offer it to <u>Smart Set</u> as a novellette. Any other magizine would cut it to pieces before they published it anyway.

Hope Wigham# is back from Paris so he can pay for this new story. Its a plot thats haunted me for two years and is like nothing I've ever read before. Of course that's against it with the American public which prefers the immemorial jaw-breakers. If this one doesn't go please let me know at once and I'll do another like <u>The Popular Girl</u>. You notice that <u>The Popular Girl</u> hasn't the vitality of my earlier popular stories even tho I've learned my tricks better now and am technically proficient. I don't believe its possible to stand still—you've either got to go ahead or slide back and in <u>The Popular Girl</u> I was merely repeating the <u>matter</u> of an earlier period without being able to capture the exuberant <u>manner</u>. Still I hope to God that <u>The Popular Girl</u> is bought by the movies.

Sincerely
F Scott Fitzgerald

P.S. I nearly forgot the whole purpose of this letter. Here it is. When I finish my play I plan to write a series of twelve articles which will ostensibly be the record of a trip to Europe but will really be a mass of impressions and heavily laden with autobiography. The first one will be called "Dawn" and will hinge apon my first [loo] view of Cherbourg, France. The twelve will not be connected and could go to different magizines if advisable, though I intend to publish them afterwards in one book.

Now I can't describe them exactly but they will be something utterly original—If you have read Hergeshiemer's <u>St. Christobal de Habana</u>, Driesers' <u>A Traveller at Forty</u> and Conrad's <u>A Personal Record</u> you will see *somewhat* what I mean. In a way they will be an attempt to capitalize what attention I [by] have recieved by being young "ect."

Now what I want to know is this. Is there any high-priced market for such stuff? I see travel articles in the <u>Post</u>—do they pay as high for those as for stories, or higher? And does any high-paying magazine except the Post buy such things?—the things will be beautifully written, they will not be radical, they will not be sexual but they will be sincere.

#Henry James Whigham, publisher of *Metropolitan Magazine*.

Write me and tell me what you think? I know you can't judge until you've seen the articles but I don't want to begin them until I see a possible market. I swear they will be, in book form, the biggest thing of their kind since "Innocense Abroad."*

As Ever

F Scott Fitzg—

ALS, 2pp. (AO)

626 Goodrich Ave
St. Paul
Feb 5th, 1922

Dear Mr. Ober—

I have your letter of Jan 30th. There are several things I want to speak to you about

(1.) My play will be done in about 10 days—two weeks. It is a wonder, I think, and should make a great deal of money.

(2.) A well-known author† who came through here last week said he thought <u>The Metropolitan</u> was on the verge of failure. As I understand they have finally paid you for my novel but have not paid for my last short story (though <u>you</u> have paid <u>me</u> for it—advanced it, I mean). If this is true do you think <u>Benjamin Button</u> should go to them until they have paid for <u>Two for a Cent</u>? I think that <u>Benjamin Button</u>, tho, like <u>The Diamond in the Sky</u>, satirical, would sell, because it does not "blaspheme" like the latter—which leads to my third point:

(3.) I should much prefer that <u>The Diamond in the Sky</u> be sent to <u>Smart Set</u> as soon as it can be re-typed with "Chap I" substituted for "I" ect. If Rascoe of Mccauls wouldn't risk it then Bridges of Scribners wouldn't. Besides he would hack it all to pieces—I once had reams of correspondence with him over a "God damn" in a story called <u>The Cut Glass Bowl</u>. Besides they would pay little more than Scribner—possibly four hundred or five hundred I should guess <u>at most</u> for a two [short] part short story—while <u>Smart Set</u>, though they pay only $35–$80 for short stories, once gave me $200.00 for a novellette when I was unknown, and I feel sure they'd give me $250.00 now.

In short I realize I <u>can't</u> get a real good price for the three weeks work that story represents—so I'd much rather get no price but reap the subtle, and nowadays oh-so-valuble dividend that comes

---

*Fitzgerald's travel series was never written.
†Probably Joseph Hergesheimer.

from Mencken's good graces. Besides, in the <u>Smart Set</u> it will be featured.

Again, I'm anxious to get it published soon so it can go in a collection I plan for next fall. I think if you offer it to them as a novellette without mentioning that its been the rounds but simply saying that I asked you to send it to them, they will take it. Of course if you'd rather not deal with <u>Smart Set</u> send it to me.

I suppose that I have been more trouble to you with less profit than any writer whose work you have yet handled but I have every confidence that when my play comes out we will square the whole thing. You have advanced me everything so far sold in America and I imagine the few pounds earned in England have been used up in type writing bills <u>ect</u>.

But I am going to call on you again to advance me, if you will, five hundred dollars on <u>Benjamin Button</u>. Don't bother to telegraph [but if] unless you <u>can't</u>. [obliterated]

I am rather discouraged that a cheap story like <u>The Popular Girl</u> written in one week while the baby was being born brings $1500.00 + a genuinely imaginative thing into which I put three weeks real entheusiasm like <u>The Diamond in the Sky</u> brings not a thing. But, by God + Lorimer, I'm going to make a fortune yet.

F Scott Fitzgerald

I note what you say about my "travel stories" I start on them in two weeks when I finish my play====F.S.F.[‡]

ALS, 3pp. (AO)

626 Goodrich Ave.
St Paul, Minn

Dear Mr Ober:

Thank you for <u>The Popular Girl</u>. I hope to God the Famous Players buy <u>The Popular Girl</u>.[§] I hope they do. I'm glad the <u>Post</u> will be hospitably disposed toward the articles. They will be like nothing ever done before in the way of a Travel Article. I expect to send you my play within 10 days now and will then begin on them. The play is fine, I think + should go big. Both Wm. Harris + Frohman are anxious for it—but more of that anon.

By now you will have recieved my letter asking you for a $500.00

[‡]This postscript is written along the left margin of page three.
[§]They did not buy it for the movies.

advance on <u>Benjamin Button</u>. I hope it's O. K. I am sending you a copy of my novel. Finishing my play has encouraged me tremendously.

As Ever
F Scott Fitzgerald

P.S.   I'm glad the Post gave me first place and good illustrations.

ALS, 1p. n.d.— February 1922. (AO)

For Harold Ober
>   from his friend
>   >   F Scott Fitzgerald
>   >   Feb 6th 1922
>   >   St. Paul, Minn.

Inscription in *The Beautiful and Damned*, which was published on 3 March, 1922. (AO)

626 Goodrich Ave.
St. Paul, Minn
Feb 11th, 1921

Dear Mr. Ober:

Thanks very much for the $500.00. I was in a tight place. I'm glad the Metropolitan came through with a $1000.00. In that case, if I'm not wrong, I'm square with you, except for this last $500. advance on <u>Benjamin Button</u>. Or does this *check from them* fully cover the last of the novel + <u>Two for a Penny</u>. This is a rhetorical question

As Ever.
F Scott Fitzgerald

ALS, 1p. (AO)

Dear Mr. Ober:

My wife read me only a part of your letter over the phone. She ommitted exactly what I wanted to know—how much the <u>Metropolitan</u> had paid you + that is why my letter was so stupid. I am still, then, over a thousand dollars in your debt.

I have written Nathan that you are sending the novellette¶

Sincerely
F Scott Fitzgerald

ALS, 1p. n.d.—received 15 February 1922. (AO)

¶"The Diamond as Big as the Ritz."

Dear Mr. Ober:

I'm glad Wigham is coming across. Play leaves here a week from today. Both Harris + Frohman are angling for it and while [Har] I should rather prefer Harris as a producer one of my best friends is in Frohman's and is anxious to get it. Its a sure fire money maker. Would it be best to send a copy to both? I'll send you two copies + let you decide.

As Ever
F Scott Fitzgerald*

ALS (pencil), 1p. n.d.—February 1922. St. Paul. (AO)

626 Goodrich Ave.
St. Paul, Minn
March 2nd 1922.

Dear Mr. Ober:

Herewith the play. Now as to placing it. As I understand you do all your play work through Alice Kauser. From all I can gather Alice Kauser is [an] a manager's agent rather than an author's: That is, that while [the] she's the best in the country, she is for the manager (producer) as against the playrite. [While you, *on the contrary*, are for the author every time as against the editor or publisher.]

Now here's the point. Both Harris + Frohman want my play. But while Harris has been at me longer Frohman is, I think, the best bet of the two. One of my great friends in college—Alexander McKaig—is assistant to Mr. Miller in Frohman's. And I think—in fact I almost know—that (and this is for your ears alone, not for Alice Kauser, for it might get him in trouble,) it can be arranged with him that I keep <u>most</u> of the movie rights. In other words Harris wants the play because he thinks it will be <u>the</u> flapper play. But with him it will be a 50–50 movie right proposition. But Frohman will, I believe, be so tickled to get any good American comedy of the type of <u>The First Year</u>† that they'll yield any point on that, I <u>believe</u>, and give me between 75% + 90% of the movie rights which I think is what the author ought to get anyways.

Now I don't know Miss Kauser. I know that several playrite friends of mine (and damm successful playrites) distrust her frightfully, so I'm asking you to see a way to put it to Frohman's (if they

---

*A note in the bottom margin, in Ober's hand, reads: "on envelope P. S. Did anything come of movie rights to Popular Girl".

†A play by actor-playwright Frank Craven, produced in 1920.

want it at all!) so that it is understood that "this is no ordinary play ect." + we have a right to expect special terms.

In any case, unless you have other plans, I'd like the original copy to go to Frohman "Attention Mr. Alex McKaig"—and the second copy to go to Mr. David Wallace of Wm. Harris Jr. either at the same time or as *soon as* the etiquette [goes] of marketing plays allows after the first copy has been sent. I believe Harris would be better than Frohman, even, at this type of play: He did so well with Clarence.‡

I should not, I suppose I should say now, want to collaborate with anyone else in a revision of this. I'm willing to revise it myself with advice from whomsovever they should designate—but I feel that Acts I + III are probably the best pieces of dramatic comedy written in English in the last 5 years and I wouldn't let them go entirely out of my possession [nie] nor permit the addition of another name to the authorship of the play.

I should like to aid in the casting—also I should like it to be produced as soon as possible with the chance of it being able to run thru the hot-weather However I will be in New York on the 9th of this month + we can discuss it then. [obliterated]§ I was surprised that <u>Smart Set</u> paid three hundred.¶

It's a good play. Act II (three scenes) are probably wretchedly constructed according to Baker and his school of Carpenters# but about every two years Craven or Tarkington come along + put Baker in his place. I will name the play later. Can't think of one just now

Into your hands, Oh Lord* I commend my playing.

As Ever
F Scott Fitzgerald

*Ober [Fitzgerald's footnote]

ALS (pencil), 6pp. (AO)

PLAY SENT SATURDAY THANKS FOR TWO HUNDRED AWFUL MESS IN CHECK BOOK CAN YOU DEPOSIT FOUR HUNDRED MORE IMMEDIATELY WILL RETURN IT WHEN ARRIVE EAST THURSDAY
S SCOTT FITZGERALD.

Wire to Reynolds office 6 March 1922. St. Paul. (AO)

---

‡Booth Tarkington's play *Clarence*, produced in 1919.
§A sentence mentioning Alice Kauser is struck out.
¶For "The Diamond as Big as the Ritz."
#Professor George Pierce Baker conducted the "47 Workshop," a playwriting course, at Harvard.

626 Goodrich
St. Paul.

Dear Mr Ober:

Thank you very much for the six hundred. I had got into somewhat of a mess due, I believe, to a raised check by an employee of
a club here. I'm trying to trace down the matter. I had intended to
leave for New York Tuesday but came down Tuesday afternoon
with severe influenza. Will leave next Tuesday and will arrange to
repay you $400.00 when I arrive in case <u>Benjamin Button</u> is not yet
sold + paid for. I hope that will be all right. The play has no doubt
reached you by this time.

As Ever
Scott Fitzg—

ALS, 1p. n.d.—received 13 March 1922. (AO)

St. Paul, 626 Goodrich Ave

Dear Mr. Ober:

Your letter relieved me enormously. I was on the point of trying
to raise some money to repay your very kind advance, having dis-
paired of selling <u>Benjamin Button</u> to anyone except the Smart Set.
According to the memo you gave me I am still in your debt by $299
after counting the $900.00 from <u>Benjamin Button</u>. but as this is covered
by 47 pounds [of] *for* English [money] *sales* + the $500.00 still due
on <u>The Beautiful + Damned</u>, I would like to let it stand until I send
you a story if it is all right with you.

I have at last finished the revision of the play to my own satisfaction. Harris already has Act I + I will send him acts II and III direct
with instructions to consult you when (and if) he is willing to talk
business. Meanwhile I am working on that scenario for Selznick
which should be finished early next week.

Sincerely
F Scott Fitzgerald

ALS, 2pp. n.d.—received 17 April 1922. (AO)

BEAUTIFUL WARNER BROS OFFER TWENTY FIVE HUNDRED
CASH[†] SAY SUCCESS PROBLEMATICAL THIS A LOW OFFER BUT
BEST WE CAN GET WIRE DECISION
HAROLD OBER.

Wire to Fitzgerald c. 19/20 April 1922. Fitzgerald pasted this telegram in his
scrapbook.

---

†For *The Beautiful and Damned.*

WOULD THEY GIVE SMALL PERCENTAGE IN ADDITION BE-
CAUSE OF LOW PRICE ACCEPT BEST OFFER ANYWAY IF YOU
THINK ADVISABLE
  F SCOTT FITZGERALD.

Wire to Reynolds office 20 April 1922. St. Paul. (AO)

Dear Mr Ober:

I'm glad Metropolitan has paid up—and enormously relieved.

About the play. I'm sending one copy today to Wm Harris Jr. +
one to the Theatre Guild who seem to be interested. No one has
seen it but Miller. Within two or three days I'm going to finish my
scenarios for Selznick + will tell him to get in touch with you if
interested.

I just had two copies of the play made this time. Told Harris to
phone you when he came to a decision

As Ever
F. Scott Fitzgerald

626 Goodrich Ave.
St Paul Minn

ALS, 1p. n.d.—received 22 April 1922. (AO)

626 Goodrich Ave.
St Paul, Minn

Dear Mr. Ober:

I am returning the Warner Bros. contract. Will you let me know
as soon as the money is deposited. I note the extra money and I
suppose it's the best arrangement we can make.‡

Now as to another matter. I sent David O. Selznick a fifteen
hundred word synopsis of a movie. If he accepts it he is to write to
me and in that case I will wire you. I'm pretty sure he will accept
it and here's what I wish you'd do as soon as I wire you. If you
would draw up a contract stating the following things:

(1.) That David Selznick (or The Selznick pictures) desire to order
from *me* an eight thousand word story, based on the synopsis submitted under the name [Selznick Com] "Trans-continental Kitty."

(2) That they agree to pay $2500 apon the delivery of the story—
That is apon <u>sight</u> of it—without looking at it. (I talked with Selznick + I think $2500.00 is a fair price—at least its the best he'd give.
Also I told him what I'm writing here and I believe he understood
me.)

---

‡The Warner Brothers contract for *The Beautiful and Damned* stipulated $2,500,
plus a bonus of $1,250 contingent upon movie receipts grossing more than $250,000.

(3) That I agree to deliver the story within three weeks from his notification to me that he approves the synopsis and is willing to order, or contract for, the complete story.

This is mixed up but no doubt you know what I mean. It's simply that when I start I want to know I'm going to get cash on delivery from him, as the synopsis should give him the material for definately making up his mind. The story will be up to specifications,

If this works out I'm going to do more of this same work as it means just about twice as much money per story, and as it seems unlikely that the satyrical short stories I feel moved to write at present (<u>Ben Button</u> + The <u>Diamond in the Sky</u>, for instance) will [never] *ever* bring me any movie money.

Meanwhile I am about half way through a travel article for the Post—not one of the European series but the account of a tour south.§

So when you get a wire from me that Selznick wants the story you will know that means to get in touch with him + draw up a contract.

As Ever

F Scott Fitzgerald

I have no word about my play either from Harris or the Guild

ALS, 3pp. n.d.—received 1 May 1922. (AO)

DO YOU THINK MONEY CAN BE DEPOSITED BY WEDNESDAY
OR IF NOT WHEN PLEASE WIRE
    F SCOTT FITZGERALD.

Wire to Reynolds office 1 May 1922. St. Paul. (AO)

ANXIOUS TO KNOW ABOUT WARNER MONEY PLEASE WIRE
    F SCOTT FITZGERALD.

Wire to Reynolds office 2 May 1922. St. Paul. (AO)

IF WARNER CANNOT DEPOSIT TWELVE HUNDRED BY THURS-
DAY NIGHT WIRE ME
    F SCOTT FITZGERALD.

Wire to Reynolds office 3 May 1922. St. Paul. (AO)

---

§"The Cruise of the Rolling Junk," *Motor*, February, March, April 1924.

626 Goodrich Ave.
St Paul, Minn

Dear Mr. Ober:

Your letter telling me of the deposit made is at hand. Thanks very much. I have not yet heard from Harris, Selznick or The Theatre Guild.

As Ever
F Scott Fitzgerald

ALS, 1p. n.d.—May 1922. (AO)

PLEASE ASK FOR IMMEDIATE DECISION FROM DAVID WAL-
LACE OF WILLIAM HARRIS JUNIOR IF HE DOES NOT WANT
PLAY OBTAIN MANUSCRIPT FROM HIM EXPECT TO HEAR FROM
SELZNICK TODAY
    F SCOTT FITZGERALD.

Wire to Reynolds office 10 May 1922. St. Paul. (AO)

626 Goodrich Ave.
St Paul, Minn
May 11th, 1922

Dear Mr. Ober:

Much to my dissapointment Selznick didn't care for the synopsis. I told him to send it to you. Viola Dana¶ of Metro might possibly like it but I don't suppose its worth trying and if you agree with me that it isn't you might as well send it on here.

I also wrote you to get an answer from Harris about the play. If he rejects it and makes any specific critisism let me know.

My travel article for the Post is almost done.

As Ever
F Scott Fitzgerald

ALS, 1p. (AO)

Dear Mr. Ober:

Your letter depresses me. Didn't Wallace even grant me the courtesy of returning the play on his own account?

Will you send it to me here? Selznick will send you the synopsis. Read it if you will.

Sincerely
F Scott Fitzgerald

ALS (pencil), 1p. n.d.—May 1922. St. Paul. (AO)

¶Actress who starred in *The Chorus Girl's Romance* ("Head and Shoulders") and *The Offshore Pirate.*

During the summer of 1922 the Fitzgeralds moved from Goodrich Avenue in St. Paul to the Yacht Club at White Bear Lake.

F. SCOTT FITZGERALD
HACK WRITER AND PLAGIARIST
[SAINT PAUL]   MINNESOTA[†]

Dear Mr. Ober:

Thanking you for your letter telling me of the deposit. I am sending you a two part travel article for the Post next Monday. It runs well over twenty thousand words. But it is about an automobile trip from Conn. to Ala. The European articles havn't materialized yet.

Note my zazzy stationary—the heading I mean. Do you think Viola Dana would be interested in that movie. She played my other two, you know. The Theatre Guild finally turned down the play. I'm going to revise it.

As Ever
F Scott Fitzgerald

New address
White Bear Yatch Club. White Bear Lake
Minn.

ALS, 1p. n.d.—received 12 June 1922. (AO)

Dear Mr Ober:

I've sent you under another cover a 25,000 word touring serial, humorous throughout, for the Post. I think they could run it as a 3 part thing in which case it'd be nice to get $2500.00 for it. If they can use it at all it seems to me it should be worth two thousand at least but of course any price you agree on will be O K with me. It is almost half again as long as The Popular Girl for which, you remember, they paid $1500. They have my permission to cut anything that displeases them—there may be a few little touches they might be afraid of but cutting them wouldn't interfere in the least with the story. My address is The Yatch Club, White Bear Lake, Minnesota.

As Ever
F. Scott Fitzgerald

ALS, 1p. n.d.—received 24 June 1922. (AO)

---

†Printed letterhead.

Dear Mr. Ober:

Glad you like <u>The Rolling Junk</u>. If Lorimer wants to make any changes tell him to go ahead.

The movie rights to <u>This Side of Paradise</u> are not tied up. Several people have nibbled at it. I was told some months ago that Marylyn Miller§ was considering buying it for Jack Pickford but nothing developed.

Sincerely
F Scott Fitzgerald

ALS, 1p. n.d.—June 1922. White Bear Lake, Minn. (AO)

WOULD NOT LIKE TO MAKE OUTRIGHT SALE WRITING
    F SCOTT FITGERALD.

Wire to Reynolds office 25 June 1922. White Bear Lake, Minn. (AO)

Dear Mr. Ober—

As I wired you I don't think I'd want to sell <u>Head + Shoulders</u> outright. I've several times been on the point of trying to make a play of it + have hesitated only because its already been a movie. Would he¶ possibly interested in a royalty arrangement. He's a clumsy butcher any how.

In regard to <u>The Cruise of the Rolling Junk</u>. I believe it could be advantageously cut in several places—so if the Post want to cut it tell them to go ahead or I will cut it myself in the proof. I refer to the part about my father's civil war adventures. My new book <u>Tales of the Jazz Age</u>. Is to be published in the fall. None of the 11 stories or playlets in it have been sold to the movies and I'm hoping that some of them may get bid for when its in book form. It includes:

The Jellybean
The Camel's Back
May Day   (Novellette in Smart Set in 1920)
Porcelain + Pink   (Playlet   "   "   "   ")
Diamond as Big as the Ritz
The Curious Case of Benjamin Button
Tarquin of Cheepside   (Smart Set)
Oh Russet Witch
The Lees of Happiness

---

§Musical comedy star, married to Jack Pickford.
¶Probably playwright Bayard Veiller, who made an offer.

Mr. Icky   (Playlet in ")
Jemima   (Vanity Fair)
   I am not republishing <u>The Popular Girl</u> or <u>Two for a Cent</u> as I never cared much for them.
   I'm working over my old comedy + intend starting another.

As Ever
F Scott Fitzgerad

ALS (pencil), 2pp. n.d.—late June 1922. (AO)

Dear Mr Ober—
   I'll send the photographs Monday. Can you do this for me? Send me a list of all my stories sold to English magazines—four or five I think—and the dates they were sold or published? I'm getting up a record *of* all my work. Am now revising my play.

As Ever
F Scott Fitzgerald

The Yatch Club, White Bear Lake, Minn.

ALS, 1p. n.d.—early July 1922. "Hack Writer and Plagiarist" letterhead. (AO)

Dear Mr. Ober:
   It was quite a blow about The <u>Rolling Junk</u>.* However, if you'll send it to me immediately as I'm wiring you, I think I can cut out 2000 words and improve it enormously. Will send it back within a week. Scribners might like it but doubt if they'd pay over $500.00 for it. I imagine Hearst is best.
   Have had picture sent you.

Sincerely
F Scott Fitzgerald

P.S.   Will you send me a list of all my stories that have been sold in England? What magazines they were sold to + how much was recieved. Sorry to bother you but am keeping a complete record of my stuff.

F S. F.

ALS (pencil and ink), 1p. n.d.—c. 13 July 1922. White Bear Lake, Minn. (AO)

PLEASE SEND ROLLING JUNK HERE IMMEDIATELY WANT TO REVISE IT
   F SCOTT FITZGERALD.

Wire to Reynolds office 13 July 1922. White Bear Lake, Minn. (AO)

---

* The Saturday Evening Post rejected the article.

Dear Mr. Ober:

Thanks for the information about my stories in England. By now you have recieved that offer for <u>Benjamin Button</u>.

Am returning the <u>Rolling Junk</u>. Perhaps Collier's could use it— or <u>McClures</u>. The Auto paper you mention wouldn't pay much would they. I think almost anything would be better than the Metropolitan until they get on their feet. What did you tell Bayard Vieller.

As Usual
F Scott Fitzgerald

The Yatch Club
White Bear Lake, Minn.

ALS, 1p. n.d.—received 24 July 1922.

The Yatch Club, White Bear Lake.

Dear Mr. Ober:

I'll try to write Hovey[‡] a story early in August. Hope he'll pay promptly. I told Scribner to send you two pictures more. [Thanks] Have been correcting proof on my fall story collection.

As Ever
F Scott Fitzgerald

ALS, 1p. n.d.—received 28 July 1922. (AO)

The Yatch Club, White Bear Lake

Dear Mr. Ober:

Sorry they didn't take <u>Benjamin Button</u>.[§] I am writing a story for the Metropolitan now which should reach you this month.

What has become of <u>The Rolling Junk</u>?

Sincerely
F Scott Fitzgerald

ALS, 1p. n.d.—received 21 August 1922. (AO)

ARTICLES FOR MCCALLS[¶] WILL REACH YOU THURSDAY OR FRIDAY
F SCOTT FITZGERALD.

Wire to Reynolds office 26 August 1922. White Bear Lake, Minn. (AO)

---

‡Carl Hovey, editor of *Metropolitan Magazine*.
§Offer unidentified—possibly for movie.
¶Probably "Does a Moment of Revolt Come Sometime to Every Married Man?" Sold to *McCall's* in 1922 but published March 1924. Companion articles by Fitzgerald and Zelda.

MCCALL ARTICLE CANNOT REACH YOU BEFORE TUESDAY
F SCOTT FITZGERALD.

Wire to Reynolds office 31 August 1922. St. Paul. (AO)

New   { The Commodore Hotel
Adress   { St. Paul, Minn

Dear Mr. Ober:

By now the article has reached you. It runs somewhat over the specified length but I am against charging them extra. Any dope on The <u>Rolling Junk</u>?

Sincerely
F Scott Fitzgerald

ALS (post card), n.d.—postmarked 6 September 1922. (AO)

{ The Commodore Hotel
New adress   { St. Paul, Minn

Dear Mr. Reynolds:

I spent a month on <u>The Rolling Junk</u> + while I realize that technicccally it isn't a success still I should hate to let it go for two hundred dollars. I think on the whole you'd better send it back + perhaps in a month or so I can manage to turn it into a short story or else incorporate it some day into a longer piece.

I hope McCalls liked the article. The story for The Metropolitan should reach you on the 13th or 14th.#

Incidentally I was amused at Sell's kind offer of publicity. Publicity won't pay the rent. It's a wonder he doesn't charge for publishing a story. Its as if a coffee company came to him + said.

"We can't pay you anything for your space but we can give you some <u>damn good ads</u>."

I know that the magazines want only flapper stories from me—the trouble you had in disposing of <u>Benjamin Button</u> + <u>The Diamond as Big as the Ritz</u> showed that.

Sincerely
F Scott Fitzgerald

ALS, 1p. n.d.—received 11 September 1922. (AO)

IF MCCALLS HAS TAKEN THE ARTICLE CAN YOU DEPOSIT NINE HUNDRED DOLLARS FOR ME WHEN YOU RECEIVE THIS TELEGRAM PERIOD IN ANY EVENT PLEASE WIRE ME CARE OF COMMODORE HOTEL STPAUL WHETHER OR NOT THEY ARE

#"Winter Dreams," *Metropolitan Magazine*, December 1922.

TAKING IT PERIOD STORY FOR METROPOLITAN WILL REACH
YOU MONDAY AT THE LATEST
    SCOTT FITZGERALD.*

Wire to Reynolds office 13 September 1922. St. Paul. (AO)

The Commodore Hotel
St. Paul, Minn.

Dear Mr. Reynolds:

The wire came and I want to thank you very much for making that deposit. If McCalls does not take the article I will of course return it immediately.

The Rolling Junk came + I think I can see my way clear to making something of it. Will you send me the list of the magazines that have refused it so I can keep the remaining market in mind while working on it. Story for Hovey leaves here Monday.

Sincerely.
F Scott Fitzgerald

ALS, 1p. n.d.—received 19 September 1922. (AO)

In September 1922 Fitzgerald's second book of short stories, Tales of the Jazz Age, *was published by Scribners.*

In October 1922 the Fitzgeralds moved to Great Neck, Long Island, in order to be closer to the New York scene for the production of

Great Neck, Long Island

Dear Mr. Ober:

I think the two people to try with this shortened version of the Rolling Junk are Century or Scribners. It was originally 25,000 words, then I cut it to 21,000 and now to 17,000. Scribners, of course, would be interested in anything of mine but then Van Doren‡ of Century has written very favorable reviews of my books +, I have heard, is paying good prices. Perhaps it would be better to try him first. All the very literary crowd have an exaggerated notion of my popular appeal. By the way I am sending you a copy of <u>Tales of the Jazz Age</u> which has sold almost 18,000 copies—pretty good for short stories. The above adress will find me for the next year. When Hovey's check comes due will you deposit any balance in the Chatham + Phenix, 30th St, + let me know.

As Ever
F Scott Fitzgerald

---

*A note at the bottom in Ober's hand reads: "We havent enough money to do this get it from McCalls?"
‡Carl Van Doren.

Perhaps the 1st page of enclosure should be retyped. It got rumpled a little in moving§

I would not care to take less than $500.00 for this but would rather let it go at that price than work on it any more.¶

FSF.

ALS (pencil), 1p. n.d.—October/November 1922. (AO)

For Harold Ober
    who fathered
        The Camel's Back
        Benjamin Button
        The Diamond as Big as the Ritz
        The Jellybean
        The Lees of Happiness
            +
        The Russet Witch
    from his gratefully
        F Scott Fitzgerald
(Note the table of contents)

Inscription in *Tales of the Jazz Age*. (AO)

Dear Ober:

Here's the scenario for Viola Dana. Will you destroy the version you have?#

When you have this typed send me a carbon please.

I'm sure its best not to try the Metropolitan on this story.* Its pretty bad stuff on second thots, but I still think it will make a magnificent movie,

Sincerely
F Scott Fitzgerald

ALS (pencil), 1p. n.d.—received 11 December 1922. Great Neck. (AO)

---

§This addition was crowded into the lower left corner of the letter.
¶This addition was written along the left margin of the letter.
#Probably a revision of "Trans-Continental Kitty."
*Ober wrote "Recklessness" at the bottom of this letter. This story was not published as "Recklessness" and has not been identified. It may possibly be "Dice, Brass Knuckles & Guitar," *Hearst's International Magazine*, May 1923.

Great Neck, L. I.
Dec 29th, 1922

Dear Mr. Ober:

I am enclosing you herewith the letter from Ray Long.[†] As you see, including the option it amounts to $1750.00 a story which seems to me a fair price.

I am all for accepting it just as it stands with a few reservations to be noted later. If I felt sure that I was going to give them what they want I might ask a little more but I am <u>not</u> sure that I can so I feel strongly <u>against</u> asking any more. Long himself is <u>not</u> particularly sold on my stuff—it is Hovey's doing + I know he got Long up to this price with some difficulty. I'm going to do these stories without fail during 1923 and if they're as good as I'll try to make them I'm sure I can jump to $2,500 in 1924. But I don't feel enough confidence in my ability to write popular fiction to force the price now. I don't want to dissapoint them as I did the Metro people in 1920. And Norman Hapgood,[‡] I know, is positively hostile to my stuff.

Confidentially I know the Post only pays Ring Lardner $1500 a story so I doubt if they'd pay me more. And I'm not awfully keen about writing fiction for McCaulls. Had you any definate agreement with Colliers? And has the Metropolitan business come out all right?

At any rate when you give him this contract + he pays you will have $1,050 coming + I will have $450.00. If you could deposit $200.00 of that Tues. morning I would be enormously obliged.

The first story for them will reach you Tuesday morning.

Another reason for signing is this—I doubt very much if my new novel will be able to be serialized at all—I'm not even sure I'll want to do it.[§]

[†]On 26 December 1922 Fitzgerald contracted with *Cosmopolitan* for an option on all his stories written during 1923. Although this contract was with Hearst's *Cosmopolitan*, the stories were all published in *Hearst's International Magazine*. Under the terms of the agreement, *Cosmopolitan* was to accept at least six stories. *Cosmopolitan* paid $1,500 for the option and agreed to pay $1,875 for each story. The following stories were submitted under this arrangement: "Dice, Brass Knuckles & Guitar" *(International)*, "Hot and Cold Blood" .*(International)*, "Our Own Movie Queen" (declined), and "One of My Oldest Friends" (declined). "The Sensible Thing" and "Rags Martin-Jones and the Pr-nce of W-les" were paid for by *International* but were later returned, and "Diamond Dick and the First Law of Woman" and "The Baby Party" were accepted in their place.
[‡]Editor of *Hearst's International Magazine*.
[§]Fitzgerald was beginning work on *The Great Gatsby* (1925).

Now, here are my reservations—all of which, no doubt they'll agree to.

(1.) If they do not serialize my new novel or if it is not offered anywhere for serialization they have no claim whatsoever on its movie rights

(2.) Have they any claims on second serial story rights?

(3.) They have no claim on movie rights of stories they refuse.

(4.) This means only six stories <u>offered</u>, doesn't it? I take it to do so.¶

———————

I guess this is all on this subject unless you know any vital reason why it shouldn't go through.

Now about Viola Dana. I'm in favor of wiring Metro Scenario dept. immediately + asking for $5000.00 which seems a fair price and asking an immediate reply. From my experience the more they wait the more reasons against it they find and if they inquire for a price a big one may scare them off. She's evidently interested and I feel that this is the psychological time + 5000.00 the psychological amount of money. Called you today + couldn't get you.

Sincerely
F Scott Fitzgerald

ALS, 3pp. (AO)

Fitzgerald's total earnings for 1922 were $25,135. He sold four stories ($2,790). This Side of Paradise earned $1,200; The Beautiful and Damned, $12,133; Flappers and Philosophers, $350; Tales of the Jazz Age, $3,056.

NEW HEARST STORY# HALL DONE CAN YOU DEPOSIT FIVE HUNDRED FOR ME IMMEDIATELY IF NOT CONVENIENT WIRE ME CARE A D SAYRE 6 PLEANSANT AVENUE MONTGOMERY ALABAMA

    T SCOTT FITZGERALD.

Wire to Reynolds office 16 March 1923. Montgomery. (AO)

———————

¶Ober noted here: "Unless you write more than 6 during 1923".

#Probably "Hot and Cold Blood," *Hearst's International Magazine*, August 1923.

6 Pleasant Ave.
Montgomery, Ala

Dear Mr. Ober:

Thanks very much for the deposit. The story will be along in a day or so.

Do you remember that $1250.00 bonus for the "Beautiful and Damned" movie? I have an idea its passed the set amount as its done very well financially. Perhaps it would be well to get in touch with them about it.

I havn't done anything about "Recklessness" as I've been working on my play which Scribners publishes April 15th

Sincerely

F Scott Fitzgerald

ALS, 1p. n.d.—received 22 March 1923. (AO)

6 Pleasant Ave
Montgomery, Ala

Dear Mr. Ober:

The Vegetable is my old play entirely revised. It won't be published until about the 15th. I hope someone will want to produce it. I am a little bit stuck on my Hearst story but I'll probably get it straightened out in a day or so.

Hope Warner Brothers will play fair on The B. + D. Heaven knows they got it cheap and it was one of their own men who told me how it was packing them in on the coast.

As Ever

F Scott Fitzgerald

ALS, 1p. n.d.—received 30 March 1923. (AO)

Dear Mr. Ober:

I got into an awful jam with my play proofs and the story's delayed again. I'll have it sure by Saturday. Meanwhile as some money came in I return the $1000.00 you were good enough to advance me on it. It's a good story but needs one more revamping.

Thanks enormously. See you Sat.

Sincerely

F Scott Fitzgerald

ALS, 1p. n.d., n.p.—received 17 April 1923. Montgomery. (AO)

Great Neck, Long Island.

Dear Mr. Ober—

I'd like to see Bercovici* any time you say—that is any time after 11 oclock any morning after Thursday. I hope he hasn't lost interest
                                    Sincerely
                                    F Scott Fitzgerald

ALS, 1p. n.d.—April/May 1923. (AO)

Great Neck, L.I.

Dear Mr. Ober—

I'm terribly sorry about missing Bercovici that morning. I had a bad case of grippe brought on by getting tight Thursday night, was in bed until yesterday and find I missed all sorts of important engagements both Sat. and Mon.

I hope you closed with him all right. I'm still anxious to talk to him, if he's not totally disgusted with me for breaking the engagement, because I've got several ideas that might aid him in mounting the skit. Enclosed is that story.† Hovey tells me Ray Long liked it.
                                    Sincerely Ashamed of my
                                    negligence, I am Yours
                                    F Scott Fitzgerald

Have there been any movie nibbles on "Dice, Brass Knuckles?"

ALS, 1p. n.d.—April/May 1923. (AO)

Great Neck, L.I.

Dear Mr. Ober—

I was away last week so I wasn't able to get to those rehearsals.‡ I'm awfully sorry I missed them.

Anything further on <u>The Beautiful and Damned</u>? I'm determined to make Warner Bros pay up more because they so mutilated the picture than for the money itself.
                                    Sincerely
                                    F Scott Fitzgerald

ALS, 1p. n.d.—received 18 May 1923. (AO)

---

*Gordon Bercovici, one of two brothers interested in producing Fitzgerald's playlet *Porcelain and Pink* on the vaudeville circuit.
†"Hot and Cold Blood."
‡Possibly for *Porcelain and Pink*.

Great Neck, L.I.

Dear Mr. Ober—

I suppose we'll have to take Warner's word for the B. + D. gross and perhaps its accurate. Am writing my novel for Hearst's magazine I think we should ask at least $25,000 for serial rights.

Did the <u>Porcelain + Pink</u> vaudeville sketch come to anything?

Sincerely
F Scott Fitzgerald

ALS, 1p. n.d.—received 21 June 1923. (AO)

Great Neck, L.I.

Dear Mr. Ober:

On rereading this story§ it doesn't seem good. I started it with one mood and plot and finished it with another and somewhere in between there is a joint that shows. However I have cut about 1800 words out of it and I think its somewhat better.

I have another one half one and meanwhile I will bring in the monagamy article¶ either tommorrow noon or early Monday Morning

Sincerely
F Scott Fitzgerald

P. S.   This had better be retyped.

ALS (ink and pencil), 1p. n.d.—received 12 November 1923. (AO)

On 19 November 1923 Fitzgerald's play The Vegetable *opened and closed at Nixon's Apollo Theatre in Atlantic City, New Jersey.*

Fitzgerald's total earnings for 1923 were $28,759.78. He sold six stories ($7,492.50). This Side of Paradise *earned $880;* Flappers and Philosophers, *$98;* The Beautiful and Damned, *$292;* Tales of the Jazz Age, *$270.43. He received an advance of $3,939 on* The Great Gatsby, *and Famous Players paid $10,000 for movie rights to* This Side of Paradise, *though the film was never made.*

---

§Possibly " 'The Sensible Thing,' " *Liberty,* 5 July 1924—or "Diamond Dick and the First Law of Woman," *Hearst's International Magazine,* April 1924.

¶"Making Monogamy Work"—syndicated under various titles; for example, " 'Why Blame It on the Poor Kiss If the Girl Veteran of Many Petting Parties Is Prone to Affairs After Marriage?' " in the *New York American,* 24 February 1924.

II
BOOM AND EUROPE

1924-1929

Dear Mr. Hovey:#

I'm delighted about the story*—I never intrinsicly lost faith in it but I began to feel that if no one wanted it my days of popular writing were about over.

I think when we get <u>The Reasonable Thing</u> back from Hovey it ought to go to Wheeler.† I had a letter from him yesterday asking me for a story and if he's buying Willa Cather he's evidently in the market for a little serious stuff. Besides its his length.

If "Our Own Movie Queen" comes back from the Tribune will you send it to me? I guess its a complete flop‡

Sincerely
F Scott Fitzgerad

ALS, 1p. n.d., n.p.—received 5 February 1924. Great Neck. (AO)

Great Neck, L.I

Dear Mr. Ober:

Here's the revised story.§ I don't know what to think of it but I'd rather <u>not</u> offer it to the Post. The ending is effective but a little sensational.

Here also is the Movie Outline.¶ When you get it typed please send a copy back to me. Thanks for that deposit this moring

As Ever.
F Scott Fitzgerald.

ALS (pencil), 1p. n.d.—17/18 March 1924. (AO)

#Harold Ober wrote in the top margin: "He means Ober".

*This is probably "Gretchen's Forty Winks," *The Saturday Evening Post*, 15 March 1924.

†John N. Wheeler, editor of *Liberty*. On 11 January Fitzgerald wrote to Hovey about his contract with *Hearst's International Magazine:* "I am to take back 'Rags Martin-Jones' . . . and I am also to buy back from you ' "The Sensible Thing" ' for the sum of $1,500, which was paid for it."

‡"Our Own Movie Queen," *Chicago Sunday Tribune*, 7 June 1925. Fitzgerald's ledger notes: "Two thirds written by Zelda. Only my climax and revision."

§"One of My Oldest Friends," *Woman's Home Companion*, September 1925.

¶Original story, "Grit," for the Film Guild, produced in 1924.

Great Neck,

Dear Mr. Ober:

This acknowledges the account + encloses the enclosure.

In haste

F Scott Fitzgerald

P. S.   The College Humor publication idea doesn't appeal to me—since for 1000 words more I could do one for Wheeler. Don't you agree?

ALS, lp. n.d.—received 12 April 1924. (AO)

Dear Mr. Ober:

The two stories are returned under separate cover.# I only made a few changes in The Unspeakable Egg (that is I made many [)] but only a few on the line they suggested.) They are welcome to make more but they ought to be careful.

I was too tired last night to do Zoebel's story (for Screenland)* I will do it on the boat + mail it from Paris on May 14th so it should reach here on the 21st. I regret this because he may have announced it and all, and I'm delaying him three weeks.

Also I'm mailing another story from Paris done on the boat.

Thank you for all your courtesy's of the past six months. As soon as I have a better adress than Guarantee Trust I will [wire] write you.

By the way, of course [today] yesterday was an exception. I mean ordinarily any money owed me ought just to be deposited in my name and not sent ᶜ/o Mr. Burnam. That was just so they'd hold the ms.

Most Sincerely

F Scott Fitzgerald

ALS, 3pp. n.d.—received 5 May 1924. Hotel Pennsylvania, New York, stationery. (AO)

#A note in the bottom margin of page three, in Ober's hand, lists three stories: "The Pusher-in-the-Face" (*Woman's Home Companion*, February 1925), "The Unspeakable Egg" (*The Saturday Evening Post*, 12 July 1924), "John Jackson's Arcady" (*The Saturday Evening Post*, 26 July 1924).

*Myron Zobel, editor of *Screenland Magazine*, had written Fitzgerald on 15 April 1924 requesting a critical article on some aspect of film production for the July 1924 issue. Fitzgerald forwarded the letter to Ober with this notation: "I told him I wanted a minimum of $200.00 for 1000 wds + referred him to you to order it. F Scott Fitzgerald". The article may have been "Why Only Ten Percent of Movies Succeed" or "The Most Pampered Men in the World," an article about directors. This article was never published.

In May 1924 the Fitzgeralds embarked on their second trip to Europe. In late May they were on the Riviera, where they lived at the Villa Marie, Valescure, St. Raphael, France. During this stay they met Gerald and Sara Murphy.

Hyerés, France
May 24th

Dear Mr. Ober;

We are living at a hotel here trying to [sublet] *rent* a villa. Living is cheap but travelling was expensive. As a weeks search hasn't produced a typist I am sending hereweth the ms. for Screenland. You'd better ask him first whether he still wants it—I'm a month and a half, or almost, behind my promise.

I hope that by this time John Jackson's Arcady is sold. I have your letter as to The Unspeakable Egg—many thanks. If we can't find a villa here we may move on so Paris is the best adress.

On second thoughts I am sending ms, under a separate cover so you can notify me if it goes astray.

As Ever
Scott F.

ALS (pencil), 1p. (AO)

Park Hotel, Hyéres, France

Dear Mr. Ober:

I hope the ms. of the article reaches you all right. If not I have a copy of it. We expect to take a villa here in a day or so if we can decide between two. Here in a hotel it has been difficult to do much work on my novel. So far I've only done one chapter and I've been gone from America almost four weeks.

Would the Sat. Eve. Post like an article on "How to live on $100.00 (or $50.00) a Month," a sort of companion piece to the other[†] telling about how we came to France to economize and what luck, good + bad, we had at it? And would they pay $1200? It would seem scarcely worth while to do it for less than that because it takes almost as long if not longer than a story by my new one or two day method.

I'm glad they liked John Jackson—I now have
1 story to appear in Hearsts[‡]

[†]"How to Live on $36,000 a Year," *The Saturday Evening Post*, 5 April 1924; "How to Live on Practically Nothing a Year," *The Saturday Evening Post*, 20 September 1924.
[‡]Possibly "The Baby Party," *Hearst's International Magazine*, February 1925.

1 " + 1 old article " McCalls[§]
2 " + 1 article " Woman's Home[¶]
3 " in Sat. Eve. Post[#]
1 Article in Screenland

I hope to Christ I get at least one movie right out of those [seven] *eight* stories (I forgot one in Jack Wheeler's Weekly) Could you tear one copy of each out of the magazines as they appear + mail them to me in envelopes. Otherwise I'll miss them. Also that story "Our Own Movie Queen" in The "Chicago Tribune". (Including the ones already published that makes exactly 19 [20] things sold in [four] five months. My God! Thats well over $20,000 worth of stuff. If only the movies liked "The Third Casket."

Scribners has pictures of me. If you phone Maxwell Perkins he'll send you some. Thanking you again for your many courtesies to me last winter and this Spring I am

As Ever Sincerely
F Scott Fitzgerald

P. S.   Your letter recieved announcing John Jackson deposit..

ALS, 2pp. n.d.—received 10 June 1924. (AO)

Villa Marie
Valescure
St. Raphael, France

Dear Mr. Ober:

If Hayward* offers $5000.00 I'd take it right away—if less use your own judgement.

I have your letter asking for a picture. As I wrote you a few days ago Scribners has some of which they'll give you as many as you want.

With Best Wishes
As Ever
F Scott Fitzgerald

ALS (pencil), 1p. n.d.—received 20 June 1924. (AO)

---

§"Rags Martin-Jones and the Pr-nce of W-les," *McCall's*, July 1924. The article was "Does a Moment of Revolt Come Sometime to Every Married Man?"

¶"One of My Oldest Friends" and "The Pusher-in-the-Face"; the article was probably "Wait Till You Have Children of Your Own," *Woman's Home Companion*, July 1924.

#"The Third Casket" (*The Saturday Evening Post*, 30 May 1924), "The Unspeakable Egg," and "John Jackson's Arcady."

*Independent producer Leland Hayward was interested in buying the film rights to "Diamond Dick and the First Law of Woman."

Villa Marie
Valescure
St. Raphael, France
June 30th, 1924

Dear Mr. Ober:

Thanks for the deposit (I refer to the $24.75 from the syndicate). I am working now on the Post Article.

Another thing. We havn't tried the <u>Beautiful + Damned</u> movie bonus for over a year—Perhaps it would be worth it. If it is ever going to gross that it should do so now for it has been exhibited in England according to a clipping I recieved.

<u>The Womans Home Companion</u> certainly seem to like the article. I hope they get results on it. I'm flattered at the full page in the Times.[†] Any news of Hayward?

Sincerely
F Scott Fitzgerald

ALS, 1p. (AO)

Villa Marie, Valescure
St. Raphael, France

Dear Mr. Ober:

I will have the Post Article to you on the 25th of July or thereabouts. This is allowing time to have it typed in Nice as there's no competent typist here.

This is to ask you to let me count on having the money from <u>Screenland</u> on July 15th—that is to ask you to deposit it for me then. This is to save an exchange of letters. Otherwise if say they paid on the 15th I would not perhaps hear about it until Aug. 5th or so. Can I count on that? In case my card went astray the above is a permanent address. "The Designer" gave Sinclair Lewis $50,000.00 for the serial rights to his new book!!![‡] My God!

Any news from Heyward as to <u>Diamond Dick</u>?

As Ever
F Scott Fitzgerald

ALS, 1p. n.d.—received 7 July 1924. (AO)

[†] *Woman's Home Companion* ran an advertisement on "Wait Till You Have Children of Your Own" in *The New York Times*, 20 June 1924.

[‡] *Arrowsmith* was serialized in *The Designer and the Woman's Magazine*, June 1924–April 1925.

Villa Marie
Valescure
St. Raphael
France

Dear Mr. Ober:

Thank you for depositing the Screenland money + for the various magazines which have safetly arrived. The article for the Post "How to Live on Practically Nothing a Year" is at the typists in Nice and will positively be mailed to you on Monday, the 21st of July.

Meanwhile the novel is almost done. Though we are living very cheaply here the getting settled is expensive and my funds are running low. I'm going to ask you if you will deposit $500.00 of the Post money (for the article) when you get this letter, or on, say, the 1st of August. The article will almost surely have reached you by then. After last winter I hate to ask you again and I am not absolutely strapped but being abroad I get nervous when the account gets low at the bank. Thanks for the news about Hayward. I hope he buys.

Sincerely
F Scott Fitzgerald

ALS, 1p. n.d.—received 28 July 1924. (AO)

Villa Marie
Valescure
St Raphael
France
July 24th 1924

Dear Mr. Ober:

I am sending you today under a separate cover my article for The S. E. P. entitled

"How to Live on Practically Nothing a Year".

If it <u>doesn't</u> reach you by, say, the 15th of *Aug.* wire me the word "Missing" and I will send another copy. This is just as a precaution

Sincerely
F Scott Fitzgerald

ALS, 1p. (AO)

Dear Mr. Ober:

In case the Post likes the article. The enclosed will give [him so] the illustrator some idea of the actual size of the car, Also—the other pictures are a plea to Mr. Blumenthal¶ if he illustrates it not to make my wife so utterly impossible looking.

I have no copies so could I have them back

Sincerely

F Scott Fitzgerald

ALS (pencil), 1p. n.d., n.p.—received 7 August 1924. St. Raphael. (AO)

Villa Marie

St Raphael, France

Dear Mr. Ober:

I cabled you today to get in touch with the Ed. Small Play Co. + wrote asking the price for movie of Unspeakable Egg. I'd be glad to get a $1000.

John Jackson's Arcady seemed pretty good to me. Hope the movies buy it. I havn't sold a movie in so long that I don't know what it feels like. Hope Post liked Article

Sincerely

P. S.   Thanks for Screenland deposit. Hope you have your money. I wrote asking you to deposit $500 of Post money if possible.

AL, 1p. n.d.—received 13 August 1924. From Fitzgerald. (AO)

Villa Marie, Valescure

St. Raphael

France

Dear Mr. Ober:

I'm glad you got so much for the "3d Casket."† *I mean so much for England* Some German Magazine wrote me and asked my price and I told them $10.00. They havn't answered so I guess its too high for them. The novel will reach you this month

Sincerely

Scott Fitzg—

P. S.   I hope Screenland came across. I think that Editor was a nervy bitch.§

ALS, 1p. n.d.—received 2 September 1924.

¶M. L. Blumenthal, illustrator for *The Saturday Evening Post*. Fitzgerald is referring to "How to Live on Practically Nothing a Year."

†$95 from *Pearson's* magazine.

§See letter received 5 May 1924. *Screenland* had commissioned an article on the movies and was holding back payment because it arrived late.

Villa Marie, Valescure
St Raphael, France
Sept 20th, 1924

Dear Mr. Ober:

The situation is as follows. I have finished my novel and will send it to you within 10 days or two weeks. It may or *may* not serialize —certainly it'd never get in the Post. Artisticly its head + shoulders over everything I've done. When I send it I'll send a letter about terms ect.

I'm about broke and as soon as the novel gets off I will write a story immediately, either for the Post or for Wheeler who has been dunning me for one violently. That story will be followed within a month by two more. The first one should reach you by October 20th or a little over two weeks after you recieve this letter—and as you have no doubt already guessed I'm going to ask you for an advance on it.

Now as I understand it I'm about $90.00 in your debt—$180.00 advanced on the Screenland article that got in too late [and] as against $90 or so due me from the English rights of the "3d casket." Here's what I fondly hope you can do:

deposit $600.00 for me on Oct 5th
" 800.00 for me on Reciept of the Story which will be about the 20th of the month. However I will write you again about the 2nd deposit when I mail the story. If this is inconvenient please drop me a cable.

Considering the fact that of the eleven stories I've written this year 4 of the 7 that have been published were run 1st in their issues I think I've had hard luck with the movies. I must try some love stories with more action this time. I'm going to try to write three that'll do for Famous-Players as well as for the Post. We are leaving for Rome about the 1st of November to spend the winter.

Sincerely
F Scott Fitzgerald

ALS, 1p. (AO)

St Raphael

Dear Mr. Ober:

Glad you got so much for the Sensible Thing in Englad.[#] Did you get my letter asking you to deposit $500.00 on Sept 6th?[¶]

Sincerely
F Scott Fitz—

$83 from *The Woman's Pictorial.*
¶ Ober noted here, "Told him twice."

P. S.   I hope you had your "daughter by preference" but I suppose by this time whichever it was you're glad

ALS, 1p. n.d.—received 27 October 1924. (AO)

Villa Marie, Valescure
St Raphael, Oct 19th

Dear Mr. Ober:

I'm glad to hear about the good English price for Rags Martin Jones.* Also thanks for the two deposits. I am in the middle of the story.† The last of the last revision of the novel is being typed.

You'd better adress me c/o Guaranty Trust Co. Paris (1 Rue des Italiens) as we leave here the day I send off the [stoo] story. I enclose a letter from Wheeler. He seems so keen that perhaps the 1st story had better go to him. This is letter number 1260 from him. I don't care about the order but my story is more of a [Post] love story than a Post story anyhow.

I will try the article on Rome as soon as I get there for the Post.‡ Intend writing at least four pieces immediately to keep me for the [wal] winter.

As Ever
F. Scott Fitzg—

ALS, 1p. (AO)

<u>St. Raphael, Oct 25th</u>
(After Nov. 3d, Care of the
American Express Co.
Rome Italy)

Dear Mr. Ober:

I am sending you today under separate cover the manuscript of my new novel <u>The Great Gatsby</u> for serialization. Whether it will serialize you will be a better judge than I. There is some pretty frank stuff in it [I] and I wouldn't want it to be chopped as Hovey chopped the <u>Beautiful + Damned</u>. Now here are my ideas:

(1.) I think the best bet by all odds is <u>Liberty</u>. It is a love story and it is sensational. Also it is only 50,000 words long which would give them ten installments of 5000 words each, just what they're looking

---

*$90 from *The Woman's Pictorial*.
†Probably "Love in the Night," *The Saturday Evening Post*, 14 March 1925.
‡"The High Cost of Macaroni," *Interim*, Nos. 1 & 2, 1954. *The Saturday Evening Post* rejected the article, which was intended as a companion piece to "How to Live on $36,000 a Year" and "How to Live on Practically Nothing a Year."

for. And moreover if they started it by February 1st it could be over in time for spring publication. I havn't had a book for almost three years now and I want Scribners to bring this out in April. I wish you would specify to John Wheeler that it must be run through by then.

(2.) Of course Ray Long will have to have first look at it according to our contract of 1923.§ But I don't want him to have it (small chance of his wanting it) because in his magazines it would drag on forever + book publication would be postponed. So I'd like to ask him $25,000 for it—a prohibitive price. But it wouldn't be worth my while to give it to him for less. For Liberty I would take $15,000 + I'm against asking more because of a peculiar situation between John + me. He told me he'd never bargain for a thing of mine again —he'd take it at the price offered or refuse it. Ring Lardner told him I was annoyed at him—anyhow its a sort of personal question as you see. So I don't think I'd want to ask him more than $15,000. When I was getting $900 a story I got $7000 or a serial, so now that I'm getting $1750, $15000 for a serial seems a fair price. Especially as its very short.

(3.) The Post I don't want to offer it to. Its not their kind of thing + I don't want to have it in there anyhow as it kills the book sale at one blow. So that's out.

(4.) In fact I think Liberty is far and away the best bet—I don't see who else could squeeze it in before April. The third chapter bars it from the womens magazines and that leaves nothing except the Red Book which would drag it out till Fall.

(5.) I've sent Scribners their copy. When you get a definate decision from Hearsts and Jack Wheeler will you phone Max Perkins and tell him as he'll be anxious to know and letters take so long. Also will you cable me.

(6.) Needless to say whether it serializes or not I will refer any and all moving picture bids on the book to you and will tell Scribners to let you know about any moving picture bids that come through them. Of course this is looking pretty far ahead.

(7.) In any case I would much appreciate your own frank opinion of the novel.

(8.) My story is now at the typist. It should reach you within the week.

As Ever
F Scott Fitzgerald

ALS, 2pp. (AO)

---

§Details of contract are in Fitzgerald's letter of 29 December 1922.

In November 1924 the Fitzgeralds traveled to Rome, where they stayed at the Hotel des Princes.

NOVEL AND STORY SENT IF YOU HAVE NOT MADE SECOND DEPOSIT CAN YOU DEPOSIT ELEVEN HUNDRED IMMEDIATELY OR THREE HUNDRED OTHER MASTE
    SCOTT

Wire to Reynolds office 3 November 1924. St. Raphael. (AO)

ᶜ/o American Express Co.
Rome, Italy

Dear Mr. Ober:

A word about the story. After reading it over very carefully I've come to the conclusion that its not one of my best. However, the one I'm working on now ought to be a wonder. The point is that I don't want to offer Wheeler "Love in the Night" as an order:

(1) because it isn't quite first rate

(2)   "   the novel will be offered him immediately [g] after I enclose, by the way, a letter which should go with the novel to Wheeler (if you think best, after reading it).

Now as to the all devastating question of money. I owe you somewhere around $200.00, [I think] (counting on Love in <u>the Night</u> being sold for $1750.00). As Í told you before I am very broke and well have to rehabilitate myself with three or four short stories, written one after the other. [This includes the one I'm working on now.] As soon as I finish *the one I'm working on now* [that] I'm afraid I'll have to wire you for some more money but I won't do it until the story is in the Post office. When the second story is sold I'll be more than square + the two or three to follow should put me ahead for the whole winter as life is very cheap, of course here in Rome. Then I'm starting another novel. My loafing days are [obliterated] over—I feel now as though I wasted 1922 + 1923.

What became of the Screenland Article + the Beautiful + *Dammed movie* bonus? Many congratulations on having a boy— though I know you wanted a girl I'm sure you're just as pleased now.

As Ever   Scott Fitzgerald

If Wheeler happens to buy novel will you kindly cable me the

news.¶ [I'm not sure] My letter to Wheeler is *not* comprehensive.
You'd better write him all the data anyhow, besides.#

ALS, 1p. n.d.—received 26 November 1924. (AO)

American Express Co.
Rome, Italy

Dear Jack:*

Reynolds is offering you my new novel for possible serialization.
It goes to Ray Long first because of a previous contract but he and
I agree very little + I doubt if he'll want it.†

Naturally, I'm mad about the book. Whether you like it or not
would you drop me a line telling me your honest opinion of it. I'd
be most interested to hear.

Mr. Ober will give you all the details about publication ect.

Sincerely
Scott Fitz—

ALS, 1p. n.d.—November 1924. (AO)

WAIT FOR REVISED VERSION OF LOVE IN NIGHT TO OFFER
POST SENDING STORY FOR RED BOOK

Wire to Reynolds office 25 November 1924. From Fitzgerald. Rome. (AO)

American Express Co. Rome
November 25th, 1924

Dear Mr. Ober:

Your telegam came today + I've answered it, telling you that I'm
sending a revised version of <u>Love in the Night</u> to be offered to the
Post. In its present form I suspect it of being no good. As to Wheeler
—the only thing to do is to offer him [Wheeler's fir] the first thing
Lorimer turns down. I can't risk my stand with Lorimer now + I
Think you are right. Also I'm sending a story which I think is a
peach, called the <u>Adjuster</u> for the Red Book order you wrote me of.‡

¶Written at the bottom of the page.
#Along the left margin. Another insert along the right margin is obliterated.
*This appears to be the letter Fitzgerald sent to Ober to be forwarded to Wheeler
with the manuscript of *The Great Gatsby*. Ober must have decided against sending it
to Wheeler.
†Long refused *The Great Gatsby* on 4 December, writing Reynolds, ". . . I don't
think it quite fits in." Wheeler refused it on 16 December, writing Reynolds, "It is
too ripe for us. Running only one serial as we do, we could not publish this story
with as many mistresses and as much adultery as there is in it."
‡*Red Book*, September 1925.

I should think the novel *(if he wants it)* would be enough for Wheeler now—anyhow tell him I wanted him to see that first. I feel I want to offer him that even if it makes Lorimer mad because I'm quite sure Lorimer wouldn't consider it. Of course you'll cable me if theres good news. I scarcely dare to hope.

We're trying to get settled + its hard as hell to write in a hotel —hence the delay on the second story. This is the "holy year" or something + appartments are hard to find

As Ever.   Scott Fitz

P. S.   Tell Wheeler the only story you got was rotten + I cabled after it not to send it anywhere till novel was decided

ALS, 1p. (AO)

OFFER NOVEL TO POST AS MATTER OF FORM THEN TO WHEELER TWO STORIES SENT DEPOSIT TWOHUNDRED SNEOTT

Wire to Reynolds office 7 December 1924. Rome. (AO)

Our adress for   { Hotel des Princes
Several Months   { Piazza di Spagna
                        { Rome, Italy

Dear Mr. Ober:

First thank you a thousand times for your telegram of congratulations + your letter about my book. It made me feel very good indeed. The book has some bad flaws in chapters VI + VII which I hope to remedy in proof but on the whole I am very proud of it. And many thanks for liking it too.

I agree with you about offering short stories to Wheeler—I don't want to be the goat of an inter-editorial row as, to a certain extent, I was in the Hovey-Ray Long race riot. As to the novel, why not offer it to the Post *as per telegram.* They will certainly refuse it + then can't kick if you give it to Wheeler.

Now as to money. I've sent you—a new story for the red book and am sending today a revised version of Love in the Night. Also I have a third story which goes to the typist tomorrow.§ I know I owe you quite a bit + am wiring you this afternoon to deposit, if possible, two hundred. When the new story arrives will you deposit $300 more? The story is excellent so you should get the Red Book money right away + get me out of the hole. In all three stories will reach

----

§"Not in the Guidebook," *Woman's Home Companion,* November 1925.

you before Xmas and one or two as soon after that as I can do them and I'm starting a new one today.

With many thanks and a prayer that this novel will put me on a financial footing where I won't be such a beggar Always I am

Most Gratefully
Scott Fitzg—

ALS, 2pp. n.d.—received 22 December 1924. (AO)

Fitzgerald's total earnings for 1924 were $20,310. He sold eleven stories ($15,868). His book royalties were $1,200.

Hotel des Princes, Rome, Italy.

Dear Mr. Ober:

By now you've got the <u>Adjuster</u>, and what is less pleasant I suppose you got that wire last week begging another two hundred. That makes about $350.00 over the Red Book story money that I owe you but the revised version of <u>Love in the Night</u> should clear it all up + leave me a balance. The third story wasn't good but I'm trying to fix it up. If I can't I'll start a new one tonight.

I'm not going to ask you for anymore until the first of the year —By that time I ought to be ahead. Eagerly awaiting bad news from the serial. I hope Wheeler takes it.

Scott Fitz—

ALS, 1p. n.d.—received 3 January 1925. (AO)

Hotel des Princes, Rome, Italy.

Dear Mr. Ober;

Tomorrow I am wiring you for three hundred more—and I hope to God that all three stories are Saleable because I owe more than I have for almost year and I'm humiliated to have to call on you again like this. As I havn't heard from I judge that Wheeler didn't want the novel which is very sad news tho it isn't really a surprise.

If two out of these three stories sell I should have a slight balance with you and if the third one does I shall be out of danger. I am beginning another one the day after Xmas.

Thank for your exceeding trust and good will in making this advance.

Sincerely
Scott Fitz—

ALS, 1p. n.d.—received 12 January 1925. (AO)

I'd rather use this {American Express Co.
for an adress {Rome, Italy

Dear Ober:

(After all these years I agree with you that it is high time to drop honorifics) 1st Thanks very much for the money, which eats well into the second story. [That takes the] I'm sure that the third story *("Not in The Guide Book")* will sell much easier than the other two. The Adjuster may seem too gloomy. However, time will tell.

I am starting a fourth story (really a sixth, for one I tore up and Love in the Night I rewrote completely, as you see. I'm a little disappointed about the novel but I suppose it did seem raw to Wheeler. He immediately wrote me the inevitable letter asking for a story.

If the novel is a big success I'm hoping my price will go up to $2000 regular. It's a neat sum and while I don't feel my stuff is worth anything like that its as good as a lot that gets much more.

I feel very old this winter. I'm twenty eight. I was twenty-two when I came to New York and found that you'd sold Head and Shoulders to the Post. I'd like to get a thrill like that again but I suppose its only once in a lifetime.

You've been awfully kind about this money. I don't know what I could have done without it. I've owed Scribner *the advance* on this novel for almost two years. Did Warner Bros. ever render a definate account on the B. + D. movie?

I hate Italy and the Italiens so violently that I can't bring myself to write about them for the Post.—unless they'd like an article called "Pope Siphilis the Sixth and his Morons" or something like that. But we're resolutely trying to econemize, so we [wouldn'tmo] wouldn't move back to France till March even if we could afford it.

Scott Fitz.

ALS, 2pp. n.d.—received 23 January 1925. (AO)

COULDNT DEFER PUBLICATION FOR LESS THAN TWENTY-THOUSAND SORRY¶
    SCOTT

Wire to Reynolds office 9 January 1925. Rome. (AO)

MUST DECLINE X SURE WOULD RUIN BOOK SALE.

Wire to Reynolds office 15 January 1925. From Fitzgerald. Rome. (AO)

¶Refers to *College Humor* offer for serialization of *The Great Gatsby*.

American Express Co.

Dear Ober:

I wired you today declining <u>College Humor</u>'s offer. Of course with the contributors you mention it couldn't be, at present, the lowsy sheet I saw a copy of last summer, but it will take it several years to live down its name. However the two chief objections were this.

(1.) That most people who saw it advertised in <u>College Humor</u> would be sure that Gatsby was a great halfback and that would kill it in book form.

(2.) While $10,000.00 is no sum to throw away lightly it postpones a turnover from book royaties and probable movie for five months, with the chance of materially decreasing the sale. I dread the gaudy and ill-advised advertising they'd give it.

I'm sure you'll agree that it would have been a foolish move. I have a strong hunch that I'm going to get about twenty five thousand for the movie rights if the book comes out now. If it waits till next fall the movie taste may change.

Regrettfully
Scott Fitzg—

ALS, 1p. n.d.—received 26 January 1925. Rome. (AO)

Hotel des Princes, Rome

Dear Ober:

Thanks for the latest deposit many times. I'm delighted that the two stories sold. The third hasn't reached you + thereby hangs a tale.# It was mailed and I went to bed for ten days with grippe. When I came too + went into the Am. Express Co. where I'd had it registered it was still there because the clerk noticed that I'd adressed it

70 5th Ave, <u>Paris, France</u>.

I opened it to have a last look + thought it was rotten so as I'd just recieved your cable about the Post story I decided to do it over. I'm working on it now.

When the Red Book pays will you [obliterated] please send me a statement so I can see how I stand with you. *I'm all mixed up but I think I'm ahead a little over $500.00* And if meanwhile I wire you to make a small deposit + you have already [made] put in the rest of

---

Probably "Not in the Guidebook."

the Red Book money just wire me that data. I think I am out of the hole now—thanks to you. I wish I could do the Post a crackerjack story.

Scott Fitz.

ALS (pencil), 1p. n.d.—received 5 February 1925. (AO)

American Express Co. Rome

Dear Ober:

Thanks for all you did about the novel. I'll try to do something for [Screenland] College Humor but 3000 words is pretty hard. Will send along a Post story—I think it'll be easier to raise my price with them (Rotten pen) after the novel is the big success I think its going to be. I've spent three extra weeks on it, clearing up that bum Plaza Hotel scene and now its really almost perfect of its kind.

God! How I hated to turn down that $10,000. If I'd been <u>one</u> <u>month</u> sooner *with it* I could have gathered it in. It makes me weep. But maybe [Ill] I'll get $25,000, for the serial.

By the way I'm writing College Humor a nice letter. *Please forward it to them.* Thanks for the deposits and I'm tickled that I'm straight at last. For the first time since last summer.

As Ever
Scott Fitz—

ALS (pencil and ink), 1p. n.d.—received 18 February 1925. (AO)

SENDING TWO STORIES MONDAY CAN YOU DEPOSIT THREE HUNDRED MORE
　　SCOTT.

Wire to Reynolds office 20 February 1925. Rome. (AO)

<u>Rome</u>

Dear Ober:

The <u>Vegetable</u> rights were controlled by Sam Harris but have now reverted to me. The second act was the biggest flop of all on the [obliterated] Atlantic City try out—and the whole thing has already cost me about a year + a half of work so I'd rather let it drop. Its honestly no good. From Feb 1922 until Nov. 1923 I was almost constantly working + patching the damn think + I don't think I could bear to look at anymore. If I ever change I'll let you know, I've never tinkered with the last act at all—oh, yes, I have + the Harris office may have it but it was flat as a pancake. I'd rather thank Mr. Goodman + let it die.

If you'll get an offer from College Humor for 3000 words one thousand dollars I'll try it but if the story does go over that I'd rather try someone else with it + then try again at the short length for them.

No news. Have one story at the typist + am trying the revise the one that wasn't good.

Thank you for all deposits

As Ever
Scott Fitzg—

ALS (pencil), 2pp. n.d.—received 2 March 1925. (AO)

Newadress { Hotel Tiberius
{ Capri

Dear Ober:

Will *be* glad to do Red Book Story. I'm delighted they liked the other.

Scott Fitz

ALS, 1p. n.d.—received 5 March 1925. (AO)

Hotel Tiberio, Capri

Dear Ober:

We've had a hell of a time here. My wifes been sick in bed three weeks + there isn't a typist nearer than Naples—the farmer who did this* kept it for 10 days at the other end of the Island. I have another ready too if he ever brings it back.

Good stories write themselves—bad ones have to be written so this took up about three weeks. And look at it. I'd rather not offer it to the Post [and] because everybody sees the <u>Post</u> but I know its saleable and I need the money. I leave it to you.

The Red Book story will be along shortly. For God's sake don't give them this. Thank you for the deposits. I don't know whats the matter with me. I can't seem to keep out of debt. Whenever I get ahead things like this sickness happen. Such is life. However two other stories will follow this thick and fast

As Ever
F Scott Fitzgerald

ALS, 1p. n.d.—March 1925. (AO)

---

*"Not in the Guidebook."

Dear Ober:

The enclosed might do for <u>Vanity Fair</u>.[†] They once paid me a hundred + now might do the same. I think its about their top price.

Hope the story about Paris reached you. I am stretching the other into a three parter called <u>The Rich Boy</u> which might bring $5000.00 or so from College Humor or the Red Book.[‡] I hope to send it on in a week.

Sincerely

Scott Fitzg

ALS, 1p. n.d.—received 13 April 1925. (AO)

MOVED ADRESSE ANY MOVIE OFFERS GATSBY HOTEL REGINA MARSEILLE CAN YOU DEPOSIT FIVE HUNDRED

Wire to Reynolds office 18 April 1925. From Fitzgerald. Naples. (AO)

Fitzgerald's third novel, The Great Gatsby, *was published by Scribners on 10 April 1925. In May the Fitzgeralds moved to Paris, where they took an apartment at 14 rue de Tilsitt. Fitzgerald first met Ernest Hemingway at this time.*

Guaranty Trust Co of New York

1–3 Rue des Italiennes

Paris, France

(Really <u>Marsielle, en route</u> to above)

Dear Ober:

Well, in my usual way, just as I had got approximately on my feet Ive succeeded in plunging into debt to you again. It must be something over 2000.00 and as I havn't heard to the contrary I gather that my suspicions were correct and <u>Not in The Guide Book</u> is unsaleable in the big markets. Also I sent you a little skit that might be worth a hundred somewhere if you care to fool with it.

We left Capri after two months of dangerous illness during which I was able to do little work. I have the three part story <u>The Rich Boy</u> finished and with a little revision I will send it to you from Paris. It is a good piece of work I think and I believe <u>College Humor</u> is the market for it.

About <u>Gatsby</u>. I have heard nothing from Scribner until today when he wired "Reviews Excellent. No data yet on Sales"—from which I gather it didn't get off to a flying start. By this time next

---

†Probably "My Old New England Farmhouse on the Erie," *College Humor*, August 1925.

‡Published in two parts by *Redbook* (January and February 1926), which paid $3,500.

week (when this arrives) it'll be obvious both whether I was a fool not to sell it serially and also whether the movies are interested. The minimum price would be $5000.00. If it goes to say fifty thousand copies I should want at least $10,000. and for anything over that, in the best-seller class I think I should get $25,000.00 which is what they seem to be getting nothing less than. However the latter situation seems unlikely at present due to two popular defects in the book—one that the title is bad and, two, that there is no important woman character and women move the fiction market outside the S. E. P.

I'd like Von Strohiem§ to do it in the movies. Do you think a wire mentioning the fact to him and asking him to read it would be of any use?

At any rate thank you for the last advance of $500.00. I'll try to get <u>The Rich Boy</u> to you on next Monday. My adress is as above

As Ever   Scott Fitzgerald

ALS, 1p. n.d.—received 2 May 1925. (AO)

CALL WILLIAM A BRADY¶
FITZGERALD.

Wire to Reynolds office 19 May 1925. Paris. (AO)

14 Rue de Tilsitt ⎱   Permanent
Paris, France   ⎰   Adress

Dear Ober:

Thank you for selling those two stories# and for the deposits and for the extra five hundred—it came in handy. We have decided that travelling saves no money, and taken an appartment here for eight months.

"What Price Macaroni?" and "The Rich Boy" (second and third versions respectively) are at the typist. Commercially the book has fallen so flat that I'm afraid there'll be no movie rights. However a book always has a chance value as a movie property. I imagine that if one movie makes a strike they buy the rights of all the other books you've written. However I'm not depressed and intend to do about five short stories this summer.

As Ever, Yours
F Scott Fitz—

ALS, 1p. n.d.—received 28 May 1925. (AO)

---

§Director Erich Von Stroheim.
¶Brady became the producer of *The Great Gatsby* play.
#Probably "Not in the Guidebook," "The Adjuster," or "Love in the Night."

IF DAVIS* MAKES DRAMATIZATION AND PLAY IS PRODUCED
WITHIN YEAR ACCEPT TERMS OFFERED BUT SINCE NOVEL AL-
READY HAS MOVIE VALUE WHICH WILL BE HELD UP INDEFI-
NATELY I WANT ONE THIRD OF ALL APICTURE RIGHTS† CAN
YOU DEPOSIT THREE HUNDRED

Wire to Reynolds office 1 June 1925. From Fitzgerald. Paris. (AO)

IF BRADY HESITATES CLINCH CONTRACT AT SIXTY FORTY.

Wire to Reynolds office 10 June 1925. From Fitzgerald. Paris. (AO)

CONTRACT AND ARTICLE‡ SENT CAN YOU DEPOSIT FIVEHUN-
DRED

Wire to Reynolds office 18 June 1925. From Fitzgerald. Paris. (AO)

IF STORY§ AND ARTICLE HAVE ARRIVED WILL YOU DEPOSIT
300 TODAY
    FITZOERALD

Wire to Reynolds office 22 July 1925. Paris. (AO)

NO WIRE RECEIVED WORRIED
FITZGERALD.

Wire to Reynolds office 24 July 1925. Paris. (AO)

14 Rue de Tilsitt
Paris, France

Dear Ober: First thanks for the hundredth time for all your
courtesy about advances. I must owe you nearly $2000.00 + I may
have to wire again next week. If you don't think the article is
saleable don't give it to the <u>Post</u> but tear it up. I have a carbon. I've
worked on it so long that it's one big mess. In any case if the <u>Post</u>
doesn't want it let it go.

The enclosed should be an excellent <u>Post</u> story.¶

<u>The Rich Boy</u> has been a scource of much trouble but its in shape
at last. I'm rewriting the 3d part this week. If its worth anything

---

*Owen Davis, playwright who adapted *The Great Gatsby* for the stage.

†The contract between Fitzgerald and William A. Brady gave Fitzgerald 40 per
cent of 5 per cent of the first $5,000; 40 per cent of 7½ per cent of the next $2,000;
40 per cent of 10 per cent in excess of $7,000; and one third of the motion picture
rights.

‡Probably "The High Cost of Macaroni."

§Probably "The Rich Boy."

¶"A Penny Spent," *The Saturday Evening Post*, 10 October 1925. Fitzgerald added
here in pencil: "It'll have to be retyped."

it should be worth [$4000.00] *3500.00* or at least $3000.00. If the Red Book doesn't want it why not try <u>College Humor</u>.

What's the dope on the <u>Liberty–Post</u> quarrel? Are they still refusing to admit each other's contributors. Had a nice letter from Owen Davis who says he'll be ready to rehearse in October.

Sincerely
F Scott Fitzgerald

ALS, 1p. n.d.—received 7 August 1925. (AO)

> THREE MANUSCRIPTS NOW SENT WILL YOU DEPOSIT TWO HUNDRED
> >FITZGERALD

Wire to Reynolds office 3 August 1925. Paris. (AO)

Memo.
Aug. 21, 1925.

Mr. Aley called up and said that he had to cut out about two hundred words in Scott Fitzgerald's story.# They changed the type of the magazine to larger type and they cut all their stories. He said he would do it very carefully. I don't think we need to say anything to Fitzgerald about it because I don't think he ever reads his stories.

H.O.

Typed Ober memo, 1p. (AO)

> PHONE MCCALLS RE OPTION NEW NOVEL FINISHED ONE YEAR PLEASE DEPOSIT THREE HUNDRED
> >SCOTT

Wire to Reynolds office 2 September 1925. Antibes. (AO)

> WHAT PRICE RICH BOY REQUEST PROMPT PUBLICATION SENDING STORY PLEASE DEPOSIT TWO HUNDRED
> >SCOTT

Wire to Reynolds office 8 September 1925. Antibes. (AO)

> PLEASE CUT AS FOWLER REQUESTS.*

Wire to Reynolds office 1 October 1925. From Fitzgerald. Paris. (AO)

Probably "Not in the Guidebook."

*Ludlow Fowler, the model for Anson Hunter of "The Rich Boy," made cuts in the story. In an undated letter during the spring of this year, Fitzgerald had written to Fowler: "I have written a fifteen thousand word story about you called <u>The Rich Boy</u>—it is so disguised that no one except you and me and maybe two of the girls concerned would recognize, unless you give it away, but it is in a large measure the story of your life, toned down here and there and symplified. Also many gaps had to come out of my imagination. It is frank, unsparing but sympathetic and I think you will like it—it is one of the best things I have ever one. Where it will appear and when, I don't as yet know." (PU)

14 Rue de Tilsitt
Paris, France

Dear Ober:

Thank you a million times for all the kind advances + for selling
The Rich Boy—I was afraid too it would be difficult. From this time
onward I'm going to keep ahead. My plans are as follows.

4 short stories to be written before the middle of November.

I think fate must have decided about the article What Price
Macaroni? I told you when I sent it that it was the lousiest thing I'd
ever written—and Im glad its lost. I have a copy and I read it over
but with discouragment. Maybe after another story—the first one
goes off tomorrow I'll have the courage to tinker with it once more.

Have you an approximate date for the out-of-town opening of the
play?[†]

Sincerely
F. Scott Fitzgerald

ALS, 1p. n.d.—received 3 October 1925. (AO)

14 Rue de Tilsitt, Paris

Dear Ober:

This is in re of several matters of which the first is to thank you
for those last two advances. I hope the Rich Boy money has come
in + also that you have no trouble in disposing of the 1st story.

Too bad about the Fowler changes—still the Red Book shouldn't
mind making them as they're both rather realistic, crude statements
for a popular magazine. It is the story of his life—he's an old friend
—we went to Princeton together + he told me those things in
confidence. Incidently he's a brilliant young lawyer + an awfully
nice fellow.

I'd rather not tell about the new novel yet—as part of it isn't clear
in my mine and I don't want it to chrystalize too soon. Did McCall
want an option so far ahead?

About the play—will you keep me posted? Also I'd like first night
tickets mailed to the following (that is if it reaches N.Y.)

J. V. Forrestal—28 Nassau St.[‡]

and six tickets to the Scribner Co. for Max Perkins to distribute as
he sees fit. Will you take care of that for me.

[†] *The Great Gatsby.*

[‡] James V. Forrestal, Princeton '15—the future Secretary of the Navy and of
Defense.

I am hard at work on the second story but it has been snarling me for a week.

Sincerely
F Scott Fitzgerald

ALS, 1p. n.d.—received 14 October 1925. (PU)

TWO STORIES SENT WILL YOU DEPOSIT TWOHUNDRED
    FITZGERALD.

Wire to Reynolds office 12 October 1925. Paris. (AO)

FOUR STORIES SENT CAN YOU DEPOSIT TWOHUNDRED POSI-
TIVELY LAST
    FITZGERALD

Wire to Reynolds office 4 November 1925. Paris. (AO)

14 Rue de Tilsitt
Paris, France

Dear Ober: Havn't written for ages but as you see have been working like a dog for six weeks. This morning comes a cable from *one* Basil Moon§ in London wanting to see me here about the "Cosmopolitan". It would cost that damn Ray Long $2500. to see any more stories of mine—maybe more. If that's what this fellow wants I'll of course wire you.

I wrote Wheeler a letter that evaded every question he asked me —a vague mention of "after my new novel was finished."

Scribners have no interest in Two for a Cent. I don't think its a good story and am never going to republish it and since its four years old now + has well yielded up its syndicate milk I told Boas + Hahn they could reprint it for nothing (tho of course I reserved all rights).¶

As far as The Vegetable is concerned anyone can use it who wants it in an amateur way but I advise strongly against their trying it. Some misguided amateurs in Baltimore came to grief on it last winter.

Magazines all arrived and thank you. Also the letter from the Women's Home Companion. Those things I leave to you—perhaps now they'd give [2500] 2,250 or MᶜCalls might. However I'm content with the Post at 2000 while the Red Book seems most hospitipal to my more serious work.

---

§Probably Basil Woon, English newspaper editor.
¶*Short Stories for Class Reading*, ed. Ralph P. Boas and Barbara M. Hahn (New York: Holt, 1925).

Thanks a million times for all your kindnesses about deposits   I
hope these stories will clear them up forever.

Sincerely

F Scott Fitzgerald

P. S.   I don't want to annoy Davis but I'd love to have a copy of
the play The Great Gatsby <u>as written</u>, both to read + for my files.
I suppose the date is now January.

ALS, 1p. n.d.—received 30 November 1925. (AO)

IF STORIES SOLD CAN YOU DEPOSIT FIVE
   FITZGERALD

Wire to Reynolds office 23 November 1925. London. (AO)

LENGEL# OFFERS EIGHT THOUSAND TWO HUNDRED FIFTY
THREE STORIES DELIVERED BEFORE JANUARY ADVISE ACCEP-
TANCE ANSWER RUSH
   FITZGERALD

Wire to Reynolds office 24 November 1925. Paris. (AO)

RE PREVIOUS TELEGRAM PLEASE WIRE ME SAYING PRICE RISE
JUSTIFIES THREE THOUSAND COSMOPOLITAN.

Wire to Reynolds office 25 November 1925. From Fitzgerald. Paris. (AO)

THIRD WIRE SUPPLANTING OTHERS STRONGLY ADVISE
THREE AT TWENTY SEVEN FIFTY IF LONG AGREES

Wire to Reynolds office 25 November 1925. From Fitzgerald. Paris. (AO)

I AGREE WITH YOUR DECISION*

Wire to Reynolds office 26 November 1925. From Fitzgerald. Paris. (AO)

ADOLESCENT MARRIAGE SENT TWO DAYS BEFORE PRESUMP-
TION OTHER WEEK LATER SENDING DUPLICATE†

Wire to Reynolds office 21 December 1925. From Fitzgerald. Paris. (AO)

*Fitzgerald's total earnings for 1925 were $18,333.61. He sold five stories
($11,025), and his* Saturday Evening Post *price was raised to $2,500. His
book royalties were $4,906.61—including $1,981.85 from* The Great
Gatsby, *above the Scribners advance.*

   # William C. Lengel of Hearst's International Magazine Co. This offer may have
been from *Cosmopolitan.*
   *Ober's decision in the *Cosmopolitan* negotiations is not known.
   †"The Adolescent Marriage." 6 March 1926, and "Presumption," 9 January 1926,
The Saturday Evening Post.

As I remember, the corrections on the other *copy* were better than these in several places, so <u>if it comes in send out the other</u>, please.

Dear Ober:

I was good and scared when I found this story hadn't arrived because I thought at first I didn't have a copy. I had given the original to a man returning to Seattle <u>who was to mail it to you on his arrival in New York</u>—that was to have been the quickest way! Then mucilage was spilled on the carbon copy—and then I got word from you that <u>Presumption</u> had arrived first. What saved me from the total loss of the story (for by wire and letter I havn't yet got a satisfactory answer from Seattle—the original seems to have been left in care of a stranger in New York who was to "wait instructions from me," whatever that means) was that the woman at the Meurice here who does my typing has the pencilled ms. It is a copy of that, corrected which is here enclosed.

I havn't any idea how much I owe you. Will you wire me any [sails] sales. It must be over $3000. I'm terribly sorry and very very grateful

Scott Fitzgerald

From nowon best adress for <u>everything</u> is Care <u>Guaranty Trust</u> Co, 1 Rue des Italiens Paris[‡]

ALS, 1p. n.d.—received 14 January 1926. (AO)

RUMOR UNFOUNDED[§] DONT TRY DANCE POST THANKS

Wire to Reynolds office 21 January 1926. From Fitzgerald. Salies-de-Béarn. (AO)

^{c}/o Guaranty Trust Co.
1 Rue des Italiens

Dear Ober:

We have come to a lost little village called Salies-de-Béarn in the Pyrenes where my wife is to take a special treatment of baths for eleven months for an illness that has run now for almost a year.[¶] Here they have the strongest salt springs in the world—and out of season nothing much else—we are two of seven guests in the only open hotel.

---

‡Written along the left margin.
§A 16 January 1926 dispatch from Paris in the *Chicago Tribune* was headlined: "Scott Fitzgerald Ill In France."
¶Zelda Fitzgerald had colitis.

We'll be here until March 1st but you'd better adress any letters to me at Paris—that's just as quick for letters. Cables about the play had better come to Fitzgerald, Bellevue
Salies-de-Bearn, France.

One Word

About the story <u>The Dance</u>,# the first detective story I've ever tried, I'm afraid its no good—(if it ever reaches you—I'm beginning to think that nothing I send ever does. That one I had registered. Did both copies of <u>Adolescent Marrige</u> come—or either) to continue —please don't offer the dance to the <u>Post</u> or <u>Red Book</u>. Why not <u>College Humor</u> for $1500. or <u>Women's Home Companion</u> (?). Tell me what you think?

I must owe you thousands—three at least—maybe more. I am forever under obligations to you for your kindness. [obliterated] From now till March 1st will be a steady stream of $2500. stories— five *more* of them. And I hope by then the play will begin to yield something on the side. I honestly think I cause you more trouble and bring you less business than any of your clients. How you tolerate it I don't know—but thank God you do. And 1926 is going to be a different story.

Did I tell you McCalls wrote again asking me about the novel. Will you talk to them? Its begun but I'm putting it aside for a month or so like I did <u>Gatsby</u> and it won't be done before the end of the year.

Someone told me Mr. Reynolds had been sick. Is that so? I hope not.

Thank you for the thousandth thousand for the thousandth time.
Scott Fitzg—

Story sent yesterday which was to have been 4th of series but was so much revised that I didn't send it from Paris after all. Have sent in all <u>seven</u> manuscripts of <u>four</u> different stories.*

ALS, 2pp. n.d.—received 4 February 1926. (AO)

AUDIENCE ENTHUSIASTIC OVER GATSBY PREDICT REAL SUC-
CESS PLAY CARRIED GLAMOR OF STORY EXCELLENTLY CAST
AND ACTED REVIEWS ALL VERY FAVORABLE WRITING
　　HAROLD OBER NEWYORK

Wire to Fitzgerald 4 February 1926. Fitzgerald pasted this telegram in his scrap-book.

#"The Dance," *Redbook*, June 1926.
*Probably included "Presumption," "The Adolescent Marriage," "The Dance."

The Owen Davis play version of The Great Gatsby *opened at the Ambas-sador Theatre in New York 2 February 1926. It starred James Rennie as Gatsby, Florence Eldridge as Daisy, and Edward H. Wever as Nick. The reviews were good, and the play ran for the season before making a road tour. Fitzgerald's share of the receipts was $7,630—plus $16,666 for the movie rights.*

Fitzgerald's third collection of short stories, All the Sad Young Men, *was published by Scribners in February 1926.*

Dear Ober:

This won't make any money—maybe $50 or a bit more but I'm awfully anxious to get it published. Its little more than a review.[†]

Will you try <u>The American Mercury</u>—I especially want [them] *Mencken* to see it first

Then The <u>Bookman</u>
    "   " [Dial N.Y.] Literary Review
    "   " <u>International</u> Book Review
I think one of these [three] *four* will take it.

Sincerely
F Scott Fitzgerald

ALS (pencil), 1p. n.d.—received 15 February 1926. Salies-de-Béarn. (AO)

PLEASE WIRE PREDICTING RUN

Wire to Reynolds office 17 February 1926. From Fitzgerald. Salies-de-Béarn. (AO)

Guaranty Trust Co.
1 Rue des Italiens

Dear Ober:

Thank you for all the dope—believe me it was most welcome. I enjoyed the clippings and your wires and the detailed accounts of everything Today I wired asking a prediction as to its run. Perhaps its already in the warehouse. Did the snow-storm hurt it?

Did you get my wire asking that the title <u>The Dance</u> be changed into <u>In a Little Town</u>? Of course its up to the Red Book.

Will you send me an account on how I stand with you? I need it for my income tax and am all mixed up in own accounts.

Please thank Mr. Reynolds, too, for writing me that dope. I thought the Davis version read pretty badly but altogether I'm

---

†"How to Waste Material A Note on My Generation," *The Bookman*, May 1926. Fitzgerald received $100 for this essay-review of Hemingway's *In Our Time*.

delighted—the production must have been great—especially Rennie. What was the "intense heat" effect they all spoke of?

If you hear that its going to be taken off wire me so I'll be prepared.

Again many thanks for keeping me so well posted

As Ever

Scott Fitzgerald

ALS, 2pp. n.d.—17 February 1926. (AO)

For Anne Ober

Hoping that none of her descendents will be sad young men

F Scott Fitzgerald

Inscription in *All the Sad Young Men*. (AO)

Salies . de . Béarn

God knows where

Dear Ober:

This§ is one of the lowsiest stories I've ever written. Just <u>terrible</u>! I lost interest in the middle (by the way the last part is typed triple space because I thought I could fix it—but I couldn't)

<u>Please</u>—and I mean this—don't offer it to the <u>Post</u>. I think that as things are now it would be <u>wretched</u> policy. Nor to the <u>Red Book</u>. It hasn't <u>one</u> *redeeming* <u>touch</u> of my usual spirit in it. I was desperate to begin a story + invented a business plot—the kind I can't handle. I'd rather have $1000, for it from some obscure place than twice that + have it seen. <u>I feel very strongly about this</u>!

Am writing two of the best stories I've ever done in my life.

As Ever—Scott Fitz—

ALS (pencil), 1p. n.d.—received 15 March 1926. (AO)

Dear Ober:

If my father from Washington, phones you in the next month or so will you have two seats to the play (best seats) left in box office for him + placed to my account?

Hope the play isn't in Joe Leblancs yet.¶

The Post made me furious by some silly cutting in <u>The Adolescent Marriage</u>. They have a right to be silly at 2500. a story but when

---

§"Your Way and Mine," *Woman's Home Companion*, May 1927, for which Fitzgerald received $1,750.

¶Leblang, a theatre agent who handled cut-rate tickets for failing shows.

two very clever paragraphes disappear of which I have no duplicate or record it makes me angry. Could you get me the ms. or an uncut proof of it so I can clip the pps. for my files? Especially the one about a church with car-cards in the pews or something.

Wasn't your way + mine terrible! Thanks for the deposits.

Always Sincerely
F Scott Fitzgerald

Glad you've moved uptown!#

ALS, 1p. n.d., n.p.—March 1926. (AO)

From March to December 1926 the Fitzgeralds were on the Riviera, at Juan-les-Pins.

Adress till   ⎧   <u>Villa Paquita</u>
June 15th   ⎨   <u>Juan-les-Pins</u>
                   ⎨   Not   { Alpes Maritime
                 ⎩ Nessessary   <u>FRANCE</u>

Dear Ober:

If a man called <u>Holger Lundberg</u>* phones you will you see that he has two seats for <u>Gatsby</u>?

Did you ever get a lousy story called <u>Your Way and Mine</u>?

Whats my average weekly return from <u>Gatsby</u>? I see its dropped from 15,500 to 14,000.† Warn me if its about to quit.

As Ever Cordially
Scott Fitzg—

ALS, 1p. n.d.—received 3 April 1926. (AO)

Gatsby picture possible offer forty five thousand advise acceptance cable quinck   Ober.

Wire to Fitzgerald c. 16 April 1926. Fitzgerald pasted this wire in his scrapbook.

ACCEPT OFFER   FITZGERALD

Wire (cc) to Reynolds office 16 April 1926. Juan-les-Pins. (AO)

LIBERTY SITUATION COMPLICATED WAIT LETTER PLEASE DEPOSIT SIX HUNDRED

Wire to Reynolds office 19 April 1926. From Fitzgerald. Antibes. (AO)

#Written along the left margin. The Reynolds agency had moved from 70 Fifth Avenue to the Scribner Building at 597 Fifth Avenue.

*A poet.

†These are gross weekly receipts for the play.

Dear Ober:

Thanks for tax blank

          "   "   statement

          "   "   story news

          "   " $1000 deposit

          "   "   mysterious telegram.

Did the article (sent many months ago) on <u>What Price Macaroni</u>? ever drift in. Not that it matters now, but I notice you didn't mention it in your list.

As to the pictures—I've been meaning for three years to have some taken—and next week I really will

As Ever
F Scott Fitzg—

P. S. Ms. of Adolescent Marriage arrived

P. S. Thanks for getting father tickets. Were all those 1st night seats free?

P. S. And many thanks for the clippings.

ALS, 1p. n.d., n.p.—received 22 April 1926. (AO)

Villa Paquita
Juan-les-Pins
Alpes Maritime
(After May 3d adress me
Villa St. Louis
Juan-les-Pins
Alpes Maritime

Dear Ober:

Naturally I was very excited about the movie opportunity. As I've heard no more I fear its fallen through—I'm anxiously awaiting news.

I have your two letters in regard to <u>Liberty</u>. Now as to the short story business alone I would rather, without qualification, stay with the <u>Post</u> at $2500. than go to <u>Liberty</u> at $3500. Not only that but I shall probably write no short stories of any kind until next autumn.

But there is another element which might force me to leave the <u>Post</u> and that is the novel serialization. The novel is about one fourth done and will be delivered for possible serialization about January 1st. It will be about 75,000 words long, divided into 12 chapters, concerning tho this is absolutely confidential such a case as that girl who shot her mother on the Pacific coast last year.# In

---

\# In January 1925 Dorothy Ellingson murdered her mother in San Francisco.

other words, like <u>Gatsby</u> it is highly sensational. Not only would this bar it from the <u>Post</u> but also they are hostile, as you know, to the general cast of thought that permeates my serious work.

On the other hand <u>Liberty</u> is evidently very much in my favor at the moment. And if they would give between $25,000 and $40,000 for the serial I'd be an idiot to throw it away. In other words with say about 30,000 for the serial + assurance that Liberty will have a stable editorial policy at least till Jan 1st 1927, I'd better swing over there. Frankly I'm at sea. Perhaps it had better depend on whether they would really contract [with] for the novel in advance. I hope to bring it home completed next December.

Wire me your advice. The trouble is that if <u>McCalls</u> or <u>Red Book</u> ran it it would take a solid year and I hate that while <u>Liberty</u> would run it in 3 mos.

Oh, hell—I hate to leave the <u>Post</u>. What is <u>Liberty</u> like anyhow? Prosperous or just subsidized?

Anxiously
F Scott Fitzgerald

ALS, 3pp. n.d.—received 3 ·May 1926. (AO)

New ⎰ Villa St. Louis
Adress ⎱ Juan-les-Pins

Dear Ober—

That's great news about the movies. I hope the play runs through May.

If the World Syndicate want to republish <u>One of My Oldest Friends</u> its O. K with me. Scribners have no jurisdiction over anything unless they've published it in a book.

With Best Wishes
Scott Fitzgerald

ALS, 1p. n.d.—received 8 May 1926. (AO)

GATSBY*

Wire to Reynolds office 6 May 1926. From Fitzgerald. Juan-les-Pins. (AO)

Villa St. Louis
Juan les Pins

Dear Ober: Hereweth the contracts.
Swanson† is imploring more stories.

---

*Ober added a note which reads: "Means Contracts signed and mailed".
†H. N. Swanson, editor of *College Humor*—later Fitzgerald's Hollywood agent.

"What Price Macaroni" has been destroyed and best pieces are in
  my note book.

What does <u>Liberty</u> say?

Needless to say I'm delighted about the movie news.

I didn't send <u>Power of Attorney</u> because I'll be home in a few
  months + nothing is liable to come up before that time.

Will you send me a sample copy of <u>McNaught's [Weekly]</u> *Monthly*?
  I'd like to see one.

I cabled you the word "Gatsby" as you suggested.

Working hard as hell.

Best Wishes, as always
Scott Fitzgerald

ALS, 1p. n.d.—received 18 May 1926. (AO)

Adress   →   Villa St.Louis
till Oct 1st   Juan-les-Pins, Alpes Maritime
                 France

Dear Ober—

  Well, its rather melancholy to hear that the run was over. However as it was something of a <u>succés d'estime</u> and put in my pocket
seventeen or eighteen thousand without a stroke of work on my part
I should be, and am, well content.

  A thousand thanks for your courtesy to my father. You went
[way] out of your way to be nice to him and he wrote me a most
pleased and entheusiastic letter. He misses me, I think, and at his
age such an outing as that was an exceptional pleasure. I am, as
usual, deeply in your debt, and now for a most pleasant + personal
reason. His own life after a rather brilliant start back in the seven-
ties has been a "failure"—he's lived always in mother's shadow and
he takes an immense vicarious pleasure in any success of mine.
Thank you.

Yours Always
Scott Fitzgerald

No stories sent since your way and mine.

ALS, 1p. n.d.—received 3 June 1926. (AO)

Paris, July 1st 1926

Dear Ober:

  I am in a lowsy little hotel near the American Hospital here
where my wife's just been delivered of an unwelcome appendix.
When I get back to Juan-les-Pins next week I'll write you at length.
This is just to say

(1.) I think the <u>Liberty</u> offer[‡] is fine. If the "end of the year" is taken to mean perhaps as late as March. I'll even consent to certain cuts but don't tell them that till they ask or they'll demand more.

(2) Have seen a lot of James Rennie here. I hope it works out so that he opens in Chicago this fall.

(3) Oh God! Mr. Swanson.

(4) Thank you for all deposits

> More Later
> Faithfully
> Scott Fitzg—

ALS, 1p. (AO)

> Villa St. Louis
> Juan-les-Pins

Dear Ober:

Home again. Many thanks for M[c]Naughts. I understand Rennie opens in Chicago in [Paris] <u>Gatsby</u>. Saw a lot of him in Paris.

Will you let me know for my files what English magazines those last two stories were sold to?[§] The last ones you mentioned.

Operation a great success. Working like hell

> Faithfully
> Scott Fitzgerald

P.S.   Hope you have luck with Hemmingways work. I think he's got a great future.

P. S.[¶] Confirming my previous letter I am all for the Liberty arrangement.

Accounts Recieved

ALS, 1p. n.d.—July 1926. (AO)

> Villa St. Louis
> Juan-les-Pins
> A—M
> France

Dear Ober:

Thanks for the wire about the deposit. Thats great news about the play.[#] Maybe I'll see it in Washington Christmas. We sail for home

---

[‡]For serial rights to the new novel.
[§]"Presumption" and "The Adolescent Marriage" were sold to *Woman's Pictorial.*
[¶]Added in pencil.
[#]Probably refers to the success of the road company.

on the <u>Conte Biancamo</u> from Genoa December 10th + spend Xmas in Alabama. Returning to New York early in January I hope to hand you the novel ms.

I never heard of the gal who claims in the <u>Telegraf</u> to be my heroine. No news.

Faithfully
Scott Fitzg—

ALS, 1p. n.d.—received 2 October 1926. (AO)

Villa St. Louis
Juan-les-Pins

Dear Ober:

Hold the book for me.* Thanks for wire about deposits. How much do those people pay for Detroit performance of <u>Gatsby</u>? I forwarded yr. note to Hemminway

In Haste
Scott Fitz

ALS, 1p. n.d.—received 14 October 1926. (AO)

Fitzgerald's total earnings for 1926 were $25,686.05. He sold only two stories ($3,375). His book royalties were $2,033.20. The movie and play income from The Great Gatsby *was $19,464.21.*

In December 1926 the Fitzgeralds returned to the United States and visited the Sayres in Montgomery. In January 1927 they went to Hollywood, where Fitzgerald worked at United Artists on a film called "Lipstick" for Constance Talmadge.

I CAN FINISH NOVEL BY MAY FIRST BUT WOULD LIKE UNTIL JUNE FIRST IF POSSIBLE PLEASE CONSULT LIBERTY AND WIRE REPLY IMMEDIATELY CARE JUDGE SAYRE SIX PLEASANT AVENUE MONTGOMERY ALA HAPPY NEW YEAR.
    SCOTT FITZGERALD.

Wire to Reynolds office 2 January 1927. Montgomery. (AO)

---

*Probably *The World's Best Short Stories of 1926*, ed. William Johnston (New York: Doran, 1926), which included "One of My Oldest Friends."

Dear Ober:

Will see you in 3 weeks. Am here trying to write an original story for Constance Talmadge. Was only 12 hrs in New York. Expect to finish novel before April 1st.

As Ever
Scott Fitzg—

ALS, 1p. n.d.—received 24 January 1927. Ambassador Hotel, Los Angeles, stationery. (AO)

Dear Ober:

Will be in New York on or about a week from today or maybe 10 days + will phone immediately.

Father still talks of your kindness to him

Sincerely
Scott Fitzg.

Roosevelt Hotel
Washington, D.C.

ALS, 1p. n.d.—received 15 March 1927. (AO)

Dear Mr. Reynolds:

When I was in Hollywood Lanes Quirk of <u>Photoplay</u> wired me asking for 500 wd editorial + offering $250.[†] His representative there stood over me in person until I handed it to him, whereapon Quirk wired that he was entheusiastic, had sent check ect. In New York he told me the same personally. But the check never arrived.

It was so smal! + so simple a matter that I didn't refer it to you —This is to ask you now to take up the matter with him + see why he doesn't come across. I believed its scheduled for an early issue.

Hope Ober is much better.

As Ever
Scott Fitzgerald

ALS, 1p. n.d.—received 7 April 1927. Hotel du Pont, Wilmington, Delaware, stationery. (AO)

In April 1927 the Fitzgeralds leased "Ellerslie" near Wilmington, Delaware, and he tried to work on his new novel, which eventually became Tender Is the Night.

[†]"Editorial on Youth" by Scott and Zelda Fitzgerald was sold to *Photoplay* in April 1927 for $500, but it was not published. *Smart Set* published it as "Paint and Powder" in May 1929.

Dear Mr. Reynolds:

Is Ober no better? Not a line from him.‡ I hope he's progressing.

How about that story I outlined to you? Do you think that it is saleable? The cigarette story, I mean.

The novel progresses fast. Finished in 2 mos. I hope.

As Ever

Scott Fitzg—

P.S. I meant, of course, to ask you to collect from Quirk on your usual terms. If his agent hadn't stood over me + snatched it out of my hands I'd have sent it through you.

FSF

Ellerslie
Edge Moor
Delaware

ALS, 1p. n.d.—received 21 April 1927. (AO)

MEMO.

April 27, 1927.

F. Scott Fitzgerald.

Fitzgerald told me about the difficulty he has been having over the moving picture deal he made. When he arrived from Europe he received wireless and telegrams from John W. Consadine, Jr., who is now with the United Artists. This is an organization with Mary Pickford, Douglas Fairbanks, Constance Talmadge, and one or two other stars—I think Charlie Chaplin. Fitzgerald said he was in New York only two or three hours. He came in to see Max Perkinsand he didn't remember that we were not still at 70 Fifth Avenue. He tried to get down there but couldn't make it, and finally decided to go ahead and make the deal with the picture people, not asking our advice. He says he is now very sorry he did.

Consadine had met him before and he at first proposed to give Fitzgerald $2500. down and give him $10,000 when his work on the picture was finished. Fitzgerald refused and finally they agreed to give him $3,500. down and $12,500. whn the picture was finished. He said, however, they did not give him all the money at once, but gave him a drawing account of $500.00 every two weeks, or something like that.

They wanted a picture of college life. His idea was for the story to be called LIPSTICK, in which a college girl is unjustly imprisoned. While she is there, she meets somebody who gives her a mysterious recipe for lipstick, which when she puts on her lips makes every man who meets her want to kiss her.

---

‡In top margin: "Ive written him thanking him for his present etc. HO".

He says they were all enthusiastic about the idea, and told him to go ahead and work it out. He did so, and turned in the manuscript which he thinks is about 8,000 words in length. Consadine said that he liked it very much and when Fitzgerald asked him if it was necessary for him to stay around any longer, he said "no."

A few days ago, which is about two months after turning in the manuscript, Fitzgerald received a long telegram which he showed me saying that they had decided not to produce the picture, and that in case he sold the story to another company they would expect him to pay back the $3,500. they had advanced him. I do not think that Fitzgerald is bound to pay any of this money back, but he says he would rather do so. He says he got into a row with Constance Talmadge for whom the story was written, and he thinks that is the reason they didn't want to do it. He says also it is a very small organization, having only five or six stars, and a bigger company would be able to do it better.

He says he spent considerably more than $3,500. while he was in Hollywood, so the thing is a complete loss to him so far. Fitzgerald says that he would like to have this offered to only two companies—Famous Players, where Consadine has suggested that Bebe Daniels would be interested, and Metro Goldwyn Mayer. He has wired to Consadine to send the manuscript to us at once.

He thinks it had better be offered on the Coast, and I told him (thinking of Landeau) we knew a man who was going out next week, and we would have him take it up. He says that if these two companies turned it down he would fix it up for College Humor. He says it is a crazy kind of story that nobody else will buy.

Typed office memo, 2pp. Almost certainly by Ober. (AO)

Dear Harold:§

Tell the agent the whole situation. The matter of the returned money he should refuse to discuss with Consedine as that is entirely unofficial and between Consedine and me.

The story is suggested for Bebe Daniels. [throu]

If for any reason Consedine refuses to hand over story ask [him] the agent to wire East.

Nobody to see story except Famous.

Don't mention Consedine's name to Famous *as suggesting Schul-*

---

§This is the first Fitzgerald letter addressing Ober by his first name. They knew and corresponded with one another for over seven years before arriving at this informality.

berg,¶ though it is no secret that it was written for Constance Talmadge.

Working hard. It was good to see you Wedensday.

As Ever
Scott Fitzg

ALS, 1p. n.d., n.p.—received 2 May 1927. "Ellerslie." (AO)

ARTICLE SENT⁺ CAN YOU DEPOSIT FOUR HUNDRED AND FIFTY.
    FITZGERALD.

Wire to Reynolds office 6 June 1927. Wilmington, Del. (AO)

LIVE IN TERROR LEST AGENT WILL OFFER LIPSTICK IN OTHER QUARTERS ESPECIALLY FOX WHICH WOULD BE TERRIBLE FOR REASONS OF UTMOST PERSONAL IMPORTANCE.#
    SCOTT FITZGERALD.

Wire to Reynolds office 9 June 1927. Wilmington, Del. (AO)

Dear Ober:

Thanks for deposit. Story along in several days.* Will you tell Swanson

(1) No changes in ms.† without permission

(2) Hold it, if he can, till October issue + he ought to sell out at Princeton.

Ever Yours
Scott Fitzg

I'll be even less popular at Harvard, Yale + Williams than at Princeton when this is published

ALS (pencil), 1p. n.d., n.p.—received 14 June 1927. "Ellerslie." (AO)

STORY SENT TOMORROW CAN YOU DEPOSIT ONE THOUSAND.
    FITZGERALD.

Wire to Reynolds office 15 June 1927. Wilmington, Del. (AO)

¶B. P. Schulberg, head of production at Paramount.
‡"Princeton," *College Humor,* December 1927.
#The reason for Fitzgerald's anxiety is not known.
*Probably "Jacob's Ladder," *The Saturday Evening Post,* 20 August 1927.
†"Princeton."

July 2, 1927.

F. Scott Fitzgerald, Esq.,
Ellerslie,
Edgemoor, Delaware,

Dear Fitzgerald:

We have sold your story entitled JACOB'S LADDER to the Post for Three Thousand Dollars ($3,000.00). They say they like the story tremendously, and are going to be very much disappointed if you don't do a lot more for them just as good.

Yours sincerely,
[Paul Revere Reynolds]

TL (cc), lp. (PU)

WOULD POST BE INTERESTED IN ARTICLE TITLE QUOTE SISSY AMERICA UNQUOTE EMBODYING IDEA OF TOO MUCH WOMAN EDUCATION AND GENERAL INEFFECTUALLY OF MALE IN ANY LINE EXCEPT BUSINESS STOP NOT PROPOSING ANY REMEDY NOR PUTTING ANY BLAME ANYWHERE BUT ON THE MAN FOR LETTING CONTROL SLIP FROM HIS HANDS YET A BITTER AND SENSATIONAL ARRAINMENT OF CONTEMPORARY MALE STOP PLEASE WIRE CAVALIER HOTEL VIRGINIABEACH VIRGINIA‡ IMMEDIATELY
   FITZGERALD.

Wire to Reynolds office 14 July 1927. Virginia Beach. (AO)

Post interested but want to know a little more about article can you send me two or three paragraph description sure it can be sold.
   Harold Ober.

Wire draft (cc) to Fitzgerald 14 July 1927. (PU)

AM SO ABSORBED IN IDEA THAT THINK I WILL WRITE IT ANY-WAY AND TRYTO CONVERT POST INTO GIVING IT A HEARING EVEN THO IT IS AT VARIANCE WITH THEIR CURRENT POLICY STOP UNLESS YOU WIRE ME THAT ON THEIR REFUSAL IT WOULD BRING LESS THAN ONE THOUSAND IN OTHER AVAIL-ABLE MARKETS.
   FITZGERALD.

Wire to Reynolds office 16 July 1927. Virginia Beach. (AO)

---

‡The Fitzgeralds were vacationing at Virginia Beach.

Have telegram from Post saying further consideration makes
them afraid of article will try Colliers unless you wire no.
Harold Ober.

Wire draft (cc) to Fitzgerald 16 July 1927. (PU)

                                    July 18, 1927.
F. Scott Fitzgerald, Esq.,
Cavalier Hotel,
Virginia Beach, Va.

Dear Scott:

I think you are wise to go ahead and write the article. I am sure
the <u>article</u> will not scare the Post as much as the <u>idea</u> did. If they
should decline it when they see it, I don't think there is ny doubt
but what we could get a thousand dollars or more for it elsewhere.

                            Yours sincerely,
                            [Harold Ober]

TL (cc), 1p. (PU)

CAN YOU DEPOSIT EIGHT HUNDRED ARTICLE FINISHED.
    FITZGERALD.

Wire to Reynolds office 21 July 1927. Norfolk, Va. (AO)

*Although the Fitzgeralds had hoped to bring some order into their lives with
the move to "Ellerslie," the ensuing wires reflect the disjointed state of
Fitzgerald's work at the time.*

CAN YOU DEPOSIT FOUR HUNDRED MORE BRING UP ARTICLE
TUESDAY
    FITZGERALD.

Wire to Reynolds office 24 July 1927. Wilmington, Del. (AO)

WILL BE UP WITH STORY FRIDAY.§
    FITZGERALD.

Wire to Reynolds office 3 August 1927. Wilmington, Del. (AO)

---

§Probably "The Love Boat," *The Saturday Evening Post*, 8 October 1927. An Ober
note reads: "He didn't come!"

TERRIBLY SORRY ABOUT DELAY BOTH STORY AND ARTICLE
ARE FINISHED AND AT TYPISTS WILL BRING THEM UP SURELY
THURSDAY CAN YOU POSSIBLY DEPOSIT THREE HUNDRED.¶
SCOTT FITZGERALD.

Wire to Reynolds office 11 August 1927. Wilmington, Del. (AO)

Please rush article Costain leaving soon and I have another
place for it if he declines.#
Harold Ober.

Wire draft (cc) to Fitzgerald 12 August 1927. (PU)

ARTICLE ROTTEN WORKING ON A TWO PART SOPHISTICATED
FOOTBALL STORY‡ ASK POST IF IT IS FINISHED IN ONE WEEK
WILL IT BE TOO LATE FOR SCHEDULE THIS FALL CAN YOU
DEPOSIT FIVE HUNDRED.
SCOTT FITZGERALD.

Wire to Reynolds office 1 September 1927. Wilmington, Del. (AO)

Not too late Post says to go ahead and finish it depositing five
hundred.
Paul R. Reynolds.

Wire draft (cc) to Fitzgerald 1 September 1927. (PU)

STORY ALMOST FINISHED CALL YOU DEPOSIT FIVE HUNDRED.
FITZGERALD.

Wire to Reynolds office 9 September 1927. Wilmington, Del. (AO)

STORY FINISHED CAN YOU DEPOSIT FIVE HUNDRED MORE.
FITZGERALD

Wire to Reynolds office 14 September 1927. Wilmington, Del. (AO)

CAN YOU DEPOSIT 300 THIS MORNING SOMEWHAT URGENT
WILL BE IN TO SEE YOU AT 215.
FITZGERALD.

Wire to Reynolds office 22 September 1927. Philadelphia, Pa. (AO)

¶An Ober note reads: "he telephoned on Wensday saying he had sent the telegram
on Teusday He raised it to 400 which I deposited HO".

#Apparently the article on "Sissy America" was never finished. Thomas B. Cos-
tain was an editor at *The Saturday Evening Post.*

‡This story was not published, but was rewritten as "The Bowl," *The Saturday
Evening Post*, 21 January 1928.

September 23, 1927.

F. Scott Fitzgerald, Esq.,
Ellerslie,
Edgemoor, Delaware.

Dear Scott:

I called you up this afternoon, but was told you were in Philadelphia. If you saw Costain or Mr. Lorimer this letter will be unnecessary.

I spoke to Costain about the football story in order to get them to get a place for it and Costain wants very much to see at least part of the story. He says that if they had half the story they could start an artist illustrating it, and in that way they might get it into the Post towards the end of November, so if you have part of the story done, no matter if it is not in finished form, could you send it along to me and I will have a copy made of it and send the original back to you to work from?

Yours sincerely,
[Harold Ober]

TL (cc), lp. (PU)

Can you send part of football story please wire.
Harold Ober.

Wire draft (cc) to Fitzgerald 26 September 1927. (AO)

WAS CALLED UNAVOIDABLE TO NEWYORK AND STOPPED OFF IN PRINCETON TWO DAYS TO WATCH FOOTBALL PRACTICE AND SEE IF I COULD GET A LITTLE LIFE INTO THAT WHICH IS THE WEAK PART OF MY STORY SO I JUST GOT YOUR TELEGRAM AND LETTER LAST NIGHT WORKING AS FAST AS I CAN BUT HATE IDEA OF SENDING PRT IS IT ESSENTIAL HOPE TO BE THROUGH MON OR TUES TERRIBLY SORRY
SCOTT FITZGERALD.

Wire to Reynolds office 30 September 1927. Wilmington, Del. (AO)

All right do best you can Post say Monday dead line for a football story but we will try to stretch it to Tuesday.
Harold Ober.

Wire draft (cc) to Fitzgerald 30 September 1927. (AO)

THE STORY IS JUST AN AWFUL MESS AND I CANT FINISH IT BY TOMMORROW FEEL TERRIBLY AT LETTING YOU AND POST DOWN ABOUT IT BUT ALSO FEEL THAT I HAVE DONE MY BEST PERHAPS I HAD BETTER TACKLE SOMETHING ELSE FOR IM-

MEDIATE PROFIT THAT IS DO A STORY THIS WEEK AND THEN
RETURN TO THE FOOTBALL STORY WITH HOPES THAT THEY
WILL BUY IT FOR PUBLICATION NEXT SEPTEMBER.
SCOTT FITZGERLA.

Wire to Reynolds office 3 October 1927. Wilmington, Del. (AO)

Saw Costain today he hopes you will finish even if it takes a
week or more STOP Knowing the football story is coming
they are keen for it STOP If you feel more like starting a new
story do that whatever you do allright with us.
Harold Ober.

Wire draft (cc) to Fitzgerald 4 October 1927. (PU)

AM GOING TO TAKE ONE MORE DAY WILL BE UP TOMORROW
INSTEAD CAN YOU STILL HAVE LUNCH WITH ME PLEASE FOR-
GIVE ME.§
SCOTT FITZGERALD.

Wire to Reynolds office 18 October 1927. Wilmington, Del. (AO)

Dear Harold:
Here's the first real ghost story I ever wrote.¶ Perhaps if not the
Post, College Humor.
It was fine seeing you

Scott

The latter pages, from 21 on better be retyped.

ALS, 1p. n.d.—late October 1927. "Ellerslie" stationery. (AO)

October 26, 1927.

F. Scott Fitzgerald, Esq.,
Ellerslie,
Edgemoor, Delaware.

Dear Scott:
Swanson of College Humor is in town and has been talking to me
for some time about you. He wants to know if you could not do him
a short story if you won't do him a two-part story. He says he will
pay Seven Thousand Dollars ($7,000.00) for a two-part story.
Of course, two-part stories are hard to sell, and if you should get
an idea for a two-part story, I suppose you could put an end to

---

§An Ober note reads: "I lunched with Fitzgerald H.O. Oct 19th 1927".
¶"A Short Trip Home," *The Saturday Evening Post*, 17 December 1927.

Swanson's agony by doing one for him. He says he is going to call you up, and if he does, I think it would be better not to tell him that you have just finished a story. If the Post declines the ghost story, we may want to offer it to Swanson, and in that case I had rather he didn't know that we had offered it to the Post first.

Yours sincerely,
[Harold Ober]

TL (cc), lp. (PU)

Dear Harold:

Please have these made very carefully.# I think they will cover any confusion and ambiguity.

Starting another story, or else back at the football story tomorrow

Scott

ALS (pencil), 3pp. n.d., n.p.—late October 1927. "Ellerslie." (AO)

CAN YOU DEPOSIT ONE HUNDRED EMERGENCY BRINGING NEW STORY MONDAY.
  FITZGERALD.

Wire to Reynolds office 27 October 1927. Wilmington, Del. (AO)

October 29, 1927.

F. Scott Fitzgerald, Esq.,
Ellerslie,
Edgemoor, Del.

Dear Scott:

Here is what the Post said about A SHORT TRIP HOME:
"Dear Ober:

Frankly, we did not find it easy to reach our decision with reference to "A Short Trip Home" by F. Scott Fitzgerald. Ghosts are rather difficult to handle in the Post, but the story is so well done that we have not been able to resist it. We have decided to publish it, and the check will be forwarded on Tuesday as usual."
and today I have another note which reads as follows:
"I neglected to mention yesterday that we may want Mr. Fitzgerald to make a change or two in the galley proofs. We felt that the scene on the train where he confronts the spook and discovers the ebbing of the force which has kept him going is perhaps a little too literal and unpleasant. However, if we feel that it is

---

Fitzgerald enclosed six revisions for "A Short Trip Home."

going to be absolutely necessary to do this, we will send something more definite with the galley proofs."
The change doesn't sound very difficult.

Sincerely yours,
[Harold Ober]

TL (cc), lp. (PU)

CAN YOU DEPOSIT ONE HUNDRED STOP I WILL BE UP WITH THE STORY THURSDAY SURE AND PERHAPS WEDNESDAY.
    SCOTT FITZGERALD.

Wire to Reynolds office 9 November 1927. Wilmington, Del. (AO)

CAN YOU DEPOSIT FOUR HUNDRED THIS MORNING THAT MAKES ALMOST TWO THOUSAND AND MY STORY HAS COLLAPSED BUT I HAVE ANOTHER ALMOST FINISHED AND WILL BRING IT UP MONDAY.
    SCOTT FITZGERALD

Wire to Reynolds office 12 November 1927. Wilmington, Del. (AO)

CAN YOU DEPOSIT TWO HUNDRED TODAY COMING IN TOMORROW MORNING BUT WITHOUT STORY.
    SCOTT FITZGERALD.

Wire to Reynolds office 18 November 1927. Wilmington, Del. (AO)

CAN YOU DEPOSIT TWO HUNDRED AND FIFTY I WILL BE IN TOMORROW MORNING WITH FOOTBALL STORY WITHOUT FAIL.*
    FITZGERALD.

Wire to Reynolds office 2 December 1927. Wilmington, Del. (AO)

December 8, 1927.

F. Scott Fitzgerald, Esq.,
Ellerslie,
Edgemoor, Delaware.

Dear Scott:

I have deposited today in your account in the Guaranty Trust Company a check for $200.00.

In Costain's letter to me he says that they feel that you have got the real spirit of the game as it has perhaps never been done before. That is very high praise.

Sincerely yours,
[Harold Ober]

TL (cc), lp. (PU)

---

*"The Bowl."

Dear Harold:

I should think the <u>Woman's Home Companion</u> might give three or four hundred for this—it isn't worth more.† If you send it to anyone else let me know first.

I have another story finished.‡ Am sending it tomorrow. Many thanks for the $1500.00

Scott Fitzg

ALS, 1p. n.d., n.p.—received 17 December 1927. "Ellerslie." (AO)

December 31, 1927.

F. Scott Fitzgerald, Esq.,
Ellerslie,
Edgemoor, Del.

Dear Scott:

Thank you for sending me the letter from McKenzie. It is certainly an extraordinary letter for an editor to write. As I think you probably know, McKenzie is no longer with Hearst.§

What is the story of the de-educated girl that he speaks about? It sounds interesting and how is the new story for the Post coming along?

I am sorry to tell you that McCall's finally decided against the little sketch you sent me.¶ One of the editors told me that she thought it delightful and tried very hard to get it accepted. Costain asked me to let the Ladies Home Journal see it next and I therefore sent it on to Schuler, the new editor. I'll let you know what he decides about it.

Sincerely yours,
[Harold Ober]

TL (cc), 1p. (AO)

Fitzgerald's total earnings for 1927 were $29,737.81. He sold five stories, all to The Saturday Evening Post *($15,300). His* Post *price was raised to $3,500. Book earnings were $5,911.64, of which $5,752.06 was an advance against his next novel.*

---

†"Outside the Cabinet Maker's," *Century Magazine*, December 1928; sold for $150.
‡"Magnetism," *The Saturday Evening Post*, 3 March 1928.
§Vernon McKenzie, associate editor in chief of the International Magazine Company, had written Fitzgerald on 9 December suggesting that he be sent the MS of Fitzgerald's novel if *Liberty* rejected it. This new novel was the work in progress that became *Tender Is the Night*.
¶"Outside the Cabinet Maker's."

CAN YOU DEPOSIT TWO HUNDRED TODAY AND WIRE ME
AMOUNT I OWE YOU SENDING STORY TODAY.
FITZGERALD.

Wire to Reynolds office 4 January 1928. Wilmington, Del. (AO)

Depositing two hundred you owe two thousand one hundred
seventyfive dollars.#
Paul R. Reynolds.

Wire draft (cc) to Fitzgerald 4 January 1928. (PU)

January 13, 1928.
F. Scott Fitzgerald, Esq.,
Ellerslie,
Edgemoor, Del.

Dear Scott:
Costain writes me as follows about your story MAGNETISM:

"Dear Ober:
As I told you over the phone today, we are taking "Magnetism"
by F. Scott Fitzgerald. It is a splendidly handled story. We like
it so much in fact that we hope Mr. Fitzgerald will decide to do
at least one more short story before settling down to the final
grind on the serial".

Sincerely yours,
[Harold Ober]

TL (cc), lp. (PU)

CAN YOU PLEASE POSSIBLY MAKE A DEPOSIT MONDAY MORN-
ING SO THAT WITH WHATEVER DEPOSIT YOU HAVE MADE
FROM POST RESIDUE TOTAL WILL AMOUNT TO SIX HUNDRED
FITZGERALD.

Wire to Reynolds office 22 January 1928. Wilmington, Del. (AO)

KINDLY DISREGARD OTHER TELEGRAM AND MAKE NEWYORK
DEPOSIT OF ONLY TWO HUNDRED AND FIFTY AND TELE-
GRAPH THREE HUNDRED AND FIFTY TO MY ACCOUNT IN THE

#An Ober note reads: "including the 200".

EQUITABLE TRUST COMPANY OF WILMINGTON DELAWARE
THIS MORNING VERY URGENT.
SCOTT FITZGERALD.

Wire to Reynolds office 23 January 1928. Montreal, Quebec.* (AO)

Dear Harold:

Enclosed find story.† Perhaps if Post doesn't want it <u>College Humor</u> would give 3000.00

"De-educated girl" is an idea that happened to strike me in Mckenzies presense. I'll probably never begin it.

About <u>Cream of the Jug</u>.§ From Carl Brandt¶ I recieved a check for $25.00. I supposed it was some small thing that he had arranged, that he had taken commission, + I thought no more about it. From what you say I gather it came thru him by accident + he took no commission. So please debit me with the 10%

Many thanks for all the advances. I hope this story will cover them

Scott Fitzg—

ALS, 1p. n.d., n.p.—January 1928. "Ellerslie" stationery. (AO)

January 27, 1928

F. Scott Fitzgerald, Esq. In account with Paul R. Reynolds

....

1927			
Aug. 25	Deposited in Guaranty		
	Trust Co. of N. Y.	500.00	500.00
Sept. 1		500.00	
8		500.00	
15		500.00	
22		300.00	1800.00
Oct. 13		200.00	
17		600.00	
25		400.00	
25		150.00	
27		100.00	1450.00

*In " 'Show Mr. and Mrs. F. to Number—' " by F. Scott and Zelda Fitzgerald, published in *Esquire* (May and June 1934), this trip is mentioned: "Next time we went, lost and driven now like the rest, it was a free trip north to Quebec. They thought maybe we'd write about it."

†"The Scandal Detectives," *The Saturday Evening Post*, 28 April 1928. The first Basil Duke Lee story.

§ *The Cream of the Jug*, ed. Grant Overton (New York: Harper, 1927), in which "The Pusher-in-the-Face" was reprinted.

¶Literary agent.

Nov. 2		700.00	
4		100.00	
9		100.00	
12		400.00	
18		200.00	
21		200.00	
25		500.00	2200.00
Dec. 2		250.00	
6		200.00	
8		200.00	
15		1500.00	
21		300.00	
28		200.00	2650.00
1928			
Jan. 5		200.00	
6		200.00	
12		100.00	
16		700.00	
23		250.00	
23	Telegraphed to Equitable Trust Co. Wilmington	350.00	
27	"	300.00	2100.00

Miscellaneous charges

Typing The Love Boat	8.08	
" The Bowl	9.24	
" Outside Cab.Makers	1.52	
" Magnetism	9.24	

Registering Assignment of copyright
Jacob's Ladder
The Love Boat 1.02
A Short Trip Home 29.10

10729.10

CREDITS
Received from Saturday Evening Post

A Short Trip Home	3500.00	
The Bowl	3500.00	
Magnetism	3500.00	

Received from Metropolitan
Newspaper Service
Your Way and Mine 153.82
Received from Golden Book
The Pusher in the Face 110.00 10763.82
Commission 10% 1076.38 9687.44
Balance due 1041.66

Typed Account, 1p. From Reynolds office. (PU)

Dear Harold:
  Will you
(1.) Notice how I fixed Scandal Bk. (P. 3)
(2.) Tell them about "sequel"
(3) Tell them I want proof
(4) Have *last four* pages [24 + 27] retyped#
                      24,25 + 27
                              Ever Yrs.
                              Scott Fitzg

ALS, 1p. n.d., n.p.—January/February 1928. "Ellerslie." (AO)

Dear Harold.
  Many things.
(1st) I will immediately do another <u>Post</u> story
(2nd) Thanks for deposits
(3d) Can you deposit $1000 more on reciept of this letter. That will
make $2000 I owe you but I have an idea + will finish story in a
week
(4th) Please debit me with $2.50 in that Brandt business. You made
the sale.
(5th) My wife got $300. apiece for articles she wrote entirely herself
for College Humor + Harpers Bazarre. The editors knew this but
insisted my name go on them with her. This is to explain why they
weren't sent *to* you. She dealt with Towne + Swanson herself.
(6th) The man who wrote <u>Coquette</u> had obviously studied <u>The
Jellybean</u> which was the first story to really recreate the modern
southern belle. [Y] Do you think some live movie agent like Packard
for instance, on the spot, could horn in on some of the success of
<u>Coquette</u> by trying to sell The <u>Jellybean</u>?
                              Yrs F. Scott Fitzgerald

ALS, 1p. n.d.—received 2 February 1928. "Ellerslie" stationery. (AO)

STARTED STORY TODAY CAN YOU POSSIBLY DEPOSIT SEVEN
HUNDRED
    SCOTT FITZGERALD.

Wire to Reynolds office 10 February 1928. Wilmington, Del. (AO)

Fitzgerald's revised pages of "The Scandal Detectives" are in the Anne Ober
papers.

WILL TRY TO GET STORY TO YOU BY MONDAY NIGHT SORRY
ABOUT DELAY
    SCOTT FITZGERALD..

Wire to Reynolds office 24 February 1928. Wilmington, Del. (AO)

February 24, 1928

F. Scott Fitzgerald, Esq.
Ellerslie
Edgemoor, Delaware

Dear Scott:
    I have your telegram and I am glad there is a chance of the story
getting in by Monday night. If it does, we can get it ready to give
to Costain on Tuesday. They are anxious to get the story, as they
have a place for a lead story in one of their early numbers.

Yours sincerely,
[Harold Ober]

TL (cc), 1p. (PU)

CAN YOU DEPOSIT THREE HUNDRED TODAY OR TOMORROW
STORY UP WEDNESDAY SURE
    SCOTT FITZGERALD.*

Wire to Reynolds office 28 February 1928. Wilmington, Del. (AO)

BRINGING MANUSCRIPT UP TODAY CAN YOU LUNCH WITH ME
    SCOTT FITZGERALD
Wire to Reynolds office 10 March 1928. Wilmington, Del. (AO)

SENDING STORY OFF THIS MORNING CONSIDERABLY IM-
PROVED IN FACT I THINK IT IS NOW VERY GOOD CAN YOU
POSSIBLY DEPOSIT CASH INSTEAD OF A CHECK THIS MORNING
    F SCOTT FITZGERALD.

Wire to Reynolds office 11 March 1928. Wilmington, Del. (AO)

DEAR HAROLD MY INCOME TAX CHECK IS DUE IN NEWYORK
TOMORROW MONDAY CAN YOU POSSIBLY DEPOSIT THREE
HUNDRED FIFTY DOLLARS TO KEEP ME OUT OF JAIL STOP
ALSO COULD I COUNT ON ABOUT TWELVE HUNDRED BEING
DEPOSITED SAY WEDNESDAY OR HAD I BETTER SAY THURS-
DAY STOP WORKING ON STORY AND WILL TRY TO GET IT TO
YOU THIS WEEK STOP YOURS IMPROVIDENTLY AS USUAL
    F SCOTT FITZGERALD.

Wire to Ober 18 March 1928. Wilmington, Del. (AO)

---

*An Ober note reads: "How much now?"

THIS SUPPLEMENTS PREVIOUS NIGHTLETTER CAN YOU POSSI-
BLY DEPOSIT FOUR HUNDRED AND FIFTY INSTEAD OF THREE
HUNDRED AND FIFTY TODAY
    SCOTT FITZGERALD.

Wire to Reynolds office 18 March 1928. Wilmington, Del. (AO)

HAVE DECIDED TO GO TO FRANCE FOR THREE MONTHS AS I
TOLD YOU IN OUR TALK FRIDAY CAN YOU DEPOSIT FOUR
HUNDRED DOLLARS CASH MONDAY MORNING HAVE THE
FIRST STORY[†] AT THE TYPISTS NOW AND SHOULD BE OFF BY
TUESDAY AFTERNOON AND I SHALL DO AT LEAST ONE MORE
BEFORE WE SAIL WHICH ACCORDING TO PRESENT PLANS WILL
BE THE TWENTY FIRST THIS MONTH
    SCOTT FITZGERALD.

Wire to Reynolds office 8 April 1928. Wilmington, Del. (AO)

SEND FIRST STORY THIS AFTERNOON CAN YOU DEPOSIT ONE
HUNDRED FIFTY AND WIRE ME WHAT TOTAL THAT MAKES
    SCOTT FITZGERALD.

Wire to Reynolds office 12 April 1928. Wilmington, Del. (AO)

NO ANSWER WAS DEPOSIT ALL RIGHT AM BRINGING STORY
PERSONALLY TOMORROW
    SCOTT FITZGERALD.

Wire to Reynolds office 13 April 1928. Wilmington, Del. (AO)

April 17, 1928

F. Scott Fitzgerald In Account with Paul R. Reynolds

....

Balance due as per statement January 27, 1928						1041.66
February	3	Guaranty Trust Co.			1000.00	
"	10	"	"	"	700.00	
"	18	"	"	"	200.00	
						1900.00
March	1	"	"	"	300.00	
"	3	"	"	"	100.00	
"	10	"	"	"	200.00	
"	15	"	"	"	100.00	
"	20	"	"	"	450.00	
"	21	"	"	"	1200.00	
"	30	"	"	"	550.00	
						2900.00

---

†Probably "The Freshest Boy," *The Saturday Evening Post*, 28 July 1928—the third
Basil story.

April	6	"	"	"		200.00	
"	9	"	"	"		400.00	
"	12	"	"	"		150.00	
"	17	"	"	"		300.00	
							1050.00
Typing THE SCANDAL DETECTIVE						8.10	8.10
							6899.76

CREDITS
Received from Saturday Evening Post For
 THE SCANDAL DETECTIVE   3500.00
Received from Metropolitan News Service
 Additional Collections
 RAGS-MARTIN JONES   1.50
                                                3501.50
 Less commission 10%   350.15   3151.35

                         Due Paul R. Reynolds   3748.41

Typed account, 1p. From Reynolds office. (PU)

In April 1928 the Fitzgeralds sailed for Europe, where they rented an apartment in the rue Vaugirard, Paris. Seeking an outlet for her own creativity, Zelda began studying ballet with Madame Lubov Egorova.

STORY FINISHED PLEASE CANCEL PREARRANGMENT AND
DEPOSIT THREEHUNDRED
 FITZGERALD.

Wire to Reynolds office 2 May 1928. Paris. (AO)

STORY PRECEEDS FRESHEST BOY.§

Wire to Reynolds office 3 May 1928. Paris. (AO)

Dear Harold:

I hope to God the <u>Post</u> waited for this before scheduling <u>The Fresh Boy</u>. If they didn't they might add a note:

This adventure of Basil Lee's *chronologically* preceeds The <u>Fresh Boy</u> which because of a delay in the mails was printed several weeks ago.

If they didn't wait + you sell it to College Humor change
[Basil Duke Lee] *Hubert Blair*   to   Dudly Kimball
[Hubert Blair] *Basil Duke Lee*   "   Howard Choate Coy

---

§"A Night at the Fair," *The Saturday Evening Post*, 21 July 1928—the second Basil story.

Elwood Leaming	"	Bill Cary
Riply Buckner	"	Fletcher Monroe

Sorry I've been such a beggar. Will write more fully tomorrow as I'm trying to catch a boat with this

Yours Ever
Scott F.—

ALS (pencil), 1p. n.d.,n.p.—c. May 1928. Paris. (AO)

FINE STORY MAILED WEDNESDAY CAN YOU DEPOSIT ONE-HUNDREDFIFTY HOPE YOU GAVE INFORMATION POST.
FITZGERALD.

Wire to Reynolds office 18 May 1928. Paris. (AO)

IF YOU RECEIVED STORY CAN YOU DEPOSIT ONEFIFTY MON-DAY AND THREEHUNDRED MORE JUNE FIRST.
FITZGERALD.

Wire to Reynolds office 28 May 1928. Paris. (AO)

June 1, 1928

F. Scott Fitzgerald, Esq.
c/o Guaranty Trust Co.
Paris, France

Dear Scott:

I have the new story, A NIGHT AT THE FAIR, and I have had it typed and it is going on to Costain tonight.

It is all right about THE FRESHEST BOY. They are holding it up and they understand that this new story is to be published first. I liked the story very much indeed and I think the Post will like it.

Yours sincerely,
[Harold Ober]

TL (cc), 1p. (PU)

TWO MORE CHAPTERS FINISHED ALL COMPLETED AUGUST*
CAN YOU DEPOSIT ONEFIFTY AT ONCE AND ONETHOUSAND
WHEN STORY IS PAID.

Wire to Reynolds office 3 June 1928. From Fitzgerald. Paris. (AO)

---

*Refers to progress on the novel that became *Tender Is the Night*.

Dear Harold

Zelda wrote this[†] for a [sydi] syndicate feature of Wheelers but it got to Wheeler a month too late, after he'd got someone else.

Could you get a few hundred for it, do you think?

Let me know.

Scott

ALS (pencil), 1p. n.d., n.p.—received 4 June 1928. Paris. (AO)

DEPOSITING ONEFIFTY TODAY THOUSAND THIRTEENTH STORY ACCEPTED.

Wire (cc) to Fitzgerald 5 June 1928. From Ober. (PU)

June 5, 1928

F. Scott Fitzgerald, Esq.
c/o Guaranty Trust Co.
Paris, France

Dear Scott:

The Post are taking A NIGHT AT THE FAIR. Costain says they would like to have another story in this series, if you decide to write another one.

I am glad you are getting along so well with the novel.

You might let me know when you have a permanent address. In the meantime I will continue to address you at the bank.

Yours sincerely,
[Harold Ober]

TL (cc), 1p. (PU)

PIRATE FINE[‡] PLEASE DEPOSIT FIVEHUNDRED SATURDAY.

Wire to Reynolds office 18 June 1928. From Fitzgerald. Paris. (AO)

June 26, 1928

F. Scott Fitzgerald, Esq.,
c/o Guaranty Trust Company,
Paris, France.

Dear Scott:

I am enclosing a copy of the option on the musical comedy rights to THE OFF SHORE PIRATE. If this is all right, will you sign

---

†"Who Can Fall in Love After Thirty?" *College Humor*, October 1928.
‡Wallace Dickson and Gordon M. Leland were interested in doing a musical comedy version of "The Offshore Pirate." The show was not produced.

this copy and return it to me? I signed one copy for you so that the authors could get to work on the story.

Yours sincerely,
[Harold Ober]

TL (cc) 1p. (AO)

WRITING STORY CAN YOU DEPOSIT TWO HUNDRED IMMEDI-
ATELY.

Wire to Reynolds office 26 June 1928. From Fitzgerald. Paris. (AO)

STORY FINISHED§ WILL TRY CATCH MONDAY BOAT WITH IT
CAN YOU POSSIBLY DEPOSIT FIVE HUNDRED IMMEDIATELY
  FITZGERALD

Wire to Reynolds office 1 July 1928. Paris. (AO)

STORY SENT CAN YOU POSSIBLY DEPOSIT THREE HUNDRED
IMMEDIATELY.
  FITZGERALD.

Wire to Reynolds office 7 July 1928. Paris. (AO)

58 Rue de Vangirard, Paris
↑
u

Dear Harold:

Terrible catastrophe—I tore up the contract + put the envelope in my pocket.¶ I'm awfully sorry I pieced it together—here it is. God help me. Sorry the story was delayed. With it ready to mail + wiring you that it was mailed I began to tinker with it + finally rewrote it. It is a wee bit disjointed, but a nessessary part of the series. Have no idea of what I owe you. Please tell me.

Novel nearly finished. Working like mad. Back in Sept.

As Ever
Scott Fitzg—

Couldn't I do some of the lyrics if I'm back in September? Better not suggest it on 2nd thot as they're all jealous as hell.

ALS, 1p. n.d.—received 4 August 1928. (AO)

---

§Probably "He Thinks He's Wonderful," *The Saturday Evening Post*, 29 September 1928.
  ¶Contract for musical version of "The Offshore Pirate."

IF STORY RECEIVED CAN YOU DEPOSIT FOUR HUNDRED IM-
MEDIATELY IF NOT WILL YOU WIRE
FITZGERALD

Wire to Reynolds office 6 August 1928. Paris. (AO)

August 8, 1928

F. Scott Fitzgerald, Esq.,
c/o Guaranty Trust Company,
Paris, France

Dear Scott:

Thank you for your note and for your story, HE THINKS HE'S
WONDERFUL. It is a very attractive story and I am sure The Post
will want it. I think you will have to write two or three more of
these stories for I shall never be satisfied until I hear more about
Basil, and I think everyone who reads the stories feels the same way.
They will make an exceedingly interesting book, I think.

Thank you for the signed contracts of THE OFF SHORE PI-
RATE. I hope something will come of this, but you have had
enough experience with the theatre to know that it is not safe to
count too much on a play until it is actually on Broadway and
earning money.

When you have any of the novel to send on, I hope you will do
so as I know you will be keen to get it out as soon as possible in book
form. The sooner we get some of the manuscript the quicker we can
arrange serialization.

Yours sincerely,
[Harold Ober]

I'll have the bookkeeper make out an account to send you. This is
in response to your request to know just how you stand. Maxwell
Perkins is back from his vacation*

TL (cc), 1p. (AO)

---

*The postscript was added in pencil.

August 6, 1928
F. Scott Fitzgerald In account with Paul R. Reynolds
....

1928						
Jan.	27	Balance due Paul R. Reynolds				
		(last statement sent)		1041.66		
Feb.	3	Guaranty Trust Company	1000.00			
	10	"	700.00			
	18	"	200.00	1900.00		
Mar.	1	"	300.00			
	3	"	100.00			
	10	"	200.00			
	15	"	100.00			
	21	"	1200.00			
	20	"	450.00			
	30	"	550.00	2900.00		
Apr.	6	"	200.00			
	9	"	400.00			
	12	"	150.00			
	17	"	300.00			
	20	"	2000.00			
	20	"	350.00	3400.00		
May	2	"	300.00			
	18	"	150.00			
	22	"	50.00			
	23	"	50.00	550.00		
June	1	"	450.00			
	4	"	150.00			
	8	"	150.00			
	13	"	350.00			
	23	"	500.00			
	26	"	200.00	2300.00		
July	2	"	500.00			
	9	"	300.00			
	13	"	100.00			
	30	"	200.00			
Aug.	6	"	400.00	1500.00	12550.00	
		Typing				
		THE SCANDAL DETECTIVE	8.10			
		THE FRESHEST BOY	8.40			
		A NIGHT AT THE FAIR	6.40			
		FALLING IN LOVE AFTER 30	1.00			
		Register Assign. Copyr.				
		THE BOWL - MAGNETISM	1.05	24.95	13616.61	

CREDITS

· Rec'd from Sat. Eve.Post For

THE SCANDAL DETECTIVE	3500.00		
Less Commission		3150.00	
THE FRESHEST BOY	3500.00		
" "		3150.00	
A NIGHT AT THE FAIR	3500.00		
" "		3150.00	
Met.News.Serv.			
YOUR WAY & MINE	15.00		
" "		13.50	9463.50
			4153.11

Less English sale for

MAGNETISM		86.94
Balance due Paul R. Reynolds		4066.17

Typed account, 1p. From Reynolds office. (PU)

DOING NEW BASEL LEE STORY IMMEDIATELY[†] CAN YOU
DEPOSIT THREE HUNDRED MORE ON WEDNESDAY
    FITZGERALD
MM QY BASIL.

Wire to Reynolds office 10 August 1928. Paris. (AO)

August 13, 1928

F. Scott Fitzgerald, Esq.,
c/o Guaranty Trust Company,
Paris, France

Dear Scott:

I am sorry I haven't had better luck with the two short things you sent us. Failing better prices elsewhere, I have had to sell OUTSIDE THE CABINET MAKER'S to The Century for $150.00, and that article entitled WHO CAN FALL IN LOVE AFTER THIRTY to College Humor for $200.00. The Century will publish your article in their December number. We haven't as yet received the money for either of these.

Yours sincerely,
[Harold Ober]

TL (cc), 1p. (PU)

CAN YOU DEPOSIT FIVE STORY FINISHED.

Wire to Reynolds office 1 September 1928. From Fitzgerald. Paris. (AO)

---

†"The Captured Shadow," *The Saturday Evening Post*, 29 December 1928.

PLEASE DEPOSIT TWO IMMEDIATELY URGENT STORY SENT.

Wire to Reynolds office 5 September 1928. From Fitzgerald. Paris. (AO)

PLEASE DEPOSIT TWO MORE STORY SENT.

Wire to Reynolds office 6 September 1928. From Fitzgerald. Paris. (AO)

DEPOSITING ONE HUNDRED FIFTY STORY UNRECEIVED DID YOU MAIL.

Wire (cc) to Fitzgerald 18 September 1928. From Ober. (PU)

VICCISITUDES DELAYED STORY AT LAST MOMENT WAS FI-NALLY MAILED THIS MORNING MARKED FOR LEVIATHAN SORRY SAILING TWENTYNINTH

Wire to Reynolds office 24 September 1928. From Fitzgerald. Paris. (AO)

In October 1928 the Fitzgeralds returned to "Ellerslie" to finish out their lease.

ARRIVING OCTOBER SEVENTH WITH SIXTH BASIL STORY§ CAN YOU DEPOSIT EIGHT HUNDRED ON RECEIPT OF FIFTH STORY OCTOBER FIRST OBLIGATIONS FOR SEVENTEEN HUNDRED ADDITIONAL WILL COME DUE OCTOBER FIFTH CAN YOU MAKE SPECIAL ARRANGEMENT WITH POST TO HANDLE THIS WIRE ME STEAMSHIP CARMANIA

Wire to Reynolds office 1 October 1928. From Fitzgerald. Paris. (AO)

October 10, 1928

F. Scott Fitzgerald, Esq.,
Ellerslie,
Edgemoor, Del.

Dear Mr. Fitzgerald:

Ober is home with an attack of the grippe, so I am writing you a line. Harry Burton, who used to be the editor of McCall's Magazine and is now editing the Hearst newspapers, told me that he wanted to get you to write a story which he would call HIP POCKETS, dealing with the flasks which young people often carry about. He would want a story not longer than fifty thousand words, and he said he would pay fifteen thousand dollars ($15,000.) for it, and he said he would want an option on the motion picture rights at fifty thousand dollars ($50,000.).

I agreed that I would lay this before you because I feel bound to

---

§"The Perfect Life," *The Saturday Evening Post,* 5 January 1929.

lay any such thing before you, as you would probably want to know about it, and also because I am doing business with Burton.

Burton said, also, that he would like to have a synopsis, or know something about the story, before confirming this offer.

There are two or three considerations. In the first place, you might possibly not want to write such a story, anyway. Secondly, it is a question of whether we couldn't get more money from some other magazine. A full length serial by you would be worth thirty-five thousand dollars ($35,000.). I believe that is what Liberty was willing to pay for the serial you are at present writing, and I suppose for a story like this, for them or somebody else, they might be willing to¶

TL (cc). From Reynolds. (PU)

STORY AT TYPIST BRINGING IT UP WEDNESDAY
    FITZGERALD.

Wire to Reynolds office 15 October 1928. Wilmington, Del. (AO)

PLEASE DEPOSIT ONE FIFTY BRINGING STORY TOMORROW OR
SATURDAY
    FITZGERALD.

Wire to Reynolds office 18 October 1928. Wilmington, Del. (AO)

October 23, 1928

F. Scott Fitzgerald In Account with Paul R. Reynolds

Statement August 6, 1928
           Balance due Paul R. Reynolds   4066.17

CHARGES

August	11	Guaranty Trust Co.	300.00	
	16	" "	500.00	
	20	" "	300.00	
	25	" "	400.00	1500.00
Sept.	4	" "	500.00	
	5	" "	200.00	
	5	" "	200.00	
	18	" "	600.00	1500.00
Oct.	2	" "	800.00	
	5	" "	1700.00	
	11	" "	150.00	
	16	" "	100.00	

¶The rest of this letter is lost. Nothing came of this proposition.

18	"	"		150.00	2900.00

Typing
HE THINKS HE'S WONDERFUL ... 7.98
THE CAPTURED SHADOW ... 9.57
Registering Assignment of Copyright
THE SCANDAL DETECTIVE ... 2.05 ... 19.60
Oct. 9 Cash advanced ... 55.00
10040.77

CREDITS

Century Magazine
OUTSIDE THE CABINET MAKERS ... 150.00
Saturday Evening Post
HE THINKS HE'S WONDERFUL ... 3500.00
THE CAPTURED SHADOW ... 3500.00
College Humor
WHO CAN FALL IN LOVE AFTER THIRTY ... 200.00
7350.00
Commission 10% ... 735.00 ... 6615.00
Balance due.............................. 3425.77
10/23 ... 200.--
3625.77

Typed account, 1p. From Reynolds office. (PU)

MISSED TRAIN ARRIVE ABOUT THREE THIRTY TERRIBLY SORRY FITZGERALD.#

Wire to Reynolds office 24 October 1928. Wilmington, Del. (AO)

November 9, 1928

F. Scott Fitzgerald, Esq.
Ellerslie
Edgemoor, Delaware

Dear Scott:

The Post are delighted that you are working on another Basil Lee story and Mr. Lorimer says that he hopes you will finish the Basil stories before you go on with other stories. If you feel like writing another story in the series after you have finished the one you are working on, I would go ahead and do it. If, however, you feel tired of the series, I would drop it.

Yours sincerely,
[Harold Ober]

TL (cc), 1p. (PU)

An Ober note reads: "he came in at 4.30 HO".

STORY ALMOST FINISHED* CAN YOU DEPOSIT ONE THOU-
SAND
FITZGERALD.

Wire to Reynolds office 11 November 1928. Wilmington, Del. (AO)

SORRY ABOUT DELAY IN STORY IT HAS STRETCHED INTO
WHAT MAY SELL FOR A TWO PARTER AND SHOULD BE IN NEW-
YORK MONDAY OR AT THE LATEST TUESDAY CAN YOU POSSI-
BLE DEPOSIT FIVE HUNDRED
FITZGERALD.

Wire to Reynolds office 22 November 1928. Wilmington, Del. (AO)

WILL BE IN WITH NEW STORY EARLY THIS AFTERNOON[†]
FITZGERALD.

Wire to Reynolds office 29 November 1928. Wilmington, Del. (AO)

I HAVE ACCIDENTALLY OVERDRAWN MY ACCOUNT DOWN
HERE I HATE TO BOTHER YOU BUT CAN YOU WIRE FIVE HUN-
DRED TO MY ACCOUNT AT THE EQUITABLE TRUST WILMING-
TON DEL
F SCOTT FITZGERALD.

Wire to Reynolds office 9 December 1928. Wilmington, Del. (AO)

STARTING STORY[‡] CAN YOU DEPOSIT THREE FIFTY
FITZGERALD.

Wire to Reynolds office 18 December 1928. Wilmington, Del. (AO)

STORY UNDER WAY CAN YOU DEPOSIT THREE
FITZGERALD.

Wire to Reynolds office 30 December 1928. Wilmington, Del. (AO)

Fitzgerald's total earnings for 1928 were $25,732.96. He sold seven stories to The Saturday Evening Post *($22,050). His income from books was $2,272.96—of which $2,129.03 was a further advance against his next novel.*

---

*Probably "The Last of the Belles," *The Saturday Evening Post*, 2 March 1929.
†An Ober note reads: "He came in HO".
‡Possibly "Forging Ahead," *The Saturday Evening Post*, 30 March 1929.

III
DEPRESSION

1929-1934

Dear Harold: Brought up ms, thinking [of] I could correct it satis-
factorily on train. But there has to be a new ending + I think its
futile to try to do it here. I'm going directly home with it + will
bring it up again tomorrow   Sorry

F Scott Fitzg—

ALS (pencil), note, n.d.—received 9 January 1929. New York. (AO)

BRINGING BASIL LEE STORY SATURDAY OR MONDAY CAN YOU
DEPOSIT FIVE
FITZGERALD.

Wire to Reynolds office 10 January 1929. Wilmington, Del. (AO)

ARRIVE ABOUT THREE WITH STORY¶
FITZGERALD.

Wire to Reynolds office 21 January 1929. Wilmington, Del. (AO)

CAN YOU POSSIBLY SUPPLEMENT THE TWO HUNDRED WITH
TWO HUNDRED MORE STORY SENT THIS AFTERNOON
FITZGERALD.

Wire to Reynolds office 8 February 1929. Wilmington, Del. (AO)

February 9, 1929

F. Scott Fitzgerald, Esq.
Ellerslie
Edgemoor, Delaware

Dear Scott:

Bennett Cerf of the Modern Library is getting up a very special
selection of short stories, which they will probably call "The Best
Modern Stories: A 20th Century Anthology". He says the book is
entirely dependent on getting one story apiece from about twelve
authors. They have permission to use stories by the following authors:

Joseph Conrad	Katharine Mansfield
E. M. Forster	Sherwood Anderson
D. H. Lawrence	Somerset Maugham

He wants a story by you and by Hemingway and one by Lardner.
I should think it would be a good thing for you to have a story in

---

¶Note in Ober's hand reads: "He did!"

this volume. You can see the quality of the volume when he told me that he did not think that Booth Tarkington was good enough to include. He tells me that he saw Mr. Arthur Scribner and he would not give him permission to use any of your stories. I judge he also refused to let them have stories by Hemingway and by Lardner. Isn't there some story of yours which Scribner has not published in a volume that you could let the Modern Library have? I don't see how the use of one of your stories could possibly hurt Scribner's and I should think it would help them in the sale of your volumes of short stories. If Maxwell Perkins were here, I cannot possibly imagine his objecting to the use of one of your stories.

They will pay a half a cent royalty per volume and they will pay $100 down against this royalty. They say they think the volume will sell steadily at the rate of about five thousand copies a year and that you ought to receive something for a good many years to come. Could you call me up about this on Monday, and do you think you could help get a story from Ernest Hemingway and one from Ring Lardner?

As you probably know, Cerf took the Modern Library over from Liveright.

Yours sincerely,#
[Harold Ober]

TL (cc), 1p. (PU)

Dear Harold.

I had no copy of this so at the last moment I thought it would be wiser to bring it up myself.*

1000 thanks for the book which arrived this morning and which looks facinating. The Modern Library man can count on a short story from me†—as soon as Max gets home I'll discuss it with him + let you know whether it'll be an old or new one. Also I'll find why they won't give Hemmingway + Lardner stories.

Yours.
F Scott F.

ALS (pencil), 1p. n.d.—received 11 February 1929. New York. (AO)

#A postscript in another hand reads: "I sent you a copy of the Undset book so don't buy one. H. O." Probably a work by Sigrid Undset.

*"Basil and Cleopatra," *The Saturday Evening Post,* 27 April 1929.

†*Great Modern Short Stories,* ed. Grant Overton. New York: Modern Library, 1930. This collection included Fitzgerald's "At Your Age" and Hemingway's "The Three-Day Blow" but nothing by Ring Lardner.

WILL YOU PLEASE HAVE THE STENOGRAPHER TAKE GREAT
PAINS TO GET AN ACCURATE COPY OF THAT MANUSCRIPT
BECAUSE IT IS SO ANNOTATED THAT IT MUST BE VERY HARD
TO FOLLOW AND ALL CHANGES ARE VERY IMPORTANT
WOULD YOU SEND ME A CARBON OF IT IF YOU LIKE IT CAN
YOU DEPOSIT THREE HUNDRED THIRTY FIVE WILL PHONE TO-
MORROW
      FITZGERALD.

Wire to Reynolds office 11 February 1929. Wilmington, Del. (AO)

February 13, 1929

F. Scott Fitzgerald, Esq.,
Ellerslie,
Edgemoor, Del.

Dear Scott:

Here is a carbon of BASIL AND CLEOPATRA.§ I found only
one or two slight changes to make. If you find anything else, let me
know.

Yours sincerely,
[Harold Ober]

TL (cc), 1p. (PU)

February 14, 1929

<u>F. Scott Fitzgerald</u>

Scott Fitzgerald said that Zelda would do six articles for College
Humor, that he would go over them and fix them up and that the
articles would be signed with both their names. He said that as he
remembers, they paid $200 for one article that Zelda did, and $250
for another. He said we had better leave the price until they did the
first article.

They are to be articles about different types of girls. I should
think they ought to pay $500 for them, if they are four or five
thousand words in length.

H.O.

Typed office memo, 1p. (AO)

---

§Ober enclosed a typed list of nineteen revisions Fitzgerald had made in this story.

February 15, 1929

F. Scott Fitzgerald, Esq.
Ellerslie
Edgemoor, Delaware

Dear Scott:

I had lunch today with Swanson of College Humor and I told him what you told me about the articles that Mrs. Fitzgerald is going to do. He is very pleased that he is going to get these and he mentioned a number of different subjects for the series, such as: the city debutante; the young married woman; the modern,southern, country club girl; the western girl; etc. He mentioned another type of girl —the New York girl who goes around to the different teas and knows all the celebrities by name.

He said he hoped the series would be story articles, not philosophical discussions of different types of girls. He thought each girl could be given a name and she could be described as a certain kind of girl because at such and such a party, she did so and so. In other words, she could be described by instances in her life, things that she did, rather than things that were said about her, etc.

He hopes very much that he will see one of the articles before you go abroad.

Yours sincerely,
[Harold Ober]

TL (cc), 1p. (PU)

GOING SOUTH TODAY FOR FIVE DAYS SENT CORRECTED PAGES TO POST AND SENT COPY OF THEM TO YOU AS I THOUGHT THAT WOULD SAVE TIME CAN YOU DEPOSIT THREE HUNDRED BEST WISHES
F SCOTT FITZGERALD.

Wire to Reynolds office 15 February 1929. Wilmington, Del. (AO)

Post taking Cleopatra like it very much I likenew ending immensely.
Harold Ober.

Wire draft (cc) to Fitzgerald 16 February 1929. (PU)

February 21, 1929

F. Scott Fitzgerald In Account with Paul R. Reynolds

....

Received from The Saturday Evening Post For

Jan 22 FORGING AHEAD		$3,500.00	
Feb 20 BASIL AND CLEOPATRA		3,500.00	
Received from The Golden Book			
Reprint			
ONE OF MY OLDEST FRIENDS		100.00	$7,100.00
Commission 10%		$ 710.00	
Dec. 17, 1928 Guaranty Trust		600.00	
19 " " "		350.00	
26 " " "		300.00	
31 " " "		300.00	
Jan. 10, 1929 " "		500.00	
16 " " "		300.00	
22 " " "		350.00	
25 " " "		300.00	
28 " " "		1,000.00	
Feb. 8 " " "		200.00	
9 " " "		200.00	
14 " " "		350.00	
15 " " "		300.00	
Typing FORGING AHEAD		8.59	
" BASIL AND CLEOPATRA		7.66	
Guaranty Trust Company		1,323.75	$7,100.00

February 21, 1929

F. Scott Fitzgerald In Account with Paul R. Reynolds

....

Metropolitan Newspaper Service			
Additional Sales & Collections			
RAGS MARTIN JONES AND			
THE PRINCE OF WALES		$25.00	
(World's Greatest Stories			
Magazine)			
Received from W. Baker & Co.			
Royalty			
JOHN JACKSON'S ARCADY		1.50	
30 copies @ 5¢ - for period			
ending Oct. 1, 1928.			$26.50
Commission 10%	$ 2.65		
Check Guaranty Trust Co.	23.85		$26.50

Typed account, 2pp. From Reynolds office. (PU)

STORY UP TUESDAY CAN YOU DEPOSIT SIX
FITZGERALD.

Wire to Reynolds office 24 February 1929. Wilmington, Del. (AO)

February 26, 1929

F. Scott Fitzgerald, Esq.
Ellerslie
Edgemoor, Delaware

Dear Scott:

Are you still planning to sail for the other side on March 2? If you
are, you will not forget, will you, about the story for the Modern
Library? You can pick out any short story that Scribner's have not
used in book form.

I am glad to know the new story will be here soon, and I hope
to see you before you sail.

Yours sincerely,
[Harold Ober]

TL (cc), 1p. (PU)

HAD HOPED TO GET STORY THROUGH TODAY BUT WILL
DELIVER THURSDAY WITHOUT FAIL EXPENSE OF LEAVING IS
VERY BIG AS USUAL CAN YOU DEPOSIT FOUR HUNDRED
SCOTT FITZGERALD.

Wire to Reynolds office 26 February 1929. Wilmington, Del. (AO)

Dear Harold: This¶ is a poor substitute for the story (tho it is a
beautifully written thing) but the story refused to be finished in the
confusion of moving + I'll have to put on the finishing touches on
the boat.

I forgot to say that this is the 1st Swanson article.

As to the story—Scribners are obdurate + won't let them (illog-
icly I think) use the Rich Boy. If Cerf wants to use Jacob's Ladder
I think it is the best available. But it will look rather sentimental
beside Conrad E. M. Forster ect. Still it is a pretty darn good story.

Goodbye for several months. I hope to God I'll have the novel
soon.

1000 Thanks for many courtesies + best wishes

Faithfully
Scott Fitz—

¶"The Original Follies Girl," *College Humor,* July 1929. This story was published
under the names of both Fitzgeralds, although it was written by Zelda.

Could you possibly deposit 200 more cash this morning. Bank hasn't recieved your check + I must cash something against it?

ALS (pencil), 2pp. n.d.—received 2 March 1929. "Ellerslie." (AO)

Early in March 1929 the Fitzgeralds went again to Europe. Arriving in Genoa, they traveled—via Nice and the Riviera—to Paris, where they settled until July. Except for the period July-October, when they stayed at the Villa Fleur des Bois in Cannes, the Fitzgeralds spent most of 1929 in Paris at 10 rue Pergolèse. Zelda resumed her dancing lessons with Madame Egorova and worked on the series of stories for College Humor, *with Fitzgerald revising and polishing her writing. Fitzgerald's drinking increased.*

March 12, 1929

F. Scott Fitzgerald, Esq.
c/o Guaranty Trust Co.
Paris, France

Dear Scott:

I have been talking to Swanson regarding the sketch you left with me, THE ORIGINAL FOLLIES GIRL. We have finally agreed that, if it is satisfactory to you, he would pay $400 for this article, with the understanding that if the others could be made a little longer, say twelve pages instead of eight, he would pay more money for the succeeding ones. Even if they aren't any longer, I think he would pay $500 for the others. He said he did not want to hold the series down to six, if you and Mrs. Fitzgerald had ideas for further articles.

Let me know where you are going to be, and if you are going to be near Paris why don't you drop me a line c/o John Farquharson, 8 Harsey House, Red Lion Square, London, W.C.1. I will get to London about March 27 and will be there two or three weeks. I might possibly get over to Paris, but I am not at all sure I can.

Yours sincerely,
[Harold Ober]

TL (cc), 1p. (PU)

STORY SENT PLEASE DEPOSIT NINE CASH URGENT

Wire to Reynolds office 14 March 1929. From Fitzgerald. Nice. (AO)

SECOND STORY# SENT CAN YOU DEPOSIT SEVEN FIFTY
FITZEGERALD

Wire to Reynolds office 29 March 1929. Nice. (AO)

MONEY DEPOSITED NEITHER STORY RECEIVED.
Reynolds.

Wire (cc) to Fitzgerald 1 April 1929. (PU)

Hotel Beau Rivage. Nice
(After Sun. % Guaranty)

Dear Harold:

We arrive in Paris April 1st, [+] have no appartment yet so will
be care of the bank. It will be fine to see you if you can get over.
The Rough Crossing has been sent + I've almost finished another.
I hope to God the novel will be done this summer.

$400. seems OK. for the sketch. My wife has too more nearly
finished—both longer.*

No news—I'm happy to be back here + if you cross the channel
will take pleasure in buying you the best dinner procurable in
France + I've become somewhat of a connessieur.

Ever Yours
F Scott Fitzg

ALS, 1p. n.d.—March/April 1929. (AO)

IF STORY SOLD CAN YOU DEPOSIT FOUR.

Wire to Reynolds office 9 April 1929. From Fitzgerald. Paris. (AO)

Dear Mr. Reynolds:

Here is my wife's second article for Swanson.†

Also, a little skit for which the New Yorker might pay something.‡
Please show it to them first as I especially want their friendship.

Sorry I've been such a beggar lately. I try to do better. Hoping
Ober comes to Paris

Yours Ever
Scott Fitzg

ALS (pencil), 1p. n.d.—received 12 April 1929. Paris. (AO)

#"The Rough Crossing," *The Saturday Evening Post*, 8 June 1929.
*The "girl" series for *College Humor*.
†"The Poor Working Girl," *College Humor*, January 1931. Published as by F. Scott
and Zelda Fitzgerald.
‡"A Short Autobiography (With Acknowledgments to Nathan)," *The New Yorker*,
25 May 1929.

April 22, 1929.

F. Scott Fitzgerald, Esq.,
c/o Guaranty Trust Company,
Paris, France.

Dear Mr. Fitzgerald:

I think Mr. Swanson of College Humor is writing you that he is taking THE POOR WORKING GIRL by you and Mrs. Fitzgerald and is willing to raise the price to five hundred dollars ($500). He writes us as follows:

"I do this with the understanding that the future ones will be at least as long as "The Poor Working Girl" and as much longer as their feeling for the material and the magazine will allow. I can use them any length, but I don't want them any shorter than this second piece."

Sincerely yours,
[Paul Revere Reynolds]

TL (cc), 1p. (PU)

NEW STORY SENT CAN YOU DEPOSIT SEVEN
FITZGERALD.

Wire to Reynolds office 22 April 1929. Paris. (AO)

DELAYED STORY MAILED LEVIATHAN ANOTHER MAILED TO-DAY§ CAN YOU DEPOSIT FOUR.

Wire to Reynolds office 13 May 1929. From Fitzgerald. Paris. (AO)

May 13, 1929

F. Scott Fitzgerald, Esq.,
c/o Guaranty Trust Company,
Paris, France.

Dear Scott:

I have an inquiry for the picture rights to THE VEGETABLE. This is probably one of those inquiries which never amount to anything. I remember also that you told me at one time that you didn't want anything whatever done with THE VEGETABLE, as you didn't like it. You didn't want the dramatic rights sold, or anything else done with it.

I meant to have written you while I was in London but I got so tied up with appointments that I couldn't get over to France. I hope to have better luck next time.

---

§One of these stories was "Majesty," *The Saturday Evening Post*, 10 July 1929.

I am glad to know that you are doing some more short stories, and I'll keep it a dark secret from Maxwell Perkins.

Yours sincerely,
[Harold Ober]

TL (cc), 1p. (PU)

CAN YOU DEPOSIT SIX FIFTY SENDING TWO STORIES.

Wire to Reynolds office 21 May 1929. From Fitzgerald. Paris. (AO)

May 28, 1929

F. Scott Fitzgerald, Esq.,
c/o Guaranty Trust Company,
Paris, France

Dear Scott:

MAJESTY came in safely and I read it at once and gave it to Costain. It is a beautifully written piece of work, and I have a note this morning from Costain saying it is a splendid story and that they are taking it.

Yours sincerely,
[Harold Ober]

TL (cc), 1p. (PU)

May 29, 1929

F. Scott Fitzgerald, Esq.
c/o Guaranty Trust Co.
Paris, France

Dear Scott:

This was in the New York Evening Post last night.¶

Sincerely,
[Harold Ober]

TL (cc), 1p. (PU)

¶The paper printed a photo of the "Loveliest Wife" selected by Fitzgerald, John Barrymore, and Cornelius Vanderbilt, Jr., for a Woodbury soap advertising campaign.

May 31, 1929

F. Scott Fitzgerald, Esq.,
C/O The Guaranty Trust Co.,
Paris, France.

Dear Scott:

Swanson asked me to send the enclosed on to you. In a note to me he says that the story* met with a great reception and he hopes the third story will be along soon.

Yours sincerely,
[Harold Ober]

TL (cc), 1p. (PU)

CONSULT AGENT MYRON SELZNICK AT BANK OF HOLLY-WOOD BUILDING REGARDING RAGS MARTINJONES FITZGERALD

Wire to Reynolds office 4 June 1929. Paris. (AO)

% Guaranty Trust
1 Rue des Italiennes

Dear Harold:

A talkie of Vegetable would be O. K with me——only no more stage representations on any account, charity or otherwise. I wouldn't feel guilty about a talkie

Sorry you didn't get over

Ever Yrs.
Scott F——

ALS, 1p. n.d.—received 5 June 1929. (AO)

STORIES† MAJESTIC AND BERENGARIA CAN YOU DEPOSIT TWO FITZGERALD

Wire to Reynolds office 11 June 1929. Paris. (AO)

June 19, 1929

Dear Scott:

The article for College Humor has just come in—the one entitled THE SOUTHERN GIRL—and I am sure that Swanson will like it.‡

---

*Probably "The Original Follies Girl."

†One of these stories was probably "At Your Age," *The Saturday Evening Post,* 17 August 1929.

‡"The Southern Girl," *College Humor,* October 1929. Published as by F. Scott and Zelda Fitzgerald.

I am sending you herewith three copies of the contract covering the talking picture rights to THE BEAUTIFUL AND DAMNED.§ I have had these contracts rewritten three or four times and have finally gotten them up to $1,000. You will remember that in the original picture contract for THE BEAUTIFUL AND DAMNED there was a clause stipulating that if the gross income from the picture reached the sum of $250,000, the company agreed to pay you an additional $1,250. In making the new contract they insisted on including the clause which you will find in the last paragraph of Clause 4, releasing them from making further payment. I have been fighting them over this for a month or two now. The lawyers say that it is impossible now under the present distribution of moving pictures to keep any kind of an accounting and tell the gross earnings of a picture. They say that they are sure that the picture has never earned anything like $250,000. I finally got them up to $1,000, but they say they will not pay any more. If we do not want to go ahead on this basis they will drop the matter. It is possible that if you refuse to sign the contract they may come up a little more, but I am inclined to think that this is their limit.

If you decide to sign the contract, sign it before an American consular officer. I can get the $1,000 as soon as you send back the signed contracts.

Yours sincerely,
[Harold Ober]

F. Scott Fitzgerald, Esq.,
c/o Guaranty Trust Company,
Paris, France.

TL (cc), 1p. (PU)

June 19, 1929

F. Scott Fitzgerald, Esq.
c/o Guaranty Trust Co.
Paris, France

Dear Scott:

Your story MAJESTY is scheduled for the July 13th issue of the Saturday Evening Post.

Yours sincerely,
[Harold Ober]

---

§Warner Brothers planned to remake *The Beautiful and Damned* with sound, but the film was never produced.

At Your Age just came in—and I have just read it. At this minute it seems to me the finest story you have ever written—and the finest I have ever read. I think I will always feel that way about it—unless you write a finer one, and I suppose you will¶

TL (cc), 1p. (PU)

POST STORY LEFT HERE ON LEVIATHAN LAST THURSDAY CAN
YOU DEPOSIT SEVENFIFTY
SCOTT FITZGERALD

Wire to Reynolds office 23 June 1929. Paris. (AO)

Dear Harold:# Did the B. + Damned Talkie come thru? Have asked for money as if it had.

I'm calling on you heavily this month (Insurance, income tax, child's adenoid + tonsil operation car, Cannes villa in advance to pay) + last American bills but am sending another story in three days which I hope will more than square us. Adress after 30th June [for emergencies]

> [Fleur des Bois]
> 12 (Boulevard) Gazagnaire
>
> unnessessary (GAZAGNAIR)
> in cables   Cannes

Excuse this scrawl but its four + I've been correcting since ten + have grown hazy with exactitude—I'd like to write this upside down. With 2nd story will have [almost] *more than* 2 clear mos. on Rivierra where we [have] will have a really inexpensive menage, for I'm damn tired of this delay about novel. for novel + if end is in sight in Sept. won't hesitate to borrow from Perkins.

My wife's 4th [schech] *sketch* along shortly. No news. Sorry you didn't get over*

> Scott Fitzg—

ALS (pencil), 2pp. n.d.—received 26 June 1929. (AO)

NEW STORY LEAVING TONIGHT CAN YOU DEPOSIT FIVE
FITZGERALD

Wire to Reynolds office 27 June 1929. Paris. (AO)

¶The holograph postscript is not in Ober's hand.
#It is impossible to reproduce this letter on a printed page exactly as it was written, so a facsimile appears in the section of illustrations.
*There is an obliterated note in the left margin of the first page.

CONTRACT[†] SENT AQUITANIA CAN YOU DEPOSIT THREE
FITZGERALD

Wire to Reynolds office 1 July 1929. Paris. (AO)

July 2, 1929

Dear Scott:

Thank you for your note that came with the last story, AT YOUR
AGE. I think I told you that I think it a beautiful piece of work.

I note that another story is coming along and that after that you
are going to take a couple of months on the novel. I know you will
be glad to finish it. If you get any of it so that you can send it over
to me, I wish you would, because, as I told you, Liberty have been
holding a place open for it for a long while and they will want to
get started on the illustrations if they are going to use it.

I know you want to have the story out in book form just as soon
as possible, so we want to do everything we can to get the story
published serially at the earliest possible date.

Yours sincerely,

[Harold Ober]

F. Scott Fitzgerald, Esq.
12 Boulevard Gazagnaire
Cannes, France

TL (cc), 1p. (PU)

July 9, 1929

Dear Scott:

I cabled you that the Post were paying $4000 for AT YOUR
AGE. I told Costain that I thought you were due for a raise and that
AT YOUR AGE was a good story to begin on. He has agreed that
it is one of your best stories and they have sent us a check for $4000
for it and they will pay us $4000 for any they get for a while now,
unless it is a very short story or one that they do not feel to be up
to your standard.

I am very much pleased that your price has come up to $4000, and
I hope you will be too.

Yours sincerely,

[Harold Ober]

F. Scott Fitzgerald, Esq.
12 Boulevard Gazagnaire
Cannes, France

TL (cc), 1p. (PU)

---

†Probably the contract for the sound movie of *The Beautiful and Damned*.

July 9, 1929

Dear Scott:

I enclose account to July 9th. The last account was sent you on February 21st when the account was exactly balanced.

I got your cable asking if we could wire one hundred dollars ($100.), and I am cabling you five hundred ($500.) as I know you must be a little short.

Yours sincerely,
[Harold Ober]

F. Scott Fitzgerald, Esq.,
12, Boulevard Gazagnaire,
Cannes, France.

TL (cc), 1p. (PU)

July 9, 1929.

F. Scott Fitzgerald In account with Paul R. Reynolds

....

Charges:

1929

Feb.	25	Deposited Guaranty Trust Co.	$600.00	
	28	"	500.00	1100.00
Mar.	1	"	500.00	
	2	"	200.00	
	9	Cabled Genoa	200.00	
	15	Deposited Guaranty Trust Co.	900.00	
	29	"	750.00	2550.00
Apr.	3	"	400.00	
	10	"	400.00	
	15	"	700.00	
	22	"	700.00	2200.00
May	6	"	700.00	
	13	"	400.00	
	22	"	650.00	
	27	"	300.00	
	31	"	1050.00	3100.00
June	6	"	200.00	
	12	"	200.00	
	14	"	500.00	
	20	"	500.00	
	24	"	750.00	
	27	"	500.00	2650.00
July	1	"	300.00	

3		"	1000.00	
8		"	500.00	1800.00

Mar. 9 Cost cabling to Genoa (200.)   5.00
    Typing:
        THE ORIGINAL FOLLIES GIRL   2.10
        THE ROUGH CROSSING   6.21
        SHORT AUTOBIOGRAPHY & THE POOR
          WORKING GIRL   2.50
    Reg. assign. copyt:
        LAST OF THE BELLES)
        CAPTURED SHADOW)
        THE PERFECT LIFE)
        FORGING AHEAD   BASIL & CLEO-
        PATRA)
        ROUGH CROSSING)   4.10
    Searching copyright records
        BEAUTIFUL AND DAMNED   1.05   20.96
                                   $13420.96

CREDITS:
    Received from College Humor
        THE ORIGINAL FOLLIES GIRL $400.00
        THE SOUTHERN GIRL   500.00
        THE POOR WORKING GIRL   500.00
    Received from Warner Brothers
        sound rights
        THE BEAUTIFUL AND DAMNED   1000.00
    Received from Saturday Evening Post
        THE ROUGH CROSSING   3500.00
        MAJESTY   3500.00
        AT YOUR AGE   4000.00
    Received from the New Yorker
        A SHORT AUTOBIOGRAPHY   100.00
    Received from Metro. News. Service
        additional collections
        YOUR WAY AND MINE   3.00
        (Indianapolis Post)
    Received from W. H. Baker Co.
        royalty
        JOHN JACKSON'S ARCADY
    (88 copies @ 5¢ to Apr. 1, 1929)   4.40
                          $13,507.40
        Commission 10%   1,350.74 $12,156.66
        Due Paul R. Reynolds   1,264.30
English Sale—OUTSIDE THE   34.56
        CABINET MAKERS—   122974

Last statement sent you Feb. 21, 1929 when we deposited $1,323.75 to balance account.

July 9, 1929

F. Scott Fitzgerald In account with Paul R. Reynolds

....

Sold in England to Storyteller Magazine
  British Serial Rights
    OUTSIDE THE CABINET MAKERS   8.8.0
    Commission 15%   1.5.2 7.2.10   4.84 $34.56
Credited to your account.

Typed account, 3pp. From Reynolds. (PU)

Dear Harold:
  Of course I was delighted with the news about the raise—which makes actually 900% in 10 yrs., you've made for me. Probably in this case by your own entheusiasm for the story. For that I thank you also. For the enormous loans you've made me I don't even dare begin.
  About the Lit. Digest.‡ I'm enclosing Outside the Cabinet Makers with the proof sent me too late for correction but which I'd like to be followed if [y] they use the story. I'll leave it to you to decide whether they use
  (1) This enclosed (Outside the ect)
  (2) Southern Girl
  (3) At Your Age (since you seem to like it so much)
Let me know which you decide to use.

                    Ever Yrs.
                    Scott
If you don't use this please return.§ [obliterated]

ALS, 1p. n.d.—received 15 July 1929. Cannes. (AO)

CAN YOU DEPOSIT FIVE POSITIVELY LAST REQUEST

Wire to Reynolds office 19 July 1929. From Fitzgerald. Cannes. (AO)

SORRY¶ AND SKETCH SENT CAN YOU DEPOSIT TWO

Wire to Reynolds office 27 July 1929. From Fitzgerald. Cannes. (AO)

---

‡This collection of stories does not seem to have been published.
§Added in pencil.
¶This story was probably "The Swimmers," *The Saturday Evening Post*, 17 October 1929.

STORIES LEFT HERE ON ISLE DE FRANCE CAN YOU POSSIBLY
DEPOSIT FOUR MONDAY
    FITZGERALD

Wire to Reynolds office 17 August 1929. Cannes. (AO)

Dear Harold:

This inexcusable delay is because this is the hardest story I ever
wrote, too big for its space + not even now [un]satisfactory. I've had
a terrible 10 days finishing it, when I thought I had *only* an hour,
+ the femme de chambre stood by all one afternoon last week to
take it to the post office. However its done + its not bad + I've got
a clear month for the goddamn novel (I don't really feel its God
damn.) and things will probably clear up eventually. Don't you
think that Zelda's Girl-the-Prince-liked thing is good?

With deathless gratitude + <u>please</u> charge interest on these exorbi-
tant loans if only to break me of the habit of having to ask for them.

                               Ever Yrs. Scott Fitzg—

P.S. (1)   Hemmingway was shocked by some offer you made him
because he'd already turned down twice that from Long. Couldn't
you find some profitable, but <u>not-exigent</u> not <u>contract-making</u> market, for the idea *of a contract* fills him with horror. <u>Let</u> <u>me</u> <u>know</u>!
P.S. (2)   When I suggested story for Lit Digest I accidently said
<u>Southern Girl</u> meaning <u>Last of the Belles</u>. However The Outside
<u>Cabinet Makers</u> will do quite well.

ALS, 2pp.—c. August 1929. Cannes. (AO)

THANKS IF STORIES RECEIVED CAN YOU POSSIBLY MANAGE
FOUR HUNDRED MORE

Wire to Reynolds office 21 August 1929. From Fitzgerald. Cannes. (AO)

                                  August 22, 1929
Dear Scott:

I have just read THE SWIMMERS and I think it is the ablest and
most thoughtful story you have ever done. I have read it twice and
I think I could get still more out of it if I read it a third time. It may
not be as popular as some of the stories you have done recently, but
I think you can very well be proud of it.

In your cable you mentioned sending <u>stories</u>. Only this one story
has come in. It came in on the Ile de France the day before yesterday. I tried to read the original copy, but it was rather difficult, so
I had it typed before I read it. You had better let me know what the

other story is, so that I can try to locate it. I thought possibly you were sending another article for College Humor.

I know Maxwell Perkins will be pleased that you are now going to finish up the novel!

I will drop you a line just as soon as the other story turns up.

I deposited $500 on the 19th and $500 again today. But you will have had my cables about this before now.

Yours sincerely,
[Harold Ober]

F. Scott Fitzgerald, Esq.
12 Boulevard Gazagnaire
Cannes, France

TL (cc), 1p. (PU)

August 26, 1929

Dear Scott:

I have just been talking over the telephone to Tom Costain and he tells me that he is taking THE SWIMMERS and thinks it is a very fine story. He is coming in tomorrow and after I have seen him I will write you more of what he says about it.

I was in Philadelphia last Thursday and had a long talk with Costain and also with Miss Neall.* They wanted to know all about you and they said you were writing some very fine stories. Mr. Lorimer is expected back from abroad and everybody there was sitting with a very expectant look and a very clean desk waiting for him to come in.

In the letter that came with THE SWIMMERS you speak of Zelda's GIRL THE PRINCE LIKED thing.† I wonder if you meant to put that in with the story and forgot to do so. Or perhaps it got off by a later boat. At any rate, it is now Monday afternoon and it has not turned up. THE SWIMMERS came in on the Ile de France on Wednesday.

P.S. - 1.   I don't understand just what you mean about Hemingway, but I will write you again about this in a few days.

P.S. - 2.   I think the Literary Digest are very lucky to get OUTSIDE THE CABINET MAKER'S, but if by any chance they

---

*Miss A. W. Neall, editor at *The Saturday Evening Post*.
†"The Girl the Prince Liked," *College Humor*, February 1930. Published as by F. Scott and Zelda Fitzgerald.

would rather have something that is more typical a story, I will let them have THE LAST OF THE BELLES.

Sincerely,
[Harold Ober]

F. Scott Fitzgerald, Esq.
12 Boulevard Gazagnaire
Cannes, France

TL (cc), 1p. (PU)

August 27, 1929

Dear Scott:

I have a letter this morning from Costain confirming what he told me over the telephone yesterday. The Post are taking THE SWIM-MERS and they are paying $4000 for it. They say the story was a little difficult for them in spots, but it was so unusually good that they could not resist it. When he says it was difficult in spots he means, of course, the part about the divorce, etc.

Yours sincerely,
[Harold Ober]

F. Scott Fitzgerald, Esq.
12 Boulevard Gazagnaire
Cannes, France

TL (cc), 1p. (PU)

GIRL PRINCE RECEIVED SWIMMERS SOLD FOUR
    OBER

Wire (cc) to Fitzgerald 28 August 1929. (PU)

IF NECESSARY I CAN MODIFI CRACK AT BUYERS ETC IN PROOF[‡]
    FITZGERALD

Wire to Reynolds office 28 August 1929. Cannes. (AO)

SENDING THREE FOURTH OF NOVEL SEPT 30 TH STARTING
NEW STORY NEXT WEEK CAN YOU DEPOSIT THREEFIFTY

Wire to Reynolds office 29 August 1929. From Fitzgerald. Cannes. (AO)

---

‡Refers to "The Swimmers."

August 30, 1929

Dear Scott:

I am sending you a copy of the revised edition of CONTEMPO-
RARY AMERICAN LITERATURE.§ You will find yourself in it.
I thought you might be interested in this.

Yours sincerely,
[Harold Ober]

F. Scott Fitzgerald, Esq.
12 Boulevard Gazagnaire
Cannes, France

TL (cc), 1p. (PU)

September 3, 1929

Dear Scott:

The Post tell me that there will not be time to send you proofs
of THE SWIMMERS and, as a matter of fact, they intend to publish
the story exactly as it stands, with perhaps a change of one or two
words. They say that Mr. Lorimer did not feel that your "cracks"
at buyers were objectionable.

Yours sincerely,
[Harold Ober]

F. Scott Fitzgerald, Esq.
12 Boulevard Gazagnaire
Cannes, France

TL (cc), 1p. (PU)

MCCALLS WILL PAY FIFTEEN HUNDRED FOR TWO THOUSAND
WORDS
   OBER

Wire (cc) to Fitzgerald 10 September 1929. (AO)

ACCEPT MCCALLS ANY PROSPECT OF RAISE FROM SWANSON
CAN YOU DEPOSIT THREE ON EIGHTEENTH

Wire to Reynolds office 11 September 1929. From Fitzgerald. Cannes. (AO)

September 18, 1929

Dear Scott:

Paul Palmer, the editor of the magazine which the New York
World publishes on Sundays, has just called me up and wants to

---

§ *Contemporary American Literature Bibliographies and Study Outlines* by John Mat-
thews Manly and Edith Rickert (New York: Harcourt, Brace and Company, 1922,
1929).

write to you about something. He wanted to know if I minded his writing direct to you and I told him I did not, so I gave him your address. He said he might write me instead of writing to you. If he does, I will let you know what he wants. He uses short articles, but I doubt if he can pay what you ought to get for an article. If he offers you a low price, let me know and perhaps I can get him up.

Yours sincerely,
[Harold Ober]

F. Scott Fitzgerald, Esq.
12 Boulevard Gazagnaire
Cannes, France

TL (cc), 1p. (PU)

> MY PARTNERSHIP REYNOLDS DISSOLVED TODAY REYNOLDS HIS WIFE AND SON CONTINUING OPENING MY OWN OFFICES 485 MADISON AVENUE YOU OWE REYNOLDS NOTHING I WILL GLADLY MAKE YOU ADVANCES WHEN NEEDED STOP TO AVOID INTERRUPTION WORK PLEASE CABLE ME AUTHORIZATION TO CONTINUE PERSUADE HEMINGWAY SEND STUFF THROUGH YOU TO ME CABLE ADRESS LITOBER NEWYORK
> HAROLD OBER

Wire (cc) to Fitzgerald 21 September 1929. (PU)

> SKETCH SENT STORY LEAVES TODAY CAN YOU MANAGE EIGHT NOW AND TWO WEDNESDAY

Wire to Ober 23 September 1929. From Fitzgerald. Cannes. (AO)

Dear Harold:

It seems to me this is worth a thousand.¶ Perhaps not from Swanson's point of view though he's running them pretty far forward in his issue—but from the point of view that most of them have been pretty strong draughts on Zelda's and my common store of material. This is Mary Hay for instance + the "Girl the Prince Liked" was Josephine Ordway both of whom I had in my notebook to use. Also they've been coming along pretty faithfully + have a culminative value.

Mailing story of my own Monday. Adress after 1st Paris.

As Ever
Scott

¶"The Girl with Talent," *College Humor*, April 1930. Published as by F. Scott and Zelda Fitzgerald.

If he can only pay $500 it seems to me Zelda's name should stand alone.

ALS (pencil), 1p. n.d.—received 8 October 1929. Cannes. (AO)

September 23, 1929

My dear Fitzgerald:

As you probably now know, Harold Ober is starting his own agency beginning with today. He has, as you know, from the start handled your work in the main and I think it would be only fair that he should go on handling it. We have been together a good many years and I am sorry that we should have decided to separate, but it seemed best for the interest of both of us.

I am writing now merely to say that although I feel that Ober, who has handled in the main your work from the start, should continue to handle it, if at any time I can give you any information or do you a good turn, I shall be glad to do it and I hope you will keep on with the success that I think your ability entitles you to.

Believe me

Sincerely yours,
[Paul Revere Reynolds]

F. Scott Fitzgerald, Esq.
12 Boulevard Gazagnaire
Cannes, France.

TL (cc), 1p. (PU)

> FOLLOWING YOU NATURALLY
> FITZGERALD
>
> Wire to Ober 24 September 1929. Cannes. (AO)

Dear Scott,

I got your cable yesterday and deposited a thousand. I had a talk with Costain to-day and he was very enthusiastic about your last stories. He says they are an advance on anything you have ever done. I told Mr. Weiss of M'Calls* that the articles had been mailed and he is very much pleased.

I'm in my new offices. I'm at the corner of 52nd Street and like them very much. I look straight down Madison Avenue from one window—over St. Patricks from another, and have a glimpse of the East River from another.

---

*Otis Wiese, editor of *McCall's*, had commissioned Fitzgerald to write an article on the "present day status of the Flapper."

Your very nice cable, saying that you are following me, "naturally" makes me very happy. It has just this moment come in.

Yours as ever,
[Harold Ober]

September 24th, 1929.

TL (cc), 1p. (PU)

SWANSON AGREES PAY EIGHT HUNDRED FUTURE ARTICLES
Ober.

Wire (cc) to Scott and Zelda Fitzgerald 30 September 1929. (PU)

F. Scott Fitzgerald, Esq.
12 Boulevard Gazagnaire
Cannes, France

Dear Scott:

Collier's Weekly want very much to have you do a short short story for them. They like stories a thousand words in length and they will pay a thousand dollars for the story, and make a definite order if you want it that way.

If you have an idea for a story of this length at any time, you might do it and send it along.

Yours sincerely,
[Harold Ober]

October 2, 1929

TL (cc), 1p. (PU)

CABLE WHEN MAILING MCCALLS ARTICLE.
Ober.

Wire (cc) to Fitzgerald 7 October 1929. (AO)

F. Scott Fitzgerald, Esq.
c/o Guaranty Trust Co.
Paris, France

Dear Scott:

There is one thing that I meant to have written you about before this, but I have been so busy moving that I neglected it.

In your last letter you write me as follows:

"Hemmingway was shocked by some offer you made him because he'd already turned down twice that from Long. Couldn't you find some profitable, but <u>not exigent</u> not <u>contract-making</u> market, for the idea of a contract fills him with horror. Let me know!"

I could not make out what this was all about until I found a memorandum, dated some time in May, showing that Reynolds' son had written a letter to Hemmingway through Maxwell Perkins giving the offer from Collier's that you probably refer to.

Your letter came in while we were in the process of terminating the partnership and I spoke to Mr. Reynolds about it, telling him that what they had done had put me in an embarrassing position with you. It was just another case of their trying to do things without letting me know about it. Of course, you told me about Ray Long's offer to Hemmingway and they knew perfectly well that I had been discussing Hemmingway with you. Reynolds said it was, of course, a mistake, but as we were still partners he thought we all ought to stand together and he begged me not to write you about the matter.

Then again, without letting me know that he was doing so, he went over to Collier's and got them to make a higher offer. I had luncheon with one of the editors the other day and he told me about the arrangement. I was very busy getting matters in shape in the Reynolds office and getting my own offices started and Reynolds and his son did a number of things like this that were decidedly unfair to me. As you know, I have always been interested in Hemmingway and I am sure I could sell his stories in a way that would satisfy him. If there is any way you can steer him my way, I should appreciate it. I know he thinks a great deal of your advice.

It is very nice of you to send me the cable you did. I like my new offices very much indeed. I received hundreds of congratulatory letters, wires and cables, and everything is starting even better than I thought it possibly could. Costain of the Post and Maxwell Perkins have both been very nice to me and have steered one or two very promising authors my way.

Some time I will tell you about the reasons for the breaking up of the old partnership.[†]

Oct 8.

TL (cc), 2pp. n.d. From Ober. (PU)

[†]The end of this letter is missing.

F. Scott Fitzgerald, Esq.,
c/o Guaranty Trust Company,
Paris, France.

Dear Scott:

The article entitled THE GIRL WITH TALENT came in safely and I have had it typed. I agree with you that it is an extremely good piece of work. I think it is the best one you and Zelda have done so far and I agree with you that it is worth more than five hundred dollars. As I cabled you the other day before the article came in, Swanson has agreed to pay eight hundred dollars ($800). I doubt if I could get him up to a thousand on the next one or two.

I agree with you that it is a mistake for you to use up material on these articles that you could use in stories. Of course as this one on Mary Hay stands, it is more of a sketch than a story, although it is a beautifully done sketch. I think that since you and Zelda have been doing these for Swanson, that we had better let him have this one at eight hundred but if you have any more ideas that will make stories, don't put them into this form.

Did you cable asking me to deposit two hundred dollars? I have just heard from the Reynolds office that they had a cable, unsigned, sent from some place that I could not make out over the telephone. They evidently received it two or three days ago. I have deposited three hundred dollars and if you did cable, I hope you will understand that I would have deposited the money right away if I had received your cable. I note by your letter that you will be in Paris after October 1st and I presume that you may have sent the cable on your way to Paris and that you didn't have my cable address or by mistake you sent it to the old address. If you didn't send it at all, there is no harm done.

Sincerely yours,
[Harold Ober]

Oct 8, 1929.

TL (cc), 1p. (PU)

MCCALL SKETCH MAILED FOR MAJESTIC TUESDAY THE SIX-
TEENTH CAN YOU DEPOSIT TWO
    FITGERALD.

Wire to Ober 14 October 1929. Paris. (AO)

F. Scott Fitzgerald, Esq.
c/o Guaranty Trust Co.
Paris, France

Dear Scott:

Your story THE SWIMMERS is in the Post for October 19th. Do
you get copies of the Post easily in France? If not, will you let me
know and I will send them over to you if you want them.

It has occured to me that you are spending more money than you
need to in cabling to me. I suggest that in future when you want
me to make a deposit that you cable me as follows:

LITOBER NEWYORK
FIVE

On receipt of such a cable I will make a deposit and cable you back
the same word, by which you will know that I have deposited the
amount you asked for. If I deposit more or less, I will cable accordingly.

If you need money in a rush and want me to cable it, merely add
the word cable before the number, as follows:

CABLE FIVE

Please do not think that such a cable will seem abrupt to me, for it
is my own suggestion and will save us both money in cabling. If for
any reason I am temporarily short and cannot make a deposit, I will,
of course, cable you at once, but I do not think such an emergency
if likely to arise.

You wrote me that you were sending a story and mailing it on
what I should think would have been a week ago Monday - October
7th. This story has not yet turned up and I hope it has not gone
astray.

I think you must be short and I am depositing $300 for you this
morning.

Sincerely,
[Harold Ober]

October 19, 1929

TL (cc), 2pp. (PU)

F. Scott Fitzgerald, Esq.,
c/o Guaranty Trust Company
Paris, France.

Dear Scott:

I have your cable today reading:

"Delayed Post story leaves Monday can you deposit threehundred".

I deposited $300. for you on Saturday as I thought you might be getting short. As you may not have received my cable of Saturday when you sent the cable I got today, I am cabling you:

"Three more deposited"

so you will understand it is not a repetition of my other cable.

Sincerely yours,

[Harold Ober]

October 21, 1929.

TL (cc), 1p. (PU)

October 21, 1929

F. Scott Fitzgerald, Esq.
c/o Guaranty Trust Co.
Paris, France

Dear Scott:

I have been talking today to Mrs. Angell‡ about the possibility of your doing some more things for the New Yorker. She is going to send me a memorandum of some things you might possibly do for them, and when I get that I will write you again. In the meantime, she wants me to ask you if you have any ideas for profiles. These are sketches of prominent people, and I am sure you have seen them in the New Yorker. It occurred to me that you might do a very amusing one of Gene Tunney. You remember one time when we were having lunch you gave me a very interesting and amusing sketch of him. Mrs. Angell, in speaking of it, said that if you did such a profile of him, she would want you to do it with "your tongue in your cheek".

As you know, the New Yorker does not pay very much, but I think they could stretch their budget a little for you. Ring Lardner has been doing quite a lot for the New Yorker and Mrs. Angell assured me that he was doing these things at their regular rates, which are not at all high. I do think, however, it would be a good thing for you to have an occasional thing in the New Yorker, which has a very different audience from the Saturday Evening Post and an audience that would be very keen to see something from you, and I think it would help you in the long run.

Mrs. Angell said you could do sketches of Americans that you see in France. Another thing she thought you could do very well would be sketches of people from different suburbs around New York,

---

‡Katherine Angell, editor at *The New Yorker*.

describing a typical person and showing the similarity between the person and the suburb. I will write you again about this when I receive the memorandum from the New Yorker. Mrs. Angell says she is going to talk the whole matter over with Mr. Ross and then write me a letter.

Sincerely,
[Harold Ober]

TL (cc), 1p. (PU)

Adress Guaranty Trust

Dear Harold:

Of course I was sorry to see the firm of Reynolds + Ober broken up, because it had become a part of my life. I hope it was settled + will turn out to your advantage + I'm sure it will.

About Hemmingway—he had recieved several offers from America thru Reynolds and while I have told him that I much preferred to remain with you, [one] I don't know what his intentions are. I think it was foolish to let him slide so long as he was so obviously a comer. I will write you at length about this later.

We are taking an appartment here for the winter + I've sworn not to come back without the novel which is really drawing to a close. Does Swanson's new price include the Mary Hay sketch?

Ever Yours
Scott Fitzg

I think only the last page of the enclosed need be typed.§

ALS (pencil), 1p. n.d.—received 23 October 1929. Paris. (AO)

F. Scott Fitzgerald, Esq.,
c/o Guaranty Trust Company,
Paris, France.

Dear Scott:

GIRLS BELIEVE IN GIRLS has just come in and it is a very thoughtful and interesting article. I hope it wasn't too difficult to write.

Let me know once in a while, won't you, how the novel is getting along, and if you can send over a portion of the manuscript, I'll take the very best possible care of it. I don't think you ought to lose the serial money and the sooner I get part of the story, the sooner we

---

§Written along left margin. Refers to "Girls Believe in Girls," written for *McCall's*, but published in *Liberty*, 8 February 1930.

can get the story into a magazine and published, so that Scribner can bring out the book and of course I know you want the book published without any more delay than is necessary. As I think you probably remember, the story goes first to Liberty at $35,000. and I don't think there is any question but what they will use it. They certainly call me up often enough about it. There are three or four other editors who are also very keen to see it and if it is possible at all as a serial, you ought to get a good sum of money for the serial rights. Then there are possible dramatic rights, and moving picture rights.

I have just received Swanson's check for THE GIRL WITH TALENT and he paid $800. for it.

Thank you for writing me about Hemingway. I have just read his new book and I think it is lengths ahead of anything that has been published here recently.

If you read any book that seems striking to you or run across any authors that you think have possibilities, I hope you will drop me a line about them. Things are going very well, indeed, for me and I am busier than I have ever been in my life but I do want to keep in touch with the younger writers and I don't know anyone who seems to have such a keen sense of values about new writers as you.

I'll keep on addressing you care of The Guaranty Trust Company but you might let me have the address of your apartment as in case of emergency I might need it. For instance, I might want to cable you during a week-end and the bank will be closed. I'll be careful not to give it to anyone who might be bothering you.

Sincerely yours,
[Harold Ober]

October 23, 1929.

TL (cc), 2pp. (PU)

F. Scott Fitzgerald, Esq.
c/o Guaranty Trust Co.
Paris, France

Dear Scott:

You may be interested in the following letter from Miss Roberts of the Woman's Home Companion:

"I was very much struck by the story of F. Scott Fitzgerald's, The Swimmers, which appears in this week's Saturday Evening Post.

"The stories which he did some time ago for us we all thought were very good and then for the last year or two it seemed to me that a good many of the stories he was publishing lacked the individual touch which had given them color.

"Reading The Swimmers made me feel awfully enthusiastic about Mr. Fitzgerald again and I wonder if you couldn't arrange to let us see something of his? That type of story with its peculiarly touching paragraphs (about America) and with the ironical scene (in the boat) I think he does so well.

"I'd appreciate your letting us know what the possibilities are."

Sincerely,
[Harold Ober]

October 25, 1929

TC (cc), 1p. (PU)

EXCELLENT POST STORY MAILED TODAY¶ FORMER ONE TURNED OUT BADLY CAN YOU DEPOSIT THREE
    FITZGERALD

Wire to Ober 26 October 1929. Paris. (AO)

F. Scott Fitzgerald, Esq.,
c/o Guaranty Trust Company,
Paris, France.

Dear Scott:

I think I wrote you a few weeks ago that Palmer, the Sunday Editor of the World, wanted your address. He has now written me as follows:

"I have written to F. Scott Fitzgerald for an article but get no reply. Can you get him to write me a fifteen hundred word story for the Sunday Magazine commenting on the 1929 flapper under some such title as "Dumber but More Beautiful"? The young lady of this year is very different from her sister of the past two or three years and I think he could do a good job describing her. I can pay $300 for the piece."

I have told him that you are very busy and that the price he offers probably would not tempt you. If you agree with me on this, you might just write no on this letter and enclose it the next time you write.

¶Probably "Two Wrongs," *The Saturday Evening Post,* 18 January 1930.

The story has not turned up yet. I hope it will be coming along soon.

Sincerely yours,

[Harold Ober]

November 7, 1929.

TL (cc), 1p. (PU)

F. Scott Fitzgerald, Esq.,

c/o Guaranty Trust Company,

Paris, France.

Dear Scott:

I am enclosing a letter from the editor of McCall's Magazine.# I think McCall's have acted very badly and I am showing the article to another editor. McCall's definitely commissioned the article and I feel very badly that I allowed you to take time from your novel and short stories to do this and then find that they are not living up to their agreement.

If I can sell it promptly to some other editor, I shall be very happy and we can then tell McCall's that we are withdrawing the article.

I am sure this article can be sold to one of the more serious magazines but as you know their prices are pretty low. If I can sell it for $1500. I'll cable you at once. I am enclosing a carbon copy of the article and if you feel like, and can, without taking too much time, lighten the article in accordance with McCall's letter, you might do it and send the article back to me and I'll be able I think to get the money from McCall's.

Sincerely yours,

[Harold Ober]

November 12, 1929.

If you don't see any sense in McCall's letter, write no on this note and mail it back to me.*

TL (cc), 1p. (PU)

#For Wiese's request for an article on the "present day status of the Flapper," Fitzgerald delivered "Girls Believe in Girls." Wiese rejected it as too serious for his magazine, saying in part: "It is not that his message is disturbing—we had expected that—so much as that some of his material is either above or alongside the general interests of our audience. I feel that the same ideas might have been expressed in the vernacular and found greater welcome among our readers. As it stands the lingo is not ours and I am afraid the going would be a bit thick."

*Postscript added in Ober's hand.

F. Scott Fitzgerald, Esq.
^c/o Guaranty Trust Co.
Paris, France

Dear Scott:

I have a letter from Mrs. Angell saying that Mr. Ross is very enthusiastic about the idea of your doing a Profile of Ring Lardner.

She says they ought to run about two thousand words, although they can run two or three hundred words over if necessary. She says they cannot give a definite order and the best price they could pay is $250, but she is sure that you can write a very good one and she says she does not think there is a chance in the world but what it would be just what they want.

Although the money paid does not amount to much, I think it might be a good idea for you to do this if you feel like it. There isn't any hurry about it and if you need any facts about Ring Lardner, there is plenty of time to write over and get them.

Sincerely,
[Harold Ober]

November 15, 1929

TL (cc), 1p. (PU)

Adress
till February 15th   }   10 Rue Pergolèse
at least   Paris

Dear Harold:

Sorry this has been so delayed. I had another called <u>The Barnaby Family</u> that I worked on to the point of madness + may yet finish, but simply lost interest. The enclosed[†] is heavy but, I think, good. Is it too heavy?[‡]

Now to answer questions ect

(1) As to Hemmingway. You (I speak of you personally, not *the old* firm) made a mistake not to help sell his stuff personally 2 yrs ago—if any success was more clearly prognosticated I don't know it. I told him the *present* situation + I know from several remarks of his that he thought *at first* he was [with] *being approached by* the same agents as mine—but he is being fought over a lot now + *is confused* + I think the wisest thing is to do nothing at present. If any

---

†"Two Wrongs." Fitzgerald circled the word "enclosed" and drew a line to the margin, where he inserted: "I mean to say separate package".

‡Fitzgerald drew a line from here to the top margin and inserted, but crossed out: "Not that it matters + on second thoughts I".

offer for *moving* pictures *of his book* for [more than] $20,000 *or more* came to you however don't hesitate to wire him as he's not satisfied with present picture offers. Simply wire him Garritus—he knows quite well who you are, ect. <u>Please</u> don't in any correspondence with him use my name—you see my relations with him are entirely friendly + not business + he'd merely lose confidence in me if he felt he was being hemmed in by any [plot] *coalition*. My guess is, and I'm not sure, that he is pretty much deferring definate action for the present on stories + serials but this may not be true by the time this reaches you and may not be at this moment)

(2) I note cable formula + will save $25 or $50 a year thereby.

(3) Post stories all available here—don't send Post.

(4) <u>World</u> offer seems small ($300.). Will answer refusing it politely myself.

(5) Of new authors this Richard Douglass[§] author of <u>The Innocent Voyage</u> (called <u>High Wind in Bermuda</u>) in England is *much* the best bet.[¶] Will try to keep you informed at the same time I usually do Scribners of anybody new *I hear of*, as, if he interests me I like to give him a chance for a hearing; but there's nobody now—but may write about that later! America will from now on give about ½ its book-buying ear to <u>serious</u> people or at any rate to people who have a backing from the sophisticated minority

(6) <u>New Yorker</u> *offers* O.K. but uninteresting—as for Mrs. Angell (whoever she is) I will gladly modify my style and subject matter for her but she will have to give me her beautiful body first and I dare say the price is too high.

(7) Did M<u>c</u><u>Calls</u> like the article "Girls believe in Girls"?

(8) Now I have two uninterrupted months on the novel and will do my best. There is no question of my not trying for the serial right + never has been.

(9) About The <u>Womans Home Companion</u>, you know.

Yours Ever in Masonry and Concubinage
Scott Fitzg—

ALS, 2pp., n.d.—received 16 November 1929. (AO)

MCCALLS CONDUCT PREPOSTEROUS BRING SUIT IF NECES-SARY[#]

Wire to Ober 20 November 1929. From Fitzgerald. Paris. (AO)

[§]Richard Hughes, author of *High Wind in Jamaica*.

[¶]Fitzgerald drew a line from here to the top margin and inserted: "but a lot of editors may have thought of that. Maybe not though!"

[#]Note in Ober's hand reads: "Cowards".

10 Rue Pergolèse, Paris
Nov 23d, 1929

Dear Harold:

McCalls letter was preposterous—no such outline was suggested to me at first. I've read of such frauds being perpretrated [on the contributer to the che so-called "cheap paper magazines" on author's who have niether means nor opportunity of defending themselves] but the rather airy way McCalls regards their agreements is something quite foriegn to any experience of mine in writing for magazines of the type that would [imply] *lay down* [obliterated] business principles in dealing with their advertisers.

Their letter asking me to put the article into baby-talk—"though they had expected and anticipated the matter being 'disturbing' " [will make juicy reading for a writer]—well, just read it over + try to make sense [out] of it. If they thot I wrote in slang, [why they have] *Their order was* simply [made] a step in the dark for which I have no intention of paying.

In any case, pale reflections of the *"disturbing"* ideas for which they presumably offered me the money, will doubtless appear in their editorial columns for some months [, or years] *to come*—so, win or loose I'd love to make this a test case.

Ever Yours
Scott Fitzg—

P.S.   Please don't offer it anywhere. Espectially not College Humor! Where was it offered? Please write me.

P. S (2)   Who is the editor of McCalls' now. Please tell me exactly —name, ect! Man or woman?

P S (3)   You'll have to investigate telegrams there as French offices keep no records once the telegram has been delivered. I tore up telegrams on your recept of article thinking of it (, as it always has been) something finished. The record is kept in one of the N. Y cable offices—i.e. W.U. or Commerial ect. They sent me a wire + you did too, both *about* same [date] *time* but theirs sent previously.

P.S (4)   A story, if its any good is always good—while an ordered, topical, timely article is an entirely different proposition, as you must know from your experience. This thing is the equivalent of: [saying:]

"You, who's time is worth two or three thousand a month, sit down + give me a month's worth of stuff—I agree to pay."

"But on second thoughts—no"

FSF

ALS, 2pp. (AO)

DONT OFFER ARTICLE TO ANYONE ELSE STOP REFUSING A
TIMELY ARTICLE ON SUCH GROUNDS IS SIMPLY OUTRAGEOUS
AND I AM ASTONISHED THAT YOU LET THEM GET AWAY WITH
IT PLEASE TAKE LEGAL MEASURES AT ONCE AM BRINGING
MATTER BEFORE AUTHORS LEAGUE AND WILL MAKE IT TEST
CASE HAVE NOT SLIGHTEST INTENTION OF COMPROMISING
OR TAKING LOSS ANSWER

Wire to Ober 24 November 1929. From Fitzgerald. Paris. (AO)

DELIGHTED FORCE MCCALLS STOP REMEMBERED YOU WOULD
NOT FORCE COSMOPOLITAN AND WAS NOT SURE YOUR POSI-
TION MAIL MCCALLS CABLE SEPTEMBER ELEVEN
    OBER

Wire (cc) to Fitzgerald 25 November 1929. (PU)

FIVE PLEASE IS STORY[†] SOLD

Wire to Ober 26 November 1929. From Fitzgerald. Paris. (AO)

LIBERTY WILL BUY GIRLS ARTICLE FIFTEEN HUNDRED ADVISE
ACCEPT DIFFICULT SUE MCCALLS BECAUSE ARTICLE SUG-
GESTS FAIRYLAND CABLE

Wire (cc) to Fitzgerald 27 November 1929. From Ober. (PU)

F. Scott Fitzgerald, Esq.,
10 Rue Pergolese,
Paris, France.

Dear Scott:

As I have cabled you, Liberty likes your article GIRLS BELIEVE
IN GIRLS and want to buy it and pay $1500. for it. I am advising
you to let Liberty have the article for several reasons:

First of all, I want to see it published. If we sue McCall's and make
them pay for the article, I am sure they would never publish it.

Liberty would pay for the article right away and it would probably take months of backing and filling to get the money out of
McCall's and possibly with lawyers' fees to eat into the amount.

We might have considerable difficulty in forcing McCall's to pay
for the article. There were several paragraphs in the article that
would be pretty strong meat for any woman's magazine. I tried to
convey this meaning to you in my cable without being too obvious.

The article will attract much more attention in Liberty and I'd
much rather see it there than in any woman's magazine.

I have talked to the Authors' League and they say they have had

---

†"Two Wrongs."

several difficulties of this kind with McCall's. In each case McCall's have fought the matter to the very end so that it has taken months to make them settle and in each case there have been several hundred dollars lawyers' fees.

Last of all, there is not much satisfaction in forcing a magazine to pay for something they don't like and on the other hand there is a lot of satisfaction in taking the story away and selling it at once to a more successful magazine.

If you agree with me in regard to the above points, I think you will be glad that the article is going to another magazine and that in the future we can tell McCall's "where to get off".

I got your cable and I am sorry that you were troubled about the whole affair. This is the first time McCall's has ever let me down this way but I always try to allow for some such occurrence as this and if I had not been almost certain that an article by you on this subject could be sold to one magazine in case another should let us down, I wouldn't have suggested your doing the article.

When I read the article I was intensely interested in it but I felt that it might be very difficult, indeed, for any woman's magazine. I hope that you will think I have acted wisely in this matter and I shall take a good deal of satisfaction in telling McCall's I have placed the article to better advantage and that as far as I am concerned I shall know what to say when they make any of their frequent and urgent requests for the sight of a story of yours.

Sincerely yours,
[Harold Ober]

November 27, 1929.

TL (cc), 2pp. (PU)

F. Scott Fitzgerald, Esq.
10 Rue Pergolese
Paris, France

Dear Scott:
I don't believe I wrote you after reading TWO WRONGS. I think it is one of the best things you have done. For some reason, the Post was a little slow in reporting on it, but they have bought it and Costain has just told me over the telephone that he likes it very much indeed.

I will have an account made up to December 1st, so you will know exactly how you stand. I have not had it checked up recently, but I think that with the money from the Post for TWO WRONGS and

from Liberty for the article GIRLS BELIEVE IN GIRLS, the
account will be fairly evenly balanced.

Yours sincerely,
[Harold Ober]

November 27, 1929

TL (cc), 1p. (PU)

AGREED IF POST NOT ALIENATED.[‡]

Wire to Ober 28 November 1929. From Fitzgerald. Paris. (AO)

ALLRIGHT WITH POST

Wire (cc) to Fitzgerald 29 November 1929. From Ober. (PU)

F. Scott Fitzgerald, Esq.
10 Rue Pergolese
Paris, France

Dear Scott:

I have your letter of November 23rd about McCall's, but as this
was written before we decided to sell the story to Liberty, I am not
going to bother you any further about the matter. I certainly agree
with all you say.

Maxwell Perkins told me today that he had a very encouraging
letter from you regarding your book. You will not forget, will you,
that it would probably save a month or two and get the book out
that much earlier if you will send over, say, half the story when you
have it done. You can send it over insured and I can get two or three
copies typed at once so that we can have one for magazine and one
for Scribner's. I could send another copy back to you if you need
it to refer to in working on the end of the story.

Sincerely,
[Harold Ober]

December 5, 1929

TL (cc), 1p. (PU)

TWELVE PLEASE FINISHING STORY

Wire to Ober 20 December 1929. From Fitzgerald. Paris. (AO)

---

‡Reply to Ober's 27 November telegram.

Dear Harold:

Would the <u>New Yorker</u> like this?[§] Be sure you have your stenographer copy everything <u>exact</u> because of the dialect—or whatever it is.

As *to* the Ring Lardner, I don't like the idea[¶]—it is hard to discuss him without bringing in the dissipation. I'd have gladly done Ernest but I see D. Parker has done him this week.

O.K. on the <u>Liberty</u> matter—you did wisely, I'm sure. Will it hurt you in any way if I nevertheless send correspondence [of] *to* Author's League Bulletin?

Working like hell on novel. Thank you for all deposits. Starting story Monday.

As Ever
Scott

Did <u>Wiess</u> of [the] M^c calls sign that letter? This if you answer this above question in the negative. Or in any case, Won't act without telling you.[#]

ALS, 1p. n.d., n.p.—received 26 December 1929. Paris. (AO)

F. Scott Fitzgerald, Esq.
10 Rue Pergolese
Paris, France

Dear Scott:

Thank you for your note, sending in the very amusing sketch entitled SALESMANSHIP IN THE CHAMPS ELLYSEE. I am sure the New Yorker will like this.

I note what you say about Ring Lardner and I will tell the editor of the New Yorker that you do not feel you could do one of him. If you think of anybody else that you would like to do at any time, you might let me know.

The letter I sent you from McCall's Magazine was signed by Otis L. Wiese, the editor. It would not hurt me in any way to have this whole correspondence published in the Authors' League Bulletin. I think, however, it might be rather embarrassing for Liberty, which is going to use the article, and I would rather not have the

---

[§]"Salesmanship in the Champs Elysees," *The New Yorker*, 15 February 1929.
[¶]Refers to a profile of Ring Lardner requested by *The New Yorker*.
[#]Added in pencil at bottom with an arrow leading back to the end of the first sentence in the third paragraph.

correspondence published until we find out how the editors of Liberty would feel about it. Some editors like to feel that anything they publish has been written directly for them and that no other editor has seen or declined anything that they use. On the whole, I would be inclined to let the matter drop. I should not be at all surprised if there was a new editor at McCall's before very long, and I don't see that you could gain very much by having the letters published in the Bulletin. If it would be a satisfaction to you to print the letters, let me know and I will see Liberty and see how they feel about it.

Sincerely,
[Harold Ober]

December 26, 1929

TL (cc), 1p. (PU)

Fitzgerald's total earnings for 1929 were $32,448.18 (including $2,430 for Zelda's sketches). He sold eight stories to The Saturday Evening Post *($27,000). His* Post *price reached the top figure of $4,000. His book royalties were $31.77.*

F. Scott Fitzgerald, Esq.
10 Rue Pergolese
Paris, France

Dear Scott:

I am glad to have your cable, although I am sorry to know that you have been ill.

You asked for $100, but I know you must be short and I am sending you $300.

Your last cables have been delayed because they have been sent over to me from the Reynolds office. You probably have the cable address "Carbonato" fixed in your mind. Perhaps you can get some new association of ideas which will fix in your mind my cable address, which is

"LITOBER".

One or two of my friends have intimated that it had an alcoholic association. This did not occur to me when they gave it to me as a cable address.

Sincerely,
[Harold Ober]

January 25, 1930

TL (cc), 1p. (AO)

F. Scott Fitzgerald, Esq.
c/o Guaranty Trust Company
Paris, France.

Dear Scott:

A MILLIONAIRE'S GIRL has just come in and I have just finished reading it.* I like it a lot and some of your lines about California are very amusing, indeed.

The story reached me with a large red stamp on the envelope "not at Park & Tilford's". You had addressed it to 485 Fifth Avenue, which evidently is the home of Park & Tilford.

Sincerely yours,
[Harold Ober]

March 5, 1930

Couldn't you send over a few Chapters of the novel. If we could get at least that much start it might be possible to publish the book this Autumn. Otherwise it means 1931.†

TL (cc), lp. (AO)

F. Scott Fitzgerald, Esq.
c/o Guaranty Trust Company
Paris, France.

Dear Scott:

Thank you for the note that reached me on March 12. I received on the same day your cable saying that another Josephine story was coming along‡ and also that you would mail half the novel on April 1. I am delighted to know that you can do this as I have been wanting for a long while to read at least part of the novel, and I think it may save a whole season in the publication of the book.

I am very pleased about selling A MILLIONAIRE'S GIRL to the Post. They have promised to send me proofs which I'll send over to you to correct.

---

*"A Millionaire's Girl," *The Saturday Evening Post*, 17 May 1930. Mostly written by Zelda, but published as by F. Scott Fitzgerald.
†Postscript added in Ober's hand.
‡"A Nice Quiet Place," *The Saturday Evening Post*, 31 May 1930.

Please don't worry about the advances I have made to you and if you don't feel like doing another Josephine story now, I think it would be wise for you to go ahead and put the time in on the novel.

Sincerely yours,

[Harold Ober]

March 14, 1930

TL (cc), lp. (AO)

F. Scott Fitzgerald, Esq.
c/o Guaranty Trust Co.
Paris, France

Dear Scott:

The second Josephine story, A NICE QUIET PLACE, came yesterday and I am delighted with it. It seems to me even better than the first.

I am glad to know that you are sending one part of the novel and I am eagerly looking forward to its getting here, so that I can read it. I will read it before I tell anyone I have it.

I am enclosing two statements; one to January 1st, and the other from January 1st to April 7th. The story, A NICE QUIET PLACE, will cover this.

I note what you say about Zelda's story that I sold to the Post. It is much too good a story for College Humor and it had so much of you in it that I am sure it would have been recognized as your story no matter under what name it was published. I guess it is all right to let Swanson have sketches if they are very short and could not possibly be made into stories, but, as I wrote you some time ago, I think it is a great mistake to waste good ideas on Swanson for such a low price. I really felt a little guilty about dropping Zelda's name from that story, THE MILLIONAIRE'S GIRL, but I think she understands that using the two names would have tied the story up with the College Humor stories and might have got us into trouble. # Will you please tell her for me that it was a mighty good piece of work. I was in Philadelphia last Monday and both Mr. Lorimer and Miss Neall inquired about you both.

I have been talking to Maxwell Perkins and I really think you ought to have a book out this autumn. Unless you are almost posi-

---

Ober made the following memo about "The Millionaire's Girl":

"On Scotts list of sales this story is listed under Zelda's writings

"I think it was meant for College Humor but came from France with Scotts handwritten changes and I thought it was his and sent it to SEP and they bought it".

tive that the novel is going to be ready, don't you think it might be well to let them do the Basil Lee stories? Of course, it would be a lot better to get the novel out this autumn, if it can be done, and I think if you once get part of it out of your hands you will be able to finish it.

By the way, O. O. McIntyre, in his column last Sunday, expressed the opinion that "Scott Fitzgerald is the best of the younger novelists—when he tries".

One more thing, then I am finished with this letter. I think the illustrations for FIRST BLOOD* were terrible and I have expressed my opinion quite freely to everybody in Philadelphia. I feel quite sure they will get somebody else to do the second Josephine story.

Sincerely,
[Harold Ober]

April 8, 1930

TL (cc), 2pp. (AO)

Dear Harold:

(1st) I will be mailing a new story about the 25th.† Glad you liked <u>A Nice Quiet Place</u>. Did you ask about the corrected proof of <u>First Blood</u>‡—I do so want to have it. Glad you put up a kick about the illustations—they were awful, with all the youthful suggestion of a G.A.R. congress

Thanks for the statements. I'm about where I feared I was.

Zelda was delighted with your compliments about the <u>Millionaire's Girl</u>.

Now—about the novel—the other night I read one great hunk of it to John Peale Bishop, and we both agreed that it would be ruinous to let <u>Liberty</u> start it uncompleted. Here's a hypothetical possibility. Suppose (as may happen in such cases) they didn't like the end + we quarreled about it—then what the hell! I'd have lost the <u>Post</u>, gained an enemy in <u>Liberty</u>—who would we turn to—Ray Long? Suppose <u>Liberty</u> didn't like even the first *part* + went around saying it was rotten before it was even finished. [So] I want to be in New York if possible when they accept it for there's that element of cutting, never *yet* discussed—are they going to cut it? Are they going to cut my stories to 5000 words or not? Are they going to pay

* *The Saturday Evening Post*, 5 April 1930.
†Probably "The Bridal Party," *The Saturday Evening Post*, 9 August 1930.
‡Line from here to top margin indicates words: "Addenda of letter covers this".

$3500. or $4000. [Zelda] At [and I] one time I was about to send four chapters out of eight done to you. Then I cut one of those chapters absolutely to pieces. I know you're losing faith in me + Max too but God knows one has to rely in the end on one's own [jude] judgement. I could have published four lowsy, half baked books in the last five years + people would [I] have thought I was at least a worthy young man not drinking myself to pieces in the south seas—but I'd be dead as Michael Arlen, Bromfield, Tom Boyd, Callaghan + the others who think they can trick the world with the hurried and the second rate. These <u>Post</u> stories <u>in</u> the <u>Post</u> are at least not any spot on me—they're honest and if [they're] *their* <u>form</u> is stereotyped people know what to *expect when* they pick up the <u>Post</u>. The novel is another thing—if, after four years I published the Basil Lee stories as a book I might as well get tickets for Hollywood immediately.

Well, that's how things are. If you'll have confidence in me I think you'll shortly see I knew what I was doing.

Ever Yours
Scott Fitz—

This letter sounds [irritable] *cross* but I'm stupid-got with work today + too tired to rewrite it. Please forgive it—it has to get tomorrow's boat.

Addenda

Zelda's been sick + not dangerously but seriously, + then I got involved in a wedding party[§] + after 2 weeks just got to work on new story yesterday but 3000 words already done—about as many as I must owe you dollars.

Meanwhile I acknowledge
(1) The account
(2) News about "the Beautiful + D——"
(3) Costain's suggestion (incidently he can go to hell). The only way I can write a decent story is to imagine no one's going to accept it + who cares. Self-consciousness about editors is <u>ruinous</u> to me. They can make their critisisms afterwards. I'm not doing *to do* another Josephine thing until I can get that out of my head. I tore [the] up the beginning of one. [I] *You* might tell him *pleasantly, of course*, that I just can't work that way—[Lorimer never made me a suggestion in his life.] Still there's no use telling him—the harms done but if he has any other ideas about writing stories please don't tell me.

---

§Powell Fowler, Ludlow's brother, was married in early May in Paris. The wedding supplied material for "The Bridal Party."

(4) I'm sorry the proofs [g] destroyed on <u>First Blood</u>. Could you get me [another] *a* copy of the magazine its in—I've lost mine. I want to fix it while I remember. By the way I don't mind *not* having [p] when I'm here on my own stories—but when I've worked on a proof its like losing a whole draft of a thing.

Yours Always
Scott

Last Word

I understand the movies are buying short stories again. Do you know a good agent in Hollywood you might persuade to interest himself in <u>Majesty</u>. Its constructed dramaticly like a play + has some damn good dramatic scenes in it

FSF

Address till July 1st
4 Rue Herran

ALS, 4pp. n.d.—received 13 May 1930. Paris. (AO)

Fitzgerald's reference to Zelda's being sick "not dangerously but seriously" was a mention of the beginning of her mental collapse. On 23 April 1930 Zelda entered Malmaison, a clinic outside Paris, in a nervous and exhausted state. She remained there only ten days, leaving against the doctor's advice on 2 May 1930.

F. Scott Fitzgerald, Esq.
4 rue Herran
Paris, France

Dear Scott:

I am very glad to have your letter about various matters and about the novel. You have convinced me that you are entirely right about the novel and I have sent you a cable to tell you so.

I have just been talking with Lou Palmer of Liberty and I have explained to him more fully than I have done before just how you feel about this novel. He wants me to write you that he wants you to take your time and get the novel just as you want it and he says that if you don't feel like sending over part of the novel before it is finished, not to do so. He wanted part of the story so that they could start a good illustrator to work on it. Good illustrations are often what hold up publication of a serial. He says he would not think of beginning the story until he had the complete manuscript.

He also wants me to tell you that there is not the least likelihood of their turning down the story and they have no intention of cutting it or of cutting short stories of yours if they are lucky enough to get them. Several years ago Liberty used almost always to cut stories but they very rarely cut them now, especially stories of authors who know how to write. As to the price of the short stories, they have agreed to pay as much as anyone else is paying and I hope that by the time their short stories come along, that they will have to pay more than $4000.

You are entirely right about the novel and I think you are right not to bring out the Basil Lee stories until after the novel is published. I have lots of confidence in you and I am sure that the novel when it appears is going to be as good a piece of work as you or anyone else has done.

A MILLIONAIRE'S GIRL is in this week's Post and I think you will agree with me that the illustrations are a great improvement on the ones for FIRST BLOOD. I am sending a copy of FIRST BLOOD herewith, taken from the Post. I am sorry about the proofs and I'll see that they are not lost again.

I'll see what can be done with the picture rights of MAJESTY.

I am sorry Zelda has been ill and I hope she is better by now.

Sincerely yours,
[Harold Ober]

May 15, 1930

P.S. Lou Palmer told me that Monk Saunders¶ told him you had read a little of the novel to him several months ago and that he was very much impressed with it.

The other evening I heard on the piano a score and some of the lyrics of a musical version of THE OFF-SHORE PIRATE. The option we gave has expired and I have given a six months option to two people connected with the Shuberts. If they don't do anything I think I'll give another option to the people whose option has just expired for they have some very original music.

TL (cc), 2pp. (AO)

Zelda did not get better. On 22 May 1930 she entered Valmont, a clinic in Switzerland. She stayed there till 4 June 1930, when she was moved to the sanitarium Les Rives de Prangins on Lake Geneva. While at Prangins, Zelda wrote at least three unpublished stories: "A Workman," "The Drought and the Flood," and "The House."

¶John Monk Saunders, novelist and screen writer.

599 Summit Ave.
St. Paul, Minn
October 28th, 1919

Mr. Paul Revere Reynolds
70 Fifth Avenue
New York City

Dear Sir:

The Scribners has accepted my first novel and I have sold several stories to Scribner's Magazine and to the Smart Set. I am not having much luck with my manuscripts in general. Mrs. Grace Flandrau suggested that I send one to you to see if you would undertake the disposal of any of my stuff.

The enclosed manuscript, West Feathers, has never been submitted anywhere. If you feel you can place it anywhere your regular terms will be satisfactory to me.

I'd liked to ask you also if you object to handling manuscripts typed in single space.

Hoping to hear from you, I am

very truly yours
F. Scott Fitzgerald.

F. Scott Fitzgerald's first letter to the Reynolds agency

Scott Fitzgerald in France—photograph
probably taken 1924

Anne Reid Ober, portrait by
Willard H. Ortlip, 1935

Harold Ober, a portrait by Willard H. Ortlip

Harold Ober with his sons Richard (left, age 14) and Nathaniel
(right, age 11) at his 35th Harvard class reunion

FORM 2TW   6-29-200M

FRENCH TELEGRAPH CABLE COMPANY

NEW YORK		PARIS
EXECUTIVE OFFICES: 60 BROAD STREET		**MAIN OFFICE: 53 RUE VIVIENNE**

60 BROAD ST. (ALWAYS OPEN) **7934 HANOVER**

PRODUCE EXCHANGE	1371 BOWLING GREEN
COTTON EXCHANGE	1289 BOWLING GREEN
PULITZER BUILDING, PARK ROW	2069 BEEKMAN
153 DUANE STREET	9696 WHITEHALL
65 FIFTH AVENUE	1135 ALGONQUIN
2 WEST 31ST STREET	2310 LACKAWANNA
545 FIFTH AVE (2 EAST 45TH STREET)	1040 LEXINGTON
5 COLUMBUS CIRCLE	0684 COLUMBUS

LONDON
MAIN OFFICE: 24 ROYAL EXCHANGE, E. C. 3

OTHER OFFICES
LIVERPOOL — HAVRE — BREST
ST. PIERRE, MIQUELON—ANTWERP
FRENCH WEST INDIES

59 CANNES 7   **SEP 24 1929**

          LCD LITOBER NY

FOLLOWING YOU NATURALLY

          FITZGERALD

          HAROLD OBER (PERSONAL) 485 MAD AVE

To reduce the risk of errors or delays, please file any answer to this message at one of the Company's own offices. Messengers may be summoned by Telephone for Cablegrams FREE OF CHARGE.
The above MESSAGE is received via FRENCH TELEGRAPH CABLE subject to the terms and conditions printed on the back hereof, which are ratified and agreed to.

Fitzgerald's response to the announcement that Ober was leaving Reynolds
to set up his own agency

The Ober home in Scarsdale, New York

The living room of the Ober home

Harold Ober having his
shoes shined in his office
at 40 East 49th Street

Harold Ober "sleeping energetically"
in his garden

JUN 26 1929

Have asked for money as if it had

Dear Harold: Did The

B. + Damned Talkie come thru?

I'm calling on you heavily
this month but am sending another
story in three days which I

(Insurance, income tax, car, Cannes
villa in advance to pay)
+ last American bills

child's absurd
tonsil operation

hope will more than square us. Address
after 30th June ~~for emergencies~~

~~Martin Line~~

12 (Boulevard) Gazagnaire
(GAZAGNAIR)

unnecessary
in cables)   Cannes

Excuse this scrawl but it's four
+ I've been correcting since ten &
have grown hazy with exactitude —
I'd like to write this upside down.

(over)

With 2nd story will have more than ~~almost~~
2 clear mos. on Rivierra for
novel + if end is in sight in
Sept. won't hesitate to borrow
from Perkins.

My wife's 4th sketch ~~scetch~~ along
shortly. No news. Sorry
you didn't get one

Scott Fitzg—

where we have will have a
really inexpensive menage, for I'm
damn tired of this delay
about novel.

A letter Fitzgerald wrote to Ober in June 1929 (see page 137)

Scott and Scottie at Salies-des-Béarn,
Pyrenees, 1926

Scott, Zelda, and Scottie on the Riviera, 1929

The Fitzgeralds at Lake Annecy, Switzerland, July 1931

Scottie at the age of nine, Lake Como, Italy

For Harold Ober
Without whose
help this world
never have been
able to be foisted
on the world
F. Scott Fitzgerald

Inscriptions in Harold Ober's
copies of (left) *Tender Is the
Night* and (below) *Tales of the
Jazz Age*

For Harold Ober
   who fathered
      The Camel's Back
      Benjamin Button
      The Diamond as Big as the Ritz
      The Jellybean
      The Lees of Happiness
      +
      The Russet Witch

   from   his gratefully
            F Scott Fitzgerald

   (note the Table of contents)

            1922

Scott and Zelda at Myrtle Beach, South Carolina, June 1937

Memo made by Harold Ober on being phoned of Scott's death by Sheila of graham

Hollywood 7730 until 2-05 in the morning
Santa Monica 53919 after 20 minutes before 3
(after 10 (California time tomorrow)) for a short time

Secretary Frances Kroll (Crestview 13704) - Los Angeles
(Executors John Biggs & Max Perkins)
Now at Pierce Bros mortuary
720 West Washington Boulevard
Los Angeles

There is a ... (about) that can be ...
Monday the Secretary will know about Insurance.
She has will and papers and rough draft of
2/3 of novel. Sheila G. says Scott intended to
rewrite the first part entirely — he wouldn't want it seen
as it is —

The will directs that the funeral shall be at the
lowest possible expense. She doesn't think he will like to
be buried in California because he really hated California. She
thinks he would like to be buried where his father is buried
because he admired him.

Sheila G. wants to know whether Scottie is coming out — I don't
think she ought to come alone — She will come back

Notes made by Harold Ober during the telephone conversation with
Sheilah Graham in which she informed him of Fitzgerald's death

with her if she wants her to.

She says the only relative Scott liked was Cousin Ceci. He liked Zelda's mother &

Scott was talking about Scotty a lot this afternoon. He had never been so happy about her as he was today. He spoke of how well she was doing at Vassar and said the one thing he wanted her to do was finish Vassar —

Two or three days ago Scott didn't feel very well and the doctor had him in bed — but for the last few days he had been feeling well and happy. Dr had told him not to do too much up and down stairs. Sheila was with him this afternoon & he was in very good spirits because he had been pleased (He had a kind of heart attack a month or two ago)

with the writing he had done recently. He was talking about (Scotty?) got up from his chair and dropped dead. She said she was sure he had no pain and that he didn't know there was anything the matter.

She said the ms of the novel was all first draft and some of it was in a confused state — but some of it was beautifully done — some of the best writing he had ever done

Harold and Anne Ober with Scottie at her wedding to Ensign Samuel J. Lanahan, February 1943

Harold and Anne Ober in their garden with Thomas A. Lanahan, Scottie's oldest son

In order to be near Zelda, Fitzgerald moved to Lausanne during the summer of 1930. By November Zelda's condition had worsened.

F. Scott Fitzgerald, Esq.
4 rue Herran
Paris, France.

Dear Scott:

Swanson has sent me a copy of a cable he has sent you about A MILLIONAIRE'S GIRL. I have just noticed that he sent it to your old address so perhaps you haven't received it, in which case you will wonder what the cable I have sent you is about.

I think Swanson is slightly crazy. He seems to be possessed with the idea that for some unknown reason he should get the best work of the best authors for a fraction of the price other magazines are willing to pay, and this seems to be a new attempt to get a Post story for $800.

I haven't seen Swanson in two months. I have not written him any letter or mentioned you or A MILLIONAIRE'S GIRL to him or any other story of yours. A Miss Reilly, who is an assistant of his, was here last week and said they hoped they could have another story. She spoke of A MILLIONAIRE'S GIRL, which was just out in the Post, and said what a fine story it was. I told her that A MILLIONAIRE'S GIRL was no longer than some of the stories they had had and I didn't think you could afford to do any more for them. Swanson must have got his idea from this conversation.

As I have cabled you, I hope you won't pay any attention to Swanson's cable or answer it in any way. I am pretty much disgusted with him. He is always begging for stories by well known authors and then offering about a quarter of what he ought to pay for them. I don't think his magazine has any great dignity and I'll be just as pleased if your name never again appeared in it.

Sincerely yours,
[Harold Ober]

May 26, 1930

TL (cc), 1p. (AO)

Dear Harold:

I havn't written for so long to you because I've been swamped with worries + anxieties here. Zelda has been in a hell of a mess, still in the sanitarium—she came within an ace of losing her mind + isn't out of the woods yet. We had a frantic time last spring +

in midsummer from the combination of worry + work my lungs sprang a leak. That's all right now thank heaven—I went up to Caux + rested for a month. All this is between you + me—even Max doesn't know. Then Scotty fell ill + I left at midnight by plane for Paris to decide about an immediate appendix operation. In short its been one of those periods that come to all men I suppose when life is so complicated that with the best will in the world work is hard as hell to do. Things are better, but no end in sight yet. I figure I've written about 40,000 words to Forel* (the psychiatrist) on the subject of Zelda trying to get to the root of things, + keeping worried families tranquil in their old age + trying to be a nice thoughtful female mother to Scotty—well, I've simply replaced letters by wires [for] wherever possible.

About Zelda's sketches, have you tried Century? They printed my little skit on Scotty. But better still—send them to the <u>New Republic</u>, attention of Edmund Wilson, under the blanket title of <u>Stories from a Swiss Clinique</u>. Failing that I'll try <u>This Quarter</u> here in Paris. Unfortunately Transition has quit. Sorry about the Enerson thing.

About money. Having wired you last week that <u>The Hotel Child</u>‡ was sent, I found on its return from the typist that it needed revision + amputation. That is done + it is back there but won't be ready till day after tomorrow. I'm sure you'll like it. I thought the last Josephine was feeble. If I press you too hard about money please try to arrange advance§ from Lorimor, telling him frankly I've never worked under such conditions of expense + pressure in my life, for when I wire you it means trouble for me if deposit isn't made. What this seems to amount too is that I am an average outstanding loan of yours of about $2000. I hope to God things will¶ be better soon. How are things going with you. Write me

> Ever Yours Gratefully
> Scott Fitzg—

Thought very little of Swanson offer. Havn't touched novel for four months, save for one week.#

ALS, 1p. n.d., n.p.—received 11 November 1930. Paris or Lausanne. (AO)

---

*Dr. Oscar Forel of Prangins.
‡ *The Saturday Evening Post*, 31 January 1931.
§Line drawn to the top margin indicates the words: "I mean cash advance, not price advance".
¶Here through the signature is written along the right margin.
#These sentences are written along the left margin.

F. Scott Fitzgerald, Esq.
c/o Guaranty Trust Company
Paris, France.

Dear Scott:

I am very glad to have your letter and I am awfully sorry that you have had such a difficult time this year. I hope Zelda will come out of the sanatorium entirely cured. I think probably you have as good doctors as can be found anywhere and that is something to be thankful for.

As I wired you, Scribner's are going to use MISS BESSIE and they will pay $150. for it.* It is a small price but it is the best I could get them to do and I thought Zelda would like to have the sketch in Scribner's. The other sketches are now with New Republic and I'll let you know when Edmund Wilson decides about them. You suggest the Century but the Century is no longer published. It became a quarterly and then it was bought by the Forum.

I have your cable telling me that your new story, THE HOTEL CHILD, has been mailed, and I presume it will be here in a day or two. I am very keen to read it as from the title I am sure it is going to be an interesting story. I didn't like the last Josephine story as well as some of the others but the Post seemed to like it very much, indeed. Of course after ONE TRIP ABROAD,† almost any story would suffer.

I am sorry you haven't been able to do anything on the novel. John Peale Bishop came in to see me not long ago and he told me he thought you had a remarkable story. He thought it a great advance on anything you have yet done. I hope things will work out so that you can finish it. Of course I can see that it has been impossible for you to do anything on it these last few months.

As you probably know, we have had a very bad year here. The stock market and business conditions were terrible and conditions in the publishing world have been very much upset. Taking everything into consideration, however, I have had a very good year, much better than I expected, and I have never for a moment regretted the change that I made a year ago last September. I am enclosing

---

*Zelda Fitzgerald's story "Miss Ella," *Scribner's Magazine,* December 1931.
† *The Saturday Evening Post,* 11 October 1930.

a list of authors I am handling as I think you may be interested in looking it over.‡

I hope that you are now in really good health yourself and that Zelda will improve just as rapidly as possible. John Peale Bishop said that he thought you might be coming over in December. Is there any possibility of that?

Sincerely yours,
[Harold Ober]

November 18, 1930

TL (cc), 2pp. (AO)

Fitzgerald's total earnings for 1930 were $33,090.10. He sold seven stories to The Saturday Evening Post *($25,200). His book income was $3,-789.94, of which $3,701.97 was a further advance against his next novel.*

Hotel de la Paix
Lausanne

Dear Harold:

I grow ashamed to write you with all this borrowing. But December's over + I've few bills (this was income tax—insurance—Xmas month) due + I'm going to write a story about Gstaad, a Swiss winter sport place where I'm taking my daughter *for the holidays* + then I hope to God the novel. Zelda was pleased with the sale of Miss Bessie. Did Edmund Wilson like the stories.§ Failing that there remains only the <u>American Caravan</u>. Send them [care] *attention* of Paul Rosenfeld. Zelda is a little better but not much.

For the moment I can't see the Lorimer article—perhaps after my next story.¶

The enclosure is O. K. with me.

Am having Scribner hand you a curious manuscript that might interest some publisher. The author is now watchman in a bank here in Paris. Did Julian Enerson come thru with any more stories? He's a lazy bastard. Did the Post like <u>The Hotel Child</u>? Practically the whole damn thing is true, bizarre as it seems. Lord Allington + the famous Bijou O'Connor were furious at me putting them in

---

‡Ober's list is missing. However, a 1937 list has been located which includes: Frederick Lewis Allen, Rex Beach, Thomas Beer, Catherine Drinker Bowen, Katharine Brush, Ben Lucien Burman, Agatha Christie, Walter D. Edmonds, Paul Gallico, Robert Herrick, Ngaio Marsh, Gouverneur Morris, Eden Phillpotts, Channing Pollock, Mari Sandoz, Arthur Train, S. S. Van Dine, Charles Wertenbaker, Ben Ames Williams, and Philip Wylie.
§Stories or sketches by Zelda Fitzgerald which were never published.
¶The subject of this article for *The Saturday Evening Post* is unknown.

+ as for the lovely jewess (real name Mimi Cohn) I don't dare tell her. [Im]

I'm impressed with the number of well-known authors on your list in such a short time.

Making lots of New Years resolves for a 50,000 a year 1931
                              Yours Always
                              Scott Fitzg

Please don't try to push <u>Post</u> up anymore *now*. I've gotten selfconscious + don't think my stuff is worth half what I get now #

<u>Very important</u> Please <u>immediately</u> send me back carbon copy of this story.* Its terribly important, because this is founded on a real quarrel with my sister-in-law + I have to square her.

ALS, 2pp. n.d.—received 2 January 1931. (AO)

F. Scott Fitzgerald, Esq.
c/o Guaranty Trust Company
Paris, France.

Dear Scott:

BABYLON REVISITED came back from the typist this morning just in time to give to Costain. I like the story very much.

You ask about THE HOTEL CHILD. Here is what Costain wrote me about this story:

" "The Hotel Child" by F. Scott Fitzgerald presented a few editorial problems in that it was not a straight-away story and that it introduced a few characters who will appear shady, to say the least, to American readers. However, it is such a splendid picture of this kind of life that we have had no hesitation in adding it to our list."

The New Republic still have Zelda's sketches. I spoke to Edmund Wilson about them and he told me that he would let me know about them as soon as he could. He says it isn't possible for them to publish very much fiction and the only chance of his using them is to hold them a little while to see if he can make an opening. If he declines them I'll show them to Paul Rosenfeld of the American Caravan.

I have a note this morning from Maxwell Perkins saying he is sending over the manuscript you spoke to me about in your last letter, and Julian Enersen came in yesterday with a manuscript which I have not yet been able to read.

He was receiving $4000 per story from *The Saturday Evening Post*.
*"Babylon Revisited," *The Saturday Evening Post*, 21 February 1931.

Don't worry about the advances. I am sure this year will be a better year for all of us. I would like to see you at the end of 1931 with ten thousand dollars saved and put away safely in a savings account. You may have to do one or two stories before you finish the novel but if you could finish the novel and put some of the serial money away, I think it would give you a feeling of security that you haven't had for some time.

I send you herewith a carbon of BABYLON REVISITED.

Sincerely yours,
[Harold Ober]

January 6, 1931

TL (cc), 2pp. (AO)

F. Scott Fitzgerald, Esq.
ᶜ/o Guaranty Trust Company
Paris, France

Dear Scott:

The Post are taking FLIGHT AND PURSUIT but they want me to tell you that they do not feel that your last three stories have been up to the best you can do. They think it might be a good idea for you to write some American stories—that is stories laid on this side of the Atlantic and they feel that the last stories have been lacking in plot.

I do not think it is necessary for a story to have a plot but I think a story must either move the reader or amuse him.

These last three stories of yours, FLIGHT AND PURSUIT, A NEW LEAF and INDECISION,‡ have been interesting to me because they were very vivid bits of life but I do feel that in these three stories you have failed to make the reader care about any one of the characters.

ON YOUR OWN§ has just come in and I have read it. I think you have improved it, especially in its construction. I am having it typed at once.

I think it is probably a mistake for me to write you this letter but the Post have definitely asked me to tell you how they feel. Although these last stories of yours may not be as good as some you

---

‡All published in *The Saturday Evening Post:* "Flight and Pursuit," 14 May 1931; "A New Leaf," 4 July 1931; "Indecision," 16 May 1931.

§"On Your Own," also titled "Home to Maryland," was rejected by *College Humor, Collier's, Good Housekeeping, Pictorial Review, Redbook, The Saturday Evening Post,* and *Woman's Home Companion* and was never published.

have done, they are so much better than most of the stories that I read, that it makes me a little angry with the Post. Perhaps the best thing for you to do is to tear this letter up and go ahead and write your stories as they come to you.

While I am about it, I want to make one more plea about your novel. I think you ought without fail to have a novel out in 1932. Can you not hide away somewhere, where you can live very cheaply, and finish the novel? Don't let anybody know where you are. I realize that you are having a tremendous lot of expense for Zelda and that must of course worry you a great deal. If the doctors there have done all they can for her perhaps it would be worth while bringing her over here and seeing what could be done in the Neurological Hospital, or the Psychiatric Institute in New York or some such place. I know that they are doing very good work here, and I imagine the expense would be very much less. I hope of course that Zelda will be well enough soon so that she won't need any more treatment of this kind.

I believe, and others who are much more competent judges than I, believe that you ought to go further than any American writer and I think now is the time for you to get down to hard work and finish the novel.

Sincerely yours,
[Harold Ober]

May 19, 1931

TL (cc), 2pp. (AO)

F. Scott Fitzgerald, Esq.
c/o Guaranty Trust Company
Paris, France

Dear Scott:

I believe I gave you a statement dated February 6 when you were in New York. I am sending you another statement to June 10 so that you will know how you stand.¶

I am also enclosing a letter that I wrote you a week or two ago but didn't send because I thought it might worry you. I think I had better send it along now as I think you ought to know the Post wants you to do American stories. If the stories that are on the way to me are not stories laid in America, it will perhaps be a good excuse for trying them on some other magazine. I'll of course give

---

¶Fitzgerald had returned to America in January for his father's funeral.

the Post a chance at them first. I feel very strongly that you ought to do the stories that you want to do and if you feel like doing stories laid in Europe, I should certainly write that kind.

I was sorry not to be able to send all the money you wanted when your cable came in yesterday. I have had a lot of extra expense lately and I may be a little short for the next month or two.

I talked to Maxwell Perkins today and he tells me has heard from you that Zelda is very much better. I am glad to hear this.

Sincerely yours,
[Harold Ober]

June 11, 1931

I shall be away for two or three weeks in July + you had better let me know a few days earlier than usual if you have to have money. If two stories get here safely + sell, everything will be all right#

TL (cc), 1p. (AO)

After a few trial trips with Fitzgerald and Scottie, Zelda was released from Prangins on 15 September 1931. The Fitzgeralds returned to America and settled at 819 Felder Avenue in Cloverdale, a suburb of Montgomery.

METRO OFFERS 750 PER WEEK PLUS RAILROAD FARE STOP*
THINK POSSIBLE ONLY PROVIDED YOU COULD DO STORIES
SAME TIME STOP ADVISE YOU WIRE ME MINIMUM WEEKLY
RATE AND I WILL MAKE COUNTER OFFER
    HAROLD OBER.

Wire to Fitzgerald 23 October 1931. (PU)

METRO INSISTS MY WIRING YOU OFFER ONE THOUSAND WEEK
SAY THEIR LIMIT STOP INQUIRY PROVES PRICES DOWN BUT
THEY EVIDENTLY WANT YOU AND IF WE HOLD OUT MAY
COME UP TO TWELVE STOP JOB IDEAL FOR YOU MIGHT LEAD
TO OTHERS STOP WIRE ME MONDAY FINAL ROCK BOTTOM
BUT I WILL FIGHT FOR TWELVE
    HAROLD OBER.

Wire to Fitzgerald 24 October 1931. (PU)

Dear Harold:

(Ink just evaporated.) I am waiting to here whether Metro will offer twelve hundred. As a matter of fact I don't want to go for a damn + don't even know whether it will be worth while at 1200. with my Hotel Expenses ect which will eat up some of it.

#Postscript added in Ober's hand.
*To work on the movie *Red-headed Woman*.

The delay in the story was because it was rotten. Begun in Washington + continued in unfavorable conditions here. So last week I began another—expect to finish it this aft + revise tomorrow.

About Zelda's story[†]—I suggest Red Bk. first. (Or <u>Post</u> if you think it has any chance of getting by morally) Then Mencken— Scribners practically told me they'd take it if revised.

[Why did you] Don't send me any more gloomy reviews like the O'Brien things. Unfavorable critisism upsets me these days—always has.

Who do you think the Metro [offer] *suggestion* came from? Katherine Brush *herself?*[§] Would I have to pay the commission of an agent in Hollywood too, like in The Great Gatsby. That would make it a still more unfavorable business. And is R. R. fare always included

I like it here, Harold—nobody talks of the depression.

Let me know any hint of <u>Post</u> price cutting as it will influence my plans.

Please send us a copy of <u>Crime Passionelle</u>.[¶]

To what English Magazines did you sell:

Jacobs Ladder 1927
Magnetism 1928
A New Leaf 1931[#]

> Ever Yours
> Scott Fitzg

ALS (pencil), 2pp. n.d., n.p.—received 29 October 1931. Montgomery. (AO)

METRO AGREE TWELVE HUNDRED PLUS FARE OUT AND RE-
TURN WIRE ME AUTHORITY SIGN CONTRACT STOP WHEN
CAN YOU LEAVE METRO SUGGEST YOU GO EARLIEST POSSIBLE
DIRECT FROM ALABAMA AND REPORT TO THALBERG PLAN
STAY SIX WEEKS ALL ABOVE PROVIDING YOU WANT TO GO
    HAROLD OBER.

Wire to Fitzgerald 6 November 1931. (PU)

DEPOSITING FIVE STOP METRO DESIRE AND EXPECT FINISH
BY DECEMBER 20 BUT ASK THAT PROVIDING UNAVOIDABLE
DELAY WORK UNFINISHED YOU COME BACK TO FINISH AFTER
RETURNING FOR WEEK IN ALABAMA STOP OF COURSE TO

---

†"There's a Myth in a Moral," not published under this title. Possibly "A Couple of Nuts," *Scribners Magazine*, August 1932.

§Author of *Red-headed Woman*.

¶An unpublished story by Zelda Fitzgerald. It was also titled "All About the Downs Case."

#In another hand are notes that "Jacob's Ladder" was not sold, that "Magnetism" was sold to *Grand Magazine*, and "A New Leaf" to Amalgamated Press.

THEIR ADVANTAGE FINISH QUICKLY STOP PLEASE WIRE SO
CONTRACT CAN BE SIGNED TOMORROW SATURDAY MORN-
ING
    HAROLD OBER.

Wire to Fitzgerald 6 November 1931. (PU)

F. Scott Fitzgerald, Esq.
819 Felder Avenue
Montgomery, Alabama

Dear Scott:

As I have wired you, Metro Goldwyn have finally come up to
$1200. a week. It evidently hurt them to do it and they say they are
not paying anything like that to anybody now but they evidently
think you are the one author to do a good job on RED-HEADED
WOMAN.

As I have wired you, they want you to go out just as soon as
possible as they are in a hurry to get to work on the picture. If you
decide to go, I think you will find it a more satisfactory experience
because you have a definite job to do and I have found Metro Goldwyn much more satisfactory to deal with than other companies.

In order to get everything fixed up, they suggested that I ask you
to wire me authority to sign the contract, but of course I will not
sign it unless I feel sure that everything is all right and if there is
any question about any of the clauses I'll wire you and if necessary
I'll send the contract down to you to look over. In order to save time
they suggested that you go directly from Alabama.

Both Lengel and Burton* have been calling me up frequently
about getting a story from you. Lengel finally wanted to know if he
couldn't send a wire direct and I told him to go ahead. He called me
up again yesterday and wanted to know if he could telegraph you
to do a twenty or thirty thousand word novelette to appear in one
number in the Cosmopolitan. I told him I didn't think there was any
chance of your doing this now, and I am telling you about this only
because he begged me to do so on the half chance that you might
have an idea for such a story.

I don't know how you feel about doing any short story or stories
for the Cosmopolitan. It is possible that you might feel like doing
a story that would not come within the Post's limitations and the
Cosmopolitan might prove a good market for such stories. I'd like,

---

*William C. Lengel and Harry Burton, editors of *Cosmopolitan*.

however, to offer the first story of this kind that you do to the Red Book on account of the fact that they took HALF A DOZEN OF THE OTHER.[†] Of course I wouldn't let them have it unless they would pay your price. By the way, Balmer[‡] tells me that you sent them direct the revised copy of this story and that it is going in the February issue.

Sincerely yours,
[Harold Ober]

November 6, 1931

TL (cc), 2pp. (AO)

In November 1931 Fitzgerald went alone to Hollywood to work on Red-headed Woman under Irving Thalberg at MGM. Zelda began working on a novel in Montgomery.

819 Felder,Mont.

Dear Harold:

Several matters. First Hollywood. I terminated the contract in 5 wks + one day my work being finished. It ended <u>last Wed. evening</u> + the document I signed abrogating the contract included that day. So please collect it. The weekly rate stands at $1200.00

I had to give one days salary[§] (I insisted on having [it] *the gift* on the $800 a wk basis as I wasn't sure of anything at that time) it ammounted to $133.00. I paid a fourth down. If they have put the rest on my studio bill + deducted it from last pay check please let me know if *from* that sum + also *from* rail road fares which were absolutely *nessessary* expenditures on my part (I still have my community chest stuff to do here) you will deduct 10%. Is it the custom. They didn't pay for a compartment for me + I had to pay all that + extra half ticket myself so the "R.R. expenses" seem almot a myth.

I'm not sorry I went because I've got a fine story about Hollywood which will be along in several days.[¶]

[Will you w] I want to know how I stand. Will you wire me on reciept of this—last word from you is a deposit of 500 for which I asked. Have you made deposits since to even our account + exactly how much.

[†]"Six of One," *Redbook*, February 1932.
[‡]Edwin Balmer, editor of *Redbook*.
[§]Fitzgerald drew a line from here to the top of the page and added the words: "to their charity".
[¶]"Crazy Sunday," *American Mercury*, November 1932.

Merry Xmas as that word goes this year.

The Post Illustrations are great. They are considering it for Joan Crawford + will act through you. #

Please send back *Zelda's* a <u>Myth + a Moral</u>—something can be done with it

> Ever Yours Faithfully
> Scott

ALS, 2pp. n.d.—received 28 December 1931. (AO)

F. Scott Fitzgerald, Esq.
819 Felder Avenue
Montgomery, Alabama

Dear Scott;

I have just received your note about the Hollywood contract. The following were the payments received on this contract:

Transportation, including
compartment, to Hollywood $143.58

1 day (November 11)	200.00
1 week to November 18 inclusive	1200.00
" " November 25 "	1200.00
" " December 2 "	1200.00
" " December 9 " (less $2.55)	1197.45
auto hire)	
5 days to December 15 inclusive	1000.00
	$5997.45

The payments were made a week after the termination of each week's work and of course reached me somewhat later than that.

The agreement terminating the contract which they sent me from the studio, which bears your signature, read as follows:

"This will confirm the agreement between us that the term of your employment under your contract of employment with us dated November 7, 1931, shall be deemed to have expired on December 15, 1931."

The letter accompanying the last check read "to and including December 15". December 15 was a Tuesday and not a Wednesday. In your letter you say that the contract ended Wednesday evening and that the document you signed included that day. You might check up on this before I ask for an extra day's payment.

Possibly refers to "Freeze Out," *The Saturday Evening Post*, 19 December 1931.

As you will see by the above statement of payments, Metro did not deduct anything for the day's salary you gave to their charities.

Let me know how much they gave you for return fare and how much the fare cost you and I will collect the difference. The original contract read that they were to pay you railroad fare and compartment both ways. I inquired from the railroad company here and found that the amount they sent me for your fare to Hollywood did include compartment.

When I make up my next statement to you I shall deduct commission only on the amount you actually received for your work. I will not, of course, take commission on your railroad fare and I won't take commission on the amount you had to give to charity.

By the way, there is another bill this morning for $1.71 for a telegram sent by you on December 10 to Montgomery. If this is all right, I can ask them to deduct it from any extra amount they may owe you for the cost of your compartment returning to Montgomery.

I'll have a statement made up to date and send it to you within a few days. I don't know when your letter was sent as it wasn't dated, but I received it only this morning as my office was closed on Saturday on account of the Christmas holidays.

I am glad to know that Joan Crawford is interested in the last Post story.

I am sending back Zelda's story THERE'S A MYTH IN A MORAL. I think she can improve it. It seems to me a very amusing sketch but it's rather slight in plot and I find that in these days when the magazines are so small they want manuscripts of this kind to be fairly short. I think a sketch of this kind ought to be considerably shorter. I'll be glad to see it again.

Sincerely yours,
[Harold Ober]

December 28, 1931

TL (cc), 2pp. (AO)

WAS TOLD I COULD GO WEDNESDAY DECEMBER SIXTEENTH FIVE OCLOCK SIGNED ABROGATION DECEMBER SEVENTEENTH THIS IS ABSOLUTELY DEFINITE.
    FITZGERALD.*

Wire (cc) to Ober 29 December 1931. Montgomery. (AO)

---

*An Ober note reads: "original sent Metro Goldwyn".

SIGNED ABROGATION CONTRACT WITHOUT READING IT
OVER BECAUSE I HAD NO REASON TO THINK THAT SCRIPT
DEPARTMENT WOULD DO ANYTHING UNFAIR AS IM SURE
THEY DID NOT DO PERSONALLY NEVERTHELESS A DAYS PAY
AND ALSO RETURN RAILROAD FARE AMOUNTED TO OVER
THREE HUNDRED DOLLARS HAS BEEN DEFINITELY CHISELED
OFF HAVE WRITTEN MARX OF SCRIPT DEPARTMENT ABOUT
DAYS PAY BUT NEVER SUSPECTED DIFFICULTY ABOUT RAIL-
ROAD FARE COUNT ON YOU TO COLLECT THAT
    FITZGERALD.

Wire to Ober 30 December 1931. Montgomery, (AO)

*Fitzgerald's total earnings for 1931 were $37,599. He sold nine stories
($31,500)—eight of them to* The Saturday Evening Post. *His book
royalties were $100. This was his peak financial year before he went to
Hollywood in 1937.*

REPORTS REACHED ME THAT KAUFFMANS OF THE I SING
COMES A LITTLE TOO CLOSE TO THE VEGETABLE TO PASS
WITHOUT ACKNOWLEDGEMENT KAUFFMAN WAS FAMILIAR
WITH THE VEGETABLE AND ADMIRED IT PLEASE MAKE DIS-
CREET INQUIRIES AS TO RESEMBLANCE AND WIRE ME
    SCOTT FITZGERALD..

Wire to Ober 5 January 1932. Montgomery. (AO)

F.Scott Fitzgerald, Esq.
819 Felder Avenue
Montgomery, Alabama

Dear Scott:

As I wrote you, Harry Burton, the new editor of the Cosmopolitan, asked me to come over to see him about several authors and
especially about you.

I saw him yesterday and had a long talk with him. He told me in
the first place that he was dropping all the confessional stuff that
Ray Long used so much of. He says he intends to make it a more
serious and better magazine and also a younger magazine. He said
he realized that the Post was your best market and he knew it would
be useless for him to try to win you entirely away from the Post.
He said, however, that to make the magazine the kind of magazine
he wants it to be, he must have you a few times a year, and he said
he would make a definite offer to take six out of eight stories, or four
out of six stories, at $5000. each. There would be nothing exclusive
about the contract and if he could get six stories in two years he
would be satisfied with that.

He also said he was very keen to get a novelette from you and he would make a contract for that, the price depending on the length. If it were the length of two short stories, which he would probably use in one number, he would probably pay $10,000. for it and more of course if it were longer.

I told him that I had mentioned the matter of a contract to you and you had told me you didn't believe you wanted to make one at the present time, but you might possibly do a novelette. He asked me if I would at least put this offer up to you, so I have done so.

As I wrote you the other day, I do not believe the Post would have any objection to your doing say three stories a year for the Cosmopolitan if they knew all the circumstances.

Costain was in today and I thought it would not do any harm to mention to him that another magazine was very keen to make a contract with you. He said the only magazine that he felt to be a direct rival of theirs at the present time was Collier's and that they didn't object to authors making contracts when they could do so with any other magazines.

In these times when many authors are getting their prices cut, I think it is very satisfying to know that your price can be increased.

Sincerely yours,
Harold Ober

January 6, 1932

P.S.   I noticed in one of the newspapers recently among the "Best similes of 1931", collected by a man named Frank J. Wilstach, the following of yours:

"Wabbling like a madeover chin in which the paraffin had run."

TLS, 2pp. (PU)

F. Scott Fitzgerald, Esq.
819 Felder Avenue
Montgomery, Alabama

Dear Scott:

I saw OF THEE I SING last night. In the first place I think it is very much over rated by the critics. I agree with Benchly that a good deal of it is very dull and the humor very heavy.

There is no doubt some similarity between this show and the second act of THE VEGETABLE. I don't believe, however, that there is enough so that there would be the slightest chance of establishing in a court that there had been plagiarism. The authors may have got the original idea from THE VEGETABLE; on the other hand, it is an idea that might come to anyone while seeing a Gilbert and Sullivan revival.

The similarity is in the fact that both are satires on political life in Washington. What story there is in OF THEE I SING is entirely different. The show begins with a campaign parade. There is a meeting of politicians in a hotel room during a political convention. They choose candidates and platform, which is to be love. They decide on a beauty contest with girls from every state and the candidate is to marry the one who is chosen to be the most beautiful. He falls in love instead with another girl and campaigns the country with her. There is a meeting in Madison Square where speeches are made that are somewhat similar but not as funny as the speech Jerry makes in THE VEGETABLE.

After the election the girl that has been turned down tries to get the president impeached and finally goes to the French Ambassador. Supreme Court Justices are called in and the president is being impeached before the Senate when the day is saved by the fact that his wife is going to have a baby.

About the only comic element in the show is the vice-president who is always turning up and whom nobody ever recognizes.

There are two or three slight points of similarity. In the show there is some mention of selling Rhode Island. This is, in a way, something like the part in THE VEGETABLE where Idaho is swapped for the Buzzard Islands. The Supreme Court Justices are slightly reminiscent of your Judge Fossile.

Finally, I should say that OF THEE I SING is much closer to Gilbert and Sullivan than it is to THE VEGETABLE and I can honestly say that I think Kaufman might have written OF THEE I SING without ever having read THE VEGETABLE. On the other hand, I can also see that after reading THE VEGETABLE it might occur to him to do a musical comedy on American political life. Whether Kaufman is entirely innocent of using THE VEGETABLE or whether he has been very clever in using it, the result, I think, is the same. I doubt, as I said in the beginning, if you could possibly have any claim against him.

I am enclosing pages from the programme.

Sincerely,
Harold Ober

January 14, 1932

TLS, 2pp. (PU)

Dear Harry Burton:

I appreciate the confidence that your offer implies.

The story CRAZY SUNDAY that I sent to Ober yesterday is going to be somewhat difficult in theme for Lorimer, I <u>think</u>, tho he's broadened in the last ten years. It's a fine story, I think, and according to all criteria I have, (my wife etc.) If he turns it down and you like it I'm suggesting to Ober that it be the first of four to be delivered within 16 months—I can't do more than that because I expect to write only two short stories in the next six and one must go to the Post.

Now:

A. The fact that the Post may take the story doesn't mean that I refuse your offer, but it means I want a few more weeks to think it over, and

B. The fact that you refuse the story does not mean that I refuse your offer—for it implies that I am mistaken, it is no good and must go into the discard.

The novelette idea is impossible at present.

Best regards to Bill Lengel. With best wishes for all the success you had with McCalls and a lot more acknowledgment of it.

Yours Faithfully,
(signed) Scott Fitzgerald

TL (cc), lp. n.d., January 1932. St. Petersburg, Fla. (AO)

During a vacation trip with Fitzgerald to St. Petersburg, Florida, in Janu-ary 1932, Zelda suffered another breakdown. On 12 February 1932 she entered the Henry Phipps Psychiatric Clinic of Johns Hopkins University in Baltimore, Maryland. Fitzgerald and Scottie remained in Montgomery. At Phipps, Zelda completed work on her novel, Save Me the Waltz.

F. Scott Fitzgerald, Esq.
819 Felder Avenue,
Montgomery, Alabama

Dear Scott:

I have your note about the income tax and I'll get the best letters I can from the Post and College Humor and send them on to you.

I enclose a list of stories sold to the Post and a list of stories sold to College Humor during the years 1929 and 1930, with the dates of sale.

The Cosmopolitan ought to let me know about CRAZY SUN-

DAY. Something is always happening to Harry Burton. The day I gave him the story he was laid up with an ulcerated tooth and since then his house has burned down. He is supposed to be back today and I'll send you a telegram the moment I get a decision from him.

Sincerely yours,

[Harold Ober]

February 10, 1932

TL (cc), lp. (AO)

Stories and Articles sold to Saturday Evening Post during 1929 and 1930 by F. Scott Fitzgerald

FORGING AHEAD	sold	January 1929	$3500.00
BASIL AND CLEOPATRA	"	February 1929	3500.00
THE ROUGH CROSSING	"	April 1929	3500.00
MAJESTY	"	May 1929	3500.00
AT YOUR AGE	"	July 1929	4000.00
THE SWIMMERS	"	August 1929	4000.00
TWO WRONGS	"	November 1929	4000.00
FIRST BLOOD	"	January 1930	4000.00
A MILLIONAIRE'S GIRL	"	March 1930	4000.00
A NICE QUIET PLACE	"	April 1930	4000.00
THE BRIDAL PARTY	"	June 1930	4000.00
A WOMAN WITH A PAST	"	July 1930	4000.00
ONE TRIP ABROAD	"	August 1930	4000.00
A SNOBBISH STORY	"	October 1930	4000.00
THE HOTEL CHILD	"	December 1930	4000.00

Stories and Articles sold to College Humor 1929 and 1930
(All written by F. Scott and Zelda Fitzgerald)

THE ORIGINAL FOLLIES GIRL	sold	March 1929	$400.00
THE POOR WORKING GIRL	"	April 1929	500.00
THE SOUTHERN GIRL	"	July 1929	500.00
THE GIRL THE PRINCE LIKED	"	Sept. 1929	500.00
THE GIRL WITH TALENT	"	Oct. 1929	800.00

F. Scott Fitzgerald, Esq.
819 Felder Avenue
Montgomery, Alabama

Dear Scott:

I have your telegram about CRAZY SUNDAY. Although it may delay offering the story for a few days I want to write you about the story before I send it to another editor.

I talked to Costain about it this week and he told me they all felt although it was beautifully written and a very accurate picture of Hollywood, that it didn't get anywhere or prove anything. They liked very much the beginning of the story but didn't think the tragedy at the end was prepared for or essentially a part of the story. He said the situation at the end would at any rate make the story very difficult for them. He said the possible use of Hollywood characters might make it dangerous for some magazines but that really would not affect them.

I told you what Burton said. They want very much to get a story of yours and Burton told me that he had planned to use it and was even planning to put it in the first open number of the magazine. Burton told me that Mr. Hearst's policy man said they wouldn't dare to use the story as they were afraid it might offend the moving picture people with whom they are affiliated. After talking to you I explained that you had been very careful about this but they still say they can't use it on this account. Burton has told me half a dozen times that he is still very keen to get stories of yours and he hopes that their declination of this story will not make you change your mind about giving them some stories.

I showed it next to Balmer of the Red Book who has been asking me frequently for another story. He told me that he had read most of your stories and he liked this story least of any of yours he had read.

I think the women's magazines are definitely ruled out because of the situation at the end of CRAZY SUNDAY. A wife who has just heard that her husband has been killed wants another man to stay with her. Collier and Liberty are the two magazines that would be most likely to use it. It is long for either of these magazines. I think I have told you how Mr. Lorimer feels about Collier. At present Collier is very definitely a rival of the Post and in a way that Liberty once was. I know that it would hurt Mr. Lorimer's feelings to see a story of yours in Collier's. When I spoke to Costain's about the possibility of offering a story of yours to Collier's he said of course they couldn't reasonably object to your selling them a story, but that it was now their one direct rival and that Mr. Lorimer liked to feel that there were certain writers that the Post readers would look for and expect to find in the Post, not in Collier's, and that you were one of those few authors.

The editor of Collier's was speaking to me the other day about getting a story of yours and I asked him what he would pay. He said that for a stray story they couldn't possibly pay more than $2500.

He said that if they could have a definite number of stories that would be a different matter for then they could look on you as a Collier author.

The question is whether it is advisable to offend Mr. Lorimer by selling the story to Collier's provided of course they like it when we show it to them.

As for Liberty, I hardly know what to say. I don't know whether you have seen the magazine lately but I do not think it is improving under Macfadden's§ ownership. They have been cutting prices just about fifty percent. On the whole I should rather offer the story to Liberty than Collier's.

What I would like to do would be to hold the story up until after you have finished the story you are working on. Then I think it is possible you might do it over again and make it one of the best stories you have ever written. I have some rather vague ideas about it that I'll be glad to send on to you if you decide to do this. If you would rather have me offer it at once to Collier or to Liberty you might send me a wire and I'll do so. As a last resort there is of course College Humor but they are paying very little now and I imagine they would offer us a very low price. Of course I think Scribner would like the story very much indeed but I think it is too bad to sacrifice it.

Sincerely yours,
[Harold Ober]

February 25, 1932

TL (cc), 3pp. (AO)

Dear Harold:

The [enclosed is for the] <u>Post</u> [(No!] story is mailed [today] tomorrow *reaches you Mon.*

Here are a whole lot of points

(1.) Are you sure my letter reached Van Cortland Enerson? It was a reference to a story idea of his I wanted to buy, + its rather important

(2.) My alternative idea for the next is to revise <u>Crazy Sunday</u>, so if you have any advice send it

---

§Bernarr Macfadden.

Nightmare¶ will never, never sell for money, in <u>any</u> times. I note there are two Clayton Magazines called "Strange Tales" + "Astounding Stories." Would either of them pay $250.00? Their rates are 2 cents a word + up.

Last + most important.

Will you write a letter to the Collector of Internal Revenue, St Paul, Minn (but send it to McNiell Seymore, Pioneer Bldg. St Paul) embodying the following points.

(1.) Who you are—long time in business ect.

(2.) Surprise at hearing that my earnings from Post ect were not accepted as earned income.

(3.) That you had never considered me a free lance author but that on the contrary my sales were arranged long in advance and that it has been understood for years among editors that my stories were written specificly [by] *for* the Post by *definate* arrangment and that I was [a Post author] what is known as a "Post Author."

(4.) Moreover *that* they conform to Post specifications as to length *and* avoidance of certain themes so that for instance they could not have been published in <u>Liberty</u> which [inste] insisted on stories not over 5000 words, + would have been inacceptable to womens magazines since they were told from the male angle. That when I contracted with another magazine such as <u>College Humor</u> the stories were different in tone + *theme*, half as long, signed in conjunction with my wife. That the <u>Post</u> made it plain that they [were] *wanted* to be offered all my work of the kind agreed apon; that [severa] they always specified that no work of mine should appear in several competing magazines. That [had even this when the Post commissions a man to go abroad + do a piece of work they do] during the years 1929 and 1930 no story of mine was rejected by the Post (The first was in February 1931, but as that year isn't in question don't mention it)

(5.) That had not the [decision] *possibility you have just been informed of (i.e. of treating* [stor] *short story money as unearned income under G.C.M. 236)* come as a completely new [departure] *attitude* all the magazines would *assurredly* have [and probably] substituted written contracts in such cases as this where the author is in fact the employee of the magazine, and [is given to understand so in t] should his [work] *story*

¶The story was declined by *College Humor, Cosmopolitan, Redbook,* and *The Saturday Evening Post* and was never published.

appear in [other] *rival* journals [That in my case there was a recent offer from another magazine for six stories of mine which you rejected] *the arrangment would be broken. It is as much a contract as a telephone conversation between two brokers. And* And no *story* order would be accepted even from a non-competing magazine without discussing it with the Post.

That's a hell of a lot to ask. Can you Send it off as soon as possible. It means a lot of money to me, as I'll explain when I see you. (Otherwise I get a reduction for having worked in Europe + paid taxes there [)]—but this only applies to <u>earned</u> income)

In Haste

Ever Yours

Scott

Also that letters + conversation were *almost* always substituted for contracts when arranging for short stories—the contrary being true as to [theatrical] *play* + picture contracts where the buyer is [considered] *often* a less stable party.#

ALS, 3pp. n.d., n.p.—received 23 April 1932. Montgomery. (AO)

STATE OF NEW YORK)

: ss.:

COUNTY OF NEW YORK)

HAROLD OBER, being duly sworn, deposes and says:

I reside in the Village of Scarsdale, County of Westchester, New York, and have an office at No. 485 Madison Avenue, in the Borough of Manhattan, City, County and State of New York, where I carry on my profession as an authors' representative. I have been engaged in this work for twenty years and represent a number of well known writers.

I have known F. SCOTT FITZGERALD, ESQ. for about ten years and have acted as his representative in dealing with editors and publishers for ten years. For the past seven years virtually all of Mr. Fitzgerald's work has been done for and at the request of The Saturday Evening Post. The stories which he first submitted to that magazine were of a type desired by the editors and were accepted, published and paid for and an arrangement made through me that I would submit all of Mr. Fitzgerald's work to the Post. During 1929 and 1930 Mr. Fitzgerald wrote a total of fifteen stories at the request

---

#Fitzgerald drew a line from this paragraph for insertion before "That's a hell of a lot to ask."

of the editors of The Saturday Evening Post, all of which were copy-righted by that publication and published therein. The arrangement, pursuant to which these stories were written for The Saturday Evening Post, specified the length of each, subject matter, avoidance of certain topics and at an agreed price for each.

The writing of these stories in conformity to the Post's specifications made them virtually unsalable to other publications financially strong enough to pay compensation suitable to an author of Mr. Fitzgerald's attainments and reputation. In other words, one magazine, which has a circulation comparable to The Saturday Evening Post, would not have been interested in these stories because it imposes a definite length limitation of 5,000 words on such stories. The Post's requirements in this connection are for stories from 5,000 to 8,000 words. The stories would not have been acceptable to certain publications known as women's magazines, which have a large circulation, since they are written from the male angle.

Mr. Fitzgerald has long been known among authors and editors as a "Post author". This reputation clearly negatives his being classified as a "free lance" writer as it would make difficult, if not impossible, the sale of these stories to other publications even conceding that the specifications according to which the stories were written for the Post should be deemed acceptable by the other publications.

In my opinion Mr. Fitzgerald was during 1929 and 1930 and for some years prior thereto virtually an employee of The Saturday Evening Post in that he wrote numerous stories for that publication as aforesaid strictly in accordance with the requirements of the publication; that he devoted virtually his entire time to this work and The Saturday Evening Post paid him a fixed sum for each story.

Sworn to before me this)

:

26th day of April, 1932)   _____

Typed deposition (cc), 2pp.

Harold Ober noted on his 5 January 1930 to 23 April 1932 file folder: "letters missing from F.S.F. April 1932 to March 23 1933." For 1932 only two Fitzgerald to Ober and four Ober to Fitzgerald letters survive; for 1933 one Fitzgerald and four Ober letters; and for 1934 six Fitzgerald and four Ober letters. Our searches have revealed one missing letter. Consequently, certain financial details for Tender Is the Night *are obscure.*

On 20 May 1932, Fitzgerald rented "La Paix" in Towson, a suburb of Baltimore. By June, Zelda was able first to divide her time between "La Paix" and Phipps and then, finally, to move completely into "La Paix."

On 14 June 1932, Zelda signed a contract with Scribners for the publication of Save Me the Waltz. *The book was published in October and sold 1,392 copies.*

Mrs. F. Scott Fitzgerald,
La Paix,
Rodger's Forge, Md.

Dear Zelda:

This is really a joint letter to you and Scott. Scott's wire came this morning and I wanted you to know that I am working on the play.* A copy has gone to Arthur Hopkins, and a copy is being read by Jed Harris' right-hand man who promised not only a quick decision but suggestions as to a competent collaborator if one seemed necessary to give a professional touch.

One copy has been sent to Washington for copyright.

As you may know it's very difficult to get play producers to read scripts quickly. They seem to think they are a chosen race (as most of them are!) who can take their time about that end of their business. For this reason, it is customary to submit copies of any one play to four or five producers at once to expedite matters. If you wanted to go to the expense of having at least three more copies of the play typed, I think it would be much more satisfactory as far as getting quick action is concerned.

Please tell Scott that I'm glad to know a new story is coming along. As usual, I'll be eager to read it. I've just been looking at ONE INTERNE in this week's Post. It's a fine story and I think the illustrations are terrible. But I guess there's nothing to be done about it.

Nothing would please me more than to sell your play, Zelda, and I'll do my best with it. Certainly the cleverness of the dialogue ought to attract some imaginative producer who might suggest a way of getting more action into the script.

Sincerely yours,
[Harold Ober]

November 1, 1932

TL (cc), lp. (AO)

---

*Possibly Zelda's *Scandalabra*, produced in Baltimore by the Junior Vagabond Players, summer 1933.

Fitzgerald's total earnings for 1932 were $15,823. This was his lowest year, financially, since 1919. He sold six stories ($14,805), five of them to The Saturday Evening Post, *which cut his price back to $3,000 and $2,500. His book royalties were $20, and he received a $480 advance on* Tender Is the Night.

F. Scott Fitzgerald, Esq.
La Paix
Rodger's Forge, Md.

Dear Scott:

This is in answer to your letter about our relations with the Post. I agree entirely with what you say and as a matter of fact I think we are both in a particularly good position with all the editors of the Post. I know that Mr. Lorimer, Miss Neall, and Tom Costain all like you and like your work. Graeme Lorimer[‡] doesn't know you so well but has a great admiration for your work.

My relations with all the editors of the Post are very happy. I have lunch with Mr. Lorimer about once a year. I see Graeme Lorimer and Tom Costain almost every week. As a matter of fact I think there is very little jealousy in that organization. At the Cosmopolitan for instance it is almost impossible not to step on someone's toes. I have never found the least conflict between Tom Costain and Graeme Lorimer. They come to New York on different days. Costain sees the larger agents and authors that he plans to keep in touch with, and Graeme Lorimer sees the smaller agents and authors that he knows. I really do not see Graeme Lorimer officially as Tom Costain is the one to keep in touch with my office but I know and like Graeme Lorimer and we have lunch together quite frequently and he always comes in the weeks that Costain doesn't come to New York. At the present moment I am engaged in finding an Airedale for Graeme Lorimer.

So I do not think either of us have to worry about this question that you have brought up. If we keep on as we have been going I think everything will be all right no matter what happens at the Post.

Sincerely yours,
[Harold Ober]

April 26, 1933

TL (cc), 1p. (AO)

---

‡George Horace Lorimer's son, an associate editor of *The Saturday Evening Post.*

F. Scott Fitzgerald, Esq.
La Paix
Rodger's Forge, Md.

Dear Scott:
   I am sending you herewith copies of the agreement for the talking
picture rights of THE GREAT GATSBY.* Both Owen Davis and
Brady have signed these agreements. I will not turn them over to
Schuyler Grey until I get the check for your share of the proceeds.
   Will you sign these before a notary and get them back to me on
Monday if possible?

Sincerely yours,
Harold Ober

May 5, 1933

P.S.   Your signature is to go just above Owen Davis' signature on
page 7 and the notary public's signature and stamp is to go on the
next page.

TLS, lp. (PU)

La Paix, Rodgers' Forge,
Towson, Maryland,
June 12, 1933.

Mr. Harold Ober,
41 East 49th Street,
New York, N. Y.

Dear Harold:
   I am enclosing a lyric which I wrote with a man down here who
composed the music. It is rather a good idea and I'd like to get it
copyrighted in case there is any money in it. Can you attend to it
for me?
   I am wiring you today to ask if you can deposit $1000. I have had
a splendid session with the novel and am now back at work on the
Interne story§ which should reach you withintthree or four days.
May do another one immediately afterwards depending on finances
but am probably going to do the article for the American Magazine.
   Houghton Mifflin did send a copy of the Best Short Stories of

---

*The film was not made.
§"What To Do About It" was rejected by *The Saturday Evening Post*, *Redbook*, and
Cosmopolitan and was never published.

'33.¶ Zelda and I had a picture taken last fall but I don't seem to have a copy. Am going to have some taken soon.

Best wishes,

F Scott Fitzgerald

Enclosure

TLS, 2pp. (AO)

Oh, Sister, Can You Spare Your Heart

Verse: I may be a What-ho, a No-can-do
        Even a banker, but I can love you
            As well as a better man
                a letter-man of fame
        As well as any Mr. Whosis you can name

———————

The little break in my voice
        —or Rolls-Royce
            take your choice
            I may lose
            You must choose
              So choose

———————

A hundred thousand in gold
        and you're sold
        to the old
        and I'm broke
        when our days a
            are gold
                I'm begging
                 begging
Oh, Sister, can you spare your heart?

****

Those wealthy goats
      In racoon coats
      can wolf you away from me
      But draw your latch
      For an honest patch
        the skin of necessity

¶ *The Best Short Stories of 1933*, edited by Edward J. O'Brien (Boston: Houghton Mifflin, 1933), included "Crazy Sunday."

(we'll make it a tent, dear)

****

The funny patch in my pants
take a chance
ask your aunts
What's a loss
You must toss
So toss!
A gap inside that's for good.
You'll be good
As you should
Touch <u>wood</u>!
I'm begging
begging
Oh, Sister, can you spare your heart?

Typescript, 2pp. (AO)

F. Scott Fitzgerald, Esq.
La Paix
Rodger's Forge, Md.

Dear Scott:

This letter is a letter of advice and if you don't feel like receiving advice you may throw it in the waste basket without reading further.

I think we have made a mistake in sending your recent stories to the Post in a very hurried fashion and I think it has been a mistake to let them know that we were in such a hurry about a decision. I think perhaps we have caused the wrong psychological effect on a possible buyer. I think we have let the Post feel that you were rushing out stories in order to get some money.

Before we show the next story to the Post I think we ought to be sure that it is just right, I think I ought to have it properly typed, and I want to try to create the impression that I am sending them a Scott Fitzgerald story, that it is a fine story and that I don't care whether they take it or not. I am sure it is a mistake for the Post to feel that you are uncertain about a story and anxious to know whether or not they like it.

I would like to start to create this new impression with this new story you are writing. I think perhaps by trying to gain a day or two we have lost a good deal. So I hope you will send the next story to me when you have it done. I'll read it right away and tell you frankly if I have any criticisms to make.

It is true that all the magazines have been harder to please this year than ever before. I feel sure that this last story of yours, WHAT TO DO ABOUT IT, would have been accepted a year or two ago by the Post and published and that many readers would have liked it. It is also true of course that a great deal is expected of an author who has written as many fine stories as you have written. An editor expects every story to compare favorably with some story of yours which he has considered your finest story. I believe you can make a very fine story out of WHAT TO DO ABOUT IT. I think you will have to make the reader care more what happens to the girl and to the doctor. To give yourself space to do this do you think it would be possible to have the girl beg the doctor to take her with him when he goes to answer the call? The boy could be hidden in the rumble seat just as you have him. This is probably a poor suggestion but I am sure you will be able to work out some way to get some feeling between the doctor and the girl.

Sincerely yours,

August 30, 1933

Dictated by Harold Ober
who left before signing.

TL (cc), 2pp. (AO)

F. Scott Fitzgerald, Esq.
La Paix
Rodger's Forge, Md.

Dear Scott:

I have been talking to my lawyer about the old Liberty contract.# He advises me not to worry about it. It was made on June 5, 1926 and when it was made Liberty belonged to the Chicago Tribune. It now belongs to Macfadden and so far as I know there is not a single editor there that used to be on the magazine. Macfadden bought Liberty early in 1931 and I feel quite certain that none of the present editors of Liberty have mentioned the story to me. It was mentioned to me since the sale to Macfadden but this was by an editor who has since left.

#For the serialization of the novel that became *Tender Is the Night*.

However, I do not feel that one should always do only what it is legal to do. I know that you are very conscientious about your obligations and I feel that way about my obligations. I think it is possible that if Scribner or the Cosmopolitan should announce publication of your novel as a serial, the editor of Liberty might call me up and ask about it so I am inclined to follow your suggestion and take the matter up now with Liberty.

Before I do this, however, I think we ought to decide one thing and that is whether you are willing to let Liberty publish the story as a serial if they insist on confirming the agreement. Macfadden has plenty of money although he is not spending as much on Liberty as Patterson used to spend. Although Macfadden has many faults, I have always found him reliable financially and prompt in payment.

I am inclined to think that I could get them to cancel the contract but there is a chance that the advertising value of having your serial would be great enough so that they would insist on what they may consider their right to accept it. Another thing we can do, and I am inclined to feel that this is the wisest course, is to do nothing until you bring the manuscript up and until I have read it.

I do not like to bother you with this question now but you raised it when you spoke to me over the telephone the other day.

I think you know, Scott, that I want to do what is best for you. If you decide that it is best not to have the book come out in Liberty or Cosmopolitan, you don't have to. I think we could get out of the Liberty arrangement by insisting that the story be published without cuts. If I understood you correctly, you said that it would be 120,000 words which is _very_ difficult for any weekly to use.

The advantage of a sale to Liberty or Cosmopolitan would be that you could pay Scribner what they have advanced you and have the remainder to live on until royalties on the book come in.

I don't believe that serial publication even in Liberty will do you any harm. I'm sure that readers of serials in magazines don't buy books and that book buyers don't read serials in magazines. And there are few authors even of the highest standing that haven't had work published by Liberty or Cosmopolitan.

Let me know how you feel about all this.

Sincerely yours,
[Harold Ober]

October 3, 1933

TL (cc), 2pp. (AO)

In October 1933 Fitzgerald delivered the Tender Is the Night *manuscript to Maxwell Perkins at Scribners. The first of four serial installments appeared in the January 1934 issue of* Scribner's Magazine.

The finances for Tender Is the Night *are obscure. Although Fitzgerald kept a detailed ledger, some of the entries reflect his personal interpretations of advances. A 1930 entry reads:*

"Further advances (Serial new Novel + 1583.06 against bk. $3701.97"
But these figures probably represent borrowings from Scribners during 1930 that Fitzgerald regarded as advances to be paid back from the earnings of his new novel. On 25 September 1933 Fitzgerald informed Maxwell Perkins: "Ober is advancing me the money to go through with it (it will probably not need more than $2000 though he has promised to go as far as $4,000) and in return I am giving him 10% of the serial rights." Perkins outlined terms for the serialization to Fitzgerald on 18 October 1933. Scribner's Magazine *paid Fitzgerald $10,000—of which $6,000 was applied to his Scribners debt. The $4,000 balance was paid in installments to Ober, who turned it over to Fitzgerald as needed. A release was obtained from* Liberty, *which had contracted for serial rights; but it is not clear whether their 1927–28 advances were repaid.*

Fitzgerald's total earnings for 1933 were $16,328.03. He sold three stories ($7,650.00). His book royalties were $30, and he received an advance of $4,200 on Tender Is the Night *and* Taps at Reveille.

F. Scott Fitzgerald, Esq.
1307 Park Avenue
Baltimore, Maryland

Dear Scott:

I tried to write you yesterday afternoon but had a busy day and didn't have a minute.

As I told you, I talked first with Maxwell Perkins and then with Charles Scribner and Max. They were both very enthusiastic about your novel and they showed me the jacket which I think is extremely attractive.

I told them your situation as you outlined it to me, and they were both very sympathetic. Charles Scribner talked at some length about the way book sales had fallen off, especially with their sub-scription books, from which they usually make a good deal of their income. He said the Galsworthy book had also been a disappoint-ment in sales. I was at Scribner's altogether for a couple of hours, I think. After several conferences Charles Scribner said that they would give me a check today for $2000. which would be returned to them out of any sale that is made of the moving picture rights. He also proposed that you pay 5% interest on this loan. He said he wanted to do this to distinguish it from advances they had made against book royalties. I didn't go into this over the telephone yes-terday as I was afraid it would make the cost of the telephone call too high.

I made at first the proposal that you made to me that they buy a share of the picture rights but both Max and Charles Scribner said they didn't want to make such an arrangement. They were against such arrangements in principle and they felt you ought to have all the money that you could get out of the dramatic rights and picture rights. I am sure that they were sincere in their reasons for not wanting to make this arrangement.

I realize that this solves our difficulties only temporarily but if you can finish rewriting the fourth section of the story in eight or ten days and then take a little rest, I think it would probably be much easier for you to do a short story and I am sure we can survive some way until that is done.

I think you are entirely right in not trying to do any short stories until the novel is entirely off your mind.

Maxwell Perkins just called up to say that the check will be ready at two o'clock this afternoon and, as we arranged yesterday, I'll deposit $1000. for you and wire you when it is done. I expect some money next week so, as we arranged, I'll keep the other $1000. in my bank and give it to you as soon as I can next week, but not later than Thursday or Friday.

I hope you and Zelda are well. You must be glad to be so near the end of your work on the novel. You might let me know when you deliver the last installment so that I can keep after Scribner and get complete proofs of the story.

Sincerely yours,
[Harold Ober]

January 5, 1934

TL (cc), 2pp. (AO)

1307 Park Avenue,
Baltimore, Maryland,
February 9, 1934.

Mr. Harold Ober,
40 East 49th Street,
New York, New York.

Dear Harold:
I don't want "The Vegetable" produced.

Scott Fitzg—

TLS, 1p. (AO)

On 12 February 1934 Zelda re-entered Phipps. This was her third break-down. In March she left Phipps and went to Craig House, a sanitarium in Beacon, New York.

WANT TO DECIDE NOW HOW TO RAISE MONEY TO TIDE ME OVER THE MONTH BEFORE FINISHING FINAL BOOK REVISION WITHOUT CONSULTING MAX CAN YOU GET OPINION OF ONE PROMINENT PLAYWRIGHT ABOUT POSSIBILITIES OF DRAMAT-IZATION OTHERWISE I WOULD RATHER SHOOT THE WORKS AND SELL TO THE PICTURES TO GET OUT OF THIS FINANCIAL HOLE IT MUST BE DECIDED IMMEDIATELY LUNCHING WITH CLARK GABLE TOMORROW AND WANT TO KNOW PRESENT STATUS OF GATSDY AS HE WOULD LIKE TO PLAY IT PLEASE WIRE IMMEDIATELY
    F SCOTT FITZGERALD.

Wire to Ober 21 February 1934. Baltimore, Md. (AO)

Feb. 23, 1934

F. Scott Fitzgerald called up and said he had decided we had better go ahead with the picture rights of TENDER IS THE NIGHT. I told him I would try one more dramatist at the same time.

He said he talked to Clark Gable. He is very keen to do GATSBY. He is going to talk to Rubin[†] of Metro Goldwyn about it, and Scott suggested I speak to Rubin about it. Scott also talked to Gable about the George Washington idea and Gable is going to talk to Rubin about that.

H.O.

Typed Ober memo. (AO)

---

†J. Robert Rubin, secretary of MGM.

F. Scott Fitzgerald, Esq.
1307 Park Avenue
Baltimore, Maryland

Dear Scott:

R.K.O. seems at the moment more excited about TENDER IS THE NIGHT than any of the other companies. I have been talking to Katharine Brown, who is the most important person in the New York offices of R.K.O.

Ann Harding, as you know, is with R.K.O. but Katharine Brown says she thinks it would be better for Katherine Hepburn and I am inclined to agree with her. She also thinks Frederick March might be possible for Dick Diver's part. She agrees with you that Robert Montgomery and Gary Cooper would be too soft for the part.

Katharine Brown wants to know if you couldn't come up Monday or Tuesday as she would like to have a talk with you about the story. She says of course there will have to be some changes in it. Katherine Hepburn is very popular just now and they want to get a really good picture for her.

Couldn't you get here early in the morning and you could go back in the afternoon. If you will let me know when you are coming up I'll meet you at the train and take you over to R.K.O. I really think it would be worth while for you to come up.

Sincerely yours,
[Harold Ober]

March 8, 1934

TL (cc), 1p. (AO)

F. Scott Fitzgerald
1307 Park Ave.,
Baltimore, Md.

Dear Scot:

The Columbia Broadcasting System want to try out DIAMOND AS BIG AS THE RITZ on a sustaining non-commercial programme and they are going to pay $50.00 for the privilege to use it once in this way.

They have been reading the stories in TALES OF THE JAZZ AGE and they say that if this story is well received they may be able to use other stories of yours on a commercial programme. They will let me know when the story is going to be used and I'll let you know so that you can hear it if you care to do so. It will be done over the whole Columbia System.

They say that sometimes it is necessary to do more than one story before they can sell the story for a commercial programme and they want to know if they can use another story or two, if it is necessary, on their sustaining programme, on the same terms as they are using this one.

Sincerely yours,
Harold Ober

March 16, 1934

They want to know Monday.‡

TLS, 1p. (PU)

For Harold Ober
Without whose help this would never have been able to be fostered on the world

F. Scott Fitzgerald

Inscription in *Tender Is the Night.* (AO)

On 19 May 1934 Zelda was transferred from Craig House to the Sheppard and Enoch Pratt Hospital outside Baltimore. By December she was able to spend Christmas with Fitzgerald and Scottie at 1307 Park Avenue in Baltimore.

F. Scott Fitzgerald, Esq.
1307 Park Avenue
Baltimore, Maryland

Dear Scott:
I couldn't get a chance to see Edwin Balmer until late yesterday afternoon. I asked him the question in your letter of November 28th and he said that he would really prefer a story of four or five thousand words to a longer one and that he would of course pay the same price for stories of that length.

As for assurance about the number of stories he can use, I am afraid there is nothing I can say that is at all definite. I think we have to remember that you have made a reputation for writing a very modern story. If an editor wants an authoratative story about modern society, you are one of the first authors that would come to his mind. The result is that when a reader picks up a magazine with one

---

‡Added in ink by Ober.

of your stories in it and finds a story about the ninth century he is going to be shocked. You will remember that I approached several magazines about this series and that is what every editor said. Balmer was the only one who was willing to try the stories and he told me yesterday that the owners of his magazine were not yet convinced that he was not partially crazy in buying these stories from you.¶

There is no question but that the stories are good stories—it has nothing to do with the quality of the stories. I am sure it is much better to let the future take care of itself. I think we have a much better chance of selling a number of stories to the Red Book if we do not press this question. After all what we want to do is to get the Red Book to take as many stories as possible. I feel sure that you have an exceedingly good book in this material so it is certainly worth while writing it. If you think this over I am sure you will feel that I am right about this. I think the stories are bound to be more and more interesting because with each story you have more material to use.

The question of scheduling the stories came up. Balmer says the value of the first story was almost entirely lost to him because he had to wait so long for the second story and although he has the second and third stories he hasn't any real faith when he will get the following stories. I don't think you can blame him for feeling this way and now I hope you won't mind if I read you a little lecture.

Up to a couple of years ago if you had sent me word that a story would arrive on a certain date, I would have been as certain that the story would arrive as that the sun would rise the next day. Lately when you have wired me that a story would be sent on a certain date I have no faith at all that it will come. I hate to say this and I hope it will not offend you in any way but if you look over the telegrams you have sent me in the last year or two you will realize that what I say is true. As far as it concerns myself I do not mind this. I know that life has been very difficult for you, that you have been working underpressure and that conditions that you could not help have prevented you from doing what you thought you could do but you have called up Balmer or have written to him telling him that you

---

¶The "Darkness" series in *Redbook:* "In the Darkest Hour," October 1934; "Count of Darkness," June 1935; "The Kingdom in the Dark," August 1935; "Gods of Darkness," November 1941. Fitzgerald intended these stories to form an episodic historical novel. The hero, Philippe, was based on Hemingway.

would deliver a story at a certain time and the story has not arrived. I have always been very proud of your dependability and as far as money goes I am still proud of it, but I do think it would be better if you would make it a rule not to call up or write to editors, and while I am on the subject I think it would be better if you did not call up or write to moving picture executives.

Sometimes I think it would be better if you would take the telephone out of your house entirely. It must cost you an enormous amount a month and I doubt if you really gain anything by its use. After all, a letter written from Baltimore will reach New York the next morning. You are apt to use the telephone when you are not in your most rational state of mind and when you do call anyone up in that way it only adds to the legend that has always been ready to crop out—that you are never sober.

Now, Scott, I hope you will not be cross with me for saying all this. I have wanted to say it for a long time but whenever you come to New York, you get started on a party and it is impossible. I have thought of driving down to Baltimore to see you but I am afraid that would be a nuisance to you.

To go back to the Red Book situation, it seems to me the only thing for you to do is to go on with the series and try to deliver about one a month until Balmer says he can't use any more. There is no reason why you shouldn't turn out a Post story occasionally in between the Red Book stories.

Balmer told me yesterday that if you had an idea for a forty or fifty thousand word story that could be used in one number he would pay ten thousand dollars for it. Of course if it were a story that could be divided into installments we could get more for it but sometime you may have an idea for a story that would not make a serial. I told Balmer I didn't think there was much chance of this —I am only letting you know about it because he brought the question up. He also said he would pay a big price for a serial by you but I said I was sure you didn't want to write a serial story at the present time.

Ask Scotty when she is going to make us another visit.

Sincerely yours,
[Harold Ober]

December 5, 1934

TL (cc), 3pp. (AO)

1307 Park Avenue,
Baltimore, Maryland,
December 6, 1934.

Mr. Harold Ober,
40 East 49th Street,
New York, New York.

Dear Harold:

Did not resent your letter one bit; or anything in it. I will accept your advice about not getting in touch with editors directly.

In the case of "Esquire" it was that Arnold Gingrich gave me two hundred dollars for [an] articles by Zelda and me and I knew that the commission on that would be of no interest to you.#

And in the case of "The Saturday Evening Post" and of "The Redbook" it has been invariably a question of either getting a quick response on their opinions of the work in question or of getting a quick decision so I would know where we would eat tomorrow.

And *on* the question of movie rights I've never been sure where you stood and how much of that sort of trade you wanted to handle. When matters come up between me and such characters as Bill Warren§ in Hollywood, and when independent people write me on their own about a story that has not been marketed there my natural tendency has been to say go ahead:

but, whenever a legitimate nibble comes you should know how quick I am to spring to you for assistance.

Since I have accepted your Sunday sermon without indignation let me accuse you in turn of lack of initiative on the movie side of the ledger. Tomorrow I am sending you as complete a record as possible of filmland. There are only two or three, the latest being Carmel Myers, and I pass them unreservedly to your hands.

With everlasting gratitude for the year that let me finish my book, with all due sense of obligation to repay you for your material loan, and with no resentment about your bawling out, I am

Ever yours,
Scott

TLS, 3pp. (AO)

"Show Mr. and Mrs. F. to Number—," *Esquire*, May and June 1934 (published as by F. Scott and Zelda Fitzgerald but written mostly by Zelda); "Auction—Model 1934," July 1934 (mostly by Zelda Fitzgerald); "Sleeping and Waking," December 1934.

§Charles Marquis Warren, with whom Fitzgerald worked on a movie treatment of *Tender Is the Night*.

1307 Park Avenue,
Baltimore, Maryland,
December 8, 1934.

Mr. Harold Ober,
40 East 49th Street,
New York, New York.

Dear Harold:

After rereading your letter there were some things I felt hadn't been sufficiently answered. The first is that I have a deep suspicion that you and Max got together at some point and decided I needed disciplining. Now I know of my fondness for you both and assume that it is reciprocated and I know also that when one man is in debt to another he is rather helpless in such matters. Nevertheless, the assumption that all my troubles are due to drink is a little too easy. Gliding over my domestic difficulties and my self indulgence on that score and not deciding which one has caused the trouble—whether the hen preceeded the egg or the egg preceeded the hen—I want to get down to a few facts: a compact "apologia pro sua vita" after all the horrors in Montgomery and the winter of '30 and '31, the return of Zelda's trouble, attacked by the family, etc (and you will find that this coincides almost exactly with my remissness in getting out MSS on specification. It became apparent to me that my literary reputation, except with the _Post_ readers, was at its very lowest ebb. I was completely forgotten and this fact was rubbed in by Zelda's inadvertently written book.* From that time on until early this spring my chief absorption was to [keep] get my book published at any cost to myself and still manage to keep the ball rolling. With yours and Max's help and some assistance from mother the thing was accomplished but at the end it left me in the black hole of Calcutta, mentally exhausted, physically exhausted, emotionally exhausted, and perhaps, morally exhausted. There seemed no time or space for recuperation. My expedition to Bermuda was a wash-out because of the pleurisy; Zelda collapsed again shortly after the holidays. The necessary "filling up" that a writer should be able to do after great struggles was impossible. No sooner did I finish the last galley on the last version of the last proof of the book proof of "Tender is the Night" than it was necessary to sit down and write a _Post_ story.

Of course any _apologia_ is necessarily a whine to some extent, a man digs his own grave and should, presumably lie on it, and I

---

*_Save Me the Waltz_ (1932).

know that the fault for this goes back to those years, which were
really years of self-in-

TL (cc)—incomplete letter from Fitzgerald. (PU)

> 1307 Park Avenue,
> Baltimore, Maryland,
> December 8, 1934.

Mr. Harold Ober,
40 East 49th Street,
New York, New York.

Dear Harold:

Everything is hereafter to go through you, hence these drawings.
They are to accompany Medieval IV, "Gods of the Darkness"
which will reach you at the latest by Tuesday. I hope to God Balmer
can use them. The little one is "Philippe's" crest and is accounted
for in the text. The others are his second castle. There are some
places where visual description fails and one must call on pictorial
representation.

> Ever yours,
> F Scott Fitzgerald

P. S.   I am sending this a day before the story goes off because it
takes longer in transport and, if possible, I would like them to reach
Balmer simultaneously, because the more I think of them, the more
important they seem to me for the understanding of the story. Do
try your best to persuade him to use them. It isn't a question of
money for the artist, because if absolutely necessary I can probably
muster enough money to pay him the bonus that I hinted at to
Balmer, which would be about twenty dollars for this set and
twenty dollars for the previous one. I have already paid him from
my own purse twenty dollars for the first set and twenty dollars for
the second. But I don't mind this, as it was done to crystal[l]ize in
my own mind, during the actual writing of the story, the evolution
of Philippe's ideas of fortification, and—as I told you before—it is
absolutely impossible, at least so far as I can determine with the
resources at hand here in Baltimore *to find out*[†] what the damn
[things] *castles* look*ed* like. So this present bastard arrangement is
partly stolen from the design in stone of Carcassonne by Violett-le-

---

[†]Although this was typed by a secretary, Fitzgerald made strikeouts and insertions
in pencil.

Duc, the French expert on restoration and military architecture. My contribution has been the building of it in wood and the general line-up that would [naturally] proceed from the exigencies of Philippe's problems, such as his failure in Illustration I, for instance, [the indication of the first unsuccessful efforts] to master the dam.

This may seem to you at first much [to do] *ado* about nothing, but working it out was responsible for more than a little of my delinquency in delivery.

You will be glad to find out that this story is much shorter than I had prophesied.

By the way, the crest is deliberately <u>Church</u> Latin, corrupt Latin, instead of Classical Latin, and really does render the idea "When the others quit, I'm just beginning."

The half-pig, half-lion will be explained in the text.

Ever Yours
Scott

3 pen + ink sketches enclosed[‡]

TLS, 3pp. (AO)

1307 Park Avenue,
Baltimore, Maryland,
December 26, 1934.

Mr. Harold Ober,
40 East 49th Street,
New York, New York.

Dear Harold:

I send you this hypothetic contract which you can amend or correct at will with the certain cooperation of young Spafford.[§] The only case in point is to protect my interest and his.

I am sure that guaranteeing him a good royalty slice is the best way of keeping him at work. Whether he is the ideal person for the job or not, is another matter, but beggars can't be choosers and since no established dramatist has offered himself as collaborator perhaps his very enthusiasm is the best thing that we can ask for. He seems anxious to devote six months of his time to the matter, knows the book thoroughly and I believe has caught a good bit of the spirit in which it is written, its comedy and pathos. I implied to him that I

---

‡Added in pencil by Fitzgerald.

§Robert Spafford adapted *Tender Is the Night* for the stage. The play was not produced.

would split the author's rights fifty-fifty but if you think that is too generous on my part I am sure he would agree to any further redistribution that seemed equitable. Likewise all the arrangements for dealing with the property are subject to your approval.

He <u>must</u>, however, have some basis to work on so as not to feel that, at any moment, I might sell the thing over his head. He would certainly be left holding the bag if we got an offer and took it after he had completed a couple of acts of a full length play. I know you are busy but I hope you will have a chance to draw up some kind of contract in which he will believe, even if only to draw up a gentlemen's agreement (for I can trust him absolutely) because I want him to get to work as soon as possible on the thing with the hope, that, if he is adequate to the work, we can go into production by mid-summer.

> Ever yours,
> Scott

TLS, 2pp. (AO)

Fitzgerald's total earnings for 1934 were $20,032.33. He sold eight stories ($12,475). Two of the stories and two essays were taken by Esquire *at $250 each. His book royalties were $58.35, and he received an advance of $6,481.98 from Scribners.*

IV
DISASTER

1935-1937

F. Scott Fitzgerald, Esq.
1307 Park Avenue
Baltimore, Maryland

Dear Scott:

You will remember that I called you up on the telephone regarding the treatment for TENDER IS THE NIGHT that was made for Miriam Hopkins.¶ I don't think I ever sent you a copy of this treatment and I am sending one herewith.

Merritt Hulburd, who is now with United Artists, is here in New York now and is going back to Hollywood in a few days. He says by the time he gets back Miriam Hopkins will be [free] *through* making BECKY SHARPE and they will then decide about the possibility of Miriam Hopkins doing TENDER IS THE NIGHT.

Merritt wants to know if you would consider going out to the coast to work on TENDER IS THE NIGHT along the lines of this treatment. He says he doesn't believe Goldwyn would actually buy the picture but what they would probably like to do would be to get an option on the picture rights of TENDER IS THE NIGHT and then pay you a salary to work on the treatment. Of course you couldn't do it unless the salary was right. If you could get a fairly good salary and could live cheaply in Hollywood it might be a good chance to mend the present state of your finances.

There is nothing definite about this yet—it depends on Samuel Goldwyn and Miriam Hopkins.

Regarding the treatment, Merritt Hulburd realizes it may seem to you rather commonplace. He says, however, that to get the book done as a picture now, it would have to be done in some such way as this. Your task would be to raise this treatment out of the commonplace.

All I want you to do now is to tell me whether in the first place you think you could work with enthusiasm on the basis I have outlined above and whether conditions in Baltimore are such that you could go out to the coast this Spring.

Sincerely yours,
[Harold Ober]

January 8, 1935

TL (cc), 1p. (AO)

¶Movie actress who specialized in dramatic roles.

1307 Park Avenue,
Baltimore, Maryland,
January 10, 1934.*

Mr. Harold Ober,
40 East 49th Street,
New York, New York.

Dear Harold:

I read the treatment of "Tender is the Night" by Mac Gown. At first, because of the coincidence of the riding incident I thought he had merely got hold of the script of our treatment (Warren's and mine) but I see I am wrong. On the whole I like the treatment, while I think it leaves out a lot of the color that Bill and I managed to put in ours it is much simpler which is an advantage. It might be possible to blend in some of our ideas into the continuity as I own all rights to our treatment. However, that is less important than the question of going to California. I hate the place like poison with a sincere hatred. It will be inconvenient in every way and I should consider it only as an emergency measure. Your letter does not suggest that I would realize any lump sum on the thing, even though it was a tremendous success and so the weekly payments to recompense me for the trip would have to be pretty big and I cannot really estimate whether it would be worth while financially until you can give me some idea what my salary would be. If, for example, it was six weeks at $1000 a week, it would be by no means worth while because I would have dispensed of a property that seems to have preserved its value for expenses, and about $3000. And I certainly do not feel inclined to dispose of "Tender of the Night" for $3000, That is what it would amount to, isn't it? I mean, if I spent $3000 I would have only $3000 over and while I am in this particular mess *of debt* my expenses *for six weeks* will certainly come to $3000.

On the contrary, if the guaranty was $2000 a week for my services, that would leave me $9000 profit and for that I believe I would, though with some regret, let the [thing] *rights* go, not that I think it isn't worth more than that, but because of the pressure of circumstances.

To revert for a moment to a sentence a little way back, I feel the thing has a natural longevity. If you will think of the matter you will see that the great proportion of the books *of* last spring are dead, perhaps perished in the films, but in any case, forgotten.

*i.e., 1935.

"Tender is the Night" on the contrary, seems to live on and to continue to grasp the imagination of people who control the entertainment business in the same way that "Gatsby," a whole year after publication, caught the imagination of Brady. This seems to me to be a very ponderable [question] item in the whole matter.

There are two more aspects. Do you remember in the "Beautiful and Damned" we had a clause saying if the profits grossed a certain amount I was to get a bonus? In that case it did not happen, but some such clause (if an inside opinion as to what an average profit was in a Goldwyn picture could be obtained) [it] might be something to follow up. By the way, who does he release through? Does he release through whoever he can get or does he release through any one company?

The last point on the subject is the question of a play. Whether Spafford, either alone or in conjunction with a technical expert, could do anything with the play is of course problematical. I got a most touching letter from Spafford this morning in which he expressed his determination to go on with it willy-nilly and begging me to reserve a final decision until he could show us a scenario and first act. I enclose his letter which tells its own story.

Tho I am not going to cut the early part of this letter. I see I made a mistake and all I would be selling would be an option to endure for some specified time. That, of course, changes the face of the situation but doesn't change my distaste for going to Hollywood. If Hulburd is still [there] *in N.Y.* tell him I liked the treatment.

So glad you liked "Travel Together."† Don't forget to send me the carbon so we can get a version together to offer the movies.

Ever yours,
Scott

P.S. I hope to God that money to be deposited Monday will be either by cash or certified check.

P. SS. Am writing Max that all future money + negotioations about prices should pass through you

P SS² There have been plays which have had runs after movie rights are sold. I am writing this to Spafford to encourage him‡

TLS, 4pp. (AO)

---

†An unpublished story.
‡All insertions and the last two postscripts were added by Fitzgerald in ink.

1307 Park Avenue,
Baltimore, Maryland,
February 1, 1935.

Dear Harold:

Enclosed find the following from Spafford (and I wish you would mail it back to me.) The man evidently has a real enthusiasm for "Tender is the Night" and anything might spring out of it. The very intensity of feeling which he has about it leads me to believe that perhaps he can do something with it. He is not a very profound character—I didn't rank him, for example, with my other protege Warren in sheer talent, but he reminds me, again and again, of Leslie Howard at the same age. Of course Leslie was on Broadway then and Spafford is still in the provinces. I gather from his letter that Constance Smith treated him rather cavalierly,§ and indeed he has only a pretty pan and a lot of enthusiasm to offer so far, but I respond, naturally, to his interest in my stuff. Can you try to keep in touch with him in this matter? Something big might break from it.

Ever yours,
[Scott]

P.S.   Note that he wants some assurance to go on with and, if you find it in your power, please drop him a note so that he won't think that he's just wasting his time. Please do this. Whatever the effort he is making is worth, he is certainly putting plenty into it.

P. S. 2.   Since writing this letter I have talked to you on the phone. There isn't even a question now of the advisability of my going away. I have honestly tried to stick it out to the end, perhaps by bad means, but even that isn't in point any more, because I am half crazy with illness and worry, and in a state where each aggravation only adds to the accumulation of anxiety, strain, self pity, or what have you.

I am going conscientiously to do what repair can be done in ten days. Perhaps passages from my story which is being written out of my heart will serve to elucidate the unfortunate state of affairs at which I seem to have arrived.#

I've had no kinder friend than you during this rotten time.

TL, 3pp. (AO)

In the early spring and summer of 1935 Fitzgerald took trips to Tryon, Hendersonville, and Asheville, North Carolina, for his health. Otherwise, he

---

§Constance Smith was Ober's assistant.
#Possibly Fitzgerald enclosed passages from "The Intimate Strangers," *McCall's*, June 1935.

was in Baltimore, staying at the Hotel Stafford or, later, the Cambridge Arms. In November 1935 he returned to Hendersonville and began writing "The Crack Up" series for Esquire.

F. Scott Fitzgerald, Esq.
Oak Hall
Tryon, N. C.

Dear Scott:

I have your note about Robert Spafford. I have talked to him once or twice over the telephone and I'll call him tomorrow and ask him to come in and I'll have another talk with him. Constance Smith tells me she was very nice to him when he came in. I would of course have seen him but I was out.

To tell the truth, I don't at all like to tie up TENDER IS THE NIGHT with an inexperienced boy like Robert Spafford. I don't like giving options on plays anyway. I gave an option a few months ago on the dramatic rights of FEBRUARY HILL, a book which I sold and which is selling very well. I gave this option to a dramatist who has had several plays produced and who has directed plays and who is known and thought well of in the theatrical world. Since then, however, I have had a chance to sell the play to several of the biggest producers, among them Max Gordon, and [Leslie] *Sidney* Howard would have done the play. I gave the option because the author knew the man and urged me to do so but it certainly was a mistake.

I had a somewhat similar experience with THE FARMER TAKES A WIFE. An option was given to an inexperienced dramatist and it took me nearly two years to get this matter straightened out and get the play into the hands of Marc Connelly and Max Gordon.

It would be a much worse mistake to tie up TENDER IS THE NIGHT with a boy like Spafford who has never had an experience. I'll ask Spafford to drop in and I'll be nice to him and look over what he has done on the play. I am keeping his letter for a few days longer as there are one or two things in it that I may want to refer to.

I hope to have a letter from you tomorrow morning and I hope that we are going to be able to arrange some way that you can stay where you are for a while longer.

Sincerely yours,
[Harold Ober]

February 14, 1935

TL (cc), 1p. (AO)

Adress Hotel Stafford <u>not</u> ᶜ/o Mrs Owens.*

Dear Harold:

I'm still here—at the last moment it appears that there is a suggestion about Zelda (three days ago was a most discouraged time) and
it means finding a very special nurse. So I wont leave till tomorrow.
On an impulse I'm sending you a letter from Zelda that came to day
—a letter from which you can guage the awful strangling heart-
rending quality of this tragedy that has gone on now more than six
years, with two brief intervals of hope. I know you'll understand the
intrusion of sending it to you—please mail it back to me, with things
so black I hang on to every scrap that is like things used to be.

————————

And with it's precise irony life continues—I went to N. Y. after
all Saturday afternoon to meet a girl—stayed 20 hrs. + got back
here Sunday night to put Scotty on the train to camp.

Now as to business—or rather finances. I owe you still somewhere around $6500. (?) + should be paying you back at the rate of
$1500 per story. But this has been a slow 6 wks—1st illness, then
unsuccessful attempt at revise of mediaval IV,† then a false start,
then <u>What You Don't Know</u>.‡ Considering that story alone for a
minute + supposing it sold for $3000. You've given me

	$500	advance
	$500	"
+	$300	Commission
	———————	
	1300	
	1700	
	3000	

Normally that would leave me $1700. And I need <u>$1000</u> for bills
due (that doesn't solve them but is "on account") + I'll need $700
on the 12th for Life Insurance. Of course I hope to have a new story
in your hands by the 15th but I hope you can see your way clear
to letting me have the whole sum this time—with the understanding that on the <u>next</u> story I will surely be able to reimburse you
$1500. (Wont need the the 700 till the <u>12th</u> but need the 1000 this

————————

*Mrs. Isabel Owens, Fitzgerald's secretary.
†"Gods of Darkness."
‡Probably published as "Fate in Her Hands," *The American Magazine*, April 1936.

week, by Friday, say, if the <u>Post</u> accepts + will put a check through.)

All this raises the ugly head of Mediaval IV. Granted that Post pays 3000.00 + you *can* complete paying me the whole sum this time—that is $1700. more—

Then shall I do Red Book revise IV first! *(it's, alas, paid for!)* + make Balmer believe in me again? (He's already published III + it reads well), or shall I do a <u>Post</u> story + begin to square things with you? Only you can decide this. I told you: Red Bk IV <u>can't</u> be revised but must be rewritten, + that <u>and</u> a new Post story will take to the end of July. I can survive till then but will it be too much of a drain on you to wait till then for further payments.

There is no use *of me* trying to rush things. Even in years like '24, '28, '29, '30 all devoted to short stories I could not turn out more than 8–9 top price stories a year. It simply is impossible—all my stories are concieved like novels, require a special emotion, a special experience—so that my readers, if such there be, know that each time it'll be something new, not in form but in substance (it'd be far better for me if I could do pattern stories but the pencil just goes dead on me.I wish I could think of a line of stories like the Josephine or Basil ones which could go faster + pay $3000. But no luck yet. If I ever get out of debt I want to try a second play. It's just possible I could knock them cold if I let go the vulgar side of my talent.)

———

So that covers [anyt] everything. Will you let me know by <u>*straight wire*</u> as soon as you've read this if I can count on these advances ($1000 this wk—$700 on the 12th) <u>if</u> the <u>Post</u> buys.

Then I can sign the checks + get off south with a clear conscience.

I want to see you + have a long talk with you under better conditions than we've found of late. You havn't seen me since I've been on my no-liquor regime.

Yrs Ever
Scott Fitzg—

Hotel Stafford
Baltimore
Mail Zelda's letter to Asheville. Thanks for yr. nice wire about story. It set me up.§

ALS (pencil), 5pp n.d.—received 2 July 1935. (AO)

———

§These sentences are written along left margin.

Dearest and always Dearest Scott:

I am sorry too that there should be nothing to greet you but an empty shell. The thought of the effort you have made over me, the suffering this <u>nothing</u> has cost would be unendurable to any save a completely vacuous mechanism. Had I any feelings they would all be bent in gratitude to you and in sorrow that of all my life there should not even be the smallest relic of the love and beauty that we started with to offer you at the end.

You have been so good to me—and all I can say is that there was always that deeper current running through my heart: my life, you.

You remember the roses in Kenney's yard—you were so gracious and I thought—he is the sweetest person in the world—and you said "darling". You still are. The wall was damp and mosey when we crossed the street and said we loved the south. I thought of the south and a happy past I'd never had and I thought I was part of the south. You said you loved this lovely land. The wistaria along the fence was green and the shade was cool and life was old.

I wish I had thought something else—but it was a confederate, a romantic and nostalgic thought. My hair was damp when I took off my hat and I was safe and home and you were glad that I felt that way and you were reverent. We were glad and happy all the way home.

Now that there isn't any more happiness and home is gone and there isn't even any past and no emotions but those that were yours where there could be my comfort—it is a shame that we should have met in harshness and coldness where there was once so much tenderness and so many dreams. Your song.

I wish you had a little house with hollyhocks and a sycamore tree and the afternoon sun imbedding itself in a silver tea-pot. Scottie would be running about somewhere in white, in Renoir, and you will be writing books in dozens of volumes. And there will be honey still for tea, though the house should not be in Granchester.

I want you to be happy—if there were justice you would be happy—maybe you will be anyway.

Oh, Do-Do Do Do—

I love you anyway—even if there isn't any me or any love or even any life—

I love you.

TL (cc), 1p. n.d. From Zelda Fitzgerald (AO)

TELEGRAM SAYS SCOTTIE ARRIVING HERE FRIDAY MAY I
TAKE HER TO VERMONT WHERE FAMILY IS
 Harold Ober

Wire (cc) to Fitzgerald 27 August 1935. (AO)

SUPPOSE SCOTTY STAYS THIS WEEK WITH YOU STOP APPRECI-
ATE YOUR HOSPITALITY SO MUCH STOP HER SHOPPING BET-
TER WAIT TILL BALTIMORE HER PLANS WILL BE DECIDED
 SCOTT FITZGERALD.

Wire to Mrs. Ober 3 September 1935. Asheville, N.C. (AO)

F. Scott Fitzgerald, Esq.
Grove Park Inn
Asheville, N. C.

Dear Scott:

The Columbia Broadcasting Company just called up to say they
are mailing me the agreement regarding the peace sketch.¶ They say
they ought to have the article by October 19th. They say this is
really the deadline and hope you can get it to them a little earlier.

I got hold of Balmer just as he was leaving town. He said that he
would not be able to read the revised story GODS OF THE DARK-
NESS until some few days after Labor Day.

I think you have done an excellent job on this and it is now a very
good story.

I got your night letter about Scotty and Max Perkins called me
up in Scarsdale yesterday saying that he had a telegram from you.
I told him that Scotty seemed to be having a good time with us and
he said as we had children she would probably have a better time
than she would with him. Anne is taking Scotty in town tomorrow
and as she wired you she will be glad to do any shopping with her
that is necessary before she goes off to school. We are very fond of
Scotty and would like to have her stay just as long as she can. As
she has probably written you, she has talked on the telephone to
both her aunts and we were delighted that they couldn't have her.

She did a very nice poem yesterday for a birthday. We are very
much in love with her and shall miss her when she goes. We hope

---

¶ "Let's Go Out and Play" was broadcast on the Squibb "World Peaceways"
program over WABC (Columbia Broadcasting Company) in New York on 3 October
1935 at 9:30 P.M.

that she will be going to boarding school somewhere near us so that we can see her once in a while.

Sincerely yours,
[Harold Ober]

September 3, 1935

TL (cc), 1p. (AO)

Personal

\+

Confidential

Dear Harold:

This letter is about several things.

1st Story: I had made 3 false starts and only now am I satisfied with what I've got (about 4,200 words).# I dont want to break it off again (broke it off once to do Red Bk + once to do radio sketch, now being typed so I think I'd better count on staying here till 12th instead of 9th as I'd planned. The story should reach you on Thurs 12th.

So if you can count on putting Scotty on the *Penn.* train for Baltimore on Fri 13th I'll meet her at the station. In Baltimore I'll go to Hotel Stafford as my plan is to move + I dont want to open up the house for only a week.

You have been a life-saver about Scotty—you may have guessed that things have gone less well here—just one day after the lung was pronounced completely well the heart went nutsey again + they sent me back to bed and I was only able to work about one day in three. I am up and around again but I dont like to allow less than five days to finish story, pack ect.

About shopping with Scotty (Mrs Ober's suggestion I mean) since I cant decide about schools, that had better wait because a child's equipment depends on that of course + I cant decide anything until I see how I stand the trip to Baltimore. If I would only die, at least she and Zelda would have the Life Insurance + it would be a general good riddance, but it seems as if life has been playing some long joke with me for the past eight months and cant decide when to leave off.

However for the moment I seem out of danger—they mean it too. I didn't want any kidding about it.

#Probably "Image on the Heart," *McCall's*, April 1936.

I like the radio skit—its original + quite powerful I think. The little corrections to be done on it wont take a day.

It goes without saying that I'll be begging for money about the 12th or 13th when you have the story in your hands. I think I can get along all right till then.

About Spafford—I promised him some money if + when the play payed anything; he seemed to think that this included the option but I wrote advising him differently—I had meant from the 1st actual royalties. Some clippings told me that the contract was signed but I dont suppose they paid more than a few hundred, did they? Spafford said you were still afraid Kirkland would be slow on the delivery. Anyhow I told Spafford I couldn't help him now—it was a [gratut] gratuitous offer merely between him + me to compensate him for his lost time + effort.*

Glad you liked the Red Bk story. Hated to do all that work for no reward but it was my fault, [but] *and* it makes the *Phillipe* series 30,000 words long, almost half enough for a book. The next step I dont know in that line. Certainly I've got to shoot at the bigger money till Im out of debt.

Ever Yours
Scott Fitzg—

ALS (pencil), 4pp. n.d., n.p.—c. 5 September 1935. Asheville. (AO)

Dear Harold:

Scotty arrived safe + happy + having had the time of her life—pleasure, variety and kindness innumerable. (She says I owe you $20. Will you charge it to my account) Of course now all she wants is a dog—I was waiting for her to say it + last night walking we saw some dogs in a window + I laughed when she said it. Or else to be a great tennis player.

I am staying in Baltimore this fall—where I don't know. I'll be here at the Stafford until I've finished at least one Post Story.

AL, 1p. n.d.—received 23 September 1935. From Fitzgerald. Hotel Stafford, Baltimore, stationery. (AO)

In the fall of 1935 Fitzgerald attempted to establish a connection with radio. His script "Let's Go Out and Play" was sold to the "World Peaceways"

---

*James Kirkland and Sam H. Grisman were producers of Jack Kirkland's dramatization of *Tobacco Road*. Grisman took an option on the dramatization of *Tender Is the Night* and wanted Jack Kirkland and Austin Parker approved as dramatists. See Ober's 2 March 1936 letter.

program for $700. At the same time he became interested in writing a radio serial about a father and his daughter. On 22 October 1935 he proposed a thirteen-week series for CBS to be called "With All My Heart." Fitzgerald submitted a sample script dealing with the daughter's staying out late one night and lying about her tardiness. Nothing resulted from this project.

The Cambridge Arms,
Charles & 34th Streets,
Baltimore, Maryland,
October 22, 1935.

Dear Graham:‡

Here is the dope for Columbia. I think it covers everything. The general title as you know is "WITH ALL MY HEART" but I don't want it to get around any more than possible until something is settled.

Thirteen weeks (three months) is all I'd want to commit myself for, and I have planned the series accordingly. The minimum price, I should think, would be $500 a broadcast, or $1000 a week. More if you think possible.

Also I should want to retain all literary rights in the playlets, the right to publish after some specific time.

Sincerely,
F. Scott Fitzgerald

TLS, 1p. (AO)

F. SCOTT FITZGERALD—RADIO

Fitzgerald has the idea of doing a series of 10 minute radio broadcasts concerning the relation of a father with his daughter. The idea is that the father will be talking to his daughter. The mother may either be dead or a mildly villainous club woman. However, the mother will be kept in good taste. In the discussions between the father and daughter the daughter will occasionally tell the father where to get off. In the first place, the father knows nothing about how to deal with this girl child of his and the first sketch will open with the story carrying from the day she is born to the day she is named?

2nd sketch in her childhood

3rd   "   Adolescence

The girl will come home late, try to explain why she is late to her worried father.

---

‡Graham Reid, an assistant in Ober's office at this time, is also Anne Ober's brother.

He suggests the following possibilities:
1. Birth
2. Honor and duty underlying.
3. Bad report card
4.
5. Before the school dance. Young boy calls for her, honks his horn and father makes him come into the house to see if he is sober.
6. Girl comes home from dance very late.
8. Her engagement.
9. The episode showing that she had made a mistake earlier in her life.
10. Just before the wedding ceremony.

Office memo, n.d.—c. October 1935. (AO)

BELIEVE SPAFFORD HAS SATISFACTORY APPROACH TO TENDER IS THE NIGHT FINALLY STOP WILL YOU TELL GRISMAN WHO HE IS AND LET ME KNOW IF GRISMAN IS INTERESTED STOP THERE IS NO USE OF SPAFFORD MAKING RENEWED EFFORT WITHOUT ENCOURAGEMENT FROM GRISMAN BUT HE THINKS HE CAN DELIVER IN FIVE WEEKS STOP HAVE WORKED WITH HIM OVER THIS TREATMENT AND BELIEVE WE HAVE A REAL SHOW STOP IF GRISMAN MAKES OTHER DEFINITE DEAL MEANWHILE I SHOULD BE NOTIFIED BY WIRE BUT WE CANT WAIT FOR KIRKLAND FOREVER STOP REGARDS
    FITZGERALD.

Wire to Ober 6 November 1935. Baltimore, Md. (AO)

F. Scott Fitzgerald, Esq.
3330 St. Paul Avenue
Baltimore, Maryland

Dear Scott:

I got back from Hollywood last week. I'll get in touch with Grisman as soon as I can and let you know what he says.

If you see Robert Spafford tell him I didn't answer his letter because it came in while I was in Hollywood.

How are you getting along with the short story that you are revising?

Sincerely yours,
[Harold Ober]

November 11, 1935

TL (cc), 1p. (AO)

STORY§ LEAVES HERE THURSDAY CAN YOU WIRE FORTY FIRST NATIONAL
          FITZGERALD.

Wire to Ober 12 November 1935. Hendersonville, N.C. (AO)

F. Scott Fitzgerald, Esq.
3330 St. Paul Avenue
Baltimore, Maryland

Dear Scott:

Grisman's option has expired. He is in trouble now over TO-BACCO ROAD. Although I have been trying to get hold of him about another matter I find it impossible to reach him. Will you ask Spafford to send me a copy of the play as soon as he has it finished —that is if he is bound to finish it. It doesn't seem to me wise for you to spend time on this play at the present moment. Any play is a gamble.

I am sending this letter to Baltimore although the telegram I got from you today came from North Carolina. If you are going to be in North Carolina for any length of time please let me know exactly what your address is.

I am glad to know that the story will be here Friday morning.

We are wiring $40.00 to the First National Bank in Baltimore the first thing in the morning. Your telegram didn't reach here in time to do it this afternoon.

Sincerely yours,
[Harold Ober]

November 12, 1935

TL (cc), 1p. (AO)

Dear Constance:

This represents a long sad tale indeed. What I am enclosing looks scrappy but is a <u>second</u> revision from what you've seen—entirely new in construction + plot at the end. I hope for this one that the <u>Post</u> might like it + am sending it this way with the hope that if it reaches you <u>Thurs.</u> you could get a quick typing + get it to them <u>Fri</u> for a wk. end decision.

The long sad tale I wont go into since everyone has one more or less of their own. Suffice to say I cracked entirely after the strain of

---

§Probably "I'd Die for You," which was originally titled "The Legend of Lake Lure." The story was never published.

doing too many things at once + simply fled down here which I had no economic right to do. But since it was that or break up again + that would be an even more expensive business to dependants [or] + creditors here I am. This is a temp. adress. Best adress me ᶜ/o Mrs Owens 5101 Roland Ave Baltimore

Ever Yours
F Scott Fitzgerald

When I know more of plans which depend on health will inform you.¶

ALS, 1p. n.d., n.p.—received 14 November 1935. Hendersonville, N.C. (AO)

F. Scott Fitzgerald, Esq.
ᶜ/o Mrs. Isobel Owens
5101 Roland Avenue
Baltimore, Maryland

Dear Scott:

I'D DIE FOR YOU came in yesterday morning. I read it and had it typed and ready for Graeme Lorimer with whom I had an appointment at three in the afternoon. He took it with him to Philadelphia yesterday afternoon.

As you know, I hadn't read the first version. It seems to me an extremely good story. There is of course a feeling that at any moment almost any one of your characters may commit suicide but you have handled the climax in a very clever way and the story ends happily. I think the Saturday Evening Post will make a mistake if they decline this story and if they do I think we can sell it well and quickly somewhere else.

Sincerely yours,
[Harold Ober]

November 15, 1935

TL (cc), 1p. (AO)

Skylands Hotel
Hendersonville. N.C.

Dear Harold:

Things rather crashed again. Since Aug 20th I have written

(1.) Practically new Red Bk Story (pd. already)#

(2.) 1st Version <u>Provençe</u> Story

¶Written along left margin.
#"Gods of Darkness."

(3) Radio Broadcast (Sold)
(4) 1st version <u>Suicice</u> Story*
(5) 2nd Version <u>Provençe</u> Story (Sold)†
(6) 2nd Version <u>Suicide</u> Story
(7) Emergency <u>Esquire</u> article for $200 (finished today)‡
(8) Most of a radio broadcast. Finish tomorrow.

Certainly a good 3 months work—but total yield has been just short of $2000. so far—of course if <u>I'd Die for You</u> sells, it will change the face of the situation.

I worked one day with Spafford on the play, gave him a new 3d act which was his weakness. He has no great talent but he works hard + has common sense + he can find the talent in the book. Sorry Kirkland didn't kick thru.

I am here till I finish a <u>Post</u> story something young + joyful. I was beginning to cough again in Baltimore with the multiplicity of events, also to drink + get irrasticable with everybody around me. Scotty is there now with Mrs. Owens.

I am living here at a $2.00 a day hotel, utterly alone, thank God! and unless something happens to upset me again should finish the story [but] by the 27th + reach Baltimore by 28th I hope for the winter this time.

Meanwhile you'll get the broadcast.

Typical of my confusion was my telling Constance Smith story should go to <u>Post</u>. It's already been there in it's first form and should have gone to <u>American</u>. Hope you overruled my suggestion.

Ever Yrs.

Scott Fitzg

The decision to leave Baltimore came when I found, after being all moved in, that a super salesman had rented me an appartment <u>next to a pianist</u>, + with clapboard walls!§

Did you see Cormack?¶

ALS (pencil), 2pp. n.d.—c. 18 November 1935. (AO)

IF SAMPLE BROADCAST SEEMS INSUFFICIENTLY FULL BODIED PERHAPS ID BETTER WORK ON IT BEFORE OFFERING IT STOP BUT IT IS NOT FINAL FORM ANYHOW ONLY A SAMPLE AND

---

*"I'd Die for You."
†Probably "Image on the Heart."
‡Possibly "The Crack-Up," *Esquire*, March 1936.
§Written along left margin of page one.
¶Bartlett Cormack, Hollywood agent, was trying to sell film rights for "Head and Shoulders." This sentence written along left margin of page two.

THE CHARACTERIZATIONS OF FATHER AND MOTHER# WILL
PRESUMABLY HAVE BEEN SET IN EARLIER BROADCASTS STOP
STARTED STORY TODAY
    F S FITZGERALD.

Wire to Ober 19 November 1935. Hendersonville, N.C. (AO)

F. Scott Fitzgerald, Esq.
Skylands Hotel
Hendersonville, N. C.

Dear Scott:

Thank you for your note written from Hendersonville. I'D DIE
FOR YOU is now at the American. Graeme Lorimer hadn't read
the story and wanted to see it but couldn't get their editors to buy
it. He let me have it back right away and I hope the American will
buy it.

I have your wire about the sample broadcast so I presume it will
come in later in the day.

I am sure I can sell I'D DIE FOR YOU fairly quickly and things
will look better when I get the money for that.

Grisman's office have called up wanting to renew the option on
TENDER IS THE NIGHT. I have told them that when they can
get hold of Grisman and assure me he is ready to get to work we
will consider whether we can give him another short option. In the
meantime there is no use tying ourselves up.

I tried to see Cormack when I was in Hollywood but didn't
manage to see him. Swanie,* however, is going to get in touch with
him but I don't think there is anything to be done for I find that the
companies very rarely are willing to release silent rights for a reasonable sum.

                                    Sincerely yours,
                                    [Harold Ober]

November 20, 1935

TL (cc), 1p. (AO)

#Ober changed "MOTHER" to "daughter".
*H. N. Swanson, fomerly editor of *College Humor,* had become a Hollywood agent.

F. Scott Fitzgerald, Esq.
Skylands Hotel
Hendersonville, N. C.

Dear Scott:

I thinkyour radio idea is very well worked out. We are having copies made and getting to work on it at once. We will keep the title to ourselves for the present. I don't think you need to do any more work on it at the present time.

Sincerely yours,
[Harold Ober]

November 21, 1935

TL (cc), 1p. (AO)

BEEN SICK IN BED POST STORY LEAVES SATURDAY CAN YOU
WIRE FIFTY TO BALTIMORE
    FITZGERALD.

Wire to Ober 5 December 1935. Hendersonville, N.C. (AO)

SORRY YOU HAVE BEEN ILL WIRING FIFTY BALTIMORE TODAY
    Harold Ober

Wire (cc) to Fitzgerald 5 December 1935. (AO)

Dear Harold:

This story is the fruit of my desire to write about children of Scotty's age.[†] (it doesn't cross the radio idea, which I gather is a dud. Will you write me about it? Also the history of the I'd Die for You) But to return to this story.

I want it to be a series if the Post likes it. Now if they do please tell them that I'd like them to hold it for another one which should preceed it, like they did once in the Basil series. I am not going to wait for their answer to start a second one about Gwen but I am going to wait for a wire of encouragment or discouragment on the idea from you. I'm getting this off Wed. It should reach you Thurs. noon. I'm going to rest Thurs. anyhow so if I hear from you Thurs night or Fri morning that you like it I'll start the other. Even if the Post didn't like the series the names could be changed + the two sold as seperate stories.

But I do think it should be offered them [seperately] *individually* before the series idea is broached to them

---

†"Too Cute for Words," *The Saturday Evening Post*, 18 April 1936. The first story about Gwen Bowers, a thirteen-year-old girl.

Money again rears its ugly head. I am getting accustomed to poverty and bankrupcy (In fact for myself I rather enjoy washing my own clothes + eating 20 cent meals twice a day, after so many years in the flesh pots—don't worry, this is only half true though I did do it for the 1st wk here to penalize myself for the expense of the journey) <u>but</u> I do object to the jails and I have almost $300 due on income tax the 15th (what a typically modern joke this is—me, with $11 in the bank at the moment.) Now can you let me have that and $200 to go with on the strength of this story? Read it first. If you can or can't please include the information in yr. telegram of Thurs. or Fri. I need $150 for Zelda + Scotty + $50 for myself— for I intend to finish the 2nd <u>Gwen</u> story + then go north for what Xmas is to be found there. If you <u>can</u> will you wire it to Baltimore to be there by Sat. morning?

If your report is favorable I shall move to Ashville *Sat.* + have the doctor go over me while I write. I arrived here weak as hell, got the grippe + spat blood again (1st time in 9 months) + took to bed for six days. I didn't dare see the Ashville doctor till I got this story off + wrote a $200 article for Gingrich[‡] on which I've been living. I'm grateful I came south when I did though—I made a wretched mistake in coming north in Sept + taking that appartment + trying 1000 things at once, + am only grateful that I got out before the blizzard, + got grippe instead of pneumonia How that part (I mean living in Balt.) is going to work out I dont know. [If] I'm going to let Scotty finish her term anyhow. For the rest things depend on health + money + its very difficult. I use up my health making money + then my money in recovering health. I got <u>well</u> last summer—but what was the use when I was broke in the fall. Dont answer—there isn't any answer If there was I'd have thought of it long ago. I am really not discouraged—I <u>enjoyed</u> writing this story which is the second time that's happened to me this year, + that's a good sign[§]

Ever Yrs.
Scott Fitzg.

P. S.   This is story number 7 for the year.[¶]

ALS (pencil), 2pp. n.d., n.p.—received 12 December 1935. Hendersonville, N.C. (AO)

---

‡Arnold Gingrich, editor of *Esquire*. The article was "The Crack-Up," February 1936. Because Fitzgerald dealt directly with Gingrich, Ober received no commission.
§This sentence written along left margin of page two.
¶P.S. written along left margin of page one.

CAN YOU WIRE FIFTY BANK AND NIGHTLETTER SUGGES-
TIONS
        FITZGERALD.

Wire to Ober 13 December 1935. Hendersonville, N.C. (AO)

Gwen story delightful but slight begins slowly and believe you
can improve it shall I send suggestions important have story
perfect before offering can your mother help over this emergency absolutely impossible for me to help during December
on account heavy expenses end year and uncollected amounts
owing me.
        Harold Ober

Wire (cc) to Fitzgerald 13 December 1935. (AO)

F. Scott Fitzgerald, Esq.
Skylands Hotel
Hendersonville, N. C.

Dear Scott:
    Both Constance Smith and I have read the story TOO CUTE
FOR WORDS and here are our suggestions:
    The first eight pages are attractively done but much longer than
they need to be to achieve their purpose of introducing Bryan
Bowers and his daughter. They are particularly unnecessary if this
is to be the second of a series, not the first.
    Mrs. Bowers is such a shadowy figure she might as well come out
—situation might be given originality by seeing lone father's
method of dealing with preadolescent daughter as compared to that
of average mother—unless you have personal reasons for not doing
that.
    Page 9 should come not later than Page 3 in story sequence.
    Couldn't you find a simpler ingress to the prom? It is chance only
that gets the girls into the prom. I think it would be better to have
them invent some clever way to get there. Perhaps they could catch
the older man and girl making love before they leave for the prom
and make them take them to watch from upstairs.
    The story trails off badly into nothing and could be strengthened,
by (A) Gwen's seeing Shorty again. at the football game—perhaps
without his recognizing her or (B) having Miss Ray belatedly arrange a party after the football game and Gwen's scorn of prep
school boys now that she has tasted the blood of "maturer men" (to
quote Samuel Hoffenstein.)

To see Shorty again is probably the best idea as it would precipitate Bryan Bowers into the situation again—he should either know or sense what has happened in order for the reader to have his reaction.

Could the man the girls dance with be a quarterback instead of an unknown freshman? He could still be small.

And finally the announcement about the jewelry theft seems a little unnatural. Perhaps the young man in his eagerness to escape his partner could remember the sheltering darkness and isolation of the balcony and accidently discover the girls.

Sincerely yours,
[Harold Ober]

December 13, 1935

TL (cc), 2pp. (AO)

HAVE SENT SUGGESTIONS SPECIAL DELIVERY WIRING BANK FIFTY TODAY
    Harold Ober

Wire (cc) to Fitzgerald 13 December 1935. (AO)

F. Scott Fitzgerald, Esq.
Skylands Hotel
Hendersonville, N. C.

Dear Scott:

I had a very busy day yesterday and didn't have time to write you as much as I wanted to. As I wired you, TOO CUTE FOR WORDS seems to me in many ways a delightful story and I think there may be a series here that will be very profitable to you. On this account it seems to me doubly important to have the first of the series that we offer an extremely good one. The need for money is apt to tempt us into rushing the story to an editor before it is just right, but by doing this we may only defeat our own ends. It is certainly better to wait a week and sell a story than it is to rush it in and not sell it.

If I possibly could I would have sent you yesterday the money you needed. December is always a difficult month—With taxes, insurance, and with Dick in Arizona# and a lot of money owing me, I

#Ober's son, Richard, who was in Arizona because of his bronchitis.

find that I can't stretch my account any further. I did manage to wire you the fifty dollars you asked for and that with what Max Perkins sent you and what you can get from your mother I hope you will be able to weather this present emergency. If you can do a little work on this first Gwen story I think there is a very good chance that we can sell it.

I liked I'D DIE FOR YOU but I am afraid it is going to be difficult to sell. The Post, American, McCall's, Cosmopolitan and Red Book have declined it. Littauer* of Collier's liked it but Chenery† didn't. Littauer, who also reads stories for the Woman's Home Companion, has turned it over to the Companion and he thinks they might possibly be able to use it. One difficulty with the story seems to be the threat of suicide all the way through the story. Cosmopolitan thought the man who was hiding from the process servers was altogether too mysterious and didn't really come to life. If the Companion doesn't buy the story I think there is a chance I can sell it to Liberty and there are of course other possibilities for it.

Columbia liked the radio idea but they haven't been able to sell it to any of their clients. We are working on it now from another angle. I think it is an extremely good idea and we are working hard on it.

I have been talking to Merritt Hulburd, who is with Samuel Goldwyn, about the possibility of your doing some work in Hollywood. They have a Somerset Maugham book which Merritt says you might be interested to work on because you know the locale and the kind of people it deals with. Do you think you would be well enough to go out there for a while early in the year? If you could do a really good job out there I think it might be the solution of your difficulties. Please don't make any plans on this as nothing may come of it but let me know if you want to go to Hollywood and if you think you are well enough. I am sure that if you live quietly there and work hard and make a business of saving money that you could do a lot to get yourself out of the hole that you are now in. A job on one story wouldn't be enough to do all this but if you do well on the first job, it would be easy to get another one and there is no reason why you couldn't get enough money ahead to give you freedom to write a novel when you get ready to write one.

---

*Kenneth Littauer, editor of *Collier's*.
†William Ludlow Chenery, editor and later publisher of *Collier's*.

I am enclosing a couple of items that I have clipped from newspapers and forgot to send you.

Sincerely yours,
[Harold Ober]

December 14, 1935

TL (cc), 2pp. (AO)

F. Scott Fitzgerald, Esq.
3330 St. Paul Avenue
Baltimore, Maryland

Dear Scott:

I called up Philadelphia and found out that the Post is going to use the story, not the Journal. The Post like the character of Gwen very much indeed and they would like to have you go ahead and do another story in the series. I think from the way they spoke they would like to have a series the way they had the Basil stories and the Josephine stories.

It is late in the afternoon and the carbon of the story has not yet come in. I hope it will be here in the morning.

Will you need all the money on this story before January 1st? If not, I think it might be well to leave all you can of it here as it will decrease the tax you will have to start to pay in March. There is another thing—I think Maxwell Perkins expects me to give him some money out of this check when it comes in.

I should think it would be a good idea for you to take only what is absolutely necessary of this check and I wouldn't mind having some of it in the bank for a little while. However, I'll do whatever you think wise.

Sincerely yours,
[Harold Ober]

December 26, 1935

TL (cc), 1p. (AO)

PLEASE WIRE ME WESTERNUNION WHEN MONEY IS DEPOSITED SO I CAN RELEASE CHECK
    SCOTT FITZGERALD.

Wire to Ober 27 December 1935. Baltimore, Md. (AO)

WILL WIRE WHEN YOU MAY RELEASE CHECK WAIT SPECIAL DELIVERY LETTER MAILED THIS MORNING
    Harold Ober

Wire (cc) to Fitzgerald 27 December 1935. (AO)

F. Scott Fitzgerald, Esq.
3330 St. Paul Avenue
Baltimore, Maryland

Dear Scott:

A check from the Post for $3000. has just come in and I am depositing it in the bank. As tomorrow is Saturday it may not be cleared until Monday morning. My bookkeeper was away yesterday when you called and I didn't have a chance to talk to her until this morning. She tells me she had been counting on some of the money out of your first check and that she will be very much embarrassed if we can't keep at least a part of it through the middle of January and perhaps a little longer.

When you get this letter will you send me a wire and let me know the minimum amount you have to have until after the 1st of January? It isn't necessary for you to call me up—I know that costs money. Will you see if you can leave $1000. out of this check for a little while? Demands on me the last part of this year have been very severe. A number of authors have been in very difficult circumstances, even more difficult than yours and I have had to help them out. The Authors' League Fund is down to zero now and it has been unable to keep up payments to a number of authors who are in desperate circumstances and needed money for food and coal so I hope you will try to get along on as little as you can until after the 1st of the year.

. Sincerely yours,
[Harold Ober]

December 27, 1935

TL (cc), 1p. (AO)

F. Scott Fitzgerald, Esq.
3330 St. Paul Avenue
Baltimore, Maryland

Dear Scott:

Yesterday I received carbon copy of pages 16 and 17 of the new story with a note saying with these I would have the complete story. I presume you mailed me a carbon of the revised version of the story but it has not yet come in.

Sincerely yours,
[Harold Ober]

December 27, 1935

TL (cc), 1p. (AO)

Cambridge Arms, Charles St.
Baltimore, Md.

Dear Harold:

You wont like what I'm confessing much but I had $5.00 in the bank + could scarcely explain to Scotty why the silver was in pawn on Xmas. So perhaps you'll understand.

I revised the story on your lines+ sent it direct to Miss Neale.§ Also I asked her if she liked it to wire me two hundred here + send the balance through you. I know this is bad policy + contrary to our agreement, but a fortnight of hemmorages make people a little unscrupulous.

Ever Yrs
F Scott Fitzgerald

I think if this series goes it will solve things.¶ I'll write you about the Hollywood matter. I'm going to try to stick Baltimore again I didn't mention a series to Miss Neale#

ALS, 1p. n.d.—received 28 December 1935. (AO)

HAVE TRIED LIFE ON SUBSISTANCE LEVEL AND IT DOESNT WORK STOP I THOUGHT IF I COULD HAVE THIS MONEY I COULD HOLD MY HEAD UP AND GO ON STOP WHAT YOU SUGGEST POSTPONES BY HALF A YEAR THE LIQUIDATION WE BOTH WANT STOP PLEASE CARRY ME OVER THE SECOND GWEN STORY AND GIVE ME TWENTY SEVEN HUNDRED
    FITZGERALD.

Wire to Ober 28 December 1935. Baltimore, Md. (AO)

Wiring five hundred mailing check for twentytwo Baltimore bank this morning regards.
    Harold Ober

Wire (cc) to Fitzgerald 28 December 1935. (AO)

---

§Adelaide Neall of *The Saturday Evening Post.*
¶The Gwen series. "Too Cute for Words" (18 April 1936) and "Inside the House" (13 June 1936) were published by *The Saturday Evening Post.* "Make Yourself at Home" and "The Pearl and the Fur" were bought by *Pictorial Review,* but the magazine died before the stories were published. "Make Yourself at Home" was published as "Strange Sanctuary" by Liberty (9 December 1939).
#This sentence was written along the left margin in pencil.

F. Scott Fitzgerald, Esq.
3330 St. Paul Avenue
Baltimore, Maryland

Dear Scott:

I have your telegram and I think you are probably right in feeling that you can't do good work if you are worrying every minute about money, with unpaid debts hanging over you, so I am wiring $500. to your Baltimore bank this morning and I am mailing a check for $2200. The Post check will be cleared by the time the check for $2200. gets to Baltimore and of course you can use the $500. right away.

The carbon of the first Gwen story came in this morning. It was addressed to 40 East 41st Street and because of the jam of Christmas mail it didn't get to me until today. I am going to take the manuscript home this afternoon to read.

I feel quite sure that this Gwen series will be the very best way to solve the present financial difficulty. The Post remembers with a great deal of pleasure the Basil stories and the Josephine stories and Graeme Lorimer told me over the telephone that his father would be very pleased to have you go on with this series.

I am breaking my word with Maxwell Perkins as I told him I would try to get him some money out of the next check I got for you, but I am sure he will understand the situation and agree with me that the best thing for all of us is for you to be free to work on this series.

We had a very nice Christmas card from Scotty. We miss her and hope she will come to see us again whenever she has a chance. I think you said over the telephone that Zelda was with you on Christmas. If she is with you now please give her my love.

I think it is much wiser for you to work on this series than to try Hollywood so lets forget that.

Sincerely yours,
[Harold Ober]

December 28, 1935

TL (cc), 2pp. (AO)

> PLEASE ASK POST TO HOLD THIS GIVEN* STORY FOR ONE TO REACH THEM JANUARY NINTH TO PROCEED THIS IN PUBLICA-TION† STOP STARTING NOW
>   SCOTT FITZGERALD. .

Wire to Ober 29 December 1935. Baltimore, Md. (AO)

---

*i.e., GWEN.
†Possibly "Make Yourself at Home," which *The Saturday Evening Post* rejected.

Cambridge Arms Apartments,
Charles & 34th Streets,
Baltimore, Maryland,
December 31, 1935.

Dear Harold:

I'd have gone to Hollywood a year ago last spring. I don't think I could do it now but I might. Especially if there was no choice. Twice I have worked out there on other people's stories—on an "original" with John Considine telling me the plot twice a week and on the Katherine Brush story—it simply fails to use what qualities I have. I don't blame you for lecturing me since I have seriously inconvenienced you, but it would be hard to change my temperament in middle-life. No single man with a serious literary reputation has made good there. If I could form a partnership with some technical expert it might be done. (That's very different from having a supervisor who couldn't fit either the technical or creative role but is simply a weigher of completed values.) I'd need a man who knew the game, knew the people, but would help me tell and sell my story—<u>not his</u>. This man would be hard to find, because a <u>smart</u> technician doesn't want or need a partner, and an uninspired one is inclined to have a dread of ever touching tops. I could work best with a woman, because they haven't any false pride about yielding a point. I could have worked with old Bess Meredith if we hadn't been in constant committees of five. I'm afraid unless some such break occurs I'd be no good in the industry.

The matter will probably solve itself—I'll either pull out of this in the next few months or else go under—in which case I might start again in some entirely new way of my own.

I know what you would do now in my situation and what the Ideal Way would be, but it simply isn't in me to do my duty blindly. I have to follow my fate with my eyes wide open.

Scotty is so well and happy. She has such faith in me and doesn't know what's happening. Tonight she and two of her admirers decorated a tree. I hope Dick is better and has a happy Christmas even out there away from his family.

Yours,
F Scott Fitzgerald

P. S. Do you think the <u>New Yorker</u> could use poem attached?‡

TLS, 3pp. (AO)

---

‡"Thousand and First Ship," first published in *The Crack Up*, 1945.

Fitzgerald's total earnings for 1935 were $16,845.16. He sold seven stories ($14,725). Four essays were taken by Esquire. *His book royalties plus an advance from Scribners came to $342.03.*

F. Scott Fitzgerald, Esq.
3330 St. Paul Avenue
Baltimore, Maryland

Dear Scott:

I have been out of the office off and on for the last week or ten days with a slight attack of grippe, otherwise I would have answered before this your note about Hollywood. Now that you are started on the Gwen stories I don't think there is any use of even thinking about Hollywood. I wrote you only because Merritt Hulburd brought up the question and it seemed a possible solution of the difficulty you were in at the time.

I have your telegram saying that the second Gwen story won't be here until the 25th. I am sure you are right in waiting until the story is just as you want it before you send it on.

I sent the poem over to the New Yorker but I haven't yet heard from them.

Max Perkins called me up the other day, said he was going to be in Baltimore and would see you.

Sincerely yours,
[Harold Ober]

Jamuary 14, 1936

TL (cc), 1p. (AO)

F. Scott Fitzgerald, Esq.
3330 St. Paul Avenue
Baltimore, Maryland

Dear Scott:

We have the following note from the New Yorker about your poem THOUSAND AND FIRST SHIP:

"We have pondered for a long while over this Scott Fitzgerald poem only to conclude reluctantly that we should not take it. As a poem, it has certain grave defects, including the non-permissible rhyme in the fourth stanza, and we don't think that as a poem it is up to what he can do.

We are sorry to send anything of his back and hope you will have something else of his for us."

I wish you would go over this verse again sometime when you have time as I am sure you can improve it.

> Sincerely yours,
> [Harold Ober]

January 20, 1936

TL (cc), 1p. (AO)

> The Cambridge Arms,
> Baltimore, Maryland,
> January 21, 1936.

Mr. Harold Ober,
40 East 49th Street,
New York, New York.

Dear Harold:

The <u>Post</u> story must go off Friday. The delay has been caused by a trip to the hospital. At least they discovered that my lung has improved even since leaving Asheville so that now there is so little infection left that I shan't have to go south again. One of the two or three pieces of good news I've had this year. It took two months to find it out. The reason for this delay being that I couldn't get the plates to compare it with because I owed the doctor in Asheville $40.00 which I couldn't pay him. Things like this have made me inclined to smile when you say that other authors have been in a worse spot than I have.

Remind the <u>Post</u> again please not to schedule "Too Cute for Words" until they get the new one. While I'm writing I want to bring up two matters:

1. If "I'd Die for You" hasn't sold you might as well send it back to me. I'm not going to touch it myself again but I know a boy here who might straighten it out for a share of the profits, if any.

2. It is of no immediate importance but I would like to know if <u>The Redbook</u> intends to publish the fourth medieval story. If it gets buried in their files and if I ever do get on with the series it will mean that it will have to be bought back from them or some such complication. I don't care about the <u>Cosmopolitan</u> holding up my article on New York§ because it's an individual piece, but the other is a more serious matter. I gather that the radio is washed up.

Anyhow, with the good news about my lung the year has started auspiciously and I should be able to pay you back $1000 a story beginning with this one.

---

§"My Lost City," *The Crack Up*, 1945.

Scottie sends her very best to you all and we hope Dick is getting along in the west.

If you read my piece in <u>Esquire</u># remember it was written last November when things seemed at their very blackest.

Best wishes always,
Scott

TLS, 2pp. (AO)

F. Scott Fitzgerald, Esq.
The Cambridge Arms
Charles + 34 Sts
Baltimore, Md.

Dear Scott:

I should have answered your note of January 21st before but I stayed in bed Friday, Saturday, and Sunday to get rid of my cold that has been hanging on since about the 1st of January. I am glad of the good news from the hospital.

I have told the Post more than once that TOO CUTE FOR WORDS is the second story in the series so I don't think there is any danger of their publishing it before the story you are now writing. By the way, this story has not yet come in but I am expecting it any moment.

I thought of offering I'D DIE FOR YOU next to Pictorial. Let me know if you want me to do this or send it back first for revision.

I'll find out when the Red Book intends to use the fourth mediaeval story and let you know.

I'll have to read that piece that is in Esquire. Several authors have asked me about you within the last day or two and I wondered why.

Dick is having a fine time in Arizona. He hasn't had a single cold so far this winter and he is getting to be a regular cowboy. We miss Scotty and hope she will visit us again just as soon as she can.

Sincerely yours,
[Harold Ober]

January 27, 1936

TL (cc), 1p. (AO)

#"The Crack-Up," which Ober had not seen before publication.

The Cambridge Arms,
Baltimore, Maryland,
January 29, 1936.

Dear Harold:

I wish you would send "I'd Die for You" right back. Please find out something more definite about the Medieval story. Can't you see how terribly important it is to me?

Ever yours,
Scott

Mr. Harold Ober,
40 East 49th Street,
New York, New York.

TLS, 1p. (AO)

F.Scott Fitzgerald Esq.,
Cambridge Arms,
Charles & 34th,
Baltimore, Md.

Dear Scott:

I have mailed you a copy of I'D DIE FOR YOU. One editor commented on the fact that the man in the story was too mysterious and this editor thought he ought to be explained. The main difficulty with the story, however, has always been that there is so much about suicide in it.

I will let you know the moment Balmer has a date for the publication of the last mediaeval story. I didn't realize and I don't think Balmer did that there was any rush about using this story. Have you done another one of these stories or are you thinking of doing one?

I read your last piece in Esquire and it seems to me a very fine piece of work. No one who had cracked up and stayed that way could possibly write as well as this.

Graeme Lorimer asked me when he was in this week when you were going to have the first Gwen story ready. He said they had scheduled the story they bought and took it out of the schedule to wait for the first story and they hope you will have it along soon.

Sincerely,
[Harold Ober]

February 1, 1936

TL (cc), 1p. (AO)

Received carbon of story did you send original to Post.
Harold Ober

Wire (cc) to Fitzgerald 6 February 1936. (AO)

TERRIBLY BROKE AND CONSEQUENTLY HAVE SENT STORY DI-
RECTLY TO POST CARBON TO YOU IF THEY LIKE IT PLEASE
SEND AT LEAST TWO THIRD STIPEND HERE TO MY CREDIT AT
FIRST NATIONAL I HOPE SO MUCH THAT YOU CAN DO THIS AS
GWEN AND I MUST GO ON
SCOTT FITZGERALD.

Wire to Ober 6 February 1936. Baltimore. (AO)

F. Scott Fitzgerald, Esq.
Cambridge Arms
Charles & 34th Streets
Baltimore, Md.

Dear Scott:
I wired you because I wasn't sure whether you had sent a copy
of MAKE YOURSELF AT HOME to the Post. Graeme Lorimer
was in this morning and I told him I thought he would find a copy
when he got back to Philadelphia and if he didn't to let me know
and I would send him my copy. My carbon copy is evidently an
uncorrected one as there are several places in it that are not clear.
I have asked Graeme Lorimer to give me a quick decision on it
and if they buy it, as I hope they will, I'll send two-thirds of the
price to your bank.

Sincerely yours,
[Harold Ober]

February 6, 1936

TL (cc), 1p. (AO)

POST REFUSED STORY CAN YOU WIRE ME TODAY YOUR REAC-
TION TO IT SHALL I REWRITE OR MERELY CHANGE NAMES
AND TRY TO SELL IT TO ANOTHER MAGAZINE REWRITING
WOULD TAKE FOUR DAYS NAMES CHANGED CAN BE DONE
IMMEDIATELY
SCOTT FITZGERALD.

Wire to Ober 7 February 1936. Baltimore. (AO)

THINK STORY NEEDS REWRITING MAILING SPECIAL DELIV-
ERY LETTER
HAROLD OBER

Wire (cc) to Fitzgerald 7 February 1936. (AO)

F. Scott Fitzgerald, Esq.
Cambridge Arms
Charles & 34th Streets
Baltimore, Maryland

Dear Scott:

As I have just wired you, I think MAKE YOURSELF AT HOME needs rewriting. The question is, however, whether you feel like rewriting it and whether you have any ideas that might make the story saleable to the Post. If you haven't, I suppose the only thing to do is to change the names and let me try it on some other magazine. I do not, however, feel very confident of placing it. The story seems to me to get too melodramatic. The two crooks in the story seem too violent for this kind of story. I am not going to send you any detailed suggestions, in the first place because I have not studied the story from that point of view, and in the second place I am not sure that you want them.

I am very sorry you sent the story direct to the Post but there is no use talking about that now. Did the editors of the Post send you any suggestions? If they did, I suppose it would be wise to try to rewrite the story according to these suggestions if you can.

I am afraid I am not being very helpful but I do not see how you can make this the first story in the Gwen series without a good deal of rewriting. Is there any reason now why we shouldn't ler the Post publish first the one they have? I am going to take this story home with me tonight and study it carefully and if I have any ideas about it and if you want them I'll be glad to send them on to you.

Sincerely yours,
[Harold Ober]

February 7, 1936

TL (cc), 1p. (AO)

The Cambridge Arms,
Charles & 34th Streets,
Baltimore, Maryland,
February 8, 1936.

Dear Harold:

The man Braun* is a plain, simple man with a true instinct toward the arts. He is of complete financial integrity and we were

---

*L. G. Braun, manager of ballerina Olga Spessivtzewa, asked Fitzgerald to write a movie for her. Fitzgerald's treatment for the ballet movie was entitled "Ballet Shoes" or "Ballet Slippers."

awfully nice to him once during a journey through North Africa and I think he is honestly fond of both Zelda and me.

I start with this because I don't want to mess up this chance with any of the inadvertencies and lack of foresight that lost me the sale of "Tender is the Night" and ruined the Gracie Allen venture.[†] You are now in touch with Hollywood in a way that you were not several years ago. This is obviously a job that I can do expertly— but it is also obviously a job that a whole lot of other people can do fairly well. Now it seems to me that the point can be sold that I am equipped to do this treatment which is the whole gist of this letter.

He has gone out [there] *to Hollywood* and they will put some hack on the thing *and* in two minutes [and] will have a poor imitation of Lily Pons deserting the stage for a poor country boy or a poor country girl named Lily Pons astounding the world in ten minutes. A hack will do exactly that with it, thinking first what previous stories dealing with the ballet and theatre have been about, and he will try to write a reasonable imitation about it. As you know Zelda and I have been through hell about the whole subject and you'll know, too, that I should be able to deliver something entirely authentic in the matter full of invention and feeling.

It seems odd having to sell you such a suggestion when once you would have taken it at my own valuation, but after these three years of reverses it seems necessary to reassure you that I have the stuff to do this job and not let this opportunity slide away with the rumor that "Scott is drinking" or "Scott is through."

You know that the merest discussion of ideas [three words omitted by the editors] would mean that they were public property. You know also as in the case of radio, (Columbia) that they want a sample. Now how on earth you can both sell the idea that I can do this job, that is, write a 5,000 word story with cash in advance, and yet be sure that the plot won't leak out, I don't know. That seems to be your problem. You remember that I lost the whole month of October on that false radio come-on where they were obviously kidding. Isn't there some way to determine whether these people are kidding or not? This man has, in a sense, come to me and I think the idea ought to be caught and trapped right now because as you may well imagine I have little [enough] energy to dissipate.

A list of suggestions follows:

First I enclose something which I wish you would read last because it has nothing to do with the present offer, but it is something

---

†Fitzgerald collaborated with Robert Spafford on a treatment for a George Burns and Gracie Allen movie, "Gracie at Sea," which was never made.

that I wrote gratuitously for a Russian dancer some years ago. Please consider that last and featuring, as it does, a male dancer rather than a female, it would certainly not fit Spessivtzewa's requirements. The other ideas which follow are the basis of a moving picture while that was for an actual ballet.

1. Zleda's awful experience of trying a difficult art too late in life to culminate with the irony that just before she cracked up she had been hoping to get little "bits" in Diaghelief's[‡] ballet and that people kept coming to the studio who she thought were emissaries of his and who turned out to be from the Folies Bergere and who thought they might make her into an American shimmy dancer. This was about like a person hoping to lead the Philadelphia Symphony being asked to be assistant conductor of Ben Bernie's band.

Please don't have anybody read Zelda's book[§] because it is a bad book! But by glancing over it yourself you will see that it contains all the material that a tragedy should have, though she was incapable as a writer of realizing where tragedy lay as she was incapable of facing it as a person. Of course the tragic ending of Zelda's story need not be repeated in the picture. One could concede to the picture people the fact that the girl might become a popular dancer in the Folies Bergere. One could conceive of a pathetic ending a la Hepburn in which because of her idealism she went on being a fifth rate "figurine" in ballets all over Europe—this to be balanced by a compensatory love story which would make up for her the failure of her work. This would seem to me to be much the best treatment of this story.

2. This idea has to do with an episode of some memoirs of Pavlova. It begins with a little girl briefly glimpsed and dancing in the Imperial ballet before the war. A scene later in Paris at the height of the flurry over the ballet and stranded finally with a ballet company in either Australia or Brazil for lack of funds. The climax would hinge on the catastrophe of the death of Diaghelief. The sorrow of it that Zelda felt, as did many others, who seemed to feel also that the ballet was ended; the old Imperial school was dead and now Diaghelief who had personally kept it alive in Paris had gone to his grave. There seemed to them no future and I know how strong that feeling was among the ballet people in '31 and '31,[¶] a sort of utter despair, a sense that they had once been under patronage of the Czar and later of an entrepreneur and that now nobody was

‡Director of the Ballet Russe.
§*Save Me the Waltz.*
¶i.e., '32.

taking care of them. They are like children to a ridiculous extent and have less practical ideas than the wildest musician imaginable. This story would end up in New York or in Hollywood, the ballet having a new renaissance under an American growing delight in that particular art as is practically true with Masine's# ballet in New York and with Trudy Schoop's* successful little trek around the country. That's idea number 2.

The third idea is more difficult in its selling aspects. In 1920 I tried to sell to D. W. Griffith the idea that people were so interested in Hollywood that there was money in a picture about that [that] and romance in the studio. He was immediately contemptuous of it, but of course, a year later <u>Merton of the Movies</u> mopped up the country. The movies seem willing always to romanticize anything from a radio broadcasting room to a newspaper office as far as the entertainment world is concerned, but are so shy about themselves that another picture can be got out of Hollywood, which is certainly one of the most romantic cities in the world. A sort of mental paralysis came over them. Do you remember how the Hearst publicity men killed my story "Crazy Sunday" for <u>Cosmopolitan</u>. That was in case someone should get hurt, that it might offend Norma Shearer, Thalberg, John Gilbert or Marion Davies,† etc. etc. As a matter of fact I had mixed up those characters so thoroughly that there was no character who could have been identified except possibly King Vidor‡ and he would have been very amused by the story.

Let me repeat that this is the most difficult idea to sell but in some ways the most interesting of the three. A Russian ballet dancer finds herself in the extra line in Hollywood; they pick her out of the crowd for her good looks, gave her bits of one kind or another but always on some other basis than the fact that she is a ballet dancer. This treatment of the general subject would have to close with a crash, at least I haven't thought any further than that. It would turn entirely on the essential tonal background of the adventures of Europeans who develop their metier in a Yiddish world (only you don't use that word except in Germany [.]) [T]that would be interesting to the people in the same rococo sense that the demand for

---

Leonide Massine was a ballet dancer and director of the Ballet National Theatre.
*The Trudi Schoop Comic Ballet was organized in 1931.
†Norma Shearer, movie actress with MGM, was the wife of Irving Thalberg, executive producer with MGM. John Gilbert was a silent screen star. Marion Davies, an actress with MGM, was William Randolph Hearst's mistress.
‡Director with MGM.

pictures about places like Shanghai and the Trans-Siberian Railroad have in the American people. Combined with it is the always fascinating Hollywood story.

I've spent the morning writing this letter because I am naturally disappointed about the <u>Post's</u> not liking the Gwen story and must rest and go to work this afternoon to try to raise some money somehow though I don't know where to turn.

Scott

TLS, 7pp. (AO)

The Cambridge Arms,
Charles & 34th Streets,
Baltimore, Maryland,
February 8, 1936.

Dear Harold:

The enclosed telegram and carbon of the letter I sent Miss Neall are self explanatory.

Ever yours,
Scott

Enclosures (2)

TLS, 1p. (AO)

WE ALL FEEL NEW STORY UNSATISFACTORY START FOR SERIES WITH NO PREVIOUS KNOWLEDGE ABOUT THE CHILD AND HER BACKGROUND IT IS RATHER BLIND AND THE INTRODUCTION OF THE CROOKS IS NOT QUITE CONVINCING AND GIVES AN UNPLEASANT FLAVOR WHEN THE READER SHOULD BE ATTRACTED INTO THE SERIES IMPORTANT THAT EACH STORY STANDS ON ITS OWN FEET AND IS COMPLETE IN ITSELF WE THINK THE OPENING STORY SHOULD DEAL MORE WITH THE CHILD AND HER FATHER IN THE WAY THE STORY WE NOW HAVE IN TYPE DOES DEEPLY SORRY THAT I CANNOT GIVE A DIFFERENT REPORT
A W NEALL.

Wire to Fitzgerald 6 February 1936. (AO)

The Cambridge Arms,
Charles & 34th Streets,
Baltimore, Maryland,
February 8, 1936.

Miss A. W. Neall,
Independence Square,
Philadelphia, Pennsylvania.

Dear Miss Neall:

Thank you for your prompt and detailed report. On thinking it over I can quite understand how you feel about the story though I would describe my reaction differently. This does not discourage me from continuing the series. It seems to me that you might as well go on with "Too Cute for Words" at your convenience. I am correcting it today and will return it to you.

My next venture with Gwen will be entirely in key with the first and as I rewrite "Make Yourself at Home" before offering it to another magazine I will eliminate any details that could possibly indicate its connection with your series. If you have any objections to this plan please tell Harold Ober as soon as you can. I still like the story and feel that after rewriting it and changing the names, of course, that no one will associate it with "Too Cute for Words."

Sincerely,
[F. Scott Fitzgerald]

TL (cc), 2pp. (AO)

F. Scott Fitzgerald, Esq.
Cambridge Arms
Charles & 34th Streets
Baltimore, Maryland

Dear Scott:

Thanks for the telegram from Miss Neall and for the copy of your letter in reply. I judge by this that you are going to write a new story in the Gwen series for the Post and that you will rewrite MAKE YOURSELF AT HOME for another magazine and that it is all right for the Post to use TOO CUTE FOR WORDS as the first story in the series.

I am sure you must have a lot of material for Gwen stories.

Sincerely yours,
[Harold Ober]

February 10, 1936

TL (cc), 1p. (AO)

F. Scott Fitzgerald, Esq.
Cambridge Arms
Charles & 34th Streets
Baltimore, Maryland

Dear Scott:

I did not receive your letter dated February 8th until yesterday. I wired your bank $100. today and I'll try to send another hundred next week. This will at least give you a little cash to go on while you are working on the new Gwen story.

Now regarding this idea for a ballet picture. I read Mr. Braun's letter over carefully and it doesn't seem to me that he has anything very definite to offer you. He says he has no authority to make any definite arrangements. I am, however, trying to get in touch with him and if he is still in Hollywood I am asking him to see Swanson. I don't believe Mr. Braun can put anybody to work on the idea because he hasn't the authority to do so. He might interest some American company in making a ballet picture using Spessivtzewa and then it might be possible for you to write the story.

At any rate, I don't think you ought to spend any more time on this matter unless someone makes a definite offer for your services. I think you are well equipped to write a story for a ballet picture and I'll make every effort to run this matter to the ground.

In the meantime I hope you are working on a new Gwen story and this time I hope you will not send it direct to the Post. It really doesn't save any time. I don't like to have the Post decline stories of yours. I would like to send them only stories that they will have to buy.

I am enclosing a clipping from O.O. McIntyre's column in this morning's paper.¶

Sincerely yours,
[Harold Ober]

February 14, 1936

TL (cc), 1p. (AO)

¶McIntyre, in his column "New York Day by Day," wrote: "F. Scott Fitzgerald, greying and chunking up, is reputedly one of the most difficult authors from whom editors may wangle stories these days. He is the literary symbol of an era—the era of the new generation—and editors continue to want stories of flask gin and courteous collegiates preceding ladies through windshields on midnight joy rides. The public has acquired this Fitzgerald taste, too. But Fitzgerald has taken an elderly and naturally serious turn. Mellowed is the term. He wants to write mellowy, too. And if they won't let him he won't write at all. So there."

F. Scott Fitzgerald, Esq.
Cambridge Arms
Charles & 34th Streets
Baltimore, Maryland

Dear Scott:

I have the manuscript of MAKE YOURSELF AT HOME with the names changed and I am showing it to an editor today. As I am wiring you, I am sending another hundred dollars to your bank in Baltimore. It isn't very much but it is all I can spare just now.

I am doing everything I can to get in touch with Mr. Braun and if he is still in Hollywood I have asked him to get in touch with Swanson and I have explained the situation to Swanson so that he can discuss the matter intelligently with him.

I hope you will be able to do a second Gwen story that will be as delightful as the first one was.

Sincerely yours,
[Harold Ober]

February 19, 1936

TL (cc), 1p. (AO)

F. Scott Fitzgerald, Esq.
Cambridge Arms
Charles & 34th Streets
Baltimore, Md.

Dear Scott:

As you know, I wrote to Swanson about your ideas of a ballerina story. He says he has not seen Mr. Braun yet. He says that David Selznick is very keen to do a ballerina story and he wants to know if it is all right to approach him with one of these ideas and it is possible that you can develop the idea here in the East.

Merritt Hulburd is in New York now and he says that they want a ballerina story for Miriam Hopkins. Do you think you could without taking too much time write a page or two about one of the ideas that you think would suit Miriam Hopkins. Samuel Goldwyn is here in New York now and will be here until March 4th.

Sincerely yours,
[Harold Ober]

February 25, 1936

TL (cc), 1p. (AO)

1 East 34th Street,
Baltimore, Maryland,
February 26, 1936.

Mr. Harold Ober,
40 East 49th Street,
New York, New York.

Dear Harold:

The carbon of those ideas seems to have been lost. Please send back copies of all the stuff that you got on the subject and I will be in a better position to say what I might do with it.

I'm almost finished the Gwen story.#

What is the exact arrangement of selling an idea if the originator of it does not go out to the coast? That is utterly out of the question at the moment for me. I mean to say, what is the down payment? I wouldn't want it to be another false venture like I've made before in pictures and radio. At any rate please send the copies of my suggestions in both my letters.

Ever yours,
Scott

TLS, 1p. (AO)

F. Scott Fitzgerald, Esq.
1 East 34th Street
Baltimore, Maryland

Dear Scott:

I am returning Mr. Braun's letter and I am also sending a copy of the parts of your letter of February 8th giving your ideas for the ballerina story. I am also returning the scenario entitled LIVES OF THE DANCERS although I am not sure you need that. All I want you to do now is perhaps elaborate a little on one of these ideas. I don't want you to make a treatment now for that is what you will be paid for if you do it. All you need to do is to write perhaps a page giving a little description of your idea, making it sound attractive and not telling too much abut it.

If Samuel Goldwyn is enthusiastic about this description he might pay $2000. or $2500. down for you to develop a twenty or

---

Possibly "Inside the House."

twenty-five page treatment on the understanding that if he liked the treatment he would pay an additional amount.

I think it is probably much more important to finish the Gwen story than it is to write out this idea but if you can do it easily without taking too much time it might be a good idea to do it now. Goldwyn is sailing for England about March 4th and if you haven't time to do it now you could do it while he is abroad and you can show it to him when he gets back.

Sincerely yours,
[Harold Ober]

February 28, 1936

TL (cc), 1p. (AO)

Harold Ober's note on his 19 February 1936–30 December 1936 file folder reads: "where are Scotts letters to me for above period one letter from Scott Oct 5, 1936". Our searches have failed to recover the missing Fitzgerald letters.

F. Scott Fitzgerald, Esq.
Cambridge Arms
34th St. & Charles Sts.
Baltimore, Maryland

Dear Scott:

Mr. Braun came in to see me this afternoon. He is just back from Hollywood and sailing on Wednesday. He says he will be back in about five weeks. You will then know exactly what the situation is regarding the ballet picture and he will come in to see me as soon as he gets to New York. He says he may bring Mlle. Spessivtzewa with him.

As you know, Sam Grisman, producer of TOBACCO ROAD has an option on TENDER IS THE NIGHT. He wants to know if we would approve of Jack Kirkland and Austin Parker as dramatists for your book. I think the combination of these two would be a very good one. I understand they have worked together very successfully. Austin Parker knows the kind of people you are writing about. He was at one time Miriam Hopkins' husband and before that he was married to Phyllis Duganne.* He has written a few plays and been very successful in Hollywood. Jack Kirkland is an

---

*Poet and short story writer.

experienced dramatist. I am assuming that you will approve this choice but you might drop me a line in confirmation.

Sincerely yours,
[Harold Ober]

March 2, 1936

TL (cc), 1p. (AO)

GOLDWYN SAILING TOMORROW EVERY MOMENT TAKEN IMPOSSIBLE COME BALTIMORE.
Harold Ober

Wire (cc) to Fitzgerald 3 March 1936. (AO)

ABSOLUTELY IMPOSSIBLE AND IMPRACTICAL SEE GOLDWYN NOW WILL ARRANGE ON HIS RETURN WRITING
Harold Ober

Wire (cc) to Fitzgerald 4 March 1936. (AO)

F. Scott Fitzgerald, Esq.
Cambridge Arms
Charles & 34th Streets
Baltimore, Maryland

Dear Scott:

I was sorry that your plan of having Samuel Goldwyn go to Baltimore was not feasible. He couldn't possibly postpone his trip. He and all his retinue had their passage arranged and had engagements in London that had to be kept. As a matter of fact I don't think it would have been of any use for him to go to Baltimore. I know Goldwyn and how he works for I spent a good many mornings with him. He always has a right-hand man who prepares everything for him—at present Merritt Hulburd is the one who does this. Merritt Hulburd used to be with the Saturday Evening Post and I have absolute confidence in him. Merritt had to go back to Hollywood yesterday. If you will let me have a short outline on the ballet picture I'll take it up with Merritt and then we can possibly arrange to see Goldwyn when he comes back from Europe.

I have been looking for the new Gwen story and I hope it will be along soon.

Sincerely yours,
[Harold Ober]

March 5, 1936

TL (cc), 1p. (AO)

PERHAPS SLIGHT COMPARED TO FIRST STORY BUT ATTRAC-
TIVE AND I LIKE IT[†]
    Harold Ober

Wire (cc) to Fitzgerald 9 March 1936.

Dear Mr. Fitzgerald:
    A COURSE IN LANGUAGES appears in the April,19336[‡] issue
of McCalls Magazine under the title IMAGE ON THE HEART.
                              Sincerely
                              HAROLD OBER
                              Per. J S S Sterling
March 9,1936

Typed post card. (AO)

F. Scott Fitzgerald, Esq.
Cambridge Arms
Charles & 34th Streets
Baltimore, Maryland

Dear Scott:
    I have sent you by special delivery this morning a carbon of the
typed copy of OUTSIDE THE HOUSE.[§] The copy you sent me
was difficult to read and I have now read over the typed copy and
it seems to me that with a few hours work you could improve the
story and this extra work might make all the difference between an
acceptance and a declination. I think it is especially important that
the Post like this story for if they don't, they might decide it is a
mistake for you to go on with the series. I feel very sure that you
can make a very fine series of the Gwen stories.
    I wish you would read the copy over carefully especially Chapter
4. The timing here is rather confused. In the first place there is no
mention of Gwen having had dinner. Then you have two accidents
to the car which seems almost too much of a coincidence. Then you
have the moving picture actress walking up and down for an hour
waiting for a taxi. Then later on when the snow is worse you have
Gwen and Jason get a taxi very easily to go a short distance.

---

    †"Inside the House."
    ‡This card was returned to Ober with the following notes written by Fitzgerald
along the bottom and left margins: "By that time I wont even remember the original
title" and "Sorry this is torn. Was amused F. S. F".
    §"Inside the House."

When Gwen and Jason finally leave the moving picture actress at the Dobies' they go to the moving picture theatre, which is evidently very near, are there only a few minutes and go back to Gwen's house. This doesn't give *enough* time for the picture actress to be at the party and go back to Gwen's house.

It also seems to me that the part about the picture house is rather confused. I thought at first that the picture was being run twice and that they had come in just at the end of the first run (on page 19 for instance you say that they were caught in a gangway of people waiting for the last of the performance). There didn't seem to be much point in their going to all the trouble of going upstairs if the picture was so nearly over.

If you go over this chapter carefully I am sure you can make it clearer and more effective. Is it really necessary to have Gwen and Jason take the picture actress to the party? If they do I think they should take her there right away and then have the difficulties getting to the picture come afterwards. I think perhaps you could simplify this chapter. As I understand the story, all you need is to have Gwen have a terrible time getting to the picture and then not see it (by the way is there any point in mentioning that she had seen the picture before?).

If you don't feel like making a final revision of the story wire me and I'll send the ribbon copy I have to the Post right away. I feel quite sure, however, that with a little more work you can make this a story that the Post will surely buy. I don't feel quite sure about it in its present shape. If you can get it back to me by Thursday I can give it to Graeme Lorimer when he is in New York and in that way there will really be no time lost.

Sincerely yours,
[Harold Ober]

March 10, 1936

TL (cc), 2pp. (AO)

F. Scott Fitzgerald, Esq.
Cambridge Arms
Charles & 34th Streets
Baltimore, Maryland

Dear Scott:

I got the revised Gwen story in time to have the pages retyped and to give it to Graeme Lorimer when he came in this morning. I also got the ballet idea and registered it at the Authors' League and sent a copy off by airmail to Merritt Hulburd. I told him I didn't want it shown to anybody but Mr. Goldwyn and Miriam Hopkins. Samuel Goldwyn's organization is quite different from the other picture companies—they do not have any Scenario Department. They make only a few pictures a year and engage writers just for the picture they are making at the time so I do not think there is any danger of the idea being seen by anyone who shouldn't see it.

I thought the idea was a good one. I thought also the changes you made in OUTSIDE THE HOUSE improved it and I hope the Post will buy it.

I received your telegram and I am registering the scenario under both titles BALLET SHOES and BALLET SLIPPERS.

> Sincerely yours,
> [Harold Ober]

March 12, 1936

TL (cc), 1p. (AO)

F. Scott Fitzgerald, Esq.
Cambridge Arms
Charles & 34th Streets
Baltimore, Maryland

Dear Scott:

I was in Philadelphia on Friday and saw both George Horace Lorimer and Graeme, and Adelaide Neall. They hadn't then read your second Gwen story and as a matter of fact I haven't had word from them yet about it. I take it from your telegram of last night that they told you they were going to buy it and I am of course very pleased. I am hoping that the check for it will come in tomorrow morning. When I get the check I'll be glad of course to keep to the arrangement we made on the story they didn't buy, and wire you $2000.

This is too obvious to mention but I presume you have considered the possibility of using in this Gwen series some of the ideas you had in the radio scenario you sent me. It seems to me that it would be a very good idea in this series to emphasize the relation between Gwen and her father.

> Sincerely yours,
> [Harold Ober]

March 17, 1936

TL (cc), 1p. (AO)

F. Scott Fitzgerald Esq.,
Cambridge Apts.,
Charles & 34th St.,
Baltimore, Md.

Dear Scott:

The latter part of January we had some correspondence about your short story I'D DIE FOR YOU, resulting in your decision to revise it before we offered it further. I sent a copy back to you on February 1st.

If after reading it you decided to start on something new and discarded further plans for rewriting, just let me know and I will remove the story from the active list.

Sincerely,
[Harold Ober]

March 30,1936

TL (cc), 1p. (AO)

BEGINNING AND END DELIGHTFUL MIDDLE NEEDS REWRITING RETURNING STORY WITH SUGGESTIONS FOR REVISION IMPORTANT THIS STORY BE JUST RIGHT.*
    OBER

Wire (cc) to Fitzgerald 6 April 1936. (AO)

F. Scott Fitzgerald, Esq.
Cambridge Arms
Charles & 34th Streets
Baltimore, Maryland

Dear Scott:

I think the beginning and the ending of the new Gwen story are delightful. The middle part of the story, however, seems to me very complicated and improbable and I think this part of the story should be rewritten before it is sent to the Post. It is most important to have the story just right because it will make a great deal of difference about the Post going on with the series. I understand that there was some division of opinion about the last story and I am sure this story will have to be better than the last to get by.

A good deal of the taxicab material seems to me improbable and two other readers independently reached the same conclusion. It doesn't seem possible that an expensive coat would be left in a

---

*"The Pearl and the Fur."

taxicab from one evening to noon of the next day. If the taxi driver went back to his company's garage reporting that something had been found, the company would take charge of the lost property.

I have checked up on the subway station at Kingsbridge and 230th Street and it is as closely settled as any part of New York City. The subways leave every four or five minutes. If anyone were in a hurry to get from 230th Street to 59th Street one would never think of taking a taxicab and there are no subway terminals that are in unpopulated districts as you describe.

Wouldn't it be simpler if Gwen found some small article like a pocketbook with the rich woman's card in it and perhaps with the tickets for the trip. She might have driven downtown and taken the cab that the rich woman had left in going to the boat. I think this middle section of the story ought to be simplified and shortened and more of it written in the style of the beginning and the end.

I hate to suggest all this just as you are leaving for Asheville but as I have said before it is much better to have a story right and have it bought than to hurry it and have it declined.

Sincerely yours,

DICTATED BY HAROLD OBER
WHO LEFT BEFORE SIGNING

April 6, 1936

ENC. THE PEARL AND THE FUR

TL (cc), 2pp. (AO)

In April 1936 Zelda left Sheppard-Pratt, and Fitzgerald took her to Highland Hospital in Asheville, North Carolina. He returned to Baltimore in May, finally moving to Grove Park Inn in Asheville during the month of July.

F. Scott Fitzgerald, Esq.
Grove Park Inn
Asheville, N. C.

Dear Scott:

As I wired you, we have sold MAKE YOURSELF AT HOME to the Pictorial and they are paying $2500. for it. I think the check will come along fairly soon and that I shall be able to send you some money in a few days.

Sincerely yours,
[Harold Ober]

April 8, 1936

TL (cc), 1p. (AO)

F. Scott Fitzgerald, Es q.
Grove Park Inn
Asheville, N. C.

Dear Scott:

I have collected the check from the Pictorial for MAKE YOUR-SELF AT HOME and on the basis of giving you $1500. of this check, I am wiring to your bank today $800. On April 6th I sent you $200., on the 9th $200., and on the 14th $300., which makes $700.-combined with the $800. I am sending you today makes up the $1500. Will this be all right until the next story comes along?

I am enclosing something that came in the mail without any address.

Sincerely yours,
[Harold Ober]

April 17, 1936

TL (cc), 1p. (AO)

> Story much improved being typed for Post.
> Harold Ober

Wire (cc) to Fitzgerald 21 April 1936. (AO)

> Is it absolutely necessary that you have four hundred now.
> Harold Ober

Wire (cc) to Fitzgerald 22 April 1936. (AO)

F. Scott Fitzgerald, Esq.
Grove Park Inn
Asheville, N. C.

Dear Scott:

I wired you yesterday that the Gwen story THE PEARL AND THE FUR was much improved and that I was having it typed for the Post. It is true that the story is improved but when I gave the new typed copy a careful reading it seemed to me to contain a great many improbabilities. I have since had other readings on the story and every reading seems to disclose further improbabilities. In your letter accompanying the new version you said you didn't feel able to do any more work on the story so we have tried to fix up the most glaring inconsistencies.

After thinking the matter over very carefully I think that it would be a great mistake to offer this story to the Post. Mr. Lorimer made it very clear to me that he could not buy another Gwen story unless it were very much better than the last one he bought. In my opinion this story is far below the first two. The story starts very well indeed but it is terribly full of holes and when you try to patch up one hole, another one appears somewhere else. I feel it is very important for your future relations with the Post that the next story they see of yours shall be an extremely good one. This is what I'd like to do: We would like to work on the story for a few days and see if we can't fix up the inconsistencies in it, then I'd like to have the story retyped changing Gwen's name to the name used in the story I just sold the Pictorial. I feel sure that you do not want to work any more on the story just now and any changes I make in the story will be merely changes of timing and correction of inaccuracies. None of your dialogue will have to be changed. Let me know how you feel about this. In the meantime I hope you will be able to start work on a new story. I think you have excellent material for these Gwen stories.

If on the other hand you want to do further work on this story let me know and I'll send you a list of the improbabilities we have found in the story. The Post is a very difficult magazine to get by with improbabilities. They ferret them out with a fine-tooth comb.

I have your telegram asking if I can deposit $400. I have wired back asking if it is absolutely necessary to have this now. I'll try to get it for you if you have to have it but I had hoped you would be able to get along for a little while on the unexpected Pictorial money.

> Sincerely yours,
> [Harold Ober]

April 22, 1936

TL (cc), 2pp. (AO)

F. Scott Fitzgerald Esq.,
Grove Park Inn,
Asheville, N.C.

Dear Mr. Fitzgerald:

Since Mr. Ober was not in this morning when your telegram arrived, I read it to him over the telephone and he asked me to tell you he would write to you early Monday. He also asked me to send you the Gwen story together with a list of the inconsistencies about which he wrote you and a list of the cuts made. The carbon is a copy of the story with the changes and cuts made in accordance with sheet No.1.

Sincerely,
[Constance Smith]

April 25,1936

TL (cc), 1p. (AO)

THE PEARL AND THE FUR
F. SCOTT FITZGERALD.

All numberings refer to original copy.

Page 4. —Direction changed because of Pier number change (Pier 97 is at foot of West 57th St. and most boats for West Indies sail from there)

Timing changed to fit further incidents.

Page 5. —Timing changed to make it logical for Mrs. TenBrook to come aboard so early. "Central Park Zoo specified - also for timing. Explains cut on page 7.

"In a new uniform" cut. N.Y.taxi drivers don't wear uniforms.

Deadhead stuff cut because seemed irrelevant and all this part had to be speeded up. (See page 6 for similar cuts)

Part about his looking up zoo cut, because of change to Central Park Zoo whose location should be known to any New Yorker.

Page 6. —Age cut because N.Y.law requires hack drivers to be 21.

Page 8. "in front of the church" cut, because they are in Park.

Page 9. —Directions changed for obvious reasons. "Chateau" changed to mansion because existence of chateaus in N.Y. doubtful.

Page 10. Cuts and changes made for timing purposes.

Page 14. Insert to explain how other taxi-driver knew about the cape.

Page 18. "windowless" changed to "dark" because doubted any room would be <u>without</u> windows.

<u>Further changes</u>: Eliminate "mention"on Page 18 of chauffeur so as not to raise question in reader's mind <u>why</u> Mrs. TenBrook went in a taxi.

1.   No girls school (from out of town) would let girls of 13 wander around New York alone.
2.   Why would anyone take a chinchilla coat to West Indies in Spring?
3.   The four boys wouldn't let girl go off in taxi with the chinchilla boat. One of them at least would go with her, or they would all go to the boat together.
4.   Gwen goes down to boat for the romance of travel(presented earlier) why doesn't she stay as long as possible to see people on board etc. Instead she gets off very early to go to the zoo—why? It isn't time for lunch.
5.   Gwen gets on board the boat—no passengers, not even a guard at gangplank—unliekly—why go so early? (page 5)
6.   Why does a rich woman board a boat several hours before it sails?
7.   Why do all four boys go back to house for coat? Why do any of them go if rich woman telephones and finds it isn't there?
8.   Exchange of drivers not plausible. I think a driver would always finish his fare and get his tip.
9.   Women do not have their names in their coats.—or addresses?
10.   Gwen after protecting coat so carefully wouldn't let driver carry it when he gets to boat.
11.   Nobody could be locked in bird house at noon?
12.   Why does rich woman go down in taxi—while the boys seems to have come back in a limousine?
13.   Taxi drivers have to be 21 in N.Y.City
14.   No taxi driver in N.Y. would start out with a passenger the first time he ever drives a cab. (Page 6)
15.   Its long after 12—boat sails at 1—boys haven't much time to dance. (Page 10)
16.   Tough taxi driver—his arriving comes as a surprise—still seems improbable—also the maids telephoning. Perhaps the rich woman should have telephoned—if she remembered taxi Co. Better say—"Rich woman telephoned to say she had left a coat in the taxi she took to the pier 97—and then word came in coat had been found in taxi? (Page 15)

17. Boat is being cleared—Rich woman says she could arrange by long distance for Gwen to sail—Pretty quick work'. (Page 18).

F. Scott Fitzgerald, Esq.
Grove Park Inn
Asheville, N. C.

Dear Scott:

I am delighted that you have decided to do a little more work on THE PEARL AND THE FUR. I am sure you can make it a story that the Post will be delighted to have.

The list of comments I sent you needs a little explanation. These were the combined comments of three readers. Some of them are trivial and some of them apply only to the changes that we made in the version we had typed.

While all of these inconsistencies might not occur to any one reader, some of them would I think be noticed by any reader of the story, so I hope you can get rid of as many of them as possible.

It seems to me that the most necessary thing to do in the story is to arrange Gwen's adventure so that it will take place in a very short space of time. A rich woman used to travelling would not board a boat very long before its time of sailing. It seems to me therefore that the finding of the coat, etc. ought to be arranged in such a way that everything could happen within the space of three-quarters of an hour or an hour.

Couldn't you have the young taxi driver lose his job for not reporting the loss of the coat? This would do away with the second taxi driver who I think is very difficult to introduce in a plausible manner.

I hope you know that no one reads your stories with more pleasure and with more partiality than I do and that I wouldn't suggest your making changes in a story unless it seemed to me important that you should do so. Of course much the easiest thing for me to do would be to have had your copy typed and send it as it was to Philadelphia but I am sure you want me to use my best judgment and so far I think we have agreed very well on the changes that are advisable to make in your stories.

Sincerely yours,
[Harold Ober]

April 27, 1936

TL (cc), 1p. (AO)

F. Scott Fitzgerald, Esq.
Grove Park Inn
Asheville, N. C.

Dear Scott:

I have a letter from Miss Neall saying she thinks you have strengthened INSIDE THE HOUSE very much by the changes you have made in it.

Sincerely yours,
[Harold Ober]

April 30, 1936

TL (cc), 1p. (AO)

WIRING TWO HUNDRED STORY READS VERY WELL NOW ON WAY TO POST
    Harold Ober

Wire (cc) to Fitzgerald 4 May 1936. (AO)

F. Scott Fitzgerald, Esq.
Cambridge Arms
Charles & 34th Streets
Baltimore, Maryland

Dear Scott:

The story came in this morning and I also have your telegram from Baltimore. How long are you going to be there? I have just finished reading THE PEARL AND THE FUR and although I have gone over it a number of times I really enjoyed it this time and I think you have done a very good job on it. It is already on the way to the Post.

I am a little short at the moment but I have wired you $200. this morning.

Did you get a letter that Paramount wants you to sign regarding the verse on the title page of THE GREAT GATSBY? They have called me up this morning to know whether we ever got the signed letter.

Dick Knight,* whom I met with you several years ago, called me this morning for your address. I gave it to him. He tells me he has had articles accepted by several magazines in the last week or two.

---

*A New York lawyer friend of the Fitzgeralds.

Let me know how Zelda is and tell Scotty we hope she is going to make us a visit sometime this summer.

Sincerely yours,
[Harold Ober]

May 4, 1936

TL (cc), 1p. (AO)

F. Scott Fitzgerald, Esq.
1 East 34th Street
Baltimore, Maryland

Dear Scott:

I'll try to get a copy of MAKE YOURSELF AT HOME within a few days. We haven't one here but I have just got from Pictorial Review the names of the characters in the first story which may help you temporarily:

You called the child Dolly Haines; her school teacher was named Grace Terhune, the boy in the story Clarke Cresswell; the maid Hazel Dawn; the uncle Charlie Craig. You mention two families, the Appletons, whom Dolly had just visited, and the Martins, whom she was supposed to visit. Major Redfern, Miss Willie and Hep Morrison were the crooks. The society girl was named Angela Duckney.

Sincerely yours,
[Harold Ober]

May 7, 1936

I hope you won't have to use any of these names on the present story!
Have you that letter Paramount wanted you to sign?[†]

TL (cc), 1p. (AO)

F. Scott Fitzgerald, Esq.
1 East 34th Street
Baltimore, Maryland

Dear Scott:

I have a note from Miss Neall this morning telling me what she has already told you about the Gwen story THE PEARL AND THE FUR. She tells me you have decided to drop the series for the

---

[†]The postscripts were added in Ober's hand.

Post but I think we will be able to sell this story to the Pictorial after you have changed the names.

I am having a copy made of the story the Pictorial bought and will send it to you by special delivery when it is ready.

Sincerely yours,
[Harold Ober]

May 8, 1936
TL (cc), 1p. (AO)

F. Scott Fitzgerald, Esq.
1 East 34th Street
Baltimore, Maryland

Dear Scott:

THE PEARL AND THE FUR is very much better than any other version and I am sorry the Post could not have seen it first in this version. However, I think you are probably right that it would be a mistake to ask them to read the story again. We are having it typed and I'll show it to the Pictorial.

I wish I could have a talk with you and I'll be glad to run down to Baltimore any time that you feel like seeing me.

If Scotty is not going to camp I hope she can have a long visit with us this summer.

Katharine Brush told me today that a year or two ago there was an article in Fortune on Metro Goldwyn. One of her friends brought the article to her and pointed out a line which said that she was one of the first imitators of Scott Fitzgerald. This friend thought she would be very angry but she told me it was the highest compliment she had ever been paid.

I'll write you again in a day or two—I haven't any more time tonight.

Sincerely yours,
[Harold Ober]

May 11, 1936
TL (cc), 1p. (AO)

F. Scott Fitzgerald, Esq.
1 East 34th Street
Baltimore, Maryland

Dear Scott:

I talked today to one of the editors of the Pictorial. The other editor is away for a day or two and I am afraid I won't have an answer on the story until the middle or latter part of the week.

The moment Swanson gets here I'll see about coming down to see you and I'll let you know when he arrives.

Sincerely yours,
[Harold Ober]

May 18, 1936

TL (cc), 1p. (AO)

F. Scott Fitzgerald, Esq.
1 East 34th Street
Baltimore, Maryland

Dear Scott:

I have been thinking about the publication of Zelda's letters and while I think it is something that should be done sometime, I do not feel sure that now is the time to do it. At any rate it seems to me a thing that ought to be done very carefully. I should think the letters would have to be edited and you yourself would have to do considerable writing to make the connection between the letters clear. It doesn't seem to me that it is a thing that you ought to put very much time on just now. I feel very sure, however, that Zelda's letters would make a very beautiful book, and sometime I hope they will be published.

R.K.O. want to have an original written for a boy star, Bobby Breen, who is starring in the picture LET'S SING AGAIN. This boy is six years old and has a fine soprano voice. If the picture has been released in Baltimore you might see it. If you think you could write an original for this boy, I think R.K.O. would pay something like $2500. down and when the treatment was finished the price would be determined before you started work. All they would need would be a rounded outline of the story. It need not be put into moving picture scenario form. I am enclosing a review of LET'S SING AGAIN from Variety.

If you think you could write a story for a boy of this age let me know and I'll see what can be done, but don't spend any time writing the story until I know whether we can get a definite order for it, and the $2500. before you begin.

Sincerely yours,
[Harold Ober]

May 21, 1936

TL (cc), 1p. (AO)

F. Scott Fitzgerald, Esq.
1 East 34th Street
Baltimore, Maryland

Dear Scott:

I can't be absolutely sure but I think I shall be able to sell the second Gwen story (with the names changed)‡ to the Pictorial. They have promised a definite decision on this by Monday and I hope to be able to wire you on Monday that it has been sold.

I am sorry you are laid up with lumbago.

I am a little doubtful whether Swanie is going to be able to get down to Baltimore. He comes to New York very rarely and cannot leave his office in California for very long and he is tied up with engagements for every day he is here. I have talked the picture situation over with him at great length and if it isn't possible for him to go down I'll go down to see you as soon as I possibly can.

We wired you fifty dollars this morning and on receipt of your second wire I am sending you another fifty dollars.

Sincerely yours,
[Harold Ober]

May 28, 1936

TL (cc), 1p. (AO)

F. Scott Fitzgerald, Esq.
1 East 34th Street
Baltimore, Maryland

Dear Scott:

I tried to get you on the telephone this afternoon but no answer.

I have been talking to the editor of the Pictorial and the best I have been able to get him to do is to say that he will pay $1000. for THE PEARL AND THE FUR and this on condition that they can make some changes in the story where it doesn't seem to them plausible. The editor says he doesn't want you to feel that he is trying to take advantage of you but he doesn't feel that this story is anywhere near as good as the first one they bought. He says he likes the character Dolly and if you have ideas for other stories about this character, he might like to have another one or two and I think he would pay the same price as he paid for the first story but he would want first a paragraph or two telling him what the story would be about. You might let me know what you want me to do

---

‡See 11 May Ober letter.

about this. I am afraid we are rather at the mercy of the Pictorial as I think it would be very difficult to change Gwen's name again and try to sell it to a third magazine.

Graeme Lorimer was in yesterday and said that you had talked on the telephone to Miss Neall about CYCLONE IN SILENT LAND¶ but he didn't know what had been decided about it. He said there were some things about the story he liked very much indeed. I presume from your telegram that Miss Neall gave you some suggestions and that you are rewriting the story.

I don't think you can count on anything from Hollywood at the present time. I think the days are over when an author with a good name can go out to Hollywood for a month or two and pick up a sizeable amount of money. They would rather have a dramatist that has written a play that is a flop, whom they can get on a long contract at a moderate salary.

I am sure you can fix up the interne story so the Post will buy it.

Sincerely yours,
[Harold Ober]

June 5, 1936

TL (cc), 1p. (AO)

F. Scott Fitzgerald Esq.,
Cambridge Apts.
Charles & 34th Sts.,
Baltimore, Md.

Dear Scott:

The new editor of College Humour has asked us for a story of yours. I find we have here four unsold ones, which we might show him. They are, TRAVEL TOGETHER, NIGHTMARE, WHAT TO DO ABOUT IT and ON YOUR OWN. of which I believe TRAVEL TOGETHER is the best of the lot.#

Since College Humour's outside price is $500.00 and since these are all old stories you may not wish to have them offered. Will you drop me a line about this?

Sincerely,
[Constance Smith]

June 15, 1936

TL (cc), 1p. (AO)

¶This story about a nurse named Trouble is not the same story as "Trouble" and was never published. Fitzgerald was attempting to start a series about a nurse.
College Humor published none of these stories.

F. Scott Fitzgerald, Esq.
1 East 34th Street
Baltimore, Maryland

Dear Scott:

I think your idea for Bobby Breen is a good one but I think it is dangerous to do anything with it in its present shape. I spoke to Costain about this and he said he thought it was dangerous to offer an idea to a picture company unless it was worked out at some length with the individuality of the characters clearly outlined. I don't believe it would pay you just now to take the time to do this. I'll see if there is any safe way of presenting the idea as it stands.

The New Yorker still has the short piece you sent.* I think they will decide about it soon.

Sincerely yours,
[Harold Ober]

June 25, 1936
I hope to get down to see you before long.†
TL (cc), 1p. (AO)

F. Scott Fitzgerald, Esq.
1 East 34th Street
Baltimore, Maryland

Dear Scott:

I have your new story and I had a talk with Graeme Lorimer today and he told me that the story had arrived safely in Philadelphia. I have read about half of the story and like it very much indeed.

Sincerely yours,
[Harold Ober]

June 29, 1936
TL (cc), 1p. (AO)

F. Scott Fitzgerald, Esq.
1 East 34th Street
Baltimore, Maryland

Dear Scott:

I am very sorry that your mother has been ill and I hope she is now better. Let me know the next time you write.

---

*"Thank You for the Light" was rejected by *The New Yorker, College Humor, Harper's Bazaar,* and *Vanity Fair* and was not published.
†Added in Ober's hand.

I finished the new interne story TROUBLE‡ last night and it seems to me a good story and if the Post should decline it I am pretty sure I can sell it elsewhere. I spoke to Graeme Lorimer this morning and he said he believed his father was going to decide on the story sometime today.

Sincerely yours,
[Harold Ober]

June 30, 1936

TL (cc), 1p. (AO)

F. Scott Fitzgerald, Esq.

Dear Scott:
You may be interested in the following in a letter from Miss Neall:

"Personally, this last piece encouraged me a great deal because it shows that Mr. Fitzgerald still can write the simple love story, free of the melodrama that he introduced into his recent manuscripts."

And here is what the New Yorker says about THANK YOU FOR THE LIGHT:

"We're afraid that this Fitzgerald story is altogether out of the question. It seems to us so curious and so unlike the kind of thing we associate with him and really too fantastic. We would give a lot, of course, to have a Scott Fitzgerald story and we hope that you will send us something that seems more suitable. Thank you, anyhow, for letting us see this."

Sincerely yours,
[Harold Ober]

July 2, 1936

TL (cc), 1p. (AO)

F. Scott Fitzgerald, Esq.
1 East 34th Street
Baltimore, Maryland

Dear Scott:
I enjoyed my short visit with you Friday and I hope you can make us a real visit sometime this summer.

---

‡ *The Saturday Evening Post*, 6 March 1937. Fitzgerald's last *Saturday Evening Post* story.

I am sending along the following paragraph from a letter I got this morning from Miss Neall:

"Mr. Fitzgerald told me on the telephone that he thought he would use his nurse "Trouble", the heroine in his last story, in another story. When I mentioned this to Mr. Lorimer he seemed to think that it would be much better to have an entirely new character, even though she, too, is a nurse. Mr. Fitzgerald said he left the ending of his story rather up in the air because he thought he might want to use "Trouble" the second time. Frankly, I think his story would have been a lot better if he had given it a little more definite ending. We have often found that when writers have a series in mind they sometimes unconsciously hold over material for a future story that could be used in the one they are working on. I thought you might be interested to know Mr. Lorimer's reaction, so, if Mr. Fitzgerald says anything to you, you can advise him to create a new heroine."

I am sorry the question went up to Mr. Lorimer at all for I think if you wrote another good story about Trouble, he would have liked it. Trouble is I think a delightful character. Perhaps you can write the next story using some other nurse and then go back to Trouble in the story after that.

Sincerely yours,
[Harold Ober]

July 6, 1936

TL (cc), 1p. (AO)

F. Scott Fitzgerald Esq.,
Grove Park Inn,
Asheville, N.C.

Dear Scott:

I have your telegram asking the shortest number of words for a Post serial. The Post buys three parters and these should be from twenty-five to thirty thousand words in length. They also like four, five and six parters.

They do not like two part stories but occasionally buy them. Stories from fifteen to twenty thousand words in length are usually put into two parters. Mr. Lorimer has told me a number of times that he doesn't like two part stories and he has asked me to discourage authors from writing them. One of the most successful stories he had last year was a story we sold him by Richard Sherman entitled TO MARY WITH LOVE, which was a two parter.

Sincerely yours,

[Harold Ober]

July 20, 1936

TL (cc), 1p. (AO)

SORRY ABOUT ACCIDENT# WIRING THREE HUNDRED
Harold Ober

Wire (cc) to Fitzgerald 28 July 1936. (AO)

F. Scott Fitzgerald, Esq.
Grove Park Inn
Asheville, N. C.

Dear Scott:

How is your shoulder. I know that a shoulder is a very complicated thing to break and I hope that it is not very painful. Get somebody to write me and let me know how you are.

Sincerely yours,

[Harold Ober]

August 6, 1936
I have a note this morning so you needn't answer this.*

TL (cc), 1p. (AO)

POSSIBILITY HOLLYWOOD JOB ON STORY OF ADOLESCENTS AROUND SEVENTEEN YEARS MINIMUM FOUR WEEKS GUARANTEE FIFTEEN HUNDRED A WEEK STOP IF JOB APPEALS AND MATERIALIZES WHEN COULD YOU LEAVE WIRE ANSWER
HAROLD OBER.

Wire to Fitzgerald 13 August 1936. (AO)

FINE STORY THINK POST WILL LIKE IT WE WANT SCOTTIE
Harold Ober

Wire (cc) to Fitzgerald 18 August 1936. (AO)

#Fitzgerald injured his shoulder while diving into a swimming pool.
*Added in Ober's hand. Fitzgerald's letter is missing.

F. Scott Fitzgerald, Esq.
Grove Park Inn
Asheville, N. C.

Dear Scott:

I like THUMBS UP† very much indeed. I think it is one of the best stories you have written for a long time. It is a little long and perhaps later on can be cut. It seems to me also that with the addition of a sentence here and there you might give a little more warmth in the relationship between Tib and Joseph. I don't think it would have harmed to have let him recognize her a little sooner.

Of course we shall be delighted to have Scotty visit us. We have been counting on it all along and we shall be very disappointed if she doesn't. My family is in Vermont at present but we expect to get back to Scarsdale about the 5th or 6th of September. When does Scotty get through at camp?

I expect to hear something from Hollywood within the next day or two and I may call you up on the telephone tonight.

> Sincerely yours,
> [Harold Ober]

August 18, 1936

TL (cc), 1p. (AO)

> THINK CAN SELL AMERICAN OR ELSEWHERE IF SHORTENED AND TWO MAIN CHARACTERS MADE MORE SYMPATHETIC SENDING THREE BUT WORRIED ABOUT AMOUNT WRITING
>   Harold Ober
>
> Wire (cc) to Fitzgerald 21 August 1936. (AO)

F. Scott Fitzgerald, Esq.
Grove Park Inn
Asheville, N. C.

Dear Scott:

As I wired you, I think the story ought to be shortened and simplified and I think you ought to see if you can't give a little more warmth to the story between the sister and Tib. If you have them recognize each other sooner you can make any conversation they

---

†This story was also titled "When This Cruel War—" and "Dentist Appointment." After being rejected by *American Magazine, Collier's, Cosmopolitan, Country Gentleman, Delineator, Ladies' Home Journal, Liberty, McCall's, Pictorial Review, Redbook, The Saturday Evening Post, Woman's Home Companion,* and *This Week,* it was published by *Collier's* as "End of Hate," 22 June 1940.

have count for more. You can make changes in pencil on your carbon of the story and I can have it typed very quickly here.

I am wiring you the $300. you ask for. I take it from the telegram that you want it sent to you at Asheville. You have enough worry without my adding to it but do you realize that this $300. makes the amount I have advanced you almost exactly $11,000.? This is a good deal of a load for me to carry but I have faith in you and I want to do everything I possibly can to help you. I wish you would, however, fix up that assignment just as soon as you possibly can. I think all you have to do is to write a letter to the insurance company and they will send you the necessary papers.‡

The moving picture deal is held up temporarily because a friend of one of the men said he had seen you in New York in December when you had been drinking. I have assured them that you have not been drinking this year and I think and hope things can be straightened out in a few days. If you could go out I think the change might be good for you and there is no reason why you couldn't save a good part of the amount you make.

Sincerely yours,
[Harold Ober]

August 21, 1936

TL (cc), 1p. (AO)

F. Scott Fitzgerald, Esq.
Grove Park Inn
Asheville, North Carolina

Dear Scott:

I had a long talk today with Knopf§ who is interested in having you go to Hollywood for Metro and I think I have convinced him that you would do a good job and that they need not worry about you. Knopf is going back to Hollywood tomorrow and will go into the matter again and let me know what is decided. Knopf told me that things worked out badly the last time you were there but he wants you and is convinced that you will work seriously.

I think those confounded Esquire articles¶ have done you a great

---

‡Fitzgerald assigned to Ober a portion of his life insurance in the event that he died before his debt to Ober was paid.
§Edwin Knopf of MGM.
¶The "Crack-Up" series.

deal of harm and I hope you won't do any more.

Sincerely,

[Harold Ober]

August 26, 1936

TL (cc), 1p. (AO)

F. Scott Fitzgerald, Esq.
Grove Park Inn
Asheville, N. C.

Dear Scott:

I have your telegram asking if I can raise $1000. and wire $300. to Baltimore immediately. I have wired $300. to the bank in Baltimore but I haven't any way of raising the additional $700. I have been trying to get a decision on THUMBS UP but I shall have to wait another day or two for this.

When do you expect the $2000. that is forthcoming from the estate? I shall need before the end of the month the $300. I have sent you today and I hope you will get the $2000. so that you can send me some money before then as I have a lot of payments coming due which have to be made.

I wish I knew where I could raise some more money. I am hoping to sell THUMBS UP before long but you know how difficult it is to predict the sale of a story.

Scotty came in to town with me yesterday and is staying for a day or two with her aunt.# She is very happy about school and she called me up just now to say that she was shopping for her uniform. She was delighted to get your letter yesterday. I am very glad that she is going to the Walker School as I know several girls who have gone there and I am sure Scotty will do very well there. She is coming back to Scarsdale with me Wednesday or Thursday and I hope she can stay with us until she starts school. Scotty says you are coming up to take her to school and if you do I hope you will come out to Scarsdale and I think we can arrange to drive you both to Simsbury if you would like to have us do so. Dick and his mother are now on their way to Exeter and Nat, my younger boy, begins school tomorrow.

Sincerely yours,

[Harold Ober]

September 22, 1936

TL (cc), 1p. (AO)

#Mrs. Newman Smith, Zelda Fitzgerald's sister Rosalind.

F. Scott Fitzgerald, Esq.
Grove Park Inn
Asheville, N. C.

Dear Scott:

If you haven't seen the enclosed you will eventually so I may as well send it along to you.* I don't believe you had any idea the reporter was going to do what he did in this article. I suppose there is nothing to be done about it now.

Scottie has just come in and I am taking her out in the train to Scarsdale and I'll do my best to keep it from her.

Sincerely yours,
[Harold Ober]

September 25, 1936
N Y Evening Post article with picture of Scott in bath robe. It shocked Scott so that he stopped drinking.†

TL (cc), 1p. (AO)

F. Scott Fitzgerald, Esq.
Grove Park Inn
Asheville, N. C.

Dear Scott:

Scottie was disappointed that you couldn't come out to Scarsdale and drive up to school with her but I explained to her that you were not well enough to do it. She drove up with Anne‡ today and I am sure she is going to be very happy at the school. Last night she showed me her new uniform and all her new purchases. She is a charming girl and we are going to miss her.

Please do not worry too much about the piece in the New York Evening Post. Only the first early afternoon edition had your picture on the front page and it is a very cheap paper and very few people read it. I sometimes think that almost any kind of publicity is good publicity. I know that you are going to write other fine novels and many fine stories—better ones than you have ever done before.

---

*Michel Mok, in "The Other Side of Paradise," *New York Post*, 25 September 1936 —an interview with Fitzgerald in Asheville, N.C., on his fortieth birthday—showed Fitzgerald as a despairing drunk.

†Added in Ober's hand.

‡Mrs. Harold Ober.

I haven't any good news for you yet regarding the Civil War story[§]—it is with the Cosmopolitan now.

I hope you can come up to New York later on in the Fall and go up to visit Scottie. We will be glad to drive you up when you go.

Sincerely yours,
[Harold Ober]

October 2, 1936

TL (cc), 1p. (AO)

(personal: Mr Ober only)

Dear Harold: I'll try to summarize all that's happened in the last two weeks. 1st about the story:[¶]

It is all corrected except one part but I'm in a quandary about getting it typed because I can't send it off as is without having even the original that being in shorthand as the arm was just a broken mess one week (before last)[#] + I had to dictate again. The two available stenographers I found between jobs. + both are engaged but I'll think of something + shoot to get it off tomorrow night [, pe] its about a cartoonist + I like it + so [does] do the people who've heard parts of it.

2nd About the article about Michael Muck. I was in bed with temp about 102 when the [obliterated] phone rang and a voice said that this party had come all the way from N. Y to interview me. I fell for this like a damn fool, got him up, gave him a drink + accepted his exterior good manners. He had some relative with mental trouble (wife or mother) so I talked to him freely about treatments symtoms ect, about being depressed at advancing age and a little desperate about the wasted summer with this shoulder and arm—perhaps more freely than if had been well. I hadn't the faintest suspicion what would happen + I've never been a publicity seeker + never gotten a rotten deal before. When that thing came it seemed about the end and I got hold of a morphine file and swallowed four grains enough to kill a horse. It happened to be an overdose and almost before I could get to the bed I vomited the whole thing and the nurse came in + saw the empty phial + there was hell to pay. [D] for awhile + afterwards I felt like a fool. And if I ever see, Mr Mock what will happen will be very swift and sudden. <u>Dont tell Perkins.</u>

[§]"Thumbs Up" ("End of Hate").
[¶]Possibly "They Never Grow Older," never published.
[#]Fitzgerald reinjured his shoulder by falling while he was still in a cast.

As to Scotty there's nothing I can say to thank you; when I'm straight there will be expenses you've undertaken for her we can allocate.

For the financial angle: I wait from day to day—unable now to buy medicines even, or to leave to the hotel because I couldn't pay a r.r fare [finance]—and twenty thousand of mine lies idle in a Baltimore Bank. Edgar Allen Poe *Jr.** the exector says he can advance me $2000 to $5000 (perhaps that much) but I wire him again and there is no news up to noon today. The hotel, doctors, Zelda's clinic ect clamor for money but there is none. By Maryland law I cant get the whole sum for six months but the other I cant understand. I want this to catch the only mail. I'll write the rest this afternoon.

> Ever
> Scott

ALS (pencil), 3pp. n.d.—received 5 October 1936. Asheville, N.C. (AO)

F. Scott Fitzgerald, Esq.
Grove Park Inn
Asheville, N. C.

Dear Scott:

I have been trying for the last day or two to write you a letter but a number of authors have been in town and I haven't had a moment to write.

Your telegram came in today and I have wired you $200. With all the troubles you are having I hate to tell you about my own but it really has seriously embarrassed me to send you the money I have been sending you recently. I have had a lot of things to meet recently what with schools and other things and I hope that you can realize on the legacy very soon and send me as much as you can. Of course it would help some if we could sell a story and I hope the new story will come along as you say within two or three days. The Civil War story is in many ways a good piece of work but it is not what editors expect from you.

We had a letter from Scottie the other day and she seems to be very happy at school.

> Sincerely yours,
> [Harold Ober]

October 8, 1936

TL (cc), 1p. (AO)

---

*Lawyer who was settling Fitzgerald's mother's estate.

F. Scott Fitzgerald, Esq.
Grove Park Inn
Asheville, N. C.

Dear Scott:

I received your special delivery letter and if you can do what you outline in that letter I think I shall be able to get along. Take your time on the story you are working on and get it just the way you want it. It is much better to have it right than to hurry it.

We received a very nice letter from Zelda and one of her watercolors. It is a very beautiful one. We also had a letter from Scottie yesterday and she seems to be getting along very well in school. She is a delightful child and she writes delightful letters.

I hope your shoulder is getting better and that everything is going as well as possible with you. I hope you are not worrying any more about the newspaper article. I think newspaper men are probably right when they say that almost any kind of publicity is better than none.

> Sincerelyyours,
> [Harold Ober]

October 14, 1936

TL (cc), 1p. (AO)

F. Scott Fitzgerald, Esq;
Grove Park Inn
Asheville, N. C.

Dear Scott:

We stopped in Simsbury yesterday and took Scottie out to lunch with us. She was prettier than I have ever seen her. She said she had lost about five pounds which she gained after she left camp. She showed us all over the school and I am sure she is very happy there. Miss Sergeant and one of her teachers told us that she was doing very good work and that everybody liked her. She is looking forward to a visit from you at Thanksgiving time.

Are you going to try to finish the story you are working on before you take your rest? Don't bother to answer this. I hope your shoulder is better.

> Sincerely yours,
> [Harold Ober]

October 19, 1936

TL (cc), 1p. (AO)

F. Scott Fitzgerald, Esq.
Grove Park Inn
Asheville, N. C.

Dear Scott:

I haven't bothered you with letters lately because I wanted you to have a complete rest from writing or even thinking about writing. I am glad, however, to have your note this morning and to know that you will be in New York either before or after Thanksgiving. This means I suppose that you are going up to see Scottie and I know she will be delighted for she has been counting on it.

I am sorry about the mixup over the $50. that was wired by Postal Telegraph to Baltimore. At the top of the telegram was written 'Asheville by way of Baltimore' so I thought you were on the way to Baltimore and that you would get the money at the Postal Telegraph office in Baltimore. If you still need the $50. let me know where to send it. I understand that you have given up your apartment in Baltimore and have no address there at the present time. Is that right?

Regarding unpublished stories: Both the McCall stories have been published. THE INTIMATE STRANGER was published in June 1935, and A COURSE IN LANGUAGES was published in April 1936 under the title IMAGE IN THE HEART. If you haven't seen copies of these magazines I'll have them for you when you get to New York.

The article MY LOST CITY which you wrote for the Cosmopolitan was one of a series. The Cosmopolitan ran a number of them and then decided that the readers might get a little tired of them so stopped publication. They tell me, however, that they are going to start very soon to publish the remaining articles in the series and your article will be published among the first.

Edwin Balmer tells me that GODS OF THE DARKNESS is now in type and that he is going to publish it within the next few months.

I am glad I am going to see you next week.

Sincerely yours,
[Harold Ober]

November 19, 1936

TL (cc), 1p. (AO)

F. Scott Fitzgerald, Esq.
Grove Park Inn
Asheville, N. C.

Dear Scott:

I don't know why I forgot about the two girl stories when I wrote you about unpublished stories. These were sold to the Pictorial Review and the editor tells me they will probably be published in the Spring not before March or April.

I am sorry not to see you but I think it would be a great mistake for you to come north in this kind of weather until you are perfectly well. I am afraid Scottie was disappointed but I am sure she doesn't want you to come up when you are not well. We hear from her quite often and will try to run up and see her the first chance we get.

The last time we saw Scottie she was hoping to go to Baltimore for Christmas because there were some dances she wanted to go to. If she doesn't go to Baltimore and there isn't any other place she particularly wants to go, we will be delighted to have her come to Scarsdale.

I hope you are getting a rest and I hope you will soon be in fine shape.

Sincerely yours,
[Harold Ober]

November 27, 1936

TL (cc), 1p. (AO)

F. Scott Fitzgerald, Esq.
Grove Park Inn
Asheville, N. C.

Dear Scott:

Of course we shall be delighted to have Scottie until you are ready for her and I'll meet her train on Friday, the 18th, and take her out to Scarsdale with me.

I am sorry you have been laid up again. I hope you will be able to get some rest before you start again to work.

I am writing Scottie a note telling her I will meet her.

Sincerely yours,
[Harold Ober]

December 9, 1936

TL (cc), 1p. (AO)

SCOTTIES SIDE KICK PEACHES¶ IS GIVING SOME PARTY IN BAL-
TIMORE ON THE NINETEENTH AND SHE IS DETERMINED TO
BE AMONG THOSE PRESENT STOP I HOPE TO HEAVEN YOU
HAVENT MADE ANY SPECIAL PREPARATIONS FOR HER IF YOU
STILL WANT HER I KNOW SHE WOULD LOVE TO BE WITH YOU
FOR COUPLE OF DAYS TOWARD THE END OF HOLIDAYS AM
COUNTING ON SEEING YOU THE TWENTY THIRD IF POSSIBLE
FITZGERALD.

Wire to Ober 17 December 1936. Asheville, N.C.

F. Scott Fitzgerald, Esq.
c/o Mrs. Isobel Owens
5101 Roland Avenue
Baltimore, Maryland

Dear Scott:

I haven't much idea where you are—I think you may be in Baltimore. I had a telegram just before Christmas from Edgar Allan
Poe, Jr. asking if I couldn't deposit $500. for you but I was absolutely
broke at the time and will be until after the first of the year. He said
you were expecting some money in a couple of days so I hope that
came through all right and relieved the difficulty.

Anne received a very attractive Christmas present from Scottie
and wants to thank her for it but doesn't know where to reach her.
We are hoping that she will stay with us before she goes back to
school. We also received a very attractive Christmas card from
Zelda and you and I want to thank you for that.

I know that 1936 has been a very bad year for you and I hope and
feel sure that 1937 is going to be a better one. If you can only get
back your health I am sure that everything will be all right.

Here is a comment from an editor who has just turned down
THUMBS UP:

"I thought it was swell but all the femmes down here said it was
horrid. The thumbs, I suppose, were too much for them."

I have talked to several editors and I think it is mostly because of
the incident about the thumbs that this story has not sold. Another
criticism of the story has been that it wanders about a good deal. Do
you think there is anything that you could substitute for the hanging by the thumbs—something that is not so harrowing? I think the
story might be salvaged if you feel like doing a little more work on
it.

¶Peaches Finney, daughter of Mr. and Mrs. Eben Finney of Baltimore.

Please drop me a line and let me know where and how you are.
                              Sincerely yours,
                              [Harold Ober]

December 30, 1936

TL (cc), 1p. (AO)

Fitzgerald's total earnings for 1936 were $10,180. He sold four stories ($7,650) and nine pieces to Esquire *($2,250). His book royalties were $81.18.*

V
HOLLYWOOD

1937-1940

Jan 2nd

Baltimore.
<u>But</u> Stafford Hotel after
tomorrow.

Dear Harold:

I've owed you a letter a long time.

1st as to money. I arranged another loan but I hope to God this new story# (last version now at typists) will sell quick as I have enough for a fortnight only + am at the end of borrowing on mother's little estate until it's settled in April.

2nd I can do no more with <u>Thumbs Up</u>. I think I told you that it's [somewhat arbitrary] shifting around was due to my poor judgement in founding it arbitrarily on two unrelated events in father's family—the Thumbs Up and the Empresses Escape. I dont think I ever put more work on a story with less return. Its early diffuseness was *due*, of course, *to* my inability to measure the length of dictated prose during the time my right arm was helpless—that's why it strung out so long.

I suggest this—send it to <u>Esquire</u>—I owe them $500. See if they'll accept this in full payment—maybe something more. They paid me 200–250 for a mere appearance (1000 to 2000 wds of any sort in any genre)—but at least twice they've published Hemmingway *long* stories—one of 6000 + one that must have been 9000 or over. At least it would clear up that debt + in dire emergency I could get a couple of hundred there instead of having to go to mechanics loan offices as has been the case this last terrible year.

3d *Scottie* I'd promised to give Scotty a little tea dance + arranged it should cost $60. Every child in Baltimore came, it seemed to me + brought their friends. Immediately afterwards she went to the country with her friend Peaches—and I came to the hospital with 104° + raging flu to spend Xmas to New Years.

I'm all right now—(back on the absolute wagon by the way) + could have gone out today except that it's sleety. My plan is have Scottie join me at The Stafford tomorrow for a day or so—I've seen nothing of her + in any case the Baltimore schools open Monday

---

#"They Never Grow Older."

so her friends can't keep her or rather they would but none of the adults are close enough to me so that she would feel quite at home there.

The alternative arises—either she comes south with me at extra expense of time + money for a week (My God why do they open these schools <u>the 11th</u>!) or she visits you or Max—I couldn't send her to what would for her be strangers just now unless it were urgent. But I know how Xmas leaves anyone, you + Anne included + be frank with me. Her aunt, Mrs Smith, is under the surgeons knife + that's out + I'm so out of touch with all other New York friends that I don't know who to ask. She has one standing invitation—but it is to a tuberculosis Chateau! (Gerald + Sara Murphy of whom you've heard me speak.*

Anyhow I'll be at the Stafford all Monday anyhow finishing the last infinitismal details of mother's affairs. Let me know what. Then I've <u>got</u> to go see Zelda.

This last is general: I can live cheaper at a hotel I know in Tryon N.C. (Oak Hall), than at Grove Park (Ashville). As far as I can plan ahead it seems better to go to the† former place for a few months. It is warmer and I am still in such wretched health that such a fact means a lot. The arm has healed right + I should be thankful. Perhaps I shall be pushing you along more hopeful indications before the first grass pushes up. Anyhow wire me (Stafford) about Scottie

F.S.F.

ALS (pencil), 2pp. (AO)

F. Scott Fitzgerald, Esq.
Hotel Stafford
Baltimore, Md.

Dear Scott:

I have no idea whether you are still in Baltimore. You say in your letter that you are going to Tryon but you don't say when.

I have your telegram and we are looking forward to seeing Scottie Saturday afternoon. Anne has wanted to write to Scottie but doesn't know where to reach her.

I have the letter you wrote me on January 2nd and I will answer

---

*The Murphys were friends from the Riviera, and Fitzgerald dedicated *Tender Is the Night* to them. Their son was in a sanitarium.
†The rest of the letter is written along the left margin.

it further when I know where you are. We wish Scottie could be
with us longer but a few days will be better than nothing.

Sincerely yours,

[Harold Ober]

January 6, 1937

TL (cc), lp. (AO)

*Attempting to pull himself together, Fitzgerald went to Tryon, North
Carolina, for the winter and spring of 1937; there, with the aid of a doctor,
he tried to stop drinking completely.*

Dear Harold:

This will reach you with the story I imagine I have no illusions
about it—it was written, delayed, rewritten, finished twice + rewritten. If you think it is <u>too</u> bad don't show it to the <u>Post</u>, but
unless you have some extraordinarily good suggestion you might
show it to some one + get a reaction.

I am located as above§—Three weeks on the absolute wagon and
comparitively well. I went over my affairs thoroughly and in consequence laid the situation before Zelda's doctor + obtained an immense reduction. At present the basic costs of the Fitzgerald family
(I mean food + board + Zelda's doctors + Scottie's school) are

Me	$35.00	American plan
Zelda	41.00	Hospital
Scotty	<u>25.00</u>	School
<u>per week</u>	101.00	

This of course doesn't include Insurance, taxes, work expenses,
clothes + extras but it should certainly give me leaway to dig into
this terrible [burden] burden of debt which has been a 3 yr. nightmare. Just think—the 1st six months of this year I made $10,000—
the second six months, after the accident, I made $500 (<u>Esquire</u>)

By the way—what of <u>Thumbs Up</u>?

And so it goes. I shall be here the rest of the winter, making a
weekly trip to Ashville.

I enjoyed meeting your family, would have enjoyed it more if I
hadn't made the trip on stimulants. A couple of nights at Hopkins
ironed me out and I shall be on the wagon as far as I can see ahead.

Ever Your-Friend

Scott Fitzg

---

§This letter has no return address.

P.S.   If I can write a couple of good stories I don't particularly care about going west. I'm not very strong yet. After this long blank period I ought to have good material in me. I feel much less desperate than at Xmas. You were damned kind.

ALS (pencil), 2pp. n.d.—received 2 February 1937. Tryon, N.C. (AO)

F. Scott Fitzgerald, Esq.
Oak Hall
Tryon, N. C.

Dear Scott:

I am going to try to sell THEY NEVER GROW OLDER but it doesn't seem to me that it is wise to offer it to the Post. The next story of yours I show them I want to be a really good Scott Fitzgerald story. If you will wait about a week and read the story over I think you will agree with me that it hasn't the quality your stories ought to have.

> Sincerely yours,
> [Harold Ober]

February 4, 1937

TL (cc), 1p. (AO)

> JOHN OHARA THE WRITER WIRES THAT MAN LOCATED AT FOUR SEVENTY WEST TWENTY FOURTH STREET IS USING MY NAME STOP WILL YOU MAKE INQUIRIES STOP PERHAPS CONTACT OHARA FOR INFORMATION
> FITZGERALD.

Wire to Ober 18 February 1937. Tryon, N.C. (AO)

F. Scott Fitzgerald, Esq.
Oak Hall
Tryon, N. C.

Dear Scott:

I received your telegram about the man who is using your name here in New York. I have put the matter in the hands of the Bureau of Investigation of the Department of Justice. They have assigned an agent to investigate it. It is possible it is the same man who has impersonated other authors here in the East for the past year or two.

> Sincerely yours,
> [Harold Ober]

February 19, 1937

TL (cc), 1p. (AO)

Dear Harold:

If you could see the pile of false starts on my desk you'd know how hard I am trying. The twin fates of worry and lack of healthy stimuli continue even when liquor is out, as it has been for almost two months. Today I tore up a story—tomorrow I begin another. What of Thumbs Up—that might sell to Esquire. Who has it. It isn't very good but it has its points. About the cartoonist story I don't care.

Also what about the impersonator? Did you trace him, or did he exist?

Ever Yours
Scott

P.S. I am in better or rather excellent health for me, which is something, or is it. Sooner or later the old fire must reemerge.

ALS (pencil), 1p. n.d., n.p.—received 2 March 1937. Tryon, N.C. (AO)

F. Scott Fitzgerald, Esq.
Oak Hall
Tryon, N. C.

Dear Scott:

Thanks for your letter which came in just as I was beginning to write to you about THUMBS UP.

I hate to let Esquire have it except as a last resort. I gave the story to Tom Costain to read. He is editing a new magazine, the first number of which will appear sometime in April.* He told me yesterday that he thought you would have a good story here if you would let it end after Josie cuts Tib down. The story would need a scene bringing it to a romantic ending. Costain thinks, as you and I do, that you tried to put two stories into one. Costain says he thinks if you do this the story ought to bring a good price from some of the magazines which like your work. He says if it doesn't sell in this shortened version, he can use it but his top price for a short story at present is about $600. and he thinks the story ought to bring more than that.

I imagine you have a carbon copy of the story and if you feel like it I wish you would take a look at it and see if you can't end it as Costain suggested. Perhaps you can add another incident in the early part of the story so that the relation between Josie and Tib could be a little further advanced.

---

*American Cavalcade.

I am glad you are feeling in better health. We had a nice note from Scottie the other day. She seems to be very busy and very happy. We are going to try to drive up to see her sometime this Spring.

Sincerely yours,
[Harold Ober]

March 2, 1937

TL (cc), 1p. (AO)

F. Scott Fitzgerald, Esq.
Oak Hall
Tryon, N. C.

Dear Scott:

I am enclosing a letter from T. B. Costain, also copy of the idea for a short short which he mentions in his letter.

I know that you usually don't like to write stories on other people's ideas but I don't think it will do any harm to let you look at this and see if you want to do it or not.

Costain has a fine list of contributors for the first issue of his magazine, among them Booth Tarkington, Katharine Brush, Alice Duer Miller. The magazine will be a monthly magazine the size of the Readers Digest but devoted to fiction and articles. The price of $250. is not very tempting but if you can do a piece quickly it might be worth while.

On receipt of this letter would you mind wiring me collect whether or not you want to try this.

Sincerely yours,
[Harold Ober]

March 3, 1937

TL (cc), 1p. (AO)

PLEASE ANSWER MY LETTER ABOUT SHORT FOR COSTAINS MAGAZINE THOMAS BEER[†] HERE SENDS REGARDS
   HAROLD OBER

Wire to Fitzgerald 6 March 1937. (AO)

CANT DO COSTAIGNES SHORT JUST GOT LETTER
   FITZGERALD.

Wire to Ober 6 March 1937. Tryon, N.C. (AO)

---

†Novelist and biographer of Stephen Crane.

Dear Harold:

1st place didn't like Costains idea + 2nd place am working desperately on another long story to get some money by the 15th.

I couldn't have done his story—I'd like to do something for him later. I'll try cutting the Thumb story as you suggest.

Costain's story isn't good. One guesses the end right away. Sorry —I couldn't do it.

Ever

Scott F.

ALS (pencil), 1p. n.d., n.p.—received 8 March 1937. Tryon, N.C. (AO)

F. Scott Fitzgerald, Esq.
Oak Hall
Tryon, N. C.

Dear Scott:

I am glad you are working on a new story and of course it would be a mistake to drop work on that to do a short short, especially when you don't like the idea. I don't blame you, I didn't think very much of it myself, but I thought possibly you might be able to do something to it to get a little money.

I have hopes of getting about £50. from England for a second serial sale of THE GREAT GATSBY.‡

I hope your health continues to improve.

Sincerely yours,

[Harold Ober]

March 9, 1937

TL (cc), 1p. (AO)

Dear Harold:

This will reach you with a story The Vanished Girl.§ It is, I think, a pretty good story—at least it reads and isn't muffed, even if the conception isn't very full-bodied.

The point is that I have to sell it right away. I mean I'd rather have a little for it now than a lot in two weeks. On Monday there is income tax—thank God very little, Scotty to get out of school hotel bills + two doctors who are driving me frantic. On a guess I can get by with about $900.00. Do you think Costain would give that— I have absolutely no way to raise the money

---

‡*Argosy*, August 1937.
§"The Vanished Girl" was rejected by *Redbook* and was never published.

I know all this is poor policy and if I could struggle along until it could get a hearing I would, but it has been struggle a plenty to get this out—a good eight hours a day for five weeks + This the only one of four starts to come through at all. I am well, not pessimistic and doing my level best, including being 2 mos. on the absolute wagon and the next one will as usual try to be a <u>Post</u> story but this just has to be sacrificed for immediate gold. Four hundred on the 15th and $500 on the 20th would do it. Isn't there some editor who would advance me that much on a delivered story. Tell them anything, tell them frankly that you've advanced me the limit but for Gods sake raise me something on this story + wire it to Baltimore. If the income tax isn't paid the 15th it has to all be paid—and as for the insurance.

There may be something left in April of mother's money—I don't know. But if health and work can do anything the old talent can't lie supine much longer.

I want to sell two Post stories and then do a play very quick.

I may take a shot at The <u>Thumbs</u> revision tomorrow.

Wont Costain come through? I mean I dont mind his knowing I've been sick and strapped—I honestly don't mind anyones knowing if I can get money by the 15th. Please wire me about the story

Ever Yours,
Scott

ALS (pencil), 2pp. n.d., n.p.—received 11 March 1937. Tryon, N.C. (AO)

STORY INTERESTING BUT DIFFICULT FOR QUICK SALE DOING MY BEST STOP ADVISE APPLY FOR EXTENSION SIXTY DAYS FOR FILING RETURN YOU CAN THEN MAKE QUARTERLY PAYMENT WITH INTEREST STOP YOUR RECENT ILLNESS SUFFICIENT EXCUSE

Harold Ober

Wire (cc) to Fitzgerald 12 March 1937. (AO)

F. Scott Fitzgerald, Esq.
Oak Hall
Tryon, N. C.

Dear Scott:

The story arrived late this afternoon and I have just finished reading it and I have sent you a telegram. As you know only too well, there are only two days before income tax returns have to be mailed and I haven't been able to find any editor who would read anything over the week-end. I guess almost everyone has left their income tax to do on Sunday. I don't think there is any possibility of getting an immediate decision on this story. If we try to get it I think we would just ruin our best chances of placing it.

As I wired you, you can apply for an extension of the time for filing your return. I know a number of authors who have done this and all you have to do is when you do file it pay the first quarterly payment on it with interest added. With the sickness you have had I am sure you have an adequate excuse.

I don't think there is much chance of selling THE VANISHING GIRL to Costain—in the first place it is too long for him, he wants stories about 2000 words in length. I shall do my best to place the story where I can get the money quickly.

We would love to have Scottie come and stay with us during her Easter vacation if she doesn't decide to go to Baltimore. I know she was very eager to go there this Easter vacation.

I'll write you again early in the week.

Sincerely yours,
[Harold Ober]

March 12, 1937

TL (cc), 1p. (AO)

ON PAGE TWENTY TWO LINE EIGHTEEN ALONG SHOULD BE
ALONE STOP ADD TO LINE NINETEEN QUOTE IM ASKING THE
DAVIS HOME TO PUT HER UP TONIGHT¶
    FITZGERALD.

Wire to Ober 12 March 1937. Tryon, N.C. (AO)

The New Yorker might like this, if typed.# Send me a carbon. It should be all on one page if possible

AL (pencil), torn from sheet of paper, n.d.—received 15 March 1937. From Fitzgerald to Ober. Tryon, N.C. (AO)

DESPITE ALL EFFORTS I AM THREE HUNDRED DOLLARS OVER-
DRAWN IN BALTIMORE STOP HAVE NO POSSIBLE METHOD OF
RAISING IT
    FITZGERALD.

Wire to Ober 18 March 1937. Tryon, N.C.

¶Revisions for "The Vanished Girl."
Poem, "Obit on Parnassus," *The New Yorker*, 5 June 1937.

F. Scott Fitzgerald, Esq.
Oak Hall
Tryon, N. C.

Dear Scott:

As I wired you, I have just paid my income tax and several other things that were due and my bank balance is down to zero. I decided to speak to Max Perkins and he said he would wire $300. to your Baltimore bank. He is advancing this to you personally and I told him that I would pay it back to him out of the first money I received for you. I told him there is a chance of your going to Hollywood.

I hope you didn't mind my speaking to Max—it was the only way I could think of, of getting the money in a hurry.

I hope the Hollywood deal will go through all right. If you get out there and do a good job on THE DUKE STEPS OUT I am sure that Metro will have another job for you to work on. They have told me that if you do a good job on this picture they may be able to increase your salary and give you more work. You will probably leave from New York and I'll see you before you leave.

Sincerely yours,
[Harold Ober]

March 18, 1937

TL (cc), 1p. (AO)

Dear Harold:

It hurt to ask you for that $300—I hope you got the money from England for Gatsby 2nd Serial.

I'm anxiously waiting for news—no news is no doubt bad news. Why don't I just go to the coast + let them see me. I havn't had a drop in two months + feel fine. There's nothing I'd like better, for immediate cash + a future foothold + I'd love to write dialogue rather than work out their intricate plots.

Meanwhile I am revising Thumbs (for one day, + then beginning a football story for the coast. Ive thought so much about it that I should do another peach.

I hope to God The [Lost] *Vanished* Girl sells but something tells me your letter either says Balmer refused it or Hollywod refused me. I don't know what the hell I'm going to do or where to turn next but for once it doesn't worry me as it usually does

Scott Fitz

ALS (pencil), 1p. n.d.—received 22 March 1937. Tryon, N.C. (AO)

F. Scott Fitzgerald, Esq.
Oak Hall
Tryon, N. C.

Dear Scott:

I have just wired you about the week's delay on the Hollywood job but the reason may not be very clear. As you know, producers at Metro Goldwyn are in different units and each unit has a supervisor. McGuinness has just been moved from the supervision of Sam Katz to that of Ed Mannix. It will take at least a week for Mannix to go over the stories that are being prepared by McGuinness and no writing assignments will be made until that has been done. Edwin Knopf wants me to explain to you that this is entirely an interstudio matter and he hopes to have definite word for you in about a week.

I think everything is going to work out all right and that you will be on your way to Hollywood in a week or two but, as you know, nothing is settled in the moving picture business until one has a check in one's pocket. It wouldn't do any good at all for you to go to Hollywood before the contract is signed for in that case you wouldn't get your transportation.out. I'll let you know the moment there is any definite news about the Hollywood job either for or against. The week will give you some time to finish the revision of THUMBS and to work on the new story.

The Red Book have not yet decided on THE VANISHING GIRL. I'll let you know just as soon as they do.

I didn't see Scottie on Friday but she had lunch with Anne and they did some shopping together. She was staying with the mother of one of the girls—a Mrs. Williams at the Hotel Delmonico. She was very excited about a tea dance they were going to.

Sincerely yours,
[Harold Ober]

March 22, 1937

P.S. It will probably be months before we get the money from England on THE GREAT GATSBY.

TL (cc), 1p. (AO)

Going to country dog shows isn't my daily occupation—it was my single appearance of that kind. I wanted you to see how different I look from Xmas.§

Dear Harold:

Here, or herewith is the revision of <u>Thumbs U</u>p. Maybe it'll go. It's an odd story—one editor says cut the thumbs episode, another says cut everything else—I've done the latter and shortened it to about 5500 words (from 8000) ± revised it thoroughly + written a new scene.

Thanks for the money—as time passes my position becomes more + more ludicrous, I mean generally. I just got a book (Books + Battles of the Twenties)¶ in which I am practically a leading character, my birthday is two column front page news as if I were 80 instead of 40#—and I sit worrying about next weeks $35.00 hotel bill! I really mean it that I'd like to go to Hollywood + let them <u>see</u> me. I wish you could see me. Weight 160 instead of 143 which was it last Xmas. And the dullest dogs making 1000 a week in Hollywood. Something has got to be done—this will end in slow ruination. Anyhow I've begun the football story but God knows where the next two weeks rent come from. I will owe $105 by Thurs. + will need cash—all in all $150. I was going to Max as a last rescourse but you have tapped that. What in hell shall I do? I want to write the football story unworried + uninterrupted. Since going on the wagon I [have lived on] *will have* written two originals, rewritten two *stories (Thumbs + the cartoon story)* and written 3 little Esquire pieces* (two of them mediochre) to live on. That will be a hard two ½ mos work. But reward there is none.

In fatalistic optimism,

Scott

Look at this Margaret Banning next to me—covered with rings, lives in a mansion + owns it. Ah me—well, perhaps I've learned wisdom at forty at last. If I ever get out of this mess![†]

ALS (pencil), 2pp. n.d., n.p.—received 23 March 1937. Tryon, N.C. (AO)

---

§Fitzgerald enclosed a newspaper photo of himself with Mrs. Margaret Culkin Banning, the Rev. Dr. C. Arthur Lincoln, and Donald Culross Peattie. The headline reads: "Noted Authors Enjoy Visit to Tryon Resort" (*Asheville Citizen-Times*, 21 March 1937).

¶*Books and Battles of the Twenties* by Irene and Allen Cleaton (Boston: Houghton Mifflin, 1937).

#Refers to Michel Mok's article in the *New York Post*, 25 September 1936.

*Possibly "The Honor of the Goon," June 1937; "In the Holidays," December 1937; and "The Guest in Room Nineteen," October 1937.

†Written along the left margin of page two.

THUMBS SENT YESTERDAY SHORT ONE HUNDRED IN BAL-
TIMORE WHAT CHANCE
　　　FITZGERALD.

Wire to Ober 24 March 1937. Tryon, N.C. (AO)

F. Scott Fitzgerald, Esq.
Oak Hall
Tryon, N. C.

Dear Scott:

Thank you for your letter of March 22nd. I am very glad to have
the picture of you—it is not very clear but you certainly look
healthy.

THUMBS UP hasn't come in yet but I am very glad to know that
you have cut it down to 5500 words. I really feel much more hopeful
of selling this than I do of selling THE VANISHED GIRL. I like
the first few pages of this very much indeed but when the girl
floated out the window, it began to be improbable and all the latter
part of the story seemed to me weak. Balmer has just declined it. I
talked to him about it and he says he is very keen to get a modern
story of yours but that this story is too crazy for him. I really don't
know where to offer it. I wish you could work the story out without
having the girl a mental case. Do you think that Esquire would take
it? That may be a way to get some immediate money for it.

I am hoping by next week we can get the Metro Goldwyn contract fixed up and you will then have a weekly check coming in. I
haven't anything I can give you at the present time. I have a lot of
obligations to meet at this time of the year and my taxes this year
are very heavy.

If you think it is a good idea to send the story to Esquire you had
better wire me and I'll send you the ribbon copy back so that you
can send it yourself. I think it would be better than for me to send
it.

　　　　　　　　　　　　　　Sincerely yours,
　　　　　　　　　　　　　　[Harold Ober]

March 24, 1937

Later: Just now your telegram was handed me saying that you are
short $100. in your Baltimore bank. I am wiring suggesting that you
send THE VANISHED GIRL to Esquire and since you need the
money right away, I am sending the story to you by special delivery.
Perhaps you can get Gingrich to wire the money to Baltimore.

TL (cc), 1p. (AO)

SORRY BUT I HAVE PRESSING OBLIGATIONS HOW ABOUT
SENDING VANISHED GIRL TO ESQUIRE FOR IMMEDIATE CASH
DOUBT ITS SELLING HERE MAILING STORY TO YOU SPECIAL
PERHAPS GINGRICH WILL WIRE MONEY TO BANK
    HAROLD OBER

Wire (cc) to Fitzgerald 24 March 1937. (AO)

Harold Ober
40 E. 49th St.

Dear Harold: <u>Please</u> have the last part typed before you read it.
Scottie is fine + sends best.
    Working daytimes on football story
<u>Scott Fitz.</u>

ALS (pencil), 1p. n.d., n.p.—received 25 March 1937. Tryon, N.C. (AO)

Alternate Titles   for "Thumbs Up"
  Two Minutes Alone   or
  Midst War's Alarms   "No Time For That"[§]
  That Can Wait
  Of All Times—

Memo (pencil), 1p. n.d.—c. 25 March 1937. Tryon, N.C. (AO)

F. Scott Fitzgerald, Esq.
Oak Hall
Tryon, N. C.

Dear Scott:
    I think you have done a very good job on the revision of
THUMBS UP. I am having this typed and will do my very best to
sell it just as soon as I possibly can.
Sincerely yours,
[Harold Ober]

March 25, 1937

TL (cc), 1p. (AO)

[§]A note added in Ober's hand.

F. Scott Fitzgerald, Esq.
Oak Hall
Tryon, N. C.

Dear Scott:

I enclose proof of LINES FOR AN URN¶ together with copy of a letter from the New Yorker and the note which this letter mentions. I imagine you will be able to fix this up.

"We were about to send you a check for the F. Scott Fitzgerald poem, which we like very much, when we discovered that there were certain errors in fact in it and thought that he had better fix it up first. It seems that he was entirely wrong about the ages of Rossetti and Scott. The last stanza on Landor raises a problem which we wish you would put up to Mr. Fitzgerald. He didn't literally linger until ninety, having died three or four months before reaching that age. Perhaps he could think of a way of rewording this stanza to make this clear, just to obviate all the letters of correction we and Mr. Fitzgerald would get. If he can't, I suppose we will just have to take it as it is, as it comes near the truth, and comes within the bounds of poetic license. Will you ask him to consider the problem? The other two changes won't be so hard for him but they do need some rewriting which we can't undertake here. In the last line of the next to the last stanza we took out one "and" to improve the meter, and hope Mr. Fitzgerald won't object to this alteration.

I enclose a note from our checkers, which you will probably want to pass on to Mr. Fitzgerald. I crossed out the queries that I thought were too captious."

Sincerely yours,
[Harold Ober]

March 26, 1937

TL (cc), 1p. (AO)

Dear Harold:

Heres the <u>New Yorker</u>. Even the check on this would help if wired to Baltimore. I want to finish the football story (almost done) without an [ti] interuption. After that sailing should be smoother—its a great story so far

Scott

ALS (pencil), 1p. n.d., n.p.—received 30 March 1937. Tryon, N.C. (AO)

¶Published as "Obit on Parnassus."

F.Scott Fitzgerald,
Oak Hall,
Tryon, N.C.

Dear Scott:

Harold is in Scarsdale today and he has asked me to write you letting you know that Swanson reports that Mr. Knopf of Metro-Goldwyn-Mayer says that the deal for your services on THE DUKE STEPS OUT looks cold. Swanson adds that there is no telling when this will be revived but he thinks you ought to know that there is little chance of anything happening on it immediately so that you will not hold up any new stories which you may have in mind.

Sincerely,
[Constance Smith]

March 29,1937

TL (cc), 1p. (AO)

F. Scott Fitzgerald, Esq.
Oak Hall
Tryon, N. C.

Dear Scott:

The proof of the New Yorker poem came in and it seems to me considerably better than in the first version. We shall get only about $30. for it but I have wired you $100. which I hope will help you to finish the story you are now on.

The New Yorker say they wish you would do more poems.

We are hoping Scottie will have a few days with us before she goes back to school, and Anne might drive her up to school when she drives Dick back to Exeter.

Sorry I had to worry you about the Hollywood job—and then have it grow cold. I think, however, that job or another may turn up again. In the meantime, I am delighted you are working on the football story.

Sincerely yours,
[Harold Ober]

March 30, 1937

TL (cc), 1p. (AO)

F.Scott Fitzgerald Esq.,
Oak Hall,
Tryon, N.C.

Dear Scott:

The New Yorker is pleased with the extensive changes in the poem but have questioned the accuracy of Chaucer's age. Their research department say that literary reference works give the date as approximately 1340 to 1400 which would mean he was only sixty when he died rather than seventy. Wolcott Gibbs says your verse is too good to be open to criticism of fact and he hopes you will not object to casting about for one more septuagenarian to take Chauser's place in stanza five. I am returning the galley proof herewith.

Incidentally Mr. Gibbs promises us a check regardless of possible further revision.

Sincerely,
[Harold Ober]

April 5,1937

TL (cc), 1p. (AO)

Dear Harold:

The Hollywood affair was a blow of course. It might have meant everything. Of course one cannot do justice to purely imaginative work when in rotten health + extreme worry. But since the health is good + the worry would be alleviated by the pay check it would have been ideal. My biggest loss is confidence.

So I hope that you'll bend all your efforts for me apon bringing about a chance in Hollywood. Week by week Things get worse financially and of course this can't go on much longer if I have to go out there + sell myself for a few hundred a week. I am finishing the football story + will start another but it would be twice as possible to work well if I could see any way out of this morass. If Swanson can't sell me how about Leland Hayward—he used to be a great friend + admirer.

Perhaps tomorrow I wont feel as low as today but at the moment things look very black. You might send me the cartoon story to look over. I hope to God you sell Thumbs—wire me if you do.

Ever Yours
Scott Fitzg

ALS (pencil), 1p. n.d., n.p.—received 6 April 1937. Tryon, N.C. (AO)

F. Scott Fitzgerald, Esq.
Oak Hall
Tryon, N. C.

Dear Scott:

Thanks for your note. I am sending you back the cartoon story. I don't feel very hopeful of this story and it doesn't seem to me wise for you to spend much time on it. The few people who have seen it haven't had a good word to say for it. The idea of the story has been used several times and it is not a very good one anyway.

You did a good job on THUMBS and I am hoping eventually to place that.

Both Swanson and I are doing our very best to get a new contract for you in Hollywood.

Sincerely yours,
[Harold Ober]

April 6, 1937

TL (cc), 1p. (AO)

READERS' REPORTS ON "THEY NEVER GROW OLDER" by F. Scott Fitzgerald[†]

This story of the comic strip—in life and in the papers—seems to me rather a clumsy parallel. The author apparently things he has a unique and clever idea but he doesn't pull it off. There never seems to be any good reason for keeping the characters apart just to draw the parallel. I don't think we'd miss this if we rejected it.

****

The pity is that they do, both Fitzgerald and his characters. This is a dreary badly written unbelievable story about a comic strip artist and his love and his rival, and by the time they've lived their comic strip till they're all fortyish I for one don't care for them or the comic.

****

One of the most cockeyed nightmarish stories I have ever read.

****

It is a confused, muddled story about a famous cartoonist, the girl he has loved since college days, and a rival who has also loved her

---

†Comments from unidentified magazines Ober offered the story to. This report may not have been shown to Fitzgerald.

all his life. For some reason which the author may know but I couldn't discover the cartoonist never proposes and the girl waits around until she is forty before they finally decide to get married. Just by way of pretending that it is a story, a madman breaks into the cartoonist's studio and shoots him in the middle of the story. This particular scene reminds us that Fitzgerald can write but it has very little connection with what should be the thread of the story.

Typed report, 1p. (AO)

Dear Harold:
　With this you will recieve the story
　　Athletic Interview‡
and a plea for another $100.00. The situation is terrible. One check has just come back to the hotel. Threats of suits come in daily from all over hell—not big sums but enormous now. Some matters as buying razor blades + even cigarettes have grown serious. There ought to be a little left from mother's estate this month but I dont know when or whether itll be a hundred or a thousand, all the rest being mortgaged away.

　I am revamping The Vanished Girl for Esquire and can't get any money for it until it gets there which won't be before next Monday. The $100 is for the hotel bill—I had to give them another check and if it comes back I'll be in the street.

　At least I have taken my time on this story as I should have started doing two years ago. My rate is never more than one a month—why I kept thinking I could do more with the added burden of illness and anxiety I don't know.

　For God's sake wire me you have been able to do something.
　　　　　　　　　　　　　　　　　　Scott

ALS (pencil), 2pp. n.d., n.p.—received 13 April 1937. Tryon, N.C. (AO)

　Please have it typed before you read it. It might be typed to look a little shorter—I mean these are huge margins. It's over 8000.
　　　　　　　　　　　　　　　　　Fitz—

Memo (pencil), n.d., n.p.—received 13 April 1937. Tryon, N.C. (AO)

---

　‡"Athletic Interview" became "Athletic Interval" and later "Offside Play." The story was rejected by *American Magazine, Collier's, Cosmopolitan, Redbook,* and *The Saturday Evening Post* and was never published.

F. Scott Fitzgerald, Esq.
Oak Hall
Tryon, N. C.

Dear Scott:

I have just finished reading ATHLETIC INTERVAL and I like it very much. I think it is a good piece of work.

I wired you $100. this afternoon and if I can I'll try to send you a little more within a day or two.

Sincerely yours,
[Harold Ober]

April 13, 1937

TL (cc), 1p. (AO)

F. Scott Fitzgerald, Esq.
Oak Hall
Tryon, N. C.

Dear Scott:

The Post has declined ATHLETIC INTERVAL. They say it is much too long for their present requirements—but this is a minor point. It is over 9000 words and ought to be cut before I show it to anyone else. (It's at the Cosmopolitan now and they can use long stories). I'm sending you a carbon and if Cosmopolitan declines I'll wire you to try and cut it to 6000 or 7000 words.

To go back to the Post. They say it lacks the warmth of your best work and that it hasn't the "incandescent" quality your readers expect. This gives me a pain. This story may not be your very best —no author can be his very best all the time; but it is so much better than 9/10 of the stories they buy that their criticism is absurd.

If Cosmopolitan declines the story I think you ought to cut it and while you are doing it perhaps you can do something to Kiki or Considine that will make them more likable. Considine is rather a shadowy character. I think the story would sell to the more popular magazines if you could make Considine an undergraduate who is not an athlete—but who has qualities that Rip lacks. And couldn't you motivate Kiki's rather hard headed business plans for Rip? All this, of course, in case Cosmopolitan doesn't buy the story.

I have managed to squeeze out another hundred and have deposited it in your bank.

As ever,
[Harold Ober]

April 20, 1937

TL (cc), 1p. (AO)

I HAVE BEEN THINKING THAT I HAD BETTER SUPPRESS THE
ACTUAL NAMES OF THE COLLEGES IN THAT STORY SO WILL
YOU SEND ME A COPY TO MAKE THE CHANGES ON STOP I AM
WORKING HARD ON ANOTHER
  SCOTT FITZGERALD.

Wire to Ober 21 April 1937. Tryon, N.C. (AO)

HAVE SENT SEVENTY THREE HUNDRED WORD VERSION
  FITZGERALD.

Wire to Ober 23 April 1937. Tryon, N.C. (AO)

Dear Harold:

I've cut it without difficulty to about 7300 instead of 9100 + it's
vastly improved. This is the way it should have been at first—
inevitable result of pressure + hurry. I think the Post might have
taken it as it is now.

Well, Im on another. I can only hope to God this goes. It is good
in form though I think, as if I'm getting back into stride.

Scott

ALS (pencil), 1p. n.d., n.p.—received 26 April 1937. Tryon, N.C. (AO)

F. Scott Fitzgerald, Esq.
Oak Hall
Tryon, N. C.

Dear Scott:

You did a good job of cutting the football story. The longer
version is at the Cosmopolitan and I am telling them that I am
sending them a shorter and improved version. I am sure you are
back in your stride.

Sincerely yours,
[Harold Ober]

April 26, 1937

TL (cc), 1p. (AO)

PLEASE TAKE ANY PRICE FOR INTERLUDE§ OVERDRAWN 150
AND WHOLE SITUATION TENSE NO HELP FROM ESTATE FOR
ANOTHER WEEK STORY ALMOST FINISHED BY CONDITIONS
OF WORK IMPOSSIBLE
  FITZGERALD

Wire to Ober 2 May 1937. Tryon, N.C. (AO)

---

§"Athletic Interval."

NO ANSWER TO TELEGRAM PLEASE WIRE SITUATION VIA POSTALTELEGRAPH
    FITZGERALD.

Wire to Ober 5 May 1937. Tryon, N.C. (AO)

NO NEWS AND NO MONEY COSMOPOLITAN STILL CONSIDERING FOOTBALL STORY IF THEY DECLINE HOPE AMERICAN WILL BUY DOING MY BEST
    Harold Ober

Wire (cc) to Fitzgerald 5 May 1937. (AO)

F. Scott Fitzgerald, Esq.
Oak Hall
Tryon, N. C.

Dear Scott:

I have just received ATHLETIC INTERVAL from Cosmopolitan. They told me that it had been touch and go whether they accepted it or not. The final verdict, I am sorry to say, has been against it and I am giving it at once to the editor of the American Magazine.

Sincerely yours,
[Harold Ober]

May 6, 1937

TL (cc), 1p. (AO)

F. Scott Fitzgerald, Esq.
Oak Hall
Tryon, N. C.

Dear Scott:

I have the following letter from Kenneth Littauer¶ regarding your story THUMBS UP:

"Thanks for giving me a look at this revised version of F. Scott Fitzgerald's story called THUMBS UP. The first half seems to me very good. The last half lacks point, if I am not mistaken. It is easy to understand that Tib should want to marry the girl but there is no good reason for his intent to murder her brother. Of course he may have been possessed but if this is so then we can't accept him as a suitable match for Miss Pilgrim. Furthermore, all this business about buying gold to fill a tooth seems irrelevant.

¶Editor of *Collier's*.

I wish Fitzgerald would end this story as it deserves to be ended. With the right conclusion I think it would make an excellent feature for us."

I talked to Littauer today and he says he would like very much to go down and see you in Tryon. He says he realizes this letter won't help you very much on this story but he thinks that in conversation some way might develop to fix the story so that Collier's could use it. He has wanted to see you for sometime and since the Post seems to have deserted us, I think it would be a very good idea for you to have a talk with Littauer. Let me know if and when you would like to see him.

Sincerely yours,
[Harold Ober]

May 7, 1937

TL (cc), 1p. (AO)

DONT WANT TO SEE LITTAUR UNDER PRESENT CONDITIONS HAVING BEEN EIGHTY DOLLARS OVERDRAWN FOR ONE WEEK NEW STORY SENT TODAY WHAT DO YOU DO WHEN THERES NOTHING TO DO BECAUSE THAT SITUATION ANSWER PLEASE YOU WILL HAVE TWO GOOD STORIES AND MORE IF IMPOSSI-BLE PRESSURE IS RELIEVED
    FITZGERALD.

Wire to Ober 9 May 1937. Tryon, N.C. (AO)

F. Scott Fitzgerald, Esq.
Oak Hall
Tryon, N. C.

Dear Scott:

I am sorry that you don't feel like seeing Littauer now for I think it might result in his buying THUMBS UP. When you do feel like seeing him, please let me know.

The new story you speak of hasn't come in but I hope it will before the end of the day.

The football story is now at the American and the editor has promised me a quick decision and I hope to have one within a day or two.

I wish I could do something about removing the pressure you are under but with me money has been going out recently and none coming in. I hope you can hold on until a story sells. As soon as any money comes in that doesn't have to go out right away I'll do what

I can to relieve the pressure but I do not see any chance for that in the immediate future.

When Scottie gets through school we shall be delighted to have her come and stay with us. We would really like to have her.

Sincerely yours,
[Harold Ober]

May 10, 1937

TL (cc), 1p. (AO)

F. Scott Fitzgerald, Esq.
Oak Hall
Tryon, N. C.

Dear Scott:

THAT KIND OF PARTY# has just come in and I have read it and it seems to me an attractive story and I hope it will find a place quickly. I am having it typed right away and I am giving it first to the editor of the Ladies Home Journal who is in town today and who said he would like very much to have a story of yours.

Sincerely yours,
[Harold Ober]

May 11, 1937

TL (cc), 1p. (AO)

TO REMAIN HERE AND EAT MUST HAVE ONE HUNDRED AND THIRTY TODAY PLEASE ASK PERKINS
FITZGERALD.

Wire to Ober 11 May 1937. Tryon, N.C. (AO)

MAX AND I WILL ARRANGE DEPOSIT BETWEEN US.
HAROLD OBER

Wire (cc) to Fitzgerald 11 May 1937. (AO)

Dear Harold:

Life had me going there for a little while. A check came back from the bank + then another + then the 1st over again. Hadn't tipped servants for 6 wks, paid typist, druggist, old doctors bills ect—every mail a threat of suite. All in all the short + simple annals of the

---

#Ober's note on the typescript of this story reads: "Once a Basil Story Rewritten in 1937 offered Ladies Home Journal + Pictorial Review author decided to rewrite but never did. . . ." The story was published in the *Princeton University Library Chronicle*, Summer 1951.

poor. It has been entirely a charity year—almost a year mind you since I've sold a story, tho I've only written five + two may yet sell. In fact if these two dont I am immediately on a worse spot than before. I have a balance of six dollars after immediately putting forth what you sent.

All that can save me now [iss] is that there may be a few hundred in the estate which will be settled in two weeks. What I need is a substantial sum 1st to pay a percentage on bills, 2nd for a full months security + 3d to take Zelda for a 3 day trip to Myrtle Beach which I've been promising for two month + which the sanitarum want her to take. She hasn't been out of hospital for 3½ years + they feel that she's well enough for a trip.

These two stories seem to me in the old line. I feel the stuff coming back as my health improves. I told you that since stopping drinking I've gained from just over 140 to [my] over 160. I sleep at last and tho my hair's grey I feel younger than for four years. I am surprisingly not depressed by all these bad breaks but I am exceedingly hampered—just sheerly finding it difficult to function. I tried to give up smoking from pure economy + did give up expensive medicines [even] [I] and treatments. Such matters as four abcessed teeth and a growth that ought to be removed honestly dont bother me—two years of fainting + spitting blood cured me physical worry, but the money difficulty if not solved soon will have more and more [pys] psycholigal influence on my work, undermining confidence and wrecking what's left of my market.

Why Littaur? I don't think the Post have been unreasonable. They've turned down some good stories from Crazy Sunday and Phillipe to Intimate Strangers but most of what they saw wasn't good. I didn't like their cutting my price but I'd like to wait till they turned down a good story for no reason at all before [leavin] deciding that Stout* just don't like me.

Well, I hope you'll have good news about a story by the time you get this.

Ever Yours Scott Fitz

It was a shame to sell the *little* story in this months Esq for $200, wasn't it.† That's a sheer result of debt.

ALS (pencil), 3pp. n.d., n.p.—received 13 May 1937. Tryon, N.C. (AO)

---

*Wesley Winans Stout succeeded George Horace Lorimer as editor of *The Saturday Evening Post* in 1937.
†"The Honor of the Goon," *Esquire*, June 1937.

SEND CARBON OF PARTY WIRE ANY GOOD NEWS EVERY HOUR
COUNTS
    FITZGERALD.

Wire to Ober 13 May 1937. Tryon, N.C. (AO)

Dear Harold:

More about Lithaur, as I just got your letter. Of course I'd like
to see him for purposes of selling a story, a specific one. [It] But I
am too poor to entertain him—I mean this is a decent little hotel but
old and not in the rôle of successful author at all. Niether is the 1927
Car which I bought last year + use for driving to see Zelda—it's
original cost to me was $95.00 so you can imagine what it looks
like.

When I can pay my bill here I move to Hendersonville + there
I think it might be practical [exce] even with the car. So far as being
"looked over" I would welcome it + give him any impression
personally that I chose to. Let us say when you sell a story I'll see
him. Put him off till then.

The enclosure doesn't get us far, though the sound rights are still
mine.‡ Will you take care of it
                  Ever   Fitzg
Thanks for the note about Scottie. I'm vague about her. If this
Myrtle Beach is cheap I might go there. She'll certainly come + see
you§

ALS (pencil), 1p. n.d., n.p.—received 14 May 1937. Tryon, N.C. (AO)

GRATEFUL FOR ANY NEWS
    FITZGERALD.

Wire to Ober 17 May 1937. Tryon, N.C. (AO)

IS SMALL BOY SERIES¶ WORTH CONTINUING PLEASE WIRE
THIS AFTERNOON
    FITZGERALD.

Wire to Ober 18 May 1937. Tryon, N.C. (AO)

If you have another story in mind advise write but make
children less precocious and more attractive can tell better
after first story sold.
    Harold Ober

Wire (cc) to Fitzgerald 18 May 1937. (AO)

---

‡Imperial Film of Paris asked about "Offshore Pirate."
§Written along left margin.
¶"That Kind of Party."

F. Scott Fitzgerald, Esq.
Oak Hall
Tryon, N. C.

Dear Scott:

I gave THAT KIND OF PARTY to the Ladies Home Journal and here is what they write me about it:

"I regret having to return Scott Fitzgerald's THAT KIND OF PARTY to you, as I'd like very much to be able to buy a Fitzgerald piece. It seemed to us, though, that the children involved in the story were both precocious and rather unpleasant, and on the whole we felt it safest to reject the piece."

I am sending it now to the Pictorial as I think it is more likely to sell there than anywhere else.

Sincerely yours,
Harold Ober

May 18, 1937
HO/P

TL, 1p. (PU)

F. Scott Fitzgerald, Esq.
Oak Hall
Tryon, N. C.

Dear Scott:

The editor of the Ladies Home Journal came in today and I talked to him further about THAT KIND OF PARTY. He says that he thinks the story might sell if the children were two or three years older and if at least one or two of the children were made more attractive. He says parents do not like to think of children ten years old being so much interested in sex. It would be easy to make the children a few years older but I think it is still more important to make the children more attractive. I like the first part of the story very much indeed and I think if you could make the latter part as good, it would surely sell. If Pictorial doesn't buy the story and if you feel like doing some rewriting on it, I think it would be a good idea. The Journal would like to see it if you rewrite it.

I am sorry to say the American doesn't like ATHLETIC INTERVAL and I have given it to Balmer of the Red Book.

Sincerely yours,
Harold Ober

May 18, 1937.
HO/P

TL, 1p. (PU)

May 24, 1937.

Athletic Interval by F. Scott Fitzgerald

Reports #

It is shorter and therefore somewhat better than formerly. . . . But it still is strangely complicated in motivation. . . . . The emotional parts are strangely UNemotional and static . . . The plot concerning the orphanage brother is frankly dragged in.

Strangely unemotional this story is, but it holds you to the end and the football element gives it an added value.

I kept feeling that it was good, then bad, then that it was going to be good—then it didn't. Actually, there's a sense of frustration and dullness and anticlimax in the girl's romances—she is pretty much deadened to emotion, and her final compromise is so routine and valueless. Worse, however, is the unfinished and unsatisfactory story of the two collegians, the football star and his orphanage "brother"—you have a feeling that the brother is still a crook, and that the girl has prostituted the football star to commercialism and has given him nothing in return—except a security income wangled out of a nitwit alumnus, for which the hero has sold all the glory which the public and his own deeds have given him. Altogether, it's unsatisfactory—although the color and background are just what we'd like.

Mr. Fitzgerald seems pretty far away from his characters in this. The idea of the plot is perfectly satisfactory but Kiki's switch from one man to the other and back again never seems very convincing and what should be a fairly emotional story is pretty cold.

Typed reports, 1p. *Cosmopolitan* letterhead. (AO)

Will you summarize what Littaur now wants of the original story. Does he consider the French episode entirely out? Adress me at Oak Hall, Tryon. It was a swell trip.*

Scott Fitz

These reports were in the Ober files, but they were probably not sent to Fitzgerald. They seem to be four reports by different readers.
*Fitzgerald had taken Zelda to Myrtle Beach, South Carolina.

That man Charles Warren is worth encouraging. Much better than Spafford.[†]
In my elation I bought this place. I think it will be good for my work
I charged it to Max[‡]

Post card (pencil)—postmarked 6 June 1937. Asheville, N.C. (AO)

F. Scott Fitzgerald, Esq.
Oak Hall
Tryon, N. C.

Dear Scott:

I am enclosing an account and, as you will see, I have given Max Perkins $365.

Littauer is ill so I can't talk to him again about THUMBS UP. I did, however, have a talk with him after he had read the last version and he said then that he thought the whole French part of the story should be cut. He also said he didn't think the episode in the theatre really helped the story along very much. He suggested the possibility of introducing another man who wants to marry Josie. He might be a friend of Josie's brother and Littauer says if he were picked out by Josie's brother he would probably be a prig. He said the story needed "warming up". He said there ought to be one or two love scenes between Josie and Tib in the middle of the story. This is, I think, about all he told me.

I have an idea that sometime you can take the French part and make a separate story out of it.

I like your new place very much! It looks as if there might be room enough for me if I come down to see you sometime.

Sincerely yours,
[Harold Ober]

June 9, 1937

TL (cc), 1p. (AO)

F. Scott Fitzgerald In account with Harold Ober

....

Balance due Harold Ober—Account			
dated June 2, 1937			12705.04
Cash in New York	June	3	20.00
		4	171.00

---

†Written along the left margin and top.
‡Written around the edges of a picture of Biltmore mansion, Asheville, North Carolina.

Wired 1st National Bank,
    Baltimore, Md.   June   9   600.06
Cost of wiring above   .59
To Maxwell Perkins   365.00   13661.69

Received from Collier's   1500.00
    On account of total price
    of 2500.00 for story to
    be delivered§

    10% Commission   150.00   1350.00

    Balance due Harold Ober June 9th   12511.69

    I trust you will find the above accounting correct.
                      HAROLD OBER
June 9, 1937
F. Scott Fitzgerald, Esq.
Oak Hall
Tryon, N. C.

Typed account (cc), 1p. (AO)

New Yorker might like this.¶ If you have it retyped please tell typist
to follow punctuation exactly, such as <u>Abraham's Sac</u>.
    I wrote it on the train coming down.

Fitzgerald note to Ober (pencil), n.d., n.p.—c. 12 June 1937. Tryon, N.C. (AO)

F. Scott Fitzgerald, Esq.
Oak Hall
Tryon, N. C.

Dear Scott:
    The piece you did for the New Yorker, A BOOK OF ONE'S
OWN is very amusing and I think they will like it.
    I am sorry to say that the Post could not use FINANCING
FINNEGAN.# They say it is amusing but do not think it would
interest a wide market. I'll see what I can do with it elsewhere.

---

§"Thumbs Up."
   ¶A humorous essay, "A Book of One's Own," published as "A Book of My Own,"
The New Yorker, 21 August 1937.
   # *Esquire*, January 1938.

We are planning to drive up to Exeter on Friday of this week and will probably return on Sunday or the latest on Monday. When are you coming up to New York?

Sincerely yours,
[Harold Ober]

June 14, 1937

TL (cc), 1p. (AO)

F. Scott Fitzgerald Esq.,
Oak Hall,
Tryon, N.C.

Dear Scott:

I don't know if you have seen the June 12,1937 issue of the Saturday Review of Literature,* but in case you haven't I'm sending you a copy.

Sincerely,
[Harold Ober]

June 16,1937

TL (cc), 1p. (AO)

> PLEASE SEND COPY OF THUMBS STORY FINAL VERSION
> FITZGERALD.

Wire to Ober 16 June 1937. Tryon, N.C. (AO)

> FOOTBALL REVISE[†] SENT CAN YOU ORDER RETYPEING AND
> SEND POST
> SCOTT.

Wire to Ober 16 June 1937. Tryon, N.C. (AO)

F. Scott Fitzgerald, Esq.
Oak Hall
Tryon, N. C.

Dear Scott:

Edwin Knopf arrived this afternoon and is to be here until Thursday night. I have made a tentative date with him for lunch next Thursday, June 24th. If that date isn't possible, we can arrange to see him some other time.

---

*Contains the article "The Minnesota Muse" by James Gray. He discusses several Minnesota writers, including Fitzgerald.
†"Athletic Interval."

I had the football story retyped and gave it to Graeme Lorimer today.

I am leaving tomorrow morning to drive up to Exeter to get Dick and will be back Monday night. We may stop tomorrow and see Scottie for a moment.

> Sincerely yours,
> [Harold Ober]

June 17, 1937

TL (cc), 1p. (AO)

Dear Anne:

Your hospitality is grand and I know Scottie wants to come visit you. Plans are taking shape gradually and by the time I come to New York I'll have a summer laid out. That will be the 25th— Scottie will join me in New York for a couple of days and I'll tell her the delightful news that she doesn't have to go to camp in July —though she may go in August—if I go to Hollywood.

There's an inexpensive place, quite child-populated near Ashville called Linville where I'm thinking of spending the summer, or at least July. After Scottie spends some days with you + a night with [some] *her* roommate (a new one) on Long Island I'll be about ready to start south + finish this play which is my next job. And since to take my wife anywhere seems out of the question this summer I suppose Scottie and I [will] *had best* get to know each other again after over a year apart. I'm looking forward to it in many ways as, now that I'm feeling better, I begin to get lonely in more human way. And in a few years she'll be gone for good. That's the July plan as near as it's formulated. I'll bet you're glad that by the time you get this you'll have your wandering boy with you.

Considering how entirely vulnerable I was the trip to New York restored my faith in human nature—it seems amazing that everyone could be so damn nice—you most of all. I feel as if I had been dragged out of the cellar, dusted off patted on the head and told that everything was all right if I'd just play safely from now on. Old friends I'd dreaded seeing were nice—practically the fatted calf— except for [50 words omitted by editors] Ah, well—that was a good record, one out of twenty.

I'm looking forward to trip two—except meeting Mr Knopf of the movies + being looked over but it will only be for a week as I feel better down here—that's the sad but undisputable truth that at my age health just doesn't come back to stay after six months.

A nice letter from Harold in hand, telling me [you] *he* liked the last story. I don't envy you the [white] *grey* roads of New England somehow, though they're beautiful + nicer than here. The road for me will always be white + dusty + leading between poplars to Provence. Till next week

Yours With Eternal Gratitude
Scott

Your spelling + typing are <u>perfect</u>.

ALS, 2pp. n.d., n.p.—dated 18 June 1937 by Mrs. Ober. Tryon, N.C.

Thurs. for lunch with Knopf O.K. Arrive Thurs morning. If you can't get <u>more than</u> $300 for Finnegan§ I want to give it to Esquire to whom I owe two pieces

Scott

Post card (pencil), n.d.—postmarked 19 June 1937. Tryon, N.C. (AO)

Dear Harold:

Will you find me hotel nearer 5th Ave than the Lexington (E. or W.) + in the Forties where I can go for $3.00 or at most $3.50. Lexington is O.K but I've promised daughter a few days in New York + I don't like Lexington location much.

Glad you liked football. I am finishing the Thumbs story—just what they want I think, + will bring it north. Arrive Thurs early + will phone so leave hotel word at your office if you're not there.

Ever Yours
Scott

Post card, n.d.—postmarked 21 June 1937. Tryon, N.C. (AO)

F. Scott Fitzgerald, Esq.¶

Dear Scott:

I have the following letter from the Post regarding OFFSIDE PLAY:#

"The new version of Scott Fitzgerald's story is a vast improvement over the first one. The writing has all the old Fitzgerald

---

§Note in another hand reads: "At American. dec by SEP."
¶This letter was probably never sent to Fitzgerald. It may have been given to him while he was in New York.
#New version of "Athletic Interval."

quality, but the plot values and psychology are a bit hazy. For that reason, we must regretfully return the story."

Sincerely yours,
[Harold Ober]

June 23, 1937

TL (cc), 1p. (AO)

After Fitzgerald's meeting with Knopf, MGM offered him $1,000 a week for six months with an option for renewal at $1,250 to come to Hollywood as a script-writer. Fitzgerald accepted and moved to the Garden of Allah in Hollywood early in July 1937. There he met Sheilah Graham, Hollywood columnist.

CAN ARRIVE LOSANGELES EASILY THURSDAY INCONVEN-
IENTLY WEDNESDAY MAILING YOU CHECK ON BALTIMORE
FOR FIVE HUNDRED FOR TICKETS PLEASE WIRE ME THAT SUM
BATTERY PARK HOTEL ASHEVILLE INFORMATION SCOTTIE
LATER
    SCOTT FITZJERALD.

Wire to Ober 2 July 1937. Asheville, N.C. (AO)

F. Scott Fitzgerald, Esq.*

Dear Scott:

We have talked again to the man who is getting up the Varsity Show for the Pontiac Motor Company.† He says that the master of ceremonies didn't have to do any plugging of the product on the program last year and he says he doesn't think it will be necessary this year. I told him that was something you couldn't do. He is putting your name up to the sponsors and I'll let you know if anything comes of it.

Sincerely yours,
[Harold Ober]

July 2, 1937

TL, 1p. (AO)

---

*A note in Ober's hand reads: "didn't send because Scott now in Hollywood".
†Thomas L. Stix of Henry Souvaine radio productions had asked if Fitzgerald would be interested in serving as master of ceremonies on the touring Pontiac Varsity Show.

The item * better not start for two or three weeks as I'll need a second hand car. So for that time add it to my expense check.

Dear Harold:
Here's the way I'd like to divide my pay check for the moment.
Per week

100   to you—commission
150   "   " on debt
  50   " Scribners on debt, as follows

        1st to paid against Perkins loan
        2nd to be paid against insurance assignment held by Charles Scribner
        3d to be paid against their movie loan on Tender
        4th to be paid against my retail bill there

* 200   to be banked by you against taxes somewhere where I can get compound interest. Perhaps you make a suggestion where

100   to be banked at 1st National Baltimore for "vacation money" for I will be taking six to 8 weeks off a year.

400   to be put to my account out of which I pay expenses + $100 insurance. For the present we will call this one the expense check + when I find a bank in California will deposit it there.

_____
$1000

(Do you like this arrangement? With those stories it should clear you and me within a year)—all percentages to go up after six months of course

Scott

ALS (pencil), 1p. n.d.—received 6 July 1937. Battery Park Hotel, Asheville, N.C., stationery. (AO)

SCOTT FITZGERALD ARRIVING WEDNESDAY MORNING WILL WIRE YOU FROM TRAIN STOP HE HAS SENT ME INSTRUCTIONS FOR DISPO-SITION OF HIS WEEKLY CHECK SO SEND INSTRUCTIONS TO NEW YOUR OFFICE FOR PREPARING CONTRACT WITH WEEKLY CHECK PAYABLE TO ME IT THIS CAN BE ARRANGED STOP SCOTT WILL GIVE YOU AUTHORIZATION IF HE WANTS IT THAT WAY AS I UNDER-STAND HE DOES
    Harold Ober

Wire (cc) to Edwin Knopf 6 July 1937. (AO)

Dear Harold: This is written on a rocky train—I hope its decipher-able.

1st When you figure what I owe you you better figure interest too for the past four years at some percentage you think proper. When I made from 25–35 thousand a year with so little negotiation I didn't mind being a story in debt to you—in fact I was rather upset when the Reynolds office made me pay a double commission on the Gatsby movie—almost 20%, remember? But this big debt is entirely another matter from those days + represents a loss for you in years of smaller profit + more expense on my account. So figure something you consider fair.‡

2nd When the pay off begins I think that you should send me a witnessed note somewhat as follows—that you will accept from the insurance assignment only such a sum as I may be in debt to you on your books at the time of my demise. This protects my *estate* as I pay back the money—I will file it with my will.

Nothing more at present. I suppose Scottie will be with you. Let me know if she arrives on that 11.30 train Thursday morning. Best to Anne + all of you. Wire me if stories sell.

Ever Yours
Scott

ALS, 3pp. n.d.—received 8 July 1937. Southern Pacific Railroad stationery. (AO)

F. Scott Fitzgerald
Care Metro-Goldwyn-Mayer
Culver City, California

Dear Scott:

I have your notes this morning. We are looking forward to seeing Scottie on Thursday, and either Anne or I will meet whatever train she comes on. I know Scottie will be delighted with a few weeks in Hollywood and, if she can go out with the Mac Arthurs,§ she will enjoy it even more. But please remember that if you do not find that plan workable, we will be glad to have her with us all summer.

I have your note about the disposition of your weekly checks, and I am sending a copy of your letter in case you did not keep one. I think this ought to work out very well: I was going to suggest to you that you pay me back a little faster than you pay Scribners, because they are a prosperous corporation and do not need the money probably as much as I do, but you have arranged it that way without my suggesting it.

I tried to get you on the telephone both Sunday and Monday. I

---

‡In top margin: "I never did charge interest HO".
§Charles MacArthur and Helen Hayes.

wanted to suggest that you go to the Garden of Allah at 8152 Sunset Boulevard, Hollywood. This place is quieter than a hotel and fairly reasonable in price. Graeme Lorimer always stays there when he is in Hollywood; Harold Lamb lives there right along and Robert Benchley often stays there.

I am not sure how your employment contract will be made out, in Hollywood or in the New York office. I believe a recent California law may require that the contract be made out in Hollywood. This arrangement was made in a hurry over the telephone, and you had better let me see it before you sign it. If there is a rush about it you can let Swanson look it over.

I judge from your note that you would like to have me take care of your check each week according to the instructions you sent me. If the check is paid to me, I will dispose of it according to these instructions: if the check is paid directly to you in California, you can endorse it over to me.

I feel sure this trip to California is going to work out happily for you in every way. I think you can live inexpensively and well, and when you are through you will be able to write the novel you want to write without financial worries.

I hope to hear from Colliers within the next day or two. I had the following letter from the New Yorker;

"I want to apologize, too, for the long delay on the Scott Fitzgerald short bit,¶ which we like very much, provided he will allow us to write a new lead paragraph and make a few other slight cuts or changes. We thought his first paragraph was cloudy and really too hard for the reader. We tried to embody his idea a little more clearly. What we did was to go ahead and set it up with a new lead paragraph, but, of course, we won't use the piece until we get his approval on our changes. I enclose our check for the piece now. His list of books is very funny."

This sketch is just two pages long, and the New Yorker has sent me fifty dollars for it. This does not seem like very much, but it is what the New Yorker pays for stories of this length.

Sincerely yours,
[Harold Ober]

July 6, 1937

TL (cc), 2pp. (AO)

AM COLLECTING FARE AND ONE DAY PAY CHECK HERE STOP
THEY CANNOT DIVIDE WEEKLY PAY CHECK HERE SO WILL

¶"A Book of My Own."

DEPOSIT HERE AND SEND YOU A BATCH OF SIGNED AND
DATED CHECKS BANK OF AMERICA FOR SIX HUNDRED EACH
STOP ALL WELL
    FITZGERALD.

Wire to Ober 11 July 1937. Hollywood, Calif. (AO)

WILL GET MY FIRST CHECK TOMORROW AND SEND YOU PART
STOP TRYING TO ARRANGE TO HAVE IT PAID YOU IN NEW-
YORK OR WHAT DO YOU RECOMMEND STOP HOW ABOUT
MACARTHURS TRIP STOP EVERYTHING GOING FINE
    SCOTT FITZGERALD.

Wire to Ober 19 July 1937. Hollywood, Calif. (AO)

Anne wrote you Saturday MacArthurs trip cancelled we do
not think Scottie should go out alone probably someone suitable will be going during summer but if not think we can keep
her happy stop suggest you keep what you need and send me
balance weekly check to distribute according to your schedule
thus keeping record of everything here Scottie fine.
    Harold Ober

Wire (cc) to Fitzgerald 19 July 1937. (AO)

F. Scott Fitzgerald, Esq.
c/o Metro-Goldwyn-Mayer
Culver City, Calif.

Dear Scott:

    I would have written you before but I have been taking about ten
days in Scarsdale. I am glad things are going well with you in
Hollywood. Swanson tells me that Edwin Knopf is very pleased
with the way you are taking hold. Your contract is being made out
here and ought to be ready for signature within a few days. The
New York office is waiting for instructions on one or two points
from Hollywood.

    I got your note written on the train and it is understood of course
that I would accept from the insurance assignment only what you
actually owed me. I'll send you a note to this effect that can be filed
with the policy.

    When I talked to Swanson the other night on the telephone I
believe he told me that you are staying at the Garden of Allah. If
you are you might let me know so that I can write you wherever
you are living instead of at the Metro Goldwyn office.

    We are enjoying Scottie and I think she is happy. She is of course

looking forward to the Hollywood trip. It doesn't make any diff-
rence to us when she goes—the important thing is that there is
someone to go out with her and someone to be with her while she
is in Hollywood.

I have a note from Littauer saying he wants to talk to me about
the two stories. I may not be able to see him until next week but
I'll write you after I have had a talk with him.

> Sincerely yours,
> [Harold Ober]

July 21, 1937

TL (cc), 1p. (AO)

HELEN MACARTHUR STARTING WEST AUGUST SECOND SHE
WILL BE AT NYACK WEDNESDAY PHONE 1010 AND SCOTTIE
SHOULD CALL HER THEN YOUR CHATTEL
 SCOTT FITZGERALD.

Wire to Anne Ober 23 July 1937. Hollywood, Calif.

F. Scott Fitzgerald, Esq.
ᶜ/o Metro-Goldwyn-Mayer
Culver City, Cal.

Dear Scott:

I received the $600. from your first salary check and am taking
care of it in accordance with your instructions.

Your telegram came yesterday and I understand Scottie is to start
for Hollywood with Helen Hayes on August 2nd or 3rd. Helen
Hayes has a broadcast in the evening of August 1st so I doubt if they
will get away until the 2nd. I'll wire you of course so that you will
know when she is leaving.

I have just had a talk with Littauer and he says neither the Civil
War story nor the football story are just right. He is going to read
over the football story and see if he can write a letter making
suggestions that he thinks will make the story all right.

He says Mr. Chenery and Mr. Colebaugh* have read the Civil
War story and they both liked the first part of it very much indeed.
They suggest that the whole time of the story cover only two or
three days. They think it should finish with the girl rescuing Tib
and going off with him. They think the girl would be through with
her brother and never want to see him again. What do you think

---

*Editors at *Collier's*.

about this? If you think you can do it I'll send you on a carbon. It will certainly be the easiest thing to do as far as the number of words you have to write. Littauer says now he thinks the whole trouble with the Civil War story was the break in time.

Sincerely yours,
[Harold Ober]

July 26, 1937

P.S. I have a refund of $6.99 from Franklin Simon's. Do you want me to deposit this in your Baltimore bank or send it to you in Hollywood?

TL (cc), 1p. (AO)

Dear Anne:

This letter is long overdue. Suffice to summarize: I have seen Hollywood—talked with Taylor, dined with March, danced with Ginger Rogers (this will burn Scottie up but its true) been in Rosalind Russel's dressing room, wise-cracked with Montgomery, drunk (gingerale) with Zukor and Lasky,[†] lunched alone with Maureen OSullivan, watched Crawford act and lost my heart to a beautiful half caste Chinese girl whos name I've forgotten. So far Ive bought my own breakfasts.

And this is to say Im through. From now on I go nowhere and see no one because the work is hard as hell, at least for me and I've lost ten pounds. So farewell Miriam Hopkins who leans <u>so</u> close when she talks, so long Claudette Clobert as yet unencountered, mysterious Garbo, glamourous Dietrich, exotic Shirley Temple— you will never know me. Except Miriam who promised to call up but hasn't. There is nothing left, girls but to believe in reincarnation and carry on.

Tell my daughter she is a vile daughter of Babylon who does not write letters but can charge $25. worth of wash dresses at Franklin Simons but nowhere else. Or if she wants Harold will advance her $25 from a check sent today to go to Saks.

Im glad she is playing tennis. I do want to see the wretched little harpy and don't let her make a mess of it. Helen will be in Nyack after the 29th—and is leaving the 2nd. No Long Island date should prevent Scottie from getting in touch with her and coming with her. All Metro could find for chaperones were the Ritz Brothers and

---

†Adolph Zukor and Jesse Lasky, studio executives.

I can't see it. They might vanish her as a practical joke.

> Yours with Gratitude + Devotion
> Scott

ALS, 2pp. n.d., n.p.—Anne Ober has dated this letter 26 July 1937. Hollywood. (MJB)

F. Scott Fitzgerald, Esq.
Garden of Allah
8152 Sunset Boulevard
Hollywood, Calif.

Dear Scott:

Scottie talked to Mrs. MacArthur last night and they are leaving on the 20th Century Tuesday, August 3rd. Mrs. MacArthur is taking care of getting the tickets and I'll see that she is paid for them.

I am enclosing a statement dated July 20th which is the last statement before your salary began. I am also enclosing two shorter statements covering your first two salary checks. I am of course taking care of Swanson's commission so you don't need to worry about that. Will you let me know if statements in this form each week will be clear to you?

Anne read me last night the letter you sent her. The only thing I didn't like about it was that you had lost ten pounds and I hope you will soon get some of this back. Anne was very pleased with the letter.

> Sincerely yours,
> [Harold Ober]

July 29, 1937

P.S. Perhaps you would rather have us send a monthly statement. I should think you might get a little tired of seeing <u>balance due</u> so often. Perhaps we can think of some way to make up the statements without showing the balance.

TL (cc), 1p. (AO)

F. Scott Fitzgerald In account with Harold Ober

....

Balance due Harold Ober June 9		12511.69
Typing:- FINANCING FINNEGAN	2.34	
" " (revised)	3.42	
No TIME FOR THAT NOW		
(new ending)	3.45	

OFFSIDE PLAY		5.58	
DENTIST APPOINTMENT		4.50	
By Western Union to Asheville,N.C.			
July 3		400.00	
Western Union charge		2.42	421.71
			12933.40
Received from New Yorker	30.00		
ODE TO PARNASSUS			
All Magazine Rights			
10% Commission	3.00	27.00	
Received from American			
Cavalcade	300.00		
EARLY SUCCESS			
1st American & Canadian			
serial rights			
10% Commission	30.00	270.00	
Received from F.S. Fitzgerald			
July 6		400.00	697.00
Balance due Harold Ober			12236.40

I trust you will find the above accounting correct.

HAROLD OBER

July 20, 1937
F. Scott Fitzgerald, Esq.
Garden of Allah
8152 Sunset Boulevard
Hollywood, Calif.

Typed account (cc), 1p. (AO)

F. Scott Fitzgerald In account with Harold Ober

Balance due Harold Ober July 20			12236.40
Received from F.S. Fitzgerald			
July 23		600.	
10% Commission on salary			
for week ending July 14	100.		
Maxwell Perkins	50.		
Savings Bank	200.		
Advanced to Scottie Fitzgerald:			
July 12	15.		
20	25.		
For Scottie's trip to California	60.	450.	150.00
Balance July 23rd			12086.40

I trust you will find the above accounting correct.

HAROLD OBER

July 23, 1937
F. Scott Fitzgerald, Esq.
Garden of Allah
8152 Sunset Boulevard
Hollywood, Calif.

Typed account (cc), 1p. (AO)

F. Scott Fitzgerald In account with Harold Ober

....

Balance due Harold Ober July 23rd			12086.40
Received from F.S. Fitzgerald			
July 28		550.	
10% Commission on salary			
for week ending July 21	100.		
Maxwell Perkins	50.		
Savings Bank	200.		
For Scottie's trip to California	50.	400.	150.00
Balance July 29th			11936.40

I trust you will find the above accounting correct.

HAROLD OBER

July 29, 1937
F. Scott Fitzgerald, Esq.
Garden of Allah
8152 Sunset Boulevard
Hollywood, Calif.

Typed account (cc), 1p. (AO)

F. Scott Fitzgerald, Esq.
Garden of Allah
8152 Sunset Boulevard
Hollywood, Calif.

Dear Scott:

What do you think about sending FINANCING FINNEGAN
to Esquire? It is possible that you have already done this as I think
the last time we spoke of it I said I thought that would probably be
the best place for it.

Sincerely yours,
[Harold Ober]

July 30, 1937

TL (cc), 1p. (AO)

Dear Harold

Better Send [me] <u>Finnegan</u> to Esquire as if it came Straight from me. I already owe them for it

Scott

Post card (pencil), n.d.—postmarked 3 August 1937. Los Angeles. (AO)

F. Scott Fitzgerald, Esq.
Garden of Allah
8152 Sunset Boulevard
Hollywood, Calif.

Dear Scott:

I have the following letter from Littauer of Collier's. You may like to have this with you when you tackle these two stories.

"Here are two stories by F. Scott Fitzgerald.

The one called DENTIST APPOINTMENT‡—which belongs to us—still leaves a great deal to be desired. For reasons too numerous to mention we don't like the new ending. Our suggestion to Mr. Fitzgerald now is that he revise the story so as to conclude the action within a very brief space of time.

The best of this story has always been the part that takes place in the farmhouse. After the conclusion of that episode nothing is of comparable interest. Why wouldn't it be possible therefore to finish the story in the place where it begins and within a period of twenty-four hours? After all, what interests us is the relationship of Tib Dulany and Josie Pilgrim. There seems to be no point in making us wait years to bring them to the happy issue. We are inclined to believe that the story will come out well if Josie rebels violently and promptly against the inhumanity of her brother and forsakes him without hesitation in favor of the man he has outraged. There might be another raid by Mosby's men to conclude the story with the rescue of Dulany and the flight of the girl at her injured lover's side.

Now a word about OFFSIDE PLAY. There is a great deal of good stuff in this story but the action is altogether too complicated. Unless we are mistaken the whole thing needs to be simplified and very sharply focused. For instance, the introduction of a co-ed wife for Van Kamp is a piece of strongarm work that ought to make a master of subtleties like Fitzgerald blush for shame. There is too much about Kiki and the Old Grads. There is too much about all sorts of major and minor irrelevancies. If this story ran a true course

---

‡A new version of "Thumbs Up."

it would end in the neighborhood of page twenty. The only thing that carries it all the way to page thirty-one is a conglomeration of ellipses and detours that do nothing but confuse the issue and bewilder the reader. Therefore, won't you ask Mr. Fitzgerald to make this the story of Alex and Rip and the girl. Tell us what they do to each other. Throw the spotlight on them in the center of the stage and shove everything else into the background or out in the wings as much as possible. Emphasize particularly the importance and poignancy of the romance of Alex and Kiki.

If you think well of the foregoing suggestions will you pass them along verbatim or in paraphrase to Mr. Fitzgerald and at the same time give him my regards and best wishes. Tell him I am sorry he had to go so far away. I had been hoping to see a lot of him during the coming year."

I am sending you under separate cover a carbon of OFFSIDE PLAY in case you haven't one with you. I sent you the other day a carbon of DENTIST APPOINTMENT.

Have you with you a copy of THAT KIND OF PARTY?

I am enclosing two receipted bills, one from Best and one from Lord & Taylor.

Sincerely yours,
Harold Ober

August 4, 1937

Love to Scottie. The house is very dull and quiet without her.¶

TLS, 2pp. (PU)

F. Scott Fitzgerald, Esq.
Garden of Allah
8152 Sunset Boulevard
Hollywood, Calif.

Dear Scott:

Richard Sherman, who wrote TO MARY WITH LOVE and a number of other stories that have been published in the Post, is working at 20th Century-Fox. His address is 338 North Barrington Avenue, Brentwood, Los Angeles. He has spoken a number of times of wanting to meet you and I think you would enjoy meeting him. He is very modest and somewhat shy and I don't believe he would make the first move. I feel very sure that you would like him and I hope you will call him up.

¶Added in Ober's hand.

I have a number of other authors working in Hollywood who I am not going to even mention to you.

I have your postcard and I have sent FINANCING FINNE-GAN to Esquire in a plain envelope.

I have also sent you a carbon of THAT KIND OF PARTY.

Sincerely yours,
[Harold Ober]

August 5, 1937

TL (cc), 1p. (AO)

F. Scott Fitzgerald In account with Harold Ober

Balance July 29			11936.40
Received from F. Scott Fitzgerald			
Aug. 3		300.00	
9		700.00	
		1000.00	
(from salary for weeks ending July 28			
Aug. 4)			
&10% Commission	200.00		
Maxwell Perkins	100.00		
Bowery Savings Bank	400.00	700.00	300.00
			11636.40
Received from F. Scott Fitzgerald			
on Aug. 17		600.00	
(from salary for week ending Aug. 11)			
10% Commission	100.00		
Maxwell Perkins	50.00		
Bowery Savings Bank	200.00		
For Scottie's trip	100.00	450.00	150.00
			11486.40
Received from F. Scott Fitzgerald			
on Aug. 17		500.00	
(from salary for week ending Aug. 18)			
10% Commission	100.00		
Maxwell Perkins	50.00		
Bowery Savings Bank	200.00	350.00	150.00
Balance Aug. 17			11336.40

August 24, 1937

Typed account, 1p. From Helen Good.* Ober agency letterhead. (PU)

---

*Helen Good, who was a bookkeeper with Ober at this time, is Anne Ober's sister.

Dear Anne:

I (we) are making our home here for a few hours till the plane comes.# Scottie will come to you about the 11th or 12th if the invitation is still open. You ask about smoking—with my record of T.B. once in college + then two years ago, + Scotties flat chest smoking would be suicidal—especially as she is not a moderate child but one who would begin with a few + then be smoking a package a day. Thank heavens she doesn't smoke at Walkers. I've asked her not to smoke + can't do much more. Of course don't tell her Ive written this but if it comes up + you ask her she'll tell you frankly, I think, that I don't want her to.

She'll give you all the news better than I could, All goes beautifully in Hollywood but I'm glad of this rest, I slept all day on the train 18 hrs straight which is how hard I've been working

Devotedly
Scott

ALS, 2pp. n.d.—dated by Mrs. Ober, September 1937. Hotel Paso del Norte, El Paso, Texas, stationery.

SCOTTIE ARRIVES NEWYORK THIS WEEK WILL PHONE STOP
AM HOLLYWOOD BOUND TONIGHT
 SCOTT.

Wire to Ober 12 September 1937. Asheville, N.C. (AO)

IS SCOTTIE WITH YOU I AM A LITTLE WORRIED AS I HAVE HEARD NOTHING STOP NOTE YOUR LETTER ASKS ABOUT UNCHAPERONED PARTIES IN NEWYORK AT NIGHT STOP AFRAID IM ABSOLUTELY OPPOSED TO THAT AT FIFTEEN STOP BEST TO ALL DEVOTEDLY
 SCOTT.

Wire to Anne Ober 18 September 1937. Beverly Hills, Calif.

September 18, 1937.

Dear Ann:

I am enclosing a letter from the Walker School. I hope the note about tutoring reached you.

I don't know whether Scottie is with you or with her Aunt Rosalyn. She hasn't bothered to write me. She really behaved herself beautifully out here and made a great hit with everyone, though I am quite sure she will be the school nuisance this term with her tales of the great and the near-great.

#Fitzgerald and Scottie were Eastbound to visit Zelda.

My holiday wasn't much of a holiday as you can imagine, but I think Zelda enjoyed it. Things had gone beautifully out here up to then, but this week it has been very hard to pick up the thread of work, and I see next week a horror trying to make up for five wasted days.

I have your letter and notice that you mentioned something else beside the smoking (I wrote you about that). I still don't believe that she should go out unchaperoned with a boy at night and have never allowed it. As for going alone somewhere after the theatre—my God! is that anywhere allowed at fifteen, or am I Rip Van Winkle? I once let her go with two boys to a dinner dance place here on condition that they would be home before midnight, but I think she understands that was an exception.

She was much too precocious in the things she did at fourteen, but after this year at Walkers, she seems much more appropriately her age, capable of amusing herself usefully and rationally without constant stimulation. I really think she's going to be all right now, though there was a time about a year and a half ago when I thought she was going to become an awful empty head. Thank God for boarding schools.

Something else I wanted to say has eluded me. I am your forever grateful and devoted henchman[†]

Scott F.

TLS, 1p. MGM letterhead.

IS SCOTTI WITH YOU PLEASE ANSWER GARDEN OF ALLAH HO-
TEL HOLLYWOOD WORRIED AFFECTIONATELY
    SCOTT.

Wire to Anne Ober 19 September 1937. Hollywood, Calif.

TERRIBLY SHOCKED AND SURPRISED TO SEE THAT TOM COS-
TAIN HAS CHANGED AND VULGARIZED MY ARTICLE[‡] STOP
THIS HAS NEVER BEEN DONE IN SEVENTEEN YEARS AND I
WANT TO BRING SUIT OR RECEIVE A SUBSTANTIAL RECOM-
PENSE STOP I AM SIMPLY NOT TAKING THIS
    SCOTT FITZGERALD.

Wire to Ober 28 September 1937. Hollywood, Calif. (AO)

[†]This paragraph added in ink.
[‡]"Early Success," *American Cavalcade*, October 1937.

F. Scott Fitzgerald, Esq.,
Garden of Allah,
8152 Sunset Boulevard
Hollywood, Calif.

Dear Scott:

I got your telegram about the short piece in American Cavalcade. I have just compared the piece word for word with my carbon copy of the manuscript. It is true that the manuscript was cut in a few places, but it hasn't been changed nor vulgarized. Nothing has been written into the article that you didn't write yourself, and it doesn't seem to me that the changes have in any way altered the meaning or the character of the article.

If you remember, your article was written when you needed money in a hurry, and all negotiations were done over the telephone. I remember, however, that the article was longer than Costain wanted, and I understood, and I think you did at the time, that it might have to be cut. The first cut was the following:

"Nickles and dimes in the hand. Did they make a dollar? Almost, but those two stamps had made the difference. And when one is under a dollar everything is different, people look different, food looks different."

The next cut was the incident of the anonymous admirer who called on you. The next few lines cut were about misspellings in THIS SIDE OF PARADISE. Next a few lines were cut where you mentioned your father being a failure.

If you want, I'll send you a copy of the manuscript, showing you exactly the cuts that were made. By the way, I found one misspelling that should have been changed and wasn't!

I really don't think you need be worried about this, and I don't think you have any ground for serious complaint. I found the article, when I reread it, thoughtful, interesting and dignified, and I don't see how anyone could find it otherwise.

                              Sincerely yours,
                              [Harold Ober]

September 28, 1937

TL (cc), 2pp. (AO)

F. Scott Fitzgerald, Esq.,
Garden of Allah,
8152 Sunset Boulevard,
Hollywood, Calif.

Dear Scott:

When you have time drop me a line and let me know what you are working on in the studio. Will you have any time in the evenings to work on stories? A little work on the Civil War story and on the football story will enable you to cash in on them. The main thing, however, at the present moment is to do a good job in the studio, and from all I hear you are doing that.

Someone called up from the Times yesterday and said that they understood you had finished a play based on TENDER IS THE NIGHT. Your much-loved newspaper, the New York Evening Post, had said that you had only the third part of the last act to finish. Drop me a line when you want to tell me about it.

Scottie is starting back to school on Thursday. She is very busy and very happy and looks very well indeed. We shall miss her when she leaves.

Sincerely yours,
[Harold Ober]

September 29, 1937

TL (cc), 1p. (AO)

F. Scott Fitzgerald In account with Harold Ober

....

Balance Aug. 17			11336.40
Received from F. Scott Fitzgerald on Aug. 31		600.00	
(from salary for ws/e Aug. 25 & Sept. 1)			
10% Commission	200.00		
Maxwell Perkins	100.00	300.00	300.00
			11036.40
Received from F. Scott Fitzgerald on Sept. 22		307.20	
(from salary for w/e Sept. 15 & July 8—one day)			
10% Commission	107.20		
Maxwell Perkins	50.00	157.20	150.00
			10886.40

Received from F. Scott Fitzgerald			
on Sept. 29		300.00	
(from salary for w/e Sept. 22)			
10% Commission	100.00		
Maxwell Perkins	50.00	150.00	150.00
			10736.40
Received from F. Scott Fitzgerald			
on Oct. 6		400.00	
(from salary for w/e Sept. 29)			
10% Commission	100.00		
Maxwell Perkins	50.00		
For Scottie's expenses	100.00	250.00	150.00
			10586.40

Typed account, 1p. From Helen Good 8 October 1937. Ober agency letterhead. (PU)

October 8, 1937.

Mr. Harold Ober
408 East 49th St.
New York, N. Y.

Dear Harold:

Will you get in touch with this woman. I understand that Mrs. Jarrett and Miss Oglebay§ are well-known writers, though I don't happen to have heard of them.

So far as I know, nothing new has happened to TENDER IS THE NIGHT—last I heard of, Kirkland's option had expired—didn't it? and the Spofford play pretty much turned down, so I think this is a good bet. Maybe they have a new approach that will solve the problem. In fact, I wish you would make an encouraging deal with them, as something must be done within the next two years to keep the book alive. Of all my books it seems the biggest cripple. I suggest the terms that we gave Owen Davis—half the paid play royalties and a third of the total moving picture rights with the manager taking a third. Or perhaps I could be content with a [full] fourth of the moving picture rights. What do you think? They are not as well known as Davis, but on the other hand, TENDER is a good deal deader than GATSBY was when Davis dramatized it.

I'm sorry about the awful row I raised about the Calvacade story. I don't know what was the matter with me that morning—I could have sworn that I hadn't written a line of it, especially that first part. I know I wrote it in an awful hurry, but it seems odd that I should

§Cora Jarrett and Kate Oglebay.

have forgotten it to that extent. Anyhow, thanks and a thousand pardons. Incidently, when I read the article over again last night, it didn't seem so bad.

I finished THREE COMRADES on my own. Mankiewicz# was enthusiastic about the first part and will report on the second part tomorrow. We are going over it together which means a rewriting of perhaps three weeks duration. They planned for it to go into production when Taylor* gets back from England sometime in November. I was two months and a week on the script, which is rather more than averagely fast time. If I do three weeks more on it, my work will still have cost them less than a fifth of what the average shooting script costs. So I seem to be a good investment— unless something untoward happens. The thing is rather dangerous politically—aside from that I think nothing stands in the way of its going through and of my getting the credit, which is a big thing out here. You have credits, or you don't have credits, and naturally I'm eager to have one in the book. What the next assignment will be, I don't know.

I'm happy here but of course the first excitement has worn off and I fret a good deal with the desire to do work on my own. Perhaps after another adaptation they will let me do an original, which will exercise the intellectual muscles in a more [agreeable] *amplified* manner.

The checks against taxes have lapsed and will continue to be absent for a while as there are more insurance payments due than I thought, and it seems to me they should be cleared up first. After all, it isn't next year that the taxes will fall so heavily but the year after, when it should be counted as a regular weekly deduction from my check.

I am also enclosing a letter in regard to the letter mailed me by Graham Reid as to THE VEGETABLE.† I think I will accept the offer. It hasn't flopped for a long time now and maybe their changes will do something with it.

In regard to the stories, I am going to do something about them but have definitely postponed it until after THREE COMRADES

Fitzgerald's first major assignment. Joseph Mankiewicz, the producer, subsequently revised Fitzgerald's script.

*Robert Taylor.

†In the top margin of page one, a note in another hand reads: "Can't find letter from Graham Reid on the Vegetable but have made note and will send it tomorrow. F S. F Per T.B." The Masque Players, a Chicago amateur group, had requested permission to "modernize" the play.

is in the bag—as I told you which is a matter of three weeks more. Then I will either take a week off or simply find time some way in the early morning. So tell Colliers not to fret about it. The longer I wait the more I am liable to get a fresh point of view. I think maybe you are dead on them and so is Collier, and I will have them both read here by someone who can put their finger on the trouble. Both of them come so near being right that I am sure the actual writing won't be any trouble. To get the right point of view is the question —which seems to be all [off] right now.

Yours, *Ever*

Scott Fitz

TLS, 2pp. MGM letterhead. (AO)

F. Scott Fitzgerald, Esq.,
Garden of Allah,
8152 Sunset Boulevard,
Hollywood, Calif.

Dear Scott:

I saw Edwin Knopf on Friday, and he told me that he and every-one at Metro-Goldwyn is delighted with the work you are doing on the picture you are now working on. I am glad everything is going well with you.

We had a letter from Scottie the other day. She seems very busy and very happy.

We are enclosing an account. If you would rather have these accounts oftener or less often, let me know. If you would rather have them once in three months, we can do it that way.

Sincerely yours,

[Harold Ober]

October 13, 1937

TL (cc), 1p. (AO)

F. Scott Fitzgerald, Esq.,
Garden of Allah,
8152 Sunset Boulevard,
Hollywood, Calif.

D ear Scott:

Thank you for your letter of October 8th and for the copy of the letter from Mrs. Pritchett and your reply.

One of these women, Mrs. Jarrett, is Cora Jarrett who wrote

NIGHT OVER FITCH'S POND, THE GANKGO TREE, and other books. She is a writer of a great deal of ability. The other one I don't know anything about but I will find out what I can about her. We'll draw up an agreement along the lines you suggest. Your share of the picture rights is now definitely determined by the minimum basic agreement. The authors now receive 60% and the managers 40%. Your share would, therefore, be 30%.

Thanks for letting me know about your work in Hollywood. I hope THREE COMRADES will be a very successful picture and that when I go to see it I shall see your name on the screen in large letters.

Sincerely yours,
[Harold Ober]

October 20, 1937

TL (cc), 1p. (AO)

F. Scott Fitzgerald, Esq.,
Garden of Allah,
8152 Sunset Boulevard,
Hollywood, Calif.

Dear Scott:

I am glad to know that Metro-Goldwyn have exercised your option.§ More often than not, options which carry increased salaries are not renewed. They certainly are not renewed unless the writer is doing good work. Everyone I see from Metro tells me you are doing exceedingly good work.

Are you coming East during the Christmas Holidays. If you come, I hope we shall see you. We had a note from Scottie saying that her vacation begins on the 17th. She will probably see us on the 18th or 19th before she goes to Baltimore. We hope she will be with us after she gets through her Baltimore parties and before she goes back to school. We shall, of course, be delighted to have you stay with us any time you can.

Sincerely yours,
[Harold Ober]

December 7, 1937

TL (cc), 1p. (AO)

---

§MGM renewed Fitzgerald's contract for twelve months at $1,250 a week.

Dear Harold:

Im glad too that they renewed the contract. Well, I've worked hard as hell—in a world where it seems to me the majority are loafers + incompetents.

If they'll let me work alone all the time, which I think they will when they have a little more confidence I think I can turn out four [or five] pictures a year by myself with months off included. <u>Then</u> I'll ask for some big money.

It is nervous work but I like it, save for the damn waiting + the time-killing conferences.

Im going to try to bring the Colliers story East at Xmas. I will come to N. Y. for at least a day + let you know my whereabouts in the meanwhile. Scottie has managed to work out some system for what looks like a good share of Baltimore dancing. Thanks for wanting her—She'll write you or I will to arrange a visit to you when its convenient of you to have her. [as of course] *I hope to have my scattered family together Xmas day somewhere More later*
Scott

ALS (pencil), 2pp. n.d.—received 14 December 1937. Garden of Allah, Hollywood, Calif., stationery. (AO)

MERRY CHRISTMAS TO TWO PEOPLE WHO MADE AN OLD YEAR
POSSIBLE AND A NEW YEAR HAPPY
   SCOTT FITZGERALD.

Wire to Mr. and Mrs. Harold Ober, n.d. 25 December 1937. Hollywood, Calif.

Dear Anne:

Thanks for your note. Scottie will be north again before school opens. As she is obviously destined to be a perpetual guest I do try to split her visits with such easily-imposed-on yaps as the Finneys and Obers into reasonable bits lest the golden gooses cease to lay—wait a minute, this metaphor has gotten entirely out of hand. Any how all I can think of is for you and Harold to spend your old age with me—and even that wont square things.

These letters or cards for Scottie come to hand—better hold them. I have high hopes of getting East <u>before</u> she goes back to school—if not I'll go to her school in January. I love it here. It's nice work if you can get it and you can get it if you try about three years. The point is once you've got it—Screen Credit 1st, a Hit 2nd and the Academy Award 3d—you can count on it forever—like Laurence Stallings¶ *does*—and know there's one place you'll be fed, without

---

¶Author of *What Price Glory?* and successful screen-writer.

[work] *being asked to even wash the dishes.* But till we get those [cre] three accolades we Hollywood boys keep trying.

That's [obliterated] [is] cynical but I'm not a bit cynical. I'm delighed with screen credit and really hopeful of a hit—the line up is good, depending on whether or not one of our principals has to have an operation. I hope none of you need even an extraction

Ever Affectionately
Scott Fitzg—

P.S. I recognized the dogs individually in your Christmas card. I'm going to have my suite photographed with the mice in the hall for next Xmas. (Im getting old and un-fertile so will put this crack in my note-book)

ALS (pencil), 2pp. n.d.—c. Christmas 1937. Los Angeles.

Dear Harold:

All is in confusion about the production date#—or rather about the script-for-production + therefore my plans are vague. Scottie's too.

In brief I can leave *here* either Mon 2nd (doubtful) + see Scottie, or else Fri 8th + go up to school + see her.

In either case will <u>you</u> look forward, if convenient, to having her with you from the 3d on or thereabouts. She went to see her mother + is now with her beloved Peaches in Baltimore. I called her on the phone today + she mentions festivities of great local import which probably involve some new boy wonder but I failed to follow it exactly except that *it* involves staying there till after New Years to go to a dance which came persistently over the phone as the "Whacknot".

She said her mother seemed well—went out for a drive with her alone.

I envy you your children for Xmas. (Dick's friend Jackson from [the] Exeter wasn't the star as prophecied.) I suppose I'll see enough of Scottie sometime + should be grateful for this summer.

Life is *now* like the end of all novels + short stories [at present] —me the only one caring, + ready to weep about it, tho that's confidential. Such statements in the East seemed aimed at a trust but here they are re-directed at individuals. Did you ever hear of a screen-writer giving out *real* interviews?

I thought I'd divide the $1250.00 (until [the] my [obliterated]

#For *Three Comrades.*

insurance ect. is finally paid up as.)

125.	Commission
75.	Scribner
200.	Debt to you
400.	
200.	Absolute deposit against taxes
600.	To you absolutely every week

Balance of 650. to me

I bet 3 Comrades is good. We go into production the 4th*

Ever Yr Devoted Friend
Scott

P. S. Check Enclosed.

ALS (pencil), 2pp. n.d., n.p.—received 31 December 1937. Los Angeles. (AO)

Fitzgerald stopped keeping his ledger in 1937. He published six stories, one poem, and two articles during that year.

WILL BE DELAYED PROBABLY UNTIL THIS WEEKEND STOP
PLEASE TELL SCOTTY THAT HER FUTURE PLANS DEPEND ON
HOW MUCH LATIN GROUNDWORK SHE CAN DO IN EIGHT
DAYS STOP BEST REGARDS ALWAYS[†]
    SCOTT.

Wire to Ober 4 January 1938. Los Angeles. (AO)

SCOTTIE HERE TUTORING ARRANGED. SURE SHE WILL BE ALL
RIGHT REMEMBER SHE IS ONLY SIXTEEN MY BOYS WILL NOT
GET TO COLLEGE UNTIL EIGHTEEN BUT I SHALL BE AS FIRM
WITH HER AS I CAN SO DO NOT WORRY
    Harold Ober

Wire (cc) to Fitzgerald 4 January 1938. (AO)

F. Scott Fitzgerald, Esq.
Garden of Allah,
8152 Sunset Boulevard,
Hollywood, Calif.

Dear Scott:

I have prepared contracts for the dramatization of TENDER IS
THE NIGHT between yourself and Cora Jarrett and Kate

---

*These two sentences, the closing, and the postscript are written along the left margin of page two.
†Scottie had failed a Latin exam.

Oglebay. You will recall that you wrote to me about this sometime ago. The contracts have been signed by the two dramatists and if you find them satisfactory, will you sign all copies and send them to me?

Briefly the contract provides that the dramatists will submit an outline of the play to you by February 8th. You will have three weeks in which to approve the outline. If you do approve it, they will then have until June 1st to write the completed dramatization. You will then have three weeks to approve the dramatization. If you approve it, the dramatists will have eighteen months in which to secure a production contract for the play, and any producer they may propose is also subject to your approval.

Cora Jarrett's latest novel is called I ASK NO OTHER THING. She has also written NIGHT OVER FITCH'S POND, THE GINKGO TREE and STRANGE HOUSES. Miss Oglebay has been connected with the theatre for sometime although she has not had anything of hers produced.

The play royalties and receipts from all other sources are to be divided equally between you and the dramatists.Under the terms of the minimum Basic Agreement, the manager receives a 40% interest in the motion picture rights, leaving a balance of 60% to the authors, of which your share would be ½ or 30%of the gross. Under the terms of the contract you are fully protected in the event this venture is unsuccessful.

Sincerely yours,
[Harold Ober]

January 11, 1938

P. S.   Will you also initial the pages of the contracts where I have made checks.

TL (cc), 2pp. (AO)

Dear Harold:

After this the checks will be $400. *or $600* as *last* Wed ended my 1st wk. under the new salary. Please check this now. In my calculation we're square—for the 1st six months (minus the week I took off in Sept.

This year I will be paying you at the rate of $850. a month so we should be clear well before Xmas.

I'll be seeing you within ten days

Scott

ALS (pencil), 1p. n.d., n.p.—received 12 January 1938. Los Angeles. (AO)

F. Scott Fitzgerald, Esq.
Garden of Allah
8152 Sunset Boulevard
Hollywood, Calif.

Dear Scott:

Thankyou for your check for $300.00 for the week ending January 5, 1937.[†] I understand from Swanson that Metro are keeping you on the old contract until January 12, 193[7]*8*, to make up the week you took off in September. The enclosed accounts do not include the $300.00 received today.

Will you let me know what disposition to make of the $50.00 from your salary from the weeks ending December 29, 1937 and January 5, 1938—the $50.00 usually set aside for Max Perkins. Your account with him, $1150.00, was paid in full with the check from your salary with the week ending December 22, 1937.

Sincerely,
[Harold Ober]

January 14, 1938

TL (cc), 1p. (AO)

F. Scott Fitzgerald, Esq.
Garden of Allah,
8152 Sunset Boulevard,
Hollywood, Calif.

Dear Scott:

I haven't heard from you but I hope you arrived safely in Hollywood. This letter is to remind you that the contract covering the dramatization of TENDER IS THE NIGHT stipulates that you must give your disapproval of the script within three weeks—or by February 17th. If no disapproval is given, the dramatization is automatically approved.

So please remember to send me a wire about this so that I shall receive it on or before the 17th of this month.

Sincerely yours,
[Harold Ober]

February 7, 1938

TL (cc), 1p. (AO)

[†]i.e., 1938.

February 9, 1938.

Mr. Harold Ober
40 East 49th St.
New York, N. Y.

Dear Harold:

I went on salary on the day I arrived, which was Monday, January 31st. The $200.00 is for the half week from Monday to Wednesday. The $400.00 is for the new week which will end today, February 9th. Beginning next week, I will be sending you $600.00 to bank $200.00 against taxes as we agreed.

I have two letters from you regarding Scottie and her expenses. I will take care of Scottie's expenses next week, or you can charge them against my general account.

It is all right about the dramatization of TENDER IS THE NIGHT, though I am returning the manuscript with some suggested changes. It seemed to me excellent. I am amazed at how much of the novel they got into it. My only fear is that there is perhaps a little too much of the novel in it, so that some of the dialogue has a Shavian voluminousness.

I am writing Ann at length. Of course, every item of expense which she incurred in going to Hartford must go on my account. I must contribute at least that to the party which Scottie described as "perfectly wonderful".

Sidney Skolsky, a columnist, says this week that: "The screen play of THREE COMRADES was written by F. Scott Fitzgerald and E. E. Paramore Jr., and there was grapevine news that it was one of the best scripts ever turned in at Metro."¶ But though one is being given many compliments, the truth of the matter is that the heart is out of the script and it will not be a great picture, unless I am very much mistaken. Tracy# has to go to the hospital and Franchot Tone plays his part, which is the final blow. I have been watching the taking of the mob scenes which ought to be excellent if they were about anything, now that the German Consul has had its say.

I am in the midst of one of those maddening weeks here where I am waiting to see Mr. Stromberg.* It seems odd to be paid for telephoning twice a day to see if I can get an appointment, but

---

¶ *The New York Daily Mirror*, 9 February 1928, p. 26.
# Spencer Tracy.
*Hunt Stromberg.

everyone says that I am lucky to be with him because when he works he goes directly to the point and is the best producer on the lot, if not in Hollywood.

I will be on the new Joan Crawford picture[†] and it looks at the moment as if I will have to write an original even though it will be founded on some play or story. There is no full length play or novel available that seems really suited for her, as she is the most difficult star to cast. Anyhow, that will be my assignment up to Easter, I think, and probably for some time afterwards.

I have a lot more to write you, but this will do for the present.

We had a terrible trip back, and the plane flew all over the South before it could buck through the winds up to Memphis, then it flew back and forth for three hours between Memphis and Nashville, trying to land. Then we got a tail-wind behind us and blew into Los Angeles only four hours late Monday morning.

I have not forgotten any of our conversations and shall try to follow your suggestions about money, work, etc.

Yours,
Scott

TLS, 2pp. MGM letterhead. (AO)

SOMEONE PRODUCING PLAY CALLED SAVE ME THE WALTZ STOP PLEASE INVESTIGATE STOP LIKE JARRET PLAY AND AM WRITING HER
    SCOTT FITZGERALD.

Wire to Ober 14 February 1938. Hollywood, Calif. (AO)

F. Scott Fitzgerald, Esq.
Garden of Allah,
8152 Sunset Boulevard,
Hollywood, Calif.

Dear Scott:

I have your telegram about SAVE ME THE WALTZ. This play is by Catherine Dayton who wrote FIRST LADY, and it is now being tried out in Washington. The notices have not been very good and it may not come to New York at all.

I have talked to Max Perkins and he thinks that about a year ago they had a request to use this title and that they consulted you and then refused. He is going to look-up the letters and send me copies.

---

†"Infidelity"—not produced.

With evidence that they had asked permission and were refused we can make a strong complaint and ask that the title be changed. I asked my lawyer and he tells me that in his opinion there is no legal way to prevent the use of this title. As you know, there is no copyright on a title. If Zelda's book were a current book and selling large numbers of copies, something could be done but it was published several years ago and the sale is over and in his opinion it would be impossible to prove damages.

I am glad you are working with Stromberg. I think he is one of the very best of the producers.

I am glad, too, that the dramatization of TENDER IS THE NIGHT was fairly satisfactory and I am pleased you are writing to the author.

Sincerely yours,
Harold Ober

February 15, 1938

TLS, 1p. (PU)

February 17, 1938.

Mr. Harold Ober
40 East 49th St.
New York, N. Y.

Dear Harold:

It has just occurred to me that that man to whom I was so rude at luncheon, was Weise of McCalls.‡ Suggest you send him the attached letter as if you were doing it without my suggestion.

If it was not Weise of McCalls, disregard this, because I don't remember any other Weise. There is no use making an enemy of an editor.

Enclosed also is a letter to Cora Jarrett about the play. It seems to me awfully talky and somewhat complicated, but they are implicit in their attempt. I think they have done a much better job than could be hoped for. I wish them the greatest of luck with it.

Yours,
F Scott Fitzgerald

P.S.   Will you please forward Mrs. Jarrett's letter to her.

TLS, 1p. MGM letterhead. (AO)

---

‡In the top margin a note with a line indicating "rude" written in Ober's hand reads: "He certainly was".

To Mrs. Edwin S. Jarrett
c/o Harold Ober

Dear Mrs. Jarrett:

The play pleases me immensely. So faithful has been your follow-ing of my intentions that my only fear is that you have been too loyal. I hope you haven't—I hope that a measure of the novel's intention can be crammed into the two hours of the play. My thanks, hope and wishes are entirely with you—it pleases me in a manner that the acting version of THE GREAT GATSBY did not. And I want especially to congratulate you and Miss Oglebay on the multiple feats of ingenuity with which you've handled the difficult geography and chronology so that it has a unity which, God help me, I wasn't able to give it.

My first intention was to go through it and "criticize it", but I see I'm not capable of doing that—too many obstacles in my own mind prevent me from getting a clear vision. I had some notes—that Rosemary wouldn't express her distaste for the battlefield trip—she had a good time and it belittles Dick's power of making things fun. Also a note that Dick's curiosity and interest in people was real—he didn't stare at them—he glanced at them and felt them. I don't know what point of the play I was referring to. Also I'm afraid some of his long Shavian speeches won't play—and no one's sorrier than I am—his comment on the battle of the Somme for instance. Also Tommy seemed to me less integrated than he should be. He was Tommy Hitchcock in a way whose whole life is a challenge—who is only interested in realities, his kind—in going to him you've brought him into the boudoir a little—I should be careful of what he says and does unless you can feel the strong fresh-air current in him. I realize you've had to use some of the lesser characters for plot transitions and convenience, but when any of them go out of charac-ter I necessarily feel it, so I am a poor critic. I know the important thing is to put over Dick in his relations to Nicole and Rosemary and if you can, Bob Montgomery and others here would love to play the part. But it must get by Broadway first.

If it has to be cut, the children will probably come out. On the stage they will seem to press, too much for taste, against distasteful events. As if Dick had let them in for it—he is after all a sort of superman, an approximation of the hero seen in overcivilized terms —taste is no substitute for vitality but in the book it has to do duty for it. It is one of the points on which he must never show weakness as Siegfried could never show physical fear. I did not manage, I think in retrospect, to give Dick the cohesion I aimed at, but in your dramatic interpretation I beg you to guard me from the exposal of this. I wonder what the hell the first actor who played Hamlet thought of the part? I can hear him say, "The guy's a nut, isn't he?" (We can always find great consolation in Shakespeare.)

Also to return to the criticism I was not going to make—I find in writing for a particular screen character here that it's convenient to suggest the way it's played, especially the timing, i.e.

At the top of page 25 it would probably be more effective—

Rosemary didn't grow up. (pause) It's better that way. (pause) etc.

But I'd better return to my thesis. You've done a fine dramatization and my gratitude to you is a part of the old emotion I put into the book, part of my life as a writer.

Most sincerely,
F. SCOTT FITZGERALD

TL (copy), 2pp. n.d.—c. 17 February 1938. Los Angeles, Calif. (AO)

F. Scott Fitzgerald, Esq.
Garden of Allah,
8152 Sunset Boulevard,
Hollywood, Calif.

Dear Scott:

I am enclosing three copies of an agreement between you and Sheila. If you want any changes in these, suppose you make them in pencil and send them back to me and I'll have them retyped.

It doesn't seem to me that there is any necessity for including a clause in which you assume responsibility for breach of the Metro contract by reason of the collaboration. I don't think that should be in the collaboration agreement as these agreements are supposed to be filed with the Dramatists' Guild. This point could be covered in a separate letter which could be signed by you.

I don't think in any case that this play could be in any way a breach of the Metro contract. You have the right to write a play and I am sure that Metro doesn't care what you do about it.

Sincerely yours,
Harold Ober

February 18, 1938

TLS, 1p. (PU)

Fitzgerald's relationship with Sheilah Graham has been thoroughly covered in her three books: Beloved Infidel *(1958),* The Rest of the Story

(1964), and College of One *(1967). They first saw each other on 14 July 1937 at Robert Benchley's apartment in the Garden of Allah, within a week of Fitzgerald's arrival in Hollywood, and met a few days later. They quickly fell in love, but maintained separate homes until shortly before his death. A divorce from Zelda was out of the question. Their relationship was marred by Fitzgerald's drinking, but Miss Graham kept him on the wagon during the last year of his life.*

When Fitzgerald discovered Miss Graham's insecurity about her lack of education, he created an elaborate college curriculum for her and tutored her assiduously. Their only substantial collaboration was a 1938 play, Dame Rumor, *which was not finished.*

F. Scott Fitzgerald, Esq.
Garden of Allah,
8152 Sunset Boulevard,
Hollywood, Calif.

Dear Scott:

Thank you for your note of February 17th. It was Weise of McCall's who spoke to us at lunch and I am sending your letter over to him. I am also sending Mrs. Jarrett the letter you wrote her.

Spafford has signed and returned to me a release I sent him in connection with the GRACIE ALLEN AT SEA story. I have told him that you would give him 20% of your net return from it if you are able to do anything with it in Hollywood.

Sincerely yours,
[Harold Ober]

February 21, 1938

TL (cc), 1p. (AO)

8152 Sunset Boulevard
Hollywood, California
March 4th, 1938

Mrs. Harold Ober
Dromore Road
Scarsdale, New York

Dear Anne:

I have just had a letter from "our" daughter, which I know I should laugh off as being merely the product of a mood. Even at that, I don't think she ought to have chosen her very gloomiest hour to write me. In it, there is not one word of cheer, hope or even a decent yielding to circumstances. One would suppose it to have emanated from some thoroughly brutalized child in an orphan asylum, who would shortly graduate from a woman's reformatory to her life's sentence in the prison of this world.

Among other points, I note that she is switching her allegiance from Vassar to Bryn Mawr. Now this might seem a slight thing, a mere vagary, but to a shrewd old diplomat like myself it has a different meaning. Bryn Mawr is an hour and a half by the clock from Baltimore, and Scotty has pictured college as a series of delightful weekends with the subdebutantes, in which she would find time of a Monday morning to slip back to Bryn Mawr to boast of her exploits. The distance of Vassar from Baltimore is a fair six hours. Moreover, in my opinion, it is safely insulated from the soft mellow breezes of the Southland and the scholars are actuated by the stern New England air—even though Poughkeepsie is just across the border.

So I wrote her that knowing her predilection for Baltimore, I was entering her—in case she failed to get into Vassar—in St. Timothy's School, so that she can be near her sacred city. St. Timothy's School happens to be a convent-like place, where the girls have to walk in twos on their Sunday outing, and patronized entirely by New Yorkers; and I'm afraid all she would ever see of Baltimore would be a few lights on the horizon at night.

The point is I am giving her her freedom proportionately as she will earn it by a serious attitude towards work. If she is going to college at sixteen, just as I went to college at sixteen, she could no more be kept in bib and tucker than I could have been kept from having a beer with my eighteen-year-old classmates. She will have earned her right to more freedom, with me praying that her judgment will keep pace with her precocity and keep her out of trouble. If, on the contrary, she is going to try to combine being a belle with getting an education, she had better stay under protection for another year. The idea is so simple that I should think she'd get it. But such phrases as "absurdly irrational" appear in her letters, applying to my attitude.

So I have become the heavy father again and lash into her. Her latest plaint is how can I expect her to get 80 in Latin when last term, doing some work, she got only 50. In other words, she has taken 50, her low mark, as a standard, instead of a passing point of 60.

I am taking off a week around the end of this month to try to establish communication with her again and see whether I have unknowingly begotten a monster of egotism, who writes me these letters.

She raved about the party. I had no idea that it was anything as elaborate as that. I thought merely it was a question of two or three girls and I would have gone utterly unprepared. But I suppose she was so indebted that she felt she had to entertain half the school to get square again. You were wonderful to her to do all that—much better than I ever could have done.

We will have to make a mass pilgrimage to her graduation this June. I am hoping her mother can come, too, and we will watch all the other little girls get diamond bracelets and Cord roadsters. I am going to a costumer's in New York and buy Scotty some phoney jewelry so she can pretend they are graduation presents. Otherwise, she will have to suffer the shame of being a poor girl in a rich girl's school. That was always my experience—a poor boy in a rich town; a poor boy in a rich boy's school; a poor boy in a rich man's club at Princeton. So I guess she can stand it. However, I have never been able to forgive the rich for being rich, and it has colored my entire life and works.

"Three Comrades" opens without Spencer Tracy, but with Margaret Sullavan doing a wonderful job. Shooting will be finished in twenty days, and the thing will be the most colossal disappointment of Metro's year. The producer wrote it over. The censors hacked at it. Finally, the German Government took a shot. So what we have left has very little to do with the script on which people still congratulate me. However, I get a screen credit out of it, good or bad, and you can always blame a failure on somebody else. This is simply to advise you stay away.

A good deal of the glow of Hollywood has worn off for me during the struggles with the first picture, but I would as soon be here as anywhere else. After forty, one's surroundings don't seem to matter as much.

Best to all of you.

> With devotion and gratitude,
> always,
> Scott

My God, What a garralous letter!#

TLS, 3pp.

#Added in ink.

8152 Sunset Boulevard
Hollywood, California

Mr. Harold Ober
40 East 49th Street
New York City

Dear Harold:

Forward this to Miss Dayton, if you think advisable.* I would like to get some correspondence from her and give it to the Authors' League. It's a pretty dirty piece of thievery, considering that Phil Barry⁺ made a financial offer for the title, which we refused. It's one hell of a good title and one very suitable to a dancing picture.

The script goes very well indeed.‡ I think I am going to have my pay check sent directly to you because there will be various other disbursements from now on and they will be easier for you to make than for me.

No special news. Thanks for Sheila contracts. Will take care of it and forward.

Ever yours,
Scott

TLS, 1p. n.d.—received 7 March 1938. (AO)

F. Scott Fitzgerald, Esq.
8152 Sunset Boulevard
Hollywood, Calif.

Dear Scott:

I'll be interested to know what you are working on now and how everything goes with you.

Anne and I drove up to the Ethel Walker School on Saturday and saw the senior play PRIDE AND PREJUDICE. Scottie played the part of Mrs. Bennett and was extremely good. She seemed much more at home on the stage than any of the other girls. The front seats were reserved for the families of the cast. The principal of the school had the middle seat in the front row and I found myself sitting on her right as the parent of one of the leading parts and the

---

*Fitzgerald's letter to Katherine Dayton refers to her use of the play title *Save Me the Waltz*; it reads: "All right, but don't, oh don't say I didn't warn you." A note in the bottom margin in Ober's hand reads: "didn't send because play flopped. Instead sent letter to Fleischer for Scott to sign. HO".
⁺Philip Barry, playwright.
‡Probably "Infidelity."

father of the other lead sitting on her left. The play was really very well done and we enjoyed seeing Scottie. We took her to tea in the afternoon and she is looking very well and seems very happy. Mrs. Lloyd said she was doing better this term. She was very enthusiastic about her French and English but she wasn't as good in Latin and mathematics.

I am enclosing an account to date.

Sincerely yours,
Harold Ober

March 7, 1938

TLS, 1p. (PU)

March 11th, 1938

Dear Anne and Harold:

It was perfectly magnificent of you to go up to Scottie's play. Thank you for the report on her success, and most sincere sympathy for having to sit next to the headmistress. Harold, I'll bet you writhed and expected at any moment to be kept after school—I know I should have. There is something about that atmosphere from which a child never really recovers.

I am a third through "Infidelity"—Crawford picture. I suspect that Hunt Stromberg is going to put the pressure on, but he isn't going to succeed. I worked myself half sick on the last picture and I am going to keep to a safe and sane schedule on this one. Also, I am not going to be kept here Easter. I'm awfully glad now that I wrote the vacations into my contract. Again, a thousand thanks.

Scott

Mr. and Mrs. Harold Ober
Dromore Road
Scarsdale, New York

TLS, 1p. Garden of Allah stationery.

March 11, 1938

Mr. Harold Ober
40 East 49th Street
New York City

Dear Harold:

These are checks for the weeks ending March 3 and March 10. Also, there is a check for $100 against Scottie's account. I notice that you have been paying Scribner's account at the rate of from $75 to

$100 a week. I would rather you paid them only $50 a week until this account of Scottie's is paid up. You will notice that there is nothing against taxes for these two weeks, because this month I have both taxes and insurance to pay. I will begin depositing against taxes again next week.

Scott

TLS, 1p. Garden of Allah stationery. (AO)

PLEASE LET SCOTTIE HAVE UP TO A HUNDRED AND MORE IF SHE HAS GOOD REASON FOR IT. WILL INCLUDE IN TOMOR-ROWS CHECK REGARDS
    FITZGERALD.

Wire to Ober 18 March 1938. Hollywood, Calif. (AO)

Dear Harold:

I will be for wires % Mrs. R. C. Taylor,# Gosnold Ave Norfolk Va. I'm not coming north unless you want especially to see me. Im pretty weary + not looking forward to this Trip.

This check is shy—to pay commission + what you advanced Scottie—will renew next week

Ever
Scott

ALS, 1p. n.d.—received 25 March 1938. Garden of Allah stationery. (AO)

THIS IS BAD MONTH AND MAY HAVE TO PAY YOU OR INSUR-ANCE FROM NEWYORK BANK FOR ANOTHER WEEK. HOW MUCH IS THERE AND HOW DO I DRAW ON IT. PLEASE ANSWER DIRECT WIRE LETTER FOLLOWS
    FITZGERALD. .

Wire to Ober 7 April 1938. Hollywood, Calif. (AO)

ACCOUNTANT GONE FOR DAY SO CANNOT WIRE AMOUNT IN BANK ALL RIGHT TO POSTPONE PAYMENTS TO ME TOO BAD TO DRAW ON SAVINGS WILL WIRE IN MORNING
    Harold Ober

Wire (cc) to Fitzgerald 7 April 1938. (AO)

ACCOUNT IS HAROLD OBER IN TRUST FOR F. SCOTT FITZ-GERALD. I CAN WITHDRAW FOR YOU AND REMIT YOUR BANK OR WHEREVER YOU WISH. SIXTEENHUNDRED IN ACCOUNT.
    Harold Ober

Wire (cc) to Fitzgerald 8 April 1938. (AO)

#Fitzgerald's favorite cousin, Ceci.

PLEASE WITHDRAW EIGHT HUNDRED AND WIRE IT TO THE
FIRST NATIONAL BANK OF BALTIMORE STOP. AM SENDING
CHECK TONITE TO COVER COMMISSIONS AND SOME DEBT
STOP. AFFAIRS NOT AS CONFUSED AS THIS SOUNDS BUT
METRO ARE RUSHING ME ON STORY STOP. IS SCOTTIE ALL
RIGHT.
    SCOTT FITZGERALD.

Wire to Ober 12 April 1938. Hollywood, Calif. (AO)

F. Scott Fitzgerald, Esq.
Garden of Allah,
8152 Sunset Boulevard
Hollywood, Calif.

Dear Scott:
    As I wired you Scottie went back to school yesterday. She has
been with us off and on during the latter part of her vacation. She
is very well and very happy and very busy. She and Dick and Nat
all went back to school saying that they are going to get good marks
for their last terms. Here's hoping they do!
    I was rather sorry that you had to withdraw on your savings
account and still sorrier to find that there was not more in your
account. I hope that during the rest of this year you can build this
up to a really good-sized amount so that when you want to get to
work on your novel you will be able to do so without worrying
about money.

                    Sincerely yours,
                    [Harold Ober]

April 13, 1938

TL (cc), 1p. (AO)

                    April 18, 1938

Mr. Harold Ober
40 East 49th Street
New York City

Dear Harold:
    I'd like to see the book* referred to here.
                    Scott Fitzg

TLS, 1p. Garden of Allah stationery. (AO)

    Assigned to Adventure by Irene Kuhn (New York: Lippincott, 1938). Autobiography of a reporter, which mentions Fitzgerald only in passing.

F. Scott Fitzgerald, Esq.
Garden of Allah,
8152 Sunset Boulevard,
Hollywood, Calif.

Dear Scott:

Scottie came back from Baltimore on the 3rd. I am very glad to have your letter although I am sorry that you are so tired. Of course, you know that Metro has let out a lot of people and all the picture companies are retrenching. In general, it is not a good time to raise prices. However, you know the circumstances better than anybody else, and if Stromberg seems very enthusiastic about the next copy you turn in, I don't think there would be any harm at all in suggesting a higher salary.

I am leaving for London tomorrow to be gone until about May 27th but I have arranged for everything to be taken care of while I am gone. I may call you up in Hollywood to night.

Sincerely yours,
[Harold Ober]

April 19, 1938

TL (cc), 1p. (AO)

F. Scott Fitzgerald, Esq.
Garden of Allah
8152 Sunset Blvd.
Hollywood, California

Dear Scott:

I am just back from a very satisfactory and pleasant trip to London and I'll be glad to have a note telling me how everything is going with you. Let me know what you are working on and how your health is.

Anne is planning to drive Zelda up to Scottie's graduation next week.

I am in a rush just now, but I will write more in a few days.

Sincerely,
[Harold Ober]

May 27, 1938

TL (cc), 1p. (AO)

SCOTTY WILL BE DELIVERED TO YOUR OFFICE LATE TOMOR-
ROW MORNING STOP REMEMBER IT IS AMERICAN AIRLINES
THE AFTERNOON SLEEPER FOR LOSANGELES STOP TREMEN-
DOUSLY OBLIGED PLEASE BE TERRIBLY DISCREET AS IT IS NOT
AS IF THIS HAPPENED DURING TERM AND IT MAY BE MINI-
MIZED[†]

    SCOTT FITZGERALD.

Wire to Ober 8 June 1938. Los Angeles. (AO)

IF SCOTTY IS TO TAKE COLLEGE BOARD EXAMINATION SHE
SHOULD BRING HER TEXT BOOKS STOP THANK YOU FOR EV-
ERYTHING

    SCOTT FITZGERALD.

Wire to Anne Ober 8 June 1938. Los Angeles.

Dear Scott,

I hope you won't mind my writing you what I feel about Scottie's
last escapade. I'm sure there was nothing "vicious" or "non social"
in it. School was over and she thought she could "get away with it".
She didn't do it out of "defiance" but because she didn't think they
would be caught. This is not to excuse her—but I think from what
you said last night that you attribute to her motives that has never
thought of.

Scottie is I am sure really sorry and ashamed of what she did and
when you talk to her I hope you will do it with affection and
understanding rather than as the "heavy father". She is only 16 and
if you and I look back to when we were 16, we shall have to admit
that we were not very wise.

I know that you expect a great deal of Scottie and you are right
to do so—but you mustn't be too dissapointed if she doesnt always
come up to your expectations. You know we don't always come up
to our own. She has done silly things—but I sincerely believe that
there is not a particle of meanness or wrong in her. I think her
feeling about the Walker school is what any lively girl feels about
that kind of school. Scottie gets into more trouble because she is
more inventive. There are so many nice things about Scottie and we
mustnt forget them when we are facing the mistakes.

I hope she can keep at work on her college boards and if she can
make it, I think she ought to be allowed to go to Vassar.

Please forgive me if I have ventured into places that are none of

---

[†]Scottie had left the Ethel Walker school grounds without permission. She had
already been graduated, but had remained at the school to study for college boards.

my business. I hope you know that I do it because I am very fond
of both you and Scottie

As ever

Harold

ALS, 2pp.—c. 8 June 1938. Probably never mailed. (PU)

Just finished talking to you on the phone. This isn't quite as bad as
if it had happened in term time but it's plenty to keep her out of
Vassar + change the whole course of her life. I don't know anything until I see her—there's no use punishing her because the
world will now be delighted to do that for me. I am very shocked
+ discouraged.

Dear Harold:

For a few weeks I'll have to reduce payments to $300. I'll resume
the other in July.

Im sorry to hear about Annes father—those things are always
nearer home than we think even if parents are old. It calls up so
much of the past

Ever

Scott

In regard to that old matter—the raise. Just as I was about to open
my mouth Mr. Breen the censor stepped in + we had no picture
at all.[‡] I'm at present on <u>The Women</u> for Norma Sheerer as Swanson may have told you

ALS (ink and pencil), 1p. n.d., n.p.—received 10 June 1938. Los Angeles. (AO)

SCOTTIE STARTING EAST TONIGHT. SHE WILL COME TO YOU
TOMORROW IF CONVENIENT TO YOU.DONT MEET HER STOP
WILL CALL YOU TONIGHT AT ELEVEN OCLOCK YOUR TIME
   SCOTT FITZGERALD.

Wire to Mr. and Mrs. Ober 14 June 1938. Culver City, Calif. (AO)

*In June 1938 Fitzgerald moved out to Malibu Beach. By September he was
back at the Garden of Allah in Hollywood. Finally he took a house at 5521
Amestoy Avenue in Encino.*

SCOTTIE LIED TO YOU STOP BALTIMORE WAS NOT MEN-
TIONED THAT NIGHT[#] STOP I AM GOING TO CALL THE EURO-
PEAN TRIP OFF AND PUT HER TO WORK STOP SHE IS NOT AT

---

‡Refers to "Infidelity."
#Scottie had gone to Baltimore without Fitzgerald's permission.

ANY FINNEYS IN BALTIMORE STOP SHE HAS COMPLETELY DIS-
APPEARED
    SCOTT FITZGERALD.

Wire to Ober 26 June 1938. Malibu Beach, Calif.

USE YOUR OWN JUDGEMENT ABOUT SCOTTIE STOP MORALLY
THIS WAS A FLAGRANT DISOBEDIENCE BUT I SUPPOSE YOU
MIGHT AS WELL GO TO EUROPE AS A MATTER OF CONVEN-
IENCE STOP SORRY ABOUT SUNDAY STOP HAVE CALMED
DOWN
    SCOTT.

Wire to Ober 28 June 1938. Malibu Beach, Calif. (AO)

THANKS FOR TELEGRAM YOUR REACTION PERFECTLY UN-
DERSTANDABLE THINK YOUR DECISION ABOUT EUROPE VERY
WISE SHALL SEE YOU IN HOLLYWOOD WITHIN FEW WEEKS MY
REGARDS
    Harold Ober

Wire (cc) to Fitzgerald 28 June 1938. (AO)

SCOTT MUCH BETTER PHYSICALLY AND SPIRITUALLY.* HOPE
EVERYTHING OK NOW
    SHEILAH.

Wire to Ober 28 June 1938. Santa Monica, Calif.

Dear Harold:

After this week checks will be larger. Added $100 to one of these
to help cover Scottie. It was an expensive episode on her part +
what I felt 1st anger, then pity, then annoyance has solidified into
a sort of disgust. I dont want ever to get so many threads of "caring"
into my hands as I did once. If she is going to be an idler I want no
part of her.—I dont even want to help her to grow up into the sort
of woman I loathe. If she doesn't get 90% to 100% in these two easy
exams they wont take her—all that makes it possible to hope is her
French that cost so many thousands. Nothing she is and does now
is her own or anything she deserves credit for. To hell with pretty
faces if there's nothing underneath. That is not to say to hell with
Scottie but I must stop worrying about her in the role of "my pride
and joy" if she just isn't.

---

*Fitzgerald had fallen off the wagon.

All is confused + trying in work at present but it may clear up
this week

Ever
Scott

ALS (pencil), 2pp. n.d., n.p.—received 28 June 1938. Malibu Beach, Calif. (AO)

SCOTTY GOT INTO VASSAR LOVE
    SCOTT.

Wire to Anne Ober 18 July 1938. Los Angeles.

Dear Harold
    When do you come?
    Will you bring or send copy of that letter of mine to Scotty?
    Thanks for telegram

Scott

ALS, 1p. n.d., n.p.—received 27 July 1938. Los Angeles. (AO)

Aug. 25th
1938

Dear Ann:

Thanks for forwarding the cards.

It was great to see Harold out here, especially sprawled in the sun
at his ease quite domestically on my little beach and playing ping
pong with great if sometimes erratic intensity. (The fact that he beat
me doesn't count.)

He said you had some way of finding what would be a suitable
budget for Scottie, to include her shoes, personal essentials and all
pleasure expenses—except for times when I will see her such as
Xmas vacation. If there were four kinds of living at Vassar I should
prefer for her to remain during Freshman year in what might be
called "the lower middle class"—not quite the poorest because that
is a nuisance and having to be careful of money in small ways
actually consumes a great deal of time. But on the contrary, her
circus last spring was very costly and she deserves little more than
sack cloth at the present. To let her buy a couple of new evening
gowns would be simply begging her to fly out and use them. For
the present I want the center of her life to be at Vassar.

Cooperatively I am stopping my accounts at Franklin Simon & Company, Best & Company and Lord & Taylor, etc. Do you know any others that she uses?

Always yours, with affection—

Scott

Mrs. Harold Ober
Dromore Road
Scarsdale
New York

TLS, 1p. MGM letterhead.

Aug. 29th
1938

Dear Harold:

Have you a copy of the fourth story I sold to **RED BOOK** of the Phillippe Series?‡ I somehow don't think you have. At least not of the last version. In that case would it be possible for me to have their copy copied. You can tell them that I am planning a few more of the series to stand as complete units or give any excuse you want. You might ask them if they ever plan to use that or would use it if they had a couple of others at hand.

Perhaps [his] *Balmers* old grudge against me has withered away in these years. [and] *Also* in regard to [that] *stories* I have a plan by which I can finish the **COLLIER** story to their satisfaction, and think I will do it this month without fail.

Ever yours—
Scott

Mr. Harold Ober
40 East 49th St
New York City
New York

P.S.   I am almost sure that if you have a copy it is an early version of the story and not the final corrected one I sent the **RED BOOK**. However, you might send me what you have and I can tell.

TLS, 1p. MGM letterhead. (AO)

---

‡"Gods of Darkness," one of the sequence of medieval stories.

F. Scott Fitzgerald, Esq.
Garden of Allah
8152 Sunset Blvd.
Hollywood, California

Dear Scott:

I haven't a copy of the fourth Phillippe story, but I'll send you one when I get one from Red Book. I have talked to Balmer about future stories and will let you know what he decides.

I have a letter from the New Yorker, asking if there is any chance of getting some verses or perhaps a short prose piece from you. They say it is more than a year since they have had anything from you and they would like to have you in the magazine again. I think it might be a good idea to have something of yours appearing in The New Yorker while you're in Hollywood.

I'm glad you see a way to fix the Collier's story. How's everything going with THE WOMEN?

Sincerely,
[Harold Ober]

September 2, 1938

TL (cc), 1p. (AO)

In the letter of 4 September 1938, to which Fitzgerald refers, Mrs. Ober advised him:

"I have tried to find out about allowances for Scottie and enclose a card from a friend whose daughter graduated this year. She has another daughter in college. They are people who are quite well off financially. I found that most of the girls here with whom I discussed budgets were getting along on 'as little as possible' but two of them told me they knew girls who were getting between $25 and $30 a month allowance and they seemed to think that was heaps. That allowance includes books, I believe, which they tell me amount to at least $50 a year.

"About Scottie's clothes. I think she should have an inexpensive fur coat, costing between $95 and $125, otherwise I don't think her clothes will amount to very much.

"She will probably want some furnishings for her room, but I imagine that expense will be shared by her roommates. . . .

"It is going to be great fun for me, having Scottie so near. It only takes an hour and a half to drive up by the parkways which makes it an easy as well as short drive and I am going to try to keep in close enough touch with her to know what is happening. I know you think Harold and I spoil her, but so far Scottie trusts me and I think I have at least part of her confidence. It is an important relationship to me and while she may not realize it, I think

it is to Scottie too. Don't for a minute think that I hesitate to blow your child up, for sometimes I think it is All I do. . . .

"PLEASE let me know what I can do and WHEN to expect my child. DON'T Worry until you have to!

"Forgive the advice"

Sept. 7th

1938

Dear Anne and Harold:

Just got your letter and wanted to thank you for the information about Vassar expenses. Today has been a nightmare of changed plans and I don't know even now how the newest one is going to work out. To make a long story short it looks as if Zelda is going to New York to meet Scottie at the boat¶ and that Scottie is then going to fly out here for two days. This plan may seem to you unwise and extravagant but remember that whatever I do with Scottie or her mother it costs about one-third less in money and infinitely less in work-morale than for me to break off here and go East. #

Meet the boat or not as you like but <u>don't ruin your Saturday doing it</u> as, unless you hear otherwise from me by telegram, her mother and sister will be there and if they are not, the Gerald Murphys, who are bringing her home* can put her on the train for Scarsdale.

Scottie returns from Hollyood on the 19th or 20th. Could a dentist's appointment be made for her on the 21st?

I still have the cottage [at] *on* the [lake] *sea* but now at a week-end price and I don't use it often. Of course everything there will be <u>quite proper</u>, and needless to say I shall try to be calm and reasonable with Scottie as I was nervous and irascible last June on the long distance telephone.

If you go to the boat—and remember I am not in favor of you spoiling your peaceful Saturday!—take her the letter I sent you airmail, and tell her[†] the instructions therein are <u>still good</u>. If you don't go to the boat, be sure and give it to her as soon as she arrives. The airplane tickets are waiting for her in Baltimore.

¶In the right margin Fitzgerald added in pencil: "the 'Paris', Sat 10th".

#Along the left margin Fitzgerald added in pencil: "Dont advance Scottie any [more than] money for clothes—<u>you</u> are really *the* softies. I am becoming hard as nails."

*Fitzgerald drew a line here and added in pencil: "from Europe".

†Fitzgerald drew a line here and added in pencil: "that".

I have stopped charge accounts at Bests, Lord & Taylor and Franklin Simon. Please give her absolute instructions about using your account.

Ever yours with gratitude and affection—

Scott

Mr. Harold Ober
40 East 49th Street
New York City
New York

P. S.   There are real reasons for all of these plan changes that were utterly out of my control, so don't think that I have lost my mind.

Sheets + pillow cases are provided by Vassar. She should have [slip] soft bedroom slippers instead of mules.

She can either dig out blankets *towels* + bathmat [+ pictures] in Baltimore with Mrs Owens (in which case Mrs Owens should get a wire to be ready) or buy new. Tell her <u>not</u> to let Mrs Owens down though if she asks her help.‡

TLS, 2pp. MGM letterhead.

IF YOU GO TO BOAT VERY IMPORTANT YOU DO NOT GIVE SCOTTIE LETTER THERE BUT WAIT TILL SCARSDALE SORRY TO BOTHER YOU. AFFECTIONATELY
    SCOTT.

Wire to Anne Ober 9 September 1938. Malibu Beach, Calif.

Sept. 28th
1938

Dear Harold:

Scottie and I had some pretty hot talk while she was out here. I wasn't at all pleased with her attitude on anything. But I rather think she went into college in a sober frame of mind and should produce some results.

I quote the following from a letter of Zelda's:

"We called on the Obers and their house seemed straight out of Longfellow or some fanciful or homely poet dreamily spun into the fragrance of orchards and tumbling down the rocky hill-side. I never saw a more enchanting child than their lanky, red-headed boy. How can we at least let them know our gratitude?"

---

‡The note after the postscript was added in pencil.

Checks will begin to get bigger again next week. (This is not an answer to Zelda's question!)¶

If Ann goes up there she might see if Scottie has rubbers and a good study lamp. I would appreciate any information, as our relations are rather cool and formal at present. I did a little too much for her and there is always a price for that luxury.

Ever yours—
Scott

Mr. Harold Ober
40 E. 49th Street
New York City

TLS, 1p. MGM letterhead. (AO)

Oct. 12th
1938

Dear Harold:

Sending this to the Post for Sheilah.§ It has just occurred to me that it might be a crack radio sketch and bring more money that way. If you know of any way to sell it, <u>absolutely protecting the idea</u>, which would be a cinch to steal, do something about it. But please act quickly. It certainly wouldn't do to send it to any office but if you know some trustworthy person who would be in a position to use it immediately you might let them look at it in your office. Otherwise, please send it on to the Post with the covering letter.

With best wishes always—

Scott

Mr. Harold Ober
40 E. 49th Street
New York City
New York

P.S.   Be sure and don't mention it to anyone. The idea is everything and you know how those things get about.

TLS, 1p. MGM letterhead. (AO)

¶Fitzgerald added the parenthetical material in pencil.
§Unidentified story or article about radio by Sheilah Graham.

F. Scott Fitzgerald, Esq.
Garden of Allah
8152 Sunset Blvd.
Hollywood, California

Dear Scott:

I received the sketch that Sheilah did and gave it at once to The Post. I think they may like it as they are not too fond of radio and may not mind making good-natured fun of it.

I don't think there will be any possibility of selling it as a radio sketch, because it is very critical of the radio. In any event, I wouldn't want to take the responsibility of showing it to any of the radio outfits for, as you say, if they did like the idea, they might lift it. Tell Sheilah I think it is a very clever and amusing sketch.

Sincerely,
[Harold Ober]

October 20, 1938

TL (cc), 1p. (AO)

F. Scott Fitzgerald In account with Harold Ober

Balance due Harold Ober—account dated July 26th, 1938			3525.02
Received from F. Scott Fitzgerald on July 27, August 10 & 19 for weeks ending July 27, August 3, 10, & 17		1600.00	
10% Commission on 4 weeks salary	500.00		
For Scribners'	200.00	700.00	900.00
			2625.02
Received on August 22, & 31 and September 9, 10, 28, 30 for weeks ending August 24, 31, September 7, 14, 21, 28 and October 5		2100.00	
10% Commission on 7 weeks salary		875.00	1225.00
			1400.02
Received on October 13 and 17 for weeks ending October 12 and 19		800.00	
10% Commission on 2 weeks salary	250.00		
For Scribners'	100.00	350.00	450.00
			950.02
Received from Random House	5.02		
AT YOUR AGE Royalty to June 30, 1938			
10% Commission	.50	4.52	
Received from Federal Theatre	25.00		

FAMILY IN THE WIND
One radio use on July 24, 1938
   10% Commission   2.50   22.50   27.02
Balance October 20th, 1938   923.00
        I trust you will find the above accounting correct.
                       HAROLD OBER

October 20, 1938
Statement of Scottie's expenses attached.

Typed account, 1p. Ober agency letterhead. (PU)

            Scottie Fitzgerald
       Expenses paid by Harold Ober

....

Due Harold Ober—July 26th, 1938   218.70
Paid:—
Bon Ton Valet—to 7/29/38   7.00
New York Telephone Co.—
Scarsdale—to 8/4/38   1.44
Anne Reid Ober:-   30.50
    Sept. 10—Name tapes   1.00
             Cash to Scottie
             for tips on arrival   2.50
    Sept. 12—Cash for trip to Baltimore   20.00
    Sept. 15—Buttons for blue
             dress   .50
             Laundry   1.50
             Shoes heeled & soled   3.00
             Trunk repaired   2.00
                       30.50   38.94
  Due Harold Ober   257.64

Typed account, 1p. Ober agency letterhead. (PU)

Miss Scottie Fitzgerald
Vassar College
Jocelyn Hall
Poughkeepsie, New York

Dear Scottie:
    Your father has asked me to send you this copy of Red Book, containing his story IN THE DARKEST HOUR. He says it is the same period you are covering in history.
    I hope we are going to see you soon.
                   Sincerely,
                   [Harold Ober]

October 28, 1938

TL (cc), 1p.

Scott Fitzgerald, Esq.
Garden of Allah
8152 Sunset Blvd.
Hollywood, Cal.

Dear Scott:

I have the following note from the New Yorker:

"I'm afraid this one won't do. There have been so many of this kind of broadcast that we are rather afraid of the formula itself. Thank you a lot. Do you think you could get Fitzgerald himself to do something for us?"

I'll see if I can't interest some other magazine in Sheilah's piece.

Sincerely,
[Harold Ober]

November 7, 1938

TL (cc), 1p. (AO)

Dear Harold:

Back at work on a new job that may be something really good— Mme. Curie for Gretta Garbo. It was quite a plum and I'm delighed after the thankless months spent on fixing up leprous stories. Knopff said I could do my original if I wanted but he strongly advised this.

Im sorry my concern about Scottie overcast that day at your house—I think Mr Haas* thought it was all about a football game, which shames me for having shown in public my dismay about the child. There is nothing much to do except let it work itself out— but I must beg you again not to give her money. I know how you feel about it—that I am cruel and unjust but remember you've gotten all your ideas on the subject from Scottie. I am under the greatest obligation to you but, if I may say so, I think the headmistress and teachers at Walkers, the Dean + professors at Vassar and I, who have been in constant communication with them and have concerned myself deeply with the child since she was seven—that we are in a better position to evaluate her character than you. I have to deal in results—points of stability and honor—you touch Scottie only on the superficial points of charm. So I ask you to let me *have* a fair chance by not giving her cash or credit—which she uses,

---

*On 21 October Fitzgerald was in Asheville visiting Zelda, and then went to New York. Donald Haas of Random House was Ober's neighbor in Scarsdale.

specificelly in the case of the evening dress—to come out into a frank defiance of me.

I do not want to bring her out here—I have written her a last letter asking for very simple concessions. We will see what we will see. So long as she lies it is all very difficult and tortuous from any point of view.

Ever Yours
Scott

ALS (pencil), 2pp. n.d., n.p.—received 9 November 1938. Los Angeles. (AO)

November 15,1938.

Dear Harold:—

Your letter was reassuring. I think that what's made me so sensitive is a hark-back to the days when Zelda was slowly wrecking herself in the Russian Ballet, growing more confused and hysterical day by day, and I couldn't get a single soul in Paris to help me or see it my way or slow her up until it was too late. I do not think there's anything the matter with Scottie at this time. Nevertheless, I think that any child of her heredity who throws herself into what amounts to dissipation and at the same time tries to carry on a college course might very well suffer a crackup which would influence her entire life. By dissipation I do not mean vice. I simply mean *beer and* chain-smoking and sitting up at all hours of the night, a sudden lack of [almost no] exercise except two compulsory hours of hockey a week, and the awful pressure on her time and nervous system of these elaborate flirtations. All this amounts to a strain and a waste, which is entirely what dissipation means.

My absolute order to her not to stay in New York Thanksgiving —at the time of the Mary Earle and Dorothy Burns' parties but to go to Baltimore immediately, is based on a very real fact. Those debutante parties in New York are the rendezvous of a group of idlers, the less serious type of college boys, young customer's men from Wall Street, parasites, hangers-on, fortune-hunters, the very riff-raff of New York who will take a child like Scottie who may have a real future, and exploit her and squeeze her out until she is a limp unattractive rag. In one more year she can cope with them. In two more years it will, I hope, be behind her, but this year it's dazzling her. She will be infinitely better off here with me than mixed up at all with those people, so I made arrangements before I left New York to have a check made on whether she is or is not at any of those parties. If she is, I'm taking her out of Vassar. I'd rather have an angry little girl on my hands for a few months than a broken neurotic for the rest of my life. I've completely made up my mind on this matter—which leaves the whole question up to Scottie. I think she knows I mean business as I have cut down her allowance until I get a categorical answer as to whether she intends to respect my wishes or not.

That's all, I'm really not worried about it. I think she will. If she doesn't, then she's already traveled pretty far along the primrose path. Together with fatherly feelings, I have a certain vast impersonality about such things.

With best *wishes* always,

Scott

P.S.   Let Sheila's piece drop. The Orson Wells broadcast has killed it entirely.

TLS, 2pp. MGM letterhead. (AO)

November 22,1938.

Dear Harold:

Is there enough in the bank in New York to square my debt with you? (All except the commissions, of course). If so, I would rather like to do it—if only as a matter of having a <u>fait accompli</u> behind me. Also, how much more will it take to redeem the insurance policy lien that Charley Scribner holds?

Thanks a lot for the magazine. I was somewhat disappointed. Edmund Wilson had led me to believe it was something extraordinary. One more thing in that line. A few months back, Life carried an article about modern housing with illustrations of modern and traditional houses at various prices. Could you find a copy of that and send it to Zelda? Her address is Highlands Hospital, Ashville, North Carolina.

Ever yours,
Scott

TLS, 1p. MGM letterhead. (AO)

F. Scott Fitzgerald, Esq.
5521 Amestoy Ave.
Encino
Los Angeles, California

Dear Scott:

Thank you for your note of November twenty-second. I am enclosing an account which shows how we stand. You have, in the savings bank, $714.69. If it would make you happier to clear off the loan by taking the money out of the savings account, you can do it, but please don't do it on my account. I hate to have you decrease the amount you have in the savings bank. As a matter of fact, I would like to see you increase it!

You have paid off $750 on the lien that Charlie Scribner holds and there is $750 still due.

I am getting the copy of Life that you asked for and sending it to Zelda.

Scottie called up just before Thanksgiving and she seemed very happy. She said she was working hard. We hope to see her during the Christmas vacation.

Corey Ford¶ has just been in and he said he saw you for a moment and that you are looking very well.

Sincerely,
[Harold Ober]

November 30, 1938

P.S. Your check for $200 just received. This is not included in the above figures.

TL (cc), 1p. (AO)

November 30,1938.

Dear Harold:

Bill Warren has been out here and has left in discouragement. He did the following story of his adventures, the names are changed but it is substantially his experiences. It is an awkward length and the ground may have been covered before, but it is very well written it seems to me and just perhaps you might know a place for it. Would you, as a favor to me, read this one piece?

His address is: 6 West Reed Street, Baltimore, Maryland. In case you have anything to say to him about it.

Best wishes, always

Scott

P.S. Since the New York balance is low think I will pay you the rest of what I owe you at the rate of $150.00 a week for the weeks that still remain on my contract. This will just about finish us up on the debt. I'm going to let the Scribner balance go until after Washington's Birthday when I will know one way or another

---

¶Humorist and screen-writer.

whether I remain at Metro or free-lance again, so all that I send you over $175.00 ($125.00 plus $50.00, should go in the New York bank. I will try to make it $200.00 a week but will begin with $125.00 which you will kindly deposit for me.)

What is the present status of "Tender Is the Night"? There is a young fellow named Francis Swann* who wants to dramatize it and I see no reason why he shouldn't if the two ladies have had no luck. Their fault was that they tried to cram the whole thing into a novel —something that was absolutely impossible. Maybe his approach is a good one. If the option has expired, give him some encouragement. I haven't his letter at the moment, but will forward it Monday.

TLS, 1p. MGM letterhead. (AO)

Dear Harold:

Scottie writes she will see you Friday. She is going to Montgomery—will you buy her a round trip ticket? I'm afraid to give her all this cash. It will cost about <u>seventy</u> *for fare*. The <u>sixty</u> that remains is her own present or money for clothes or what she wills. Maybe Anne can advise her how to spend it.

No news. Curie goes along but today I am a little sick + overworked.

She has (Scottie) enough expense money for berth, meals ect. ect. but if there's anything left over from the seventy she can have that too.

> Ever Yours with
> Best Xmas Wishes
> Scott

Excuse writing—am in bed.
She knows you have this + will get in touch with you

Would you get her a lower, Balt to Montgomery for the 23d—train leaving Baltimore between 5 and 6. [But please] <u>Not</u> *the later train.* But <u>she</u> should pay for this—I mean deduct it from the $60 for she already has expense money for [that] berths.‡

ALS, 1p. n.d.—received 14 December 1938. Los Angeles. (AO)

---

*A young writer Fitzgerald knew in Baltimore.
‡Note written on envelope flap.

December 16,
1938

Dear Ann:

I divided up Scottie's time as follows: two or three nights at the beginning or end with you. Four or five nights with her mother in Montgomery, two nights on the train and ten nights on the dance floors of youth. I suppose she will be a broken reed when she gets back to Vassar but I'm not even thinking of asking her to tutor in spite of the probation. I've done my best. I wanted to keep her out of New York this autumn—now let nature take its course.

With affection always,

Scott

TLS, 1p. MGM letterhead.

DO LET ME KNOW IF THERE IS ANY SERIOUS CHANGE IN SCOT-TIES CONDITION YOU WERE VERY KIND TO TAKE HER HAPPI-EST CHRISTMAS TO YOU ALL
    SCOTT.

Wire to Anne Ober 19 December 1938. Van Nuys, Calif. (AO)

Dear Harold:

Thanks about Scottie. Did she seem at all sobered by the proba-tion. I dont expect sackcloth but I hope to God she's come down a peg since Sept.

Happy Holidays to you all. It must be fine to be together

Scott

ALS (pencil), 1p. n.d., n.p.—received 21 December 1938. Los Angeles. (AO)

METRO NOT RENEWING TO MY GREAT PLEASURE BUT WILL FINISH CURIE THERES LOTS OF OTHER WORK OFFERED STOP HOWEVER PLEASE SAY NOTHING WHATEVER TO PERKINS OR TO SCOTTIE WHO WOULD NOT UNDERSTAND STOP AM WRIT-ING
    SCOTT.

Wire to Ober 26 December 1938. Van Nuys, Calif. (AO)

Dear Harold:

As I wrote you the contract wasn't renewed. Why I dont know —but not on account of the work. It seems sort of funny—to entrust me alone with their biggest picture, + <u>continue</u> me on it with a "your services will not be required". Finally Eddie§ said that when

§Edwin Knopf.

I finished it he hoped he'd have good contract for me. O.K. If <u>Curie</u> is a hit I'd go back for $2000 a week. Baby am I glad to get out! Ive hated the place ever since Monkeybitch rewrote 3 Comrades!

Glad Scottie was nice.

Shielah sends her best

Ever
Scott

ALS (pencil), 1p. n.d.—received 29 December 1938. Los Angeles. (AO)

F. Scott Fitzgerald; Esq.
5521 Amestoy
Encino
Los Angeles, Calif.

Dear Scott:

I talked to Eddie Knopf for a moment on the phone today and I'm having lunch and a long talk with him on Wednesday. He says he hopes you will be working on GONE WITH THE WIND.# That is something you could do better than anyone I can think of.

If you can get an attractive and well paid job, do you think it might be well to take it and get some money in the bank before you go back to your real job of writing? I'm sure a good picture job can be found.

We are expecting Scottie Tuesday.

Happy New Year to you!

Sincerely,
[Harold Ober]

December 30, 1938

TL (cc), 1p. (AO)

The only story Fitzgerald published in 1938 was "Financing Finnegan."

F. Scott Fitzgerald, Esq.
5521 Amestoy Avenue
Encino
Los Angeles, Cal.

Dear Scott:

I had a couple of talks with Eddie Knopf while he was in New York. He told me that the only reason that they were not renewing your contract was that they weren't paying anybody $1500 if they

---

Fitzgerald worked for two weeks on this script.

could help it. He said you had done fine work on THREE COM-RADES and admitted that Metro had made a mistake in not doing the picture the way you wrote it. If you want to work in Hollywood, after the expiration of the Metro contract, I feel sure that you can do so. I have written Swanie about this and I presume you have talked to him.

I hope you can get back to your own writing but you may feel that it is wise to work in Hollywood a little longer and get some money put by so that you can write without worry. I think you have done wonderfully well to get so many of your debts cleared up and I hope that if you do take another Hollywood job, you will be able to put most of the money in the bank for yourself. I know that it doesn't pay any author to work in Hollywood, unless he can keep his expenses down to where they would be somewhere else and keep a large part of what he makes for the future.

Scottie went back to Vassar with a bad cold and was in the infirmary for a few days. Anne talked to her on the phone a few days ago and she seemed to be all right.

I am enclosing an account up to the end of the year.

Sincerely,
[Harold Ober]

January 11, 1939

TL (cc), 1p. (AO)

Dear Harold:
   Enclosed 2456.31
3 Commissions $375.
Debt   100.   or whatever it is
Balance for bank 1981. which will make about $3000 there against my income tax.

Working with Selznick[†] is like being raised from the jungle to the court. I like Eddie but I hope I may never see the Metro factory again

Ever Yours
Scott

ALS (pencil), 1p. n.d., n.p.—received 18 January 1939. Los Angeles. (AO)

---

†David O. Selznick, producer of *Gone with the Wind*.

Dear Harold:

Herewith the last on the Metro + Selznick time—the latter ended on <u>Tues the 24th</u>, completing a 5 day instead of a <u>six</u> day week so $105.00 should square us. Does this fit in your books?

I hear nothing from you + worry that you may have grippe or something. My plans are uncertain here. I may go to work *at Universal* Tuesday and may not, depending on several factors which I will write in detail when *I've* decided. Am in touch with Swanie at all times—he has good hard sense.

Ever Yours
Scott

ALS (pencil), 1p. n.d., n.p.—received 1 February 1939. Los Angeles. (AO)

Scott Fitzgerald, Esq.
5521 Amestoy Avenue
Encino
Los Angeles, Cal.

Dear Scott:

Thank you for your note. I haven't written you lately because we understood from Scottie that you were going to be in New York this coming weekend. I was out of the office with a cold for a couple of days last week, but except for that, I have been in the best of health.

I'm glad you're planning to work in Hollywood a little longer as the weather is very cold here and there doesn't seem to be much point in coming back here just now.

I would like to see you cut down expenses just as much as you can and put away all the money you possibly can for the remaining time you are in Hollywood. This doesn't mean that I think you have been living extravagantly but there is always a period of readjustment after working in Hollywood and I would like to have you leave there with excessive security. I think you have done remarkably well to clear up so many obligations while you have been in Hollywood.

I am enclosing a memo about savings banks. If you'll be sure to let me know a week in advance of the time you leave Hollywood, I shall feel freer in writing to you. I always hate to send letters to Hollywood unless I know that the person I have addressed is to be there. There is no telling what may happen to it.

We talked to Scottie a day or two ago on the phone and she said that she is over her cold and that she is working very hard.

Please remember me to Sheila.

Sincerely,
[Harold Ober]

February 1, 1939

TL (cc), 2pp. (PU)

In February 1939 Fitzgerald traveled with Budd Schulberg to Dartmouth to work on the film Winter Carnival *for Walter Wanger. Fitzgerald went on a drunk and ended up in a New York hospital. Schulberg's novel* The Disenchanted *(1950) is based on this trip.*

F. Scott Fitzgerald, Esq.
5521 Amestory Avenue
Encino
Los Angeles, Cal.

Dear Scott:

I'm glad to have your note and sorry that I had to leave for New Hampshire so that I couldn't see you off for Hollywood.

I sent the papers to the insurance company by air mail and they should have received them Friday night or Saturday morning.

I'm glad you're finishing up the Collier's story as I know you'll feel better with it off your mind. When that is done, you can start work on your picture idea with nothing to bother you. Let me know how you are and I'll be interested to know from time to time how you are getting along with the picture idea.

Sincerely,
[Harold Ober]

February 27, 1939

TL (cc), 1p. (AO)

5521 Amestoy
Encino, California
March 2, 1939

Mr. Harold Ober
40 E. 49th Street
New York, New York

Dear Harold:

Here at last is my thumbs story, with, a [story] *good* ending. I think I was right about the Swanie's attitude on originals. He rather wavers both ways in believing in them, or not believing in them, and what he is really concerned with, is my attitude—whether I am writing with interest and competence in the field or only trying it as a lazy man's job to make quick money.

I hope you're not being at the office means you being ill again.

For the present, let what I am doing be wrapt in profound secrecy —I may add that I have not quite decided between several plans myself. But all is serene here and I have not felt more like working.

Ever yours,
Scott Fitzgerald

P. S.   I think I owe you some fractional sum of money and I have lost the letter which says how much it is. Will you just carry it on your books for awhile and take it out on the next sum due me.

TLS, 1p. (AO)

5521 Amestoy
Encino, California
March 2, 1939

Mr. Kenneth Littauer
Collier's Weekly
250 Park Avenue
New York, New York

Dear Kenneth:

Finishing this story§ was a somewhat harder job than writing "Tender is the Night", because

- (a) When a conception goes wrong repair work is twice as hard as building a new story.
- (b) because the 5,000 word length is terribly difficult for me. It seems to mean sacrifice of humor and description—or else if I give these little leeway it means forshortening of plot into melodrama in the end.

But I think this version answers your previous strictures. It moves neither to Paris nor to the West and it seems to have unity of feeling as well. I hope you like it.

While I am writing you let me ask if the following might be a way of getting around the length situation—which I know is going to haunt me. If my stories ran 8,000 or 9,000 words could you publish them as "two-parter[']s". The length may seem to you a compara-

---

§"Thumbs Up."

tively unimportant thing but from my angle it interferes with the sweep of the job and I believe it would take a dozen or so stories and a year's work before I would feel at home in the 5,000 word form.

Best wishes always
Scott Fitzg

P. S.   Have seen something of Budd Schulberg whom I liked immensely, and who spoke of you so pleasantly.

TLS, 1p. Never sent to Littauer. (AO)

PLEASE HOLD STORY FOR REVISED VERSION LEAVING HERE TOMORROW STOP CERTAIN CHANGES MAY MAKE ALL THE DIFFERENCE STOP WORKING ON GOOD PICTURE¶ FOR FOUR WEEKS BEST WISHES
    F SCOTT FITZGERALD.

Wire to Ober 5 March 1939. Van Nuys, Calif. (AO)

F. Scott Fitzgerald, Esq.
5521 Amestoy Avenue
Encino
Los Angeles, Cal.

Dear Scott:
    I am holding the copy of the thumbs story and waiting for the new version which you wired me you were sending.
    Swanie tells me you are working again so there may be some delay in your sending on the revisions but I hope you can send them before long.
    I'm glad you're feeling so much better. I have hardly been ill all winter. I was out of the office a couple of days with a cold but that was all.
    Please give my best to Sheila and when you have time, tell me how you like the job you working on.

Sincerely,
[Harold Ober]

March 10, 1939

TL (cc), 1p. (AO)

While never fully recovering, Zelda had several periods of stability, and in April 1939 she and Fitzgerald took a trip to Cuba. Fitzgerald went on another drunk, and they finally ended up in New York City. Zelda had

---

¶*Air Raid* for Paramount. In March Fitzgerald also worked on an untitled movie for Madeleine Carroll and Fred MacMurray at Paramount.

Fitzgerald put in Doctor's Hospital and returned to Highland Hospital on her own.

PLEASE WIRE ME TWO HUNDRED IF POSSIBLE TO ATLANTA
AIRPORT IMMEDIATELY WILL BE IN NEWYORK TOMORROW
WILL CALL
    SCOTT FITZGERALD.

Wire to Ober 21 April 1939. Miami, Fla. (AO)

Miss Frances S. Fitzgerald
Vassar College
Poughkeepsie, New York

Dear Scottie:
I have two letters from Mademoiselle.# In the letter to me, Mr. Waller wants to know if you will send your answer by special delivery.

Your father came in Thursday morning and left in the afternoon by plane. He seemed very cheerful. I hope you'll come down to see us soon.

> Sincerely,
> [Harold Ober]

May 1, 1939

TL (cc), 1p.

Mrs. F. Scott Fitzgerald
Highland Hospital
Ashville, N. C.

Dear Zelda:
Scott came to see me last Thursday just before he took the plane back to California. He seemed very cheerful and full of plans about getting to work on his novel.

It was very nice to see you in New York and I hope the next time you are in Scarsdale, you will be able to stay longer. Let me know if there is anything I can do for you here.

> Sincerely yours,
> [Harold Ober]

May 4, 1939

TL (cc), 1p.

Scottie had been asked to write an article by *Mademoiselle.* "A Short Retort," July 1939.

F. Scott Fitzgerald, Esq.
5521 Amestoy Avenue
Encino
Los Angeles, California

Dear Scott:

I am enclosing a letter from your friend, the taxi-cab driver.* He
brought it to the house and I told him that I would forward it to
you. I didn't tell him where you were.

Sincerely,
[Harold Ober]

May 4, 1939

TL (cc), 1p. (AO)

May 13 1939

Mr. Harold Ober
40 East 49th Street
New York, New York

Dear Harold:—

At long last, here's a revision of the "Tib" story which I think I
won't be ashamed to let Mr. Littauer see. For God's sake, if you
don't agree, send it back to me—or rather, don't show it. It's been
a year and a half since I have written the story and certainly if this
seems to you a secondary performance, I don't want to publish it.

Handled the bill you sent me from the Algonquin direct. If there
are any further bills, please pay them unless there is any doubt in
your mind about them, in which case communicate with me. They
have been awfully nice and in this regard, after the Algonquin
business is finished, I wish you would transfer the remains of my
account in the New York bank to the Bank of America, Culver City
and send me some notification.

I got that curious letter that you forwarded from the eye-slugger.
I have no intention of doing anything about it. If he'll send me his
watch, I'll send him my eye. That is positively my last word on the
subject. It was a sucker blow and I am just ashamed of myself for
having taken it.

---

*Fitzgerald had gotten into a fight with a cab driver who took him to Ober's home.

With best regards to Ann and best remembrances to the children.

Ever yours,
Scott

5521 Amestoy Avenue
Encino, California

TLS, 1p. (AO)

F. Scott Fitzgerald, Esq.
5521 Amestoy Avenue
Encino
Los Angeles, Cal.

Dear Scott:

It seems to me that you have done a very good job in your last version of the Thumbs story. I have given it to Littauer and I'll let you know his decision just as soon as I get it.

I hope everything is going well with you. Drop me a line when you have time and tell me what you are doing.

Sincerely,
Harold

May 22, 1939

TLS, 1p. (PU)

May 29 1939

Mr. Harold Ober
40 East 49th Street
New York City

Dear Harold:—

This letter is going to be full of information, some of which I may have let drop in New York or which you may have guessed. In the first place, as I suspected, I have been ill with a touch of the old malady from [the]§ *about the* time I came off "Gone With the Wind". [and] I knew I should not have taken on those last two pictures both of which were terrors and far beyond my strength at the time.¶ [A] *The* sudden outburst of drink was a result of an attempt to keep up my strength for an effort of which I was not capable. After consultations here I have been condemned, in no uncertain terms, to a

---

§Fitzgerald made pencil corrections and additions to this letter.
¶ *Winter Carnival* and *Air Raid*.

period at home some of which has to be spent in bed. This doesn't mean that I am not working—I am allowed three to four hours a day for that, but I have told Swanie to sign me off any available list. (This Hitchcock from England seems to have had me first on the list to do "Rebecca") But Swanie evidently realized that I really wasn't up to anything (for observed on [the] *a* list by Sheilah who happened to see it in Hitchcock's office at Selznick's was, "Unavailable —gone to Cuba.")

Well, "Unavailable—gone to Cuba" is as good as anything else. So to friends in the East I would rather not have it known that I was ill. Any story that I have gone away into the California mountains to write a novel will cover the situation because if I should want to go back to actual picture making next Fall, I would not want anyone to be able to say, "Well—that Fitzgerald, I understand he *'s* [has] been sick and we don't want anyone that's liable to break down on this picture." In other words, it would do me a damage here which it would not do in the East, as this is a hot bed of gossip. I even prefer Swanie to think that I am a bluffing hypochondriac than to know the whole truth. I think I told him that I had a little mild heart trouble. I am cut off here in Encino from anything and anybody who might disturb me, under the charge of an excellent doctor. There's no taint of alcoholism to confuse the issue and my only visitor is Shielah who comes out two or three times a week. We are friends again, even intimates—though we stick to our old resolution not to go back to the same basis as before.

Now, I wish you could airmail me [some] *The following* information and please do not spare me in this, because my morale is high and I want to know the exact situation [of] where I stand with the magazines—notably the <u>Post</u>. As in our previous discussions I told you that that five thousand word length is likely to be a terror for me and while I realize that Collier's has the right to see some stories still I cannot somehow see it as a permanent relation. I have planned my work in the following order:

<u>First</u>, I *have* blocked out my novel# completely with a rough sketch of every episode and event and character so that under proper circumstances I could begin writing it tomorrow. It is a short novel about fifty thousand words long and should take me three to four months.

However, for reasons of income tax I feel I should be [rather] more secure before I launch into such a venture—*but* [and] it will

---

The Last Tycoon.

divide easily into five thousand word lengths and <u>Collier's</u> might take a chance on it where the <u>Post</u> would not. They might at least be promised a first look at it when it's finished—possibly some time late in the Fall. <u>Secondly</u>, I have hesitated between the idea of those picture originals which I discussed with you and the idea of doing some short stories and have decided on the second because since I haven't done a short story for over two years I feel rather full of material and rather enthusiastic about doing a few. What I want to know most [of all] is how much the <u>Post</u> would pay me. I want to know frankly from their contact man what [his] *is the* opinion of the new editor [is] *of* of my work and as specifically as possible the sum they would [want to] offer. After this long lapse—(it has now been four years since I was their prize boy)—I do not expect $4000., naturally, but if he suggested any such sum as $2000., it would lead me to believe that he did not especially like my work, or *else* felt that I had fallen off and gone Hollywood or wants to make a clean sweep of Lorimer's old authors. Whatever you cannot find out specifically, I wish you would write me the <u>feel</u> of.

Also [Now,] in regard to other magazines. <u>*The* Pictorial Review</u> has not published those two Gwen stories. They weren't good stories—were written at a bad time, and I don't blame them. Perhaps later I can either revise those stories or send them another to go with them which will make it an interesting series. That, however, is out for the present as I feel that everything I wrote in '35 was all covered with a dust of gloom and illness. Likewise with Balmer whom I suppose has never forgiven me for the dilatory arrival of the Red Book stories. [Now] What does that leave as possible high-priced markets in New York? As I say, I feel I have from two to four short stories in me which will be in my own manner. And now let me [say again] *repeat* that if you could airmail me this information or as much of it as you can collect, it would be of inestimable value at this moment.

I warned you this would be a long letter. With warmest regards to you and Ann and the children.

Ever,
Scott Fitzg

5521 Amestoy Avenue
Encino, California

TLS, 2pp. (AO)

F. Scott Fitzgerald, Esq.
5521 Amestoy Avenue
Encino
Los Angeles, Cal.

Dear Scott:

Thank you for your letter of May twenty-ninth. Collier's likes the new ending to the Civil War story* and they will be paying me One Thousand Dollars which is the amount still due on this story. Littauer says he is very keen to get more stories by you and he indicated that he might increase the Twenty-Five Hundred Dollar price. I'll have a talk with one of the editors of The Post on Tuesday and I'll write you as soon as I have done so. I don't think I'll get anything definite from them until I have a story of yours to show them and I'd rather wait to talk about price when I show them the story.

I'm delighted to hear that you are going to do some more stories as I think it is time that your name should be appearing again, and I don't think there is any reason for your coming down to Two Thousand Dollars and I din(t think any magazine will ask you to.

I'm glad to know that you have the novel mapped out and I am sure I can get a fine price for it when the time comes.

I'll find out about those two Gwen stories. Pictorial Review suspended publication last year and most of their stories are being taken over by Good Housekeeping or Cosmopolitan. Besides The Post and Collier's, there are a number of other magazines that would pay well for your stories,—American, Cosmopolitan, Ladies Home Journal, Woman's Home Companion and some of the other women's magazines.

Sincerely,
Harold

June 2, 1939

TLS, 2pp. (PU)

Miss Frances Fitzgerald
Josselyn Hall
Vassar College
Poughkeepsie, New York

Dear Scottie:

Here is the thirty dollars I promised to send you.

I called up the editor of Mademoiselle and she said that the

---

*"Thumbs Up," published as "End of Hate," *Collier's*, 22 June 1940.

voucher has been put through, but that it may be some time before the check is drawn. I imagine you will surely get it within a week or two.

I'm glad we're going to see you on Thursday.

Sincerely,
[Harold Ober]

June 5, 1939

TL (cc), 1p.

> YOU DID NOT MENTION BALANCE IN BOWERY BANK IF ANY AND WHETHER YOU HAD IT TRANSFERRED REGARDS ALWAYS SCOTT.

Wire to Ober 8 June 1939. Van Nuys, Calif. (AO)

> MAILING CHECK FOR 897.88. WILL TRANSFER OTHER MONDAY Harold Ober

Wire (cc) to Fitzgerald 9 June 1939. (AO)

F. Scott Fitzgerald, Esq.
5521 Amestoy Avenue
Encino
Los Angeles, Cal.

Dear Scott:

I am enclosing a check for Two Hundred and Twenty-five Dollars and twenty-one cents which is the amount left in your account at The Bowery Savings Bank. I am also enclosing your Pass Book. The account is entirely closed up now.

Your telegram sounded as if you had asked me previously to transfer this amount. If you wrote me asking me to do this, I cannot find the letter. I am sending the check direct to you as I am not sure what bank you are now using.

Scottie came down from Vassar on Friday, looking very well and very pretty. I don't know whether she's told you, but she got an A in Philosophy and she thinks she has a B average in all her other courses which I think is pretty good!

Sincerely,
[Harold Ober]

June 12, 1939

TL (cc), 1p. (AO)

> 14 THOUSAND WORD STORY LEAVES HERE AIR MAIL THURS-DAY. COULD YOU ADVANCE 500 BY WIRE TO BANK OF AMERICA

CULVERCITY ANSWER SO ONLY I CAN UNDERSTAND. GET-
TING UP IN TWO WEEKS
SCOTT FITZGERALD.

Wire to Ober 20 June 1939. Encino, Calif. (AO)

GLAD STORY IS COMING PLANNED COMING HOLLYWOOD BUT
POSTPONING BECAUSE HAVE JUST PAID TAXES AND INSUR-
ANCE AND FUNDS ARE LOW. SCOTTIE LEFT FOR ASHEVILLE
Harold Ober

Wire (cc) to Fitzgerald 20 June 1939. (AO)

*MGM allowed Fitzgerald's contract to expire at the end of 1938, after
eighteen months and some $90,000. In his 1 February 1939 letter to Fitz-
gerald, Ober indicated his anxiety about starting a new debt cycle: "I would
like to see you cut down expenses just as much as you can and put away all
the money you possibly can for the remaining time you are in Hollywood."
Early in 1939 Fitzgerald had three short movie assignments—*Gone with
the Wind, Winter Carnival, *and* Air Raid. *In March Fitzgerald revised
"Thumbs Up" ("The End of Hate"), for which* Collier's *had already made
a down payment. On 20 June Fitzgerald wired Ober for $500 against his
next story—"The Women in the House" or "Temperature," which was never
sold. Ober sent the money and composed a letter—*which he did not mail
*—clearly warning that no more advances against unsold stories would be
forthcoming. It is unlikely that the warning would have deterred Fitzgerald;
however, the fact that he was unprepared for Ober's refusal of his next request
accounts for the force of his reaction. Fitzgerald quite simply did not expect
to be turned down by Ober after twenty years of advances and after he had
paid his debts. In trying to spare Fitzgerald the hurt of the warning letter,
Ober set him up for a greater hurt. Perhaps Ober understood that, warning
or no warning, Fitzgerald would ask for advances and that an estrangement
was inevitable.*

F. Scott Fitzgerald, Esq.
5521 Amestoy Avenue
Encino
Los Angeles, California

Dear Scott:‡

I was short of money when your telegram came because I had just
paid up all my taxes and paid some money on a mortgage and some
money that I owed on my insurance. I am still short, but I managed

---

‡In the top margin a note in Ober's hand reads: "never sent".

to wire to the Culver City Bank the Five Hundred Dollars you needed. I think, however, it would be a great mistake for us to get back into the position we were in. I think it is bad for you and difficult for me. The margin of profit in the agency business is very narrow. The expenses are many and high and I reckon the net profit is only about three per cent. I hope, therefore, we can keep things on a "Pay as we go" basis.

I think you can do that if you will follow the old adage about "Watching the pennies and letting the dollars take care of themselves." I notice that both Scottie and you would always rather send a telegram or make an expensive telephone call than send a letter for three cents. You give tips four and five times as large as you need to. On the other hand, you are very economical about some of the larger expenses. I am sure that if you could look back over the years with some kind of a celestial bookkeeper to note down your expenses, you would find that a large part of the money you have earned has gone for things that brought you no return.

You will probably say that I have no business to read you this kind of a lecture, but I hope you will understand that I am doing it only because I am very fond of you and of Scottie.

Speaking of Scottie. I think it would be a great deal better for her if she knew at all times exactly what your financial condition is. I think it is your fault rather than hers that she acts as if she were the daughter of a millionaire. She just doesn't think about the cost of anything. I approve entirely of your giving her the best education you can give her, but I think she ought to know that you're not very well and she ought to learn to be economical.

In any case, I think I ought to let you know that I cannot start loaning you money which means my borrowing money which is expensive and which is a thing I do not like to do.

Now for pleasanter things! I am glad you're sending me a story and I am very eager to read it.

Scottie was with us for a few days and we all liked her better than we have ever liked her before which is saying a good deal! She looked very well and very pretty and she was more thoughtful of others and more sensible than she has ever been. She finished up with a B average which is an extremely good mark at Vassar. She got an A in a difficult Philosophy course and I think you should be proud of what she has done.

She has gone to Ashville to have her appendicitis operation and we shall keep in touch with her. We hope she can come back and see us either before or after she goes to California. She says you want her to go out for a while. I think she'd rather go to California right after the operation and then come back and make us a visit , but anytime this summer will be all right for us. I think it would do her good to stay in the country with us and get in some tennis and lead a fairly quiet life.

Sincerely,
[Harold Ober]

June 21, 1939

TL, 2pp. (AO)

DO YOU LIKE STORY?
SCOTT.

Wire to Ober 28 June 1939. Van Nuys, Calif. (AO)

STORY JUST RECEIVED AND READ. MUCH TOO LONG FOR SUB-JECT. ADVISE CUTTING TO SIX THOUSAND WORDS WILL OF-FER AS IS IF YOU INSIST BUT THINK VERY UNWISE. WRITING.
Harold Ober

Wire (cc) to Fitzgerald 29 June 1939. (AO)

F. Scott Fitzgerald, Esq.
5521 Amestoy Avenue
Encino
Los Angeles, Cal.

Dear Scott:

I'm returning THE WOMEN IN THE HOUSE by airmail so that you can cut it as much as possible. As I tried to tell you over the telephone last night, this is in my opinion, a story that would be very difficult to divide into two parts. It is a light, amusing story and hasn't enough suspense. It is also too long for any magazine that I know of to use as a short story and it is not long enough for a novelette.

I know from experience that it is the length of story that the Post finds it very difficult to use. And since it is some time since you have shown the Post a story, I think it is important to show them a story that there is a chance of their buying.

I hope you will cut it just as much as you can. It is a light, farcical story and such stories do not stand a lot of words. I think the closet scene and a lot about the nurses could be cut. Also the part of the story where Monsen is intoxicated. The first part is really good, but after that it seemed to me to get rather exaggerated.

Sincerely,
Harold

June 30, 1939

TLS, 1p. (PU)

DO YOU KNOW SCOTTYS ADDRESS WOULD DEEPLY APPRECI-
ATE ANY INFORMATION WOULD YOU ANSWER COLLECT TO
322 SAYRE STREET MONTGOMERY ALABAMA KINDEST RE-
GARDS
ZELDA FITZGERALD.

Wire to Anne Ober 1 July 1939. Mongomery.

SCOTTIE WIRED FROM BOSTON YESTERDAY BUT GAVE NO AD-
DRESS SUGGEST WRITE HER CARE HARVARD COLLEGE SUM-
MER SCHOOL CAMBRIDGE SORRY NOT TO BE MORE HELPFUL
REGARDS
ANNE OBER

Draft of wire written on verso of Zelda Fitzgerald's 1 July wire.

July 3, 1939

Mr. Harold Ober
40 East 49th Street
New York City

Dear Harold:

I made a first cut from the original 14,500 words (58 pages) that I sent you, to 10,850 words and now at the last moment I have made an additional cut to 9,350 words which is the last that can be pried out of the story.(by this old hand)§

I don't see how the incident of Emmet getting the brandy bottle can <u>possibly</u> be eliminated, and I know it's a difficult length, but unfortunately that's the way the story was.

Ever yours
Scott Fitzg --

5521 Amestoy Avenue
Encino, California

TLS, 1p. (AO)

---

§Added in ink by Fitzgerald.

On or about 3 July Fitzgerald asked for another advance. His request and Ober's reply are lost. But on this day he wired Maxwell Perkins:

HAVE BEEN WRITING IN BED WITH TUBERCULOSIS UNDER DOCTORS NURSES CARE SIS ARRIVING WEST. OBER HAS DECIDED NOT TO BACK ME THOUGH I PAID BACK EVERY PENNY AND EIGHT THOUSAND COMMISSION. AM GOING TO WORK THURSDAY IN STUDIO AT FIFTEEN HUNDRED CAN YOU LEND ME SIX HUNDRED FOR ONE WEEK BY WIRE TO BANK AMERICAN CULVERCITY. SCOTTIE HOSPITAL WITH APPENDIX AND AM ABSOLUTELY WITHOUT FUNDS. PLEASE DO NOT ASK OBERS COOPERATION *(Scribners Archives, PU).*

Scott Fitzgerald, Esq.
5521 Amestoy Avenue
Encino
Los Angeles, Cal.

Dear Scott:

I got a telegram this morning asking me to hold the story a day and just now the cut version of the story has come in. I understand from the telegram that you want me to hold it another day so I am doing so. In the meantime, I'll look this version over.

Sincerely,
[Harold Ober]

July 6, 1939

TL (cc), 1p. (AO)

July 7, 1939

Mr. Harold Ober
40 East 49th Street
New York City

Dear Harold:—

This is about right, I think. I took one more whack at it. My God, what a waste of energies. What I cut out is long enough for another short story, only it might not fit together. Littauer gave me to understand that they had nothing at all against the two-parter. I know there was no trouble with the <u>Red Book</u> with the "Rich Boy" or the <u>Post</u> with the "Popular Girl".

However, I must admit that there was a lot of waste material in this one. One's pencil gets garrulous after that snail's pace movie writing.

> Best wishes,
> Scott

5521 Amestoy Avenue
Encino, California

TLS, 1p. (AO)

NEW AND SHORTER VERSION MAILED FRIDAY
  SCOTT.

Wire to Ober 8 July 1939. Van Nuys, Calif. (AO)

> July 8 1939

Mr. Harold Ober
40 E. 49th St.
New York City

Dear Harold:—

Will you kindly make these changes in the final (3rd) version of the story:

Page 13—Line 17 should read: "I lie on my right side——

Page 16—Line7 should read: "With the exception of Hedy LaMarr
  she made the swiftest——

Page 21—Line 1 should read: —in anticipation of preparing
  ″ 2   and eating him.

Page 31—Line 11 should read: and down drains, and inside
  books——"

Page 31—Line 15 should read: "Monsen may have been trying to get
  at the stuff.

(The italics, of course, are just for your aid)¶

> Sincerely,
> Scott

P.S.   Thought Scottie's article in Mademoiselle is in very bad taste. She said something about writing for Harper's Bazaar. I would like to see anything she wants to publish for the present; [because] I

¶Added in ink by Fitzgerald.

didn't like the idea of her sitting on my shoulder and beating my head with a wooden spoon.#

5521 Amestoy Ave.
Encino, Cal.

TLS, 1p. (AO)

F. Scott Fitzgerald, Esq.
5521 Amestoy Avenue
Encino
Los Angeles, California

Dear Scott:

The third version of your story now called TEMPERATURE has just come in and I have made the corrections that you sent. It is a better length now and I'll show it to The Post tomorrow. I'll read the story through before I give it to one of the editors who is coming in in the morning.

I didn't see Scottie's piece in Mademoiselle until it was in print. Harper's Bazaar wanted Scottie to do a piece about the kind of clothes girls are going to wear in college next fall. This request came just as she was leaving for her operation. The magazine has now given up the idea of using such an article. I don't think there is anything else of Scottie's that will be appearing in the magazines.

Sincerely,
[Harold Ober]

July 10, 1939

TL (cc), 1p. (AO)

HOW DO YOU LIKE IT NOW
    SCOTT.

Wire to Ober 11 July 1939. Van Nuys, Calif. (AO)

#Scottie's "A Short Retort" prompted Fitzgerald's reply, "My Generation," which was not published until October 1968 in *Esquire.* Her article was by-lined: "by Frances Scott Fitzgerald, daughter of F. Scott Fitzgerald, whose novels of the Jazz Age are definitive records of an era." Her article does not mention her father. Speaking of her generation, she states "in the speakeasy era that followed, we were left pretty much to ourselves and allowed to do as we pleased. And so, we 'know the score.'"

F. Scott Fitzgerald, Esq.
5521 Amestoy Avenue
Encino
Los Angeles, Cal.

Dear Scott:

The story is a lot better now that you have shortened it but I do not think and I do not believe you think that it is anywhere near one of your best stories. A slight story like this one cannot stand the length that a more important story would. That is why I was sure you ought to cut it down before we showed it to anyone. It is true that magazines sometimes use a two-part story but here again it is necessary that the story be one that will divide and has suspense enough to hold over for a week or a month as the case may be.

Sincerely,
[Harold Ober]

July 12, 1939

TL (cc), 1p. (AO)

STILL FLABBERGASTED AT YOUR ABRUPT CHANGE IN POLICY AFTER 20 YEARS ESPECIALLY WITH STORY IN YOUR HANDS STOP MY COMMERCIAL VALUE CANT HAVE SUNK FROM 60 THOUSAND TO NOTHING BECAUSE OF A SLOW HEALING LUNG CAVITY STOP AFTER 30 PICTURE OFFERS DURING THE MONTHS I WAS IN BED SWANSON NOW PROMISES NOTHING FOR ANOTHER WEEK STOP CANT YOU ARRANGE A FEW HUNDRED ADVANCE FROM A MAGAZINE SO I CAN EAT TODAY AND TOMORROW STOP WONT YOU WIRE
SCOTT.¶

Wire to Ober sent 13 July 1939. Van Nuys, Calif. Received in New York 3:56 A.M., 14 July. (AO)

SORRY COLLECTIONS SLOW AND IMPOSSIBLE MAKE ADVANCE NOW SUGGEST ASKING SWANSON GET ADVANCE ON JOB
HAROLD OBER.

The insult to my intelligence in the phrase "collections slow" makes me laugh.
FSF*

Wire to Fitzgerald 14 July 1939. Received in California 10:26 A.M. (PU). This wire and the next one may have crossed.

¶This wire seems to be the third in a series, beginning about 3 July. Fitzgerald's initial request for money and Ober's refusal—both lost—preceded this reaction by Fitzgerald, which he sent late 13 July California time.
*Fitzgerald apparently returned this wire to Ober with his comment.

WONT YOU PLEASE WIRE
   SCOTT.

Wire to Ober 14 July 1939. Van Nuys, Calif. Received in New York 1:46 P.M. (AO)

THINK IT IS BETTER NOT TO OFFER TEMPERATURE AGAIN AT
PRESENT SEND ME BACK COPY WHICH I WILL LOOK AT LATER
   SCOTT.

Wire to Ober 14 July 1939. Van Nuys, Calif. Received by Ober 17 July. (AO)

Scott Fitzgerald, Esq.
5521 Amestoy Avenue
Encino
Los Angeles, Cal.

Dear Scott:

I have the following letter from The Post regarding your last short story, TEMPERATURE:

"There is, it seems to us, a real story idea in Scott Fitzgerald's TEMPERATURE, but the thing has been so garbled in the telling that you can't see the story for the words. You, I know, realized this yourself when you gave the manuscript to me.

I wish you'd tell Scott that we are anxious to see more stories of his and suggest to him to put this away for awhile and have another try at it later."

I also have your telegram suggesting that I do not offer the story further. The story, even now, is about 8,200 words in length which is worse for other magazines than it is for the Post. I think you have enough material for a very light, very short, amusing story, but it isn't a good story now and I don't think it would help you to offer it.

I'm sorry that you are short of money again and I'm sorry that I cannot advance any more money just now. My expenses are increasing right along and I have two boys to send to college and I must save some money to do this with.

The margin of profit in the agency business is small and I think all the agents have found that it is impossible to run an agency and loan money at the same time. I should think that your best plan at present would be to take on a few more jobs in Hollywood and save some money so that when you get ready to write, you will have something to live on.

I haven't lost faith in your being able to write. I do know though that without exception every author I have ever known who has worked in Hollywood has had a transitional period of several months in which it has been difficult for him to get away from the motion picture technique of writing.

Sincerely,
Harold

July 18, 1939

P.S.   I am returning TEMPERATURE under separate cover.

TLS, 2pp. (PU)

July 19 1939

Mr. Harold Ober
40 East 49th Street
New York City

Dear Harold:—

This is not a request for any more backing—there will be no more requests. I am quite sure you would be as stubborn in any decision that I am through as you were up to 1934 about the value of my stories. Also I am writing this letter with, I hope, no touch of unpleasantness—simply from a feeling that perhaps you share, that I have depended too long on backing and had better find out at the source whether my products are considered deficient and why.

As I said in my telegram, the shock wasn't so much at your refusal to lend me a specific sum, because I know the demands on you and that you may not have felt able to do so at that time—it was rather "the manner of the doing", your sudden change of policy in not lending me up to the limit of what a story would sell for, a custom which had obtained between us for over a dozen years. The consequence here is of little interest now—I turned down several picture offers under the conviction that you could tide me over until I got through to a magazine (and this a few months after telling me there was no hurry about paying back that money and just after a year and a half during which I paid your firm over ten thousand dollars in commissions and you personally thirteen thousand dollars in advances.) Sick as I was I would have taken those offers rather than go along on two loans which melted immediately into medical bills and has left me most of the past seven weeks with bank balances of between eighty and fourteen dollars.

You were not here; long distance calls are unsatisfactory and telegrams suddenly did not deserve more than an airmail answer from you so I had no choice but to come to the conclusion that you were through with me in a big way. I repeat, I don't blame you. Every time I've come East I have gone on a binge, most often after a time with Zelda, and the last time I brought a good deal of inconvenience into your settled life. Though you were very nice and polite about it (and I can scarcely remember twice in our relations when there has been any harshness between us—certainly never any harsh feeling on my side) and my unwritten debt to you is terribly large and I shall always be terribly aware of it—your care and cherishing of Scottie during the intervals between school and camp in those awful sick years of '35 and '36. I have wanted someday to be able to repay that to your boys with the same instinct that made me want to give the little Finney girl a trip out here.

But Harold, I must never again let my morale become as shattered as it was in those black years—and the situation resolves itself into this: it is as if a man had once trekked up into the Arctic to save a partner and his load, and then when the partner became lost a second time, the backer was not able or willing to help him get out. It doesn't diminish the lost man's gratitude for former favors, but rather than perish, he must find his own way out—and quickly. I had to sell a 2400 word story to <u>Esquire</u> # that I think <u>Liberty</u> would have paid a thousand for because three Fitzgeralds needed surgeons, psychiatrists and T.B. doctors and medicines at the same time.

I feel less hesitation in saying this because it is probably what you wanted for some time. You now have plenty of authors who produce correctly and conduct their affairs in a business-like manner. On the contrary, I have a neurosis about anyone's uncertainty about my ability that has been a principal handicap in the picture business. And secondly, the semi-crippled state into which I seem to get myself sometimes (almost like the hero of my story "Financing Finnegan") fill me, in the long nights, with a resentment toward the absurd present which is not fair to you or to the past. Everything I have ever done or written is me, and who doesn't choose to accept the whole cannot but see the wisdom of a parting. One doesn't change at 42 though one can grow more tired and even more acquiescent—and I am very close to knowing how you feel about it all: I realize there is little place in this tortured world for any exhibition of shattered nerves or anything that illness makes people do.

So goodbye and I won't be ridiculous enough to thank you again. Nothing would ever make me forget your many kindnesses and the good times and laughs we have had together. With very best to Ann and the children.

Ever yours, gratefully,

"Design in Plaster," *Esquire*, November 1939.

P.S.   I know you are not worrying about the $500., but I will pay you out of the first money I make, which probably won't be long now.

5521 Amestoy Avenue
Encino, California

TL (cc), 2pp. From Fitzgerald. (PU)

There is no surviving Ober reply to Fitzgerald's letters of 19 July and 2 August. It seems unlikely that any were written, for Ober kept his distress to himself. But it was necessary for Fitzgerald to justify his position. On 19 July—the same day he wrote to Ober—Fitzgerald notified Perkins of the break:—

"*The main point of this letter is confidential for the most important reasons. Harold Ober and I are parting company. Whether he is throwing me over or me him may be a subject of controversy—but not on my part. . . . Also I shall be forever grateful to Harold for his part of the help in backing me through that long illness, but his attitude has changed and I tell you this without any anger, but after a month's long and regretful consideration. He is a single-tracked man and the feeling that he once had of definite interest combined with forgiveness of my sins, has changed to a sort of general disapproval and a vague sense that I am through—this in spite of the fact that I paid him over ten thousand dollars in commissions in the last year-and-a half and refunded the whole thirteen thousand that I owed him.*

"*I think something to do with it is the fact that almost every time I have come to New York lately I have just taken Zelda somewhere and have gone on more or less of a binge, and he has formed the idea that I am back in the mess of three years ago.*

"*Anyhow, it is impossible to continue a relation which has become so strained and difficult. Even though there has been no spoken impoliteness there is a new fashion of discussing my stories as if he was a rather dissatisfied and cranky editor and of answering telegrams with delayed airmails and, most of all, completely changing his old policy of backing me up to the limit of what the next story will probably be sold for which makes it impossible to go on. He fairly earned the fifty thousand dollars or so of commissions that I've paid him and nothing snows one under quicker than a send of disbelief and disillusion in anyone close. The final touch was when I had to sell two stories to Esquire at $250., when I wanted cash quick—one of them was worth at least $1000., from Liberty if he could have given me enough advance to survive the wait.*

"*So while I feel regret I have no moral compunction. This is a matter of survival. A man lost in the Arctic for the second time cannot sit waiting while a former rescuer refuses to send out another relief expedition. I would rather deal personally with the editors, as I deal always with you, and get opinions at the source. Harold's greatest help was when I lived in Europe. As you know we have never been very close either intellectually or emotionally (save for his kindness to Scottie). . . . I stuck with him, of course, when he left Reynolds, but now he has many correct and conventional Agatha Christies, etc., on his list who never cause any inconvenience, so I doubt if I will be missed.*

"I thought you should know this—know also that he has always treated me fairly and generously and is above reproach as an agent. The blame which brought about this situation is entirely mine. But it is no such illogical step as the one which made Tom Wolfe leave Scribner's. A few weeks ago when three Fitzgeralds at once were in the hands of the medical profession he found it inconvenient to help and under the circumstances of the last year and a half the episode served to give me a great uncertainty as to his caring what becomes of me.

"Above all things I wish you wouldn't discuss this with him. I have not, nor will ever say, nor could say anything against him either personally or professionally, but even the fact that I have discussed the matter with you might upset him and give him ideas that I had, and turn what should be a peaceful cleavage into an unpleasant affair."

Apparently Perkins did not react to this letter, for Fitzgerald wrote mentioning the Ober break again on 22 and 24 July. Perkins wrote on 26 July urging Fitzgerald to stay with Ober: "But, Scott, I think that Harold Ober is one of the very best and most loyal friends you have in the world. I hope to God you will stand by him. I don't know what misunderstanding you may have had, but I do know what he thinks of you, and that he has always been absolutely true to you in every sense. I do not think a man has any business to interfere in relations between other people, but if you will allow me in this case, I should say that something very serious would have to have happened before you would think of turning away from Harold."

On 18 July Fitzgerald began negotiating directly with Kenneth Littauer of Collier's:

"I would like to send the story <u>directly to you</u>, which amounts to a virtual split with Ober. This is regrettable after twenty years of association but it had better be asked under the anonymity of 'one of those things.' Harold is a fine man and has been a fine agent and the fault is mine. Through one illness he backed me with a substantial amount of money (all paid back to him now with Hollywood gold), but he is not prepared to do that again with growing boys to educate—and, failing this, I would rather act for a while as my own agent in the short story just as I always have with Scribners. But I much prefer, both for his sake and mine, that my sending you the story

direct should be a matter between you and me. For the fact to reach him through your office might lead to an unpleasant cleavage of an old relationship. I am writing him later in the week making the formal break on terms that will be understood between us, and I have no doubt that in some ways he will probably welcome it. Relationships have an unfortunate way of wearing out, like most things in this world."

Later in July Fitzgerald wrote Littauer:

"The second thing is my relation to Ober. It is completely vague. I've very seldom taken his advice on stories. I have regarded him as a mixture of friend, bill collector and for a couple of sick years as backer. So far as any editorial or financial dealing, I would much rather, as things are now, deal directly with an editor. For instance, if this sort of story is worth less to you than a story of young love, I would be perfectly willing to accept less. I would not want any agent to stand in my way in that regard. I think all the agents still act as if we were back in the 1920s in a steadily rising market."

July 22 1939

Harold Ober Office
40 East 49th Street
New York City

Dear Sirs:—

From lack of communication in regard to my story "Temperature", I am assuming that Mr. Ober is on his vacation. I wired about a week ago directly to the <u>Post</u>. They answered suggesting some specific changes whereupon I wired you to return the manuscript to me and have expected it by airmail daily.

As I said in the wire, I want to do a revision before showing it to any other magazine.

Sincerely,
F. Scott Fitzgerald

P.S.   Would you please wire me collect whether the manuscript is on its way to me?[†]

5521 Amestoy Avenue
Encino, California

TLS, 1p. (AO)

[†]Immediately following the P.S. a note in Ober's hand reads: "This was sent to him on July 19th (last Wednesday) by Express."

F. Scott Fitzgerald, Esq.
5521 Amestoy Avenue
Encino, California

Dear Scott:

The copy of TEMPERATURE was shipped to you on the day you asked me for it. I hope you have it by now. Let me know if you don't receive it and I'll send out a tracer for it. I didn't send it airmail because you said you might look it over later on.[‡]

Sincerely yours,
[Harold Ober]

July 24, 1939

TL (cc), 1p. (AO)

August 2 1939

Dear Harold:—

I have been and still am somewhat shocked by your sudden and most determined reversal of form. Only six months ago you were telling me "not to be in too much of a hurry to pay you back" but instead try to save some money. It was something of a counter-blast to find that my credit was now worth much less than I loaned Charles Warren and other young authors last year.

Your advice that I should have "taken on some movie work" with a lung cavity and a temperature of 102° was a new slant. The cavity evidently began to form about the time I started on "Air Raid", and your implication that I had been loafing must have been based on those two day binges in New York, several months apart. Anyhow, when the temperature was still a hundred and the cavity still crackling I was asking Swanie to get me work and meanwhile putting in five hours a day on a bed-desk.

Being in need, I make no apology for having sent the original of the enclosed[§] directly to the <u>Post</u>, with the request that they communicate by wire to me as well as by letter to you. I had a fifteen day wait on "Temperature"—it is hard to remember there was a time your cables reached me in North Africa. Sending a story direct may be bad policy but one doesn't consider that when one is living on money from a hocked Ford—every day counts, less in the material matter of eating than in the inestimable question of morale. Swanie turned down a dozen jobs for me when I was sick in bed—but there just haven't been any since the cavity began to heal.

---

‡A note quoting Fitzgerald's second 14 July telegram is added in Ober's hand in the bottom margin.

§"Director's Special," published as "Discard," *Harper's Bazaar*, January 1948.

I don't have to explain that even though a man has once saved another from drowning, when he refuses to stretch out his arm a second time the victim has to act quickly and desperately to save himself. For change you did, Harold, and without warning—the custom of lending up to the probable yield of a next short story obtained between us for a dozen years. Certainly you haven't just discovered that I'm not any of the things a proper business man should be? And it wasn't even a run around—it was a walk-around that almost made me think the New York telegraph was closed. Finally I had to sell a pair of stories[1] to <u>Esquire</u> the longer one of which (2800 words) might have brought twice as much from <u>Liberty</u>.

Whatever I am supposed to guess, your way of doing it and the time you chose, was as dispiriting as could be. I have been all too hauntingly aware during these months of what you did from 1934 to 1937 to keep my head above water after the failure of <u>Tender</u>, Zelda's third collapse and the long illness. But you have made me sting none the less. Neither Swanson nor Sheilah nor Eddie Knopf have any idea but that I have labored conscientiously out here for twenty months and every studio (except Wanger, but including Metro!) asked for, according to Swanson, me at some time during April and May.

Your reasons for refusing to help me were all good, all praiseworthy, all sound—but wouldn't they have been equally so any time within the past fifteen years? And they followed a year and a half in which I fulfilled all my obligations.

If it is of any interest to you I haven't had a drink in two months but if I was full of champagne I couldn't be more confused about you than I am now.

Ever yours,
Scott

P.S. "Temperature" turned up yesterday at the Van Nuys Railway Express—and in case you think that's incredible I forward the evidence.

5521 Amestoy Avenue
Encino, California

TLS, 2pp. (AO)

---

[1] Probably "Design in Plaster," *Esquire*, November 1939, and "The Lost Decade," December 1939.

Fitzgerald's 3 August reply to Maxwell Perkins's plea to reconsider the break indicates that he was still very hurt and he wanted some sign of Ober's confidence in him. The fact of Ober's support mattered as much to Fitzgerald as the money did:

"Thanks for your letter of July 26. The attached was enclosed with a carbon copy of a manuscript sent to Harold Ober. I chose a moderate course. If he wants to break it is all right with me. In reading my letter keep in mind that during the last year and a half I have paid his firm $9,000. in commissions as well as returning to him $13,000., the entire sum I owed him, the process beginning even before I went to Hollywood. . . .

[14 lines omitted by the editors]

"P.S. Don't think that your advice wasn't valuable. I had composed a much harsher and less just letter to Harold which I did not send. After all, part of his function is to encourage me rather than play the disapproving schoolmaster."

The Fitzgerald-Ober wound never healed. Later in 1939 when Fitzgerald was trying to sell the serial rights for The Last Tycoon, *he acted as his own agent. However, Scottie continued to stay with the Obers, and Fitzgerald and Ober corresponded cordially enough about her. After Fitzgerald died, the Obers continued to look after Scottie; and Ober saw to it, with help from Perkins, that she finished Vassar.*

F. Scott Fitzgerald, Esq.
5521 Amestoy Avenue
Encino
Los Angeles, Cal.

Dear Scott:

I am pleased with DIRECTOR'S SPECIAL and hope The Post will like it. Whether they do or not, it's a good piece of work. I'll write you again in a few days.

Sincerely,
[Harold Ober]

August 7, 1939

TL (cc), 1p. (AO)

F. Scott Fitzgerald, Esq.
5521 Amestoy Avenue
Encino
Los Angeles, California

Dear Scott:

One of the editors of The Post was in today and talked to me about DIRECTOR'S SPECIAL. He said they all felt that this would be a story for The Post if you could make it less obscure—especially at the beginning and the end. I think the first part could be fixed with a little cutting in the first two or three pages and a little more explanation of where everybody is and what they are doing. The first paragraph, for instance, is a little difficult to understand.

The ending is clear enough to me but The Post evidently would like to have you make it clearer that Dolly comes out on top. Perhaps you could build up a little more to the fact that The Portrait of a Lady is a very important one to get. If The Post doesn't like the story after you have done this, or even if you don't feel like doing anything more with it, I think I can sell it to Collier's.

> Sincerely,
> [Harold Ober]

August 8, 1939

TL (cc), 1p. (AO)

DONHOFFER DIRECTORS SPECIAL UNTIL YOU GET REVISED VERSION REGARDS
　　FITZGERALD.

Wire to Ober 9 August 1939. Encino, Calif. (AO)

August 12 1939

Mr. Harold Ober
40 East 49th Street
New York City

Dear Harold:—

This revise follows most of the suggestions you sent me in addition to some by Scottie. It is not quite a top story—and there's nothing much I can do about it. The reasons are implicit in the structure which wanders a little. If you really think the <u>Post</u> sounded interested you might give them another shot at it, but the note I received from them did not sound very hopeful. It was from a man I've never met as Adelaide Neall seems to be away.

In any case, please don't offer it to <u>Collier's</u> under any conditions.# It simply couldn't stand any cutting whatsoever and one of the reasons for its faults is that I was continually conscious in the first draft of that <u>Collier'</u> length and left out all sorts of those sideshows that often turn out to be highspots.

Couldn't you try the <u>Cosmopolitan</u> or some of those other magazines you mentioned? It certainly seems to me to be a woman's story and my impression is that Stout* likes women's stories less than Lorimer did.

It is quite probably that I am set for a picture job the beginning of this week.†

Ever yours,
F Scott Fitz—

P.S. Please have any pages that look bad typed over.

5521 Amestoy Ave.
Encino, California

TLS, 1p. (AO)

Scott Fitzgerald, Esq.
5521 Amestoy Avenue
Encino, California

Dear Scott:

I have the revision of **DIRECTOR'S SPECIAL**. One of the editors of the Post was in this morning and I let him take it back to Philadelphia with him, although I don't feel sure that it is changed enough to change their decision. They have just discovered that they need a few stories that will interest women so perhaps this will get there at just the right time.

If The Post doesn't buy the story Collier's is, in my opinion, the best market for it. The story is a very good length for Collier's and I think it should be offered there next. You may remember that when Collier's advanced some of the money that helped you get to Hollywood I agreed they would have a chance at your stories. I think they would be surprised and hurt to see the story in any other magazine than the Post.

#Fitzgerald had attempted to sell "Director's Special" to Kenneth Littauer of *Collier's* in July.

*Wesley Winan Stout, editor of *The Saturday Evening Post*.

†Probably *Open That Door* (based on the novel *Bull by the Horns*) for Universal.

Please give our love to Scottie. We hope she will come to make us a visit before she goes back to college.

Sincerely,
[Harold Ober]

August 15, 1939

TL (cc), 1p. (AO)

> PLEASE WIRE ME COLLECT WHO HAS STORY AND WHEN I MAY EXPECT DECISION REGARDS
> FITZGERALD.

Wire to Ober 15 August 1939. Van Nuys, Calif. (AO)

> STORY AT POST EXPECT DECISION NEXT WEEK
> Harold Ober

Wire (cc) to Fitzgerald 16 August 1939. (AO)

August 16 1939

Mr. Harold Ober
40 East 49th Street
New York City

Dear Harold:—

Thanks for the wire. If the <u>Post</u> still doesn't like it, *would*‡ rather you would show it to any other magazine except <u>Collier's</u>.

It seems to take the[m] *Post* much longer to decide than it used to, doesn't it? Scottie sends her best.

Yours
Scott

5521 Amestoy Avenue
Encino, California

TLS, 1p. (AO)

> DONT OFFER STORY COLLIER. WRITING
> SCOTT.

Wire to Ober 17 August 1939. Van Nuys, Calif. (AO)

F. Scott Fitzgerald, Esq.
5521 Amestoy Ave.
Encino, California

Dear Scott:

The Post declined DIRECTOR'S SPECIAL for the second time.

---

‡Fitzgerald made corrections in ink.

The editors tell me that none of them could make head nor tail out of it. I think the story is clear if anyone takes the trouble to think about it, but I think it is true now more than ever before that readers read for pleasure and would rather read an obvious story than a too subtle one. I am showing this story to other editors and hope to find someone who will like it.

If I sell it to some other magazine, I shall have to explain to Collier's why I did not show it to them. You may have forgotten but just before you went to Hollywood, when you needed money very badly, Collier's gave us some money on the Civil War story although it was not in shape so that they could use it. To induce them to do this, I promised that I would give them, for a reasonable length of time, an equal chance with the Post at your stories. I told you this at the time and I think we have to live up to our agreement. I still think that Collier's would be more likely to buy this story than any other magazine.

I hope the job at Universal has relieved your necessity. Please tell Scottie that we are looking forward to a visit from her.

Sincerely,
[Harold Ober]

August 28, 1939

TL (cc), 1p. (AO)

WHERE IS STORY REGARDS
    SCOTT FITZGERALD.¶

Wire to Ober 28 August 1939. Van Nuys, Calif. (AO)

STORY AT COSMOPOLITAN
    Harold Ober

Wire (cc) to Fitzgerald 29 August 1939. (AO)

YOU MIGHT AS WELL SEND THE STORY BACK HERE STOP MOST OF MY PLANS HAVE GONE COMPLETELY ASTRAY STOP WILL WRITE YOU
    FITZGERALD.

Wire to Ober 11 September 1939. Encino, Calif. (AO)

¶Note in another hand reads: "story in office".

Scott Fitzgerald, Esq.
5521 Amestoy Ave.
Encino
Los Angeles, Cal.

Dear Scott:
  DIRECTOR'S SPECIAL is now at Cosmopolitan. If they decline it, I'll send it back to you.
  I'm glad to know that you have a job with Samuel Goldwyn and I'll be glad to hear from you when you have a chance to write me. #

Sincerely,
[Harold Ober]

September 14, 1939

TL (cc), 1p. (AO)

September 19 1939

Dear Harold:
  The job at Goldwyn's lasted <u>one week</u>. Goldwyn and Wood* had a fight on the set, and Wood said he'd quit if he had to rehearse the characters in new dialogue. Eddie Knopf told Swanson my stuff was grand and that he'll get me back some way.
  Very encouraging. Almost as much fun as the war. I've had two picture offers since I began to walk again last July. Each for one week. The last one paid the income tax and left a cash balance of $38.00. I've never asked Swanie for money <u>unless</u> I was working— he told me in advance that he never lent money to writers. Once I used to write him pieces for <u>College Humor</u> as a favor. You always thought it was rather foolish. I guess you were right.
  And so it goes. I can't possibly pay Scottie's Vassar tuition of $615.00. I'm working today on an Esquire story to get her back here. The situation is all so preposterous that I can't even discuss it any more. <u>Because</u> I made $68,000 last year, <u>because</u> Swanie won't offer me for less than fifteen hundred, I can't keep Scottie in school.

Ever yours,
Scott

5521 Amestoy Avenue
Encino, California

TLS, 1p. (AO)

#Fitzgerald was working on the film *Raffles*.
*Director Sam Wood.

YOU CAN REGISTER AT VASSAR STOP IT COST A HEMORRHAGE
BUT I RAISED SOME MONEY FROM ESQUIRE AND ARRANGED
WITH COMPTROLLER TO PAY OTHER HALF OCTOBER 15TH IF
YOU DONT PLAY STRAIGHT THIS WILL BE ALL STOP FORGIVE
ME IF UNJUSTLY CYNICAL REMEMBER HARMONY MORE PRAC-
TICAL THAN MUSIC HISTORY ALSO OTHER CHANGE STOP RE-
TURN ME FORMER CHECK AIR MAIL LOVE
    DADDY.

Wire to Scottie Fitzgerald 21 September 1939. Encino, Calif.

HAVE OFFER ONE MORNING BROADCAST OF GREAT GATSBY
YOUR SHARE $250 OWEN DAVIS ARRANGING WITH HIS PLAY
ETHAN FROME SHALL I ACCEPT
    HAROLD OBER

Wire (cc) to Fitzgerald 2 October 1939. (AO)

ALL RIGHT WITH ME ABOUT GATSBY. PLEASE AIR MAIL ME
WHEN AND WHAT STATION
    F SCOTT FITZGERALD.

Wire to Ober 2 October 1939. Van Nuys, Calif. (AO)

IF YOU CAN SEND HALF THAT RADIO MONEY TO THE COMP-
TROLLER AT VASSAR IT WOULD HELP STOP SITUATION NOT
IMPROVED HERE
    SCOTT FITZGERALD.

Wire to Ober 2 October 1939. Van Nuys, Calif. (AO)

Scott Fitzgerald, Esq.
5521 Amestoy Avenue
Encino
Los Angeles, Cal.

Dear Scott:

I don't know when the radio money will be along but I'll send
One Hundred and Twenty-five Dollars now to the Comptroller at
Vassar.

Cosmopolitan has returned DIRECTOR'S SPECIAL with the
following letter:

"It's really heart-breaking to return a Scott Fitzgerald story. I
think everybody in our kind of work today really gets a thrill from
seeing that name in print or on a manuscript. I read DIRECTOR'S
SPECIAL with the highest hope and was terribly disappointed that
I could not whole-heartedly recommend it. That opinion seemed to
be general here, I regret to say."

I believe you asked me to return it to you so I am sending it back,
under separate cover. As I told you, the Post thought it still very

difficult to understand even after you had revised it. I still think it would sell much more quickly and for a better price if you would simplify it. And by this I mean to make it a little more obvious. It isn't a story that the average reader can get his teeth into. The very first page is difficult to understand until the reader has read half the story.

The editor of Collier's told me a few days ago that you had sent a story direct to him. I really don't think you are helping yourself by sending stories off direct to editors. Every author I know has difficulty in his writing after working for a time in Hollywood. This is so true that I have heard a great many editors comment on it. Most of them think that working in Hollywood ruins an author. I know that it needn't ruin an author permanently but I think it is important to get a story just right before offering it.

I have written you a couple of letters and then I have torn them up. I think, however, I have explained as well as I can the reason why I cannot go on advancing money. I don't think any agent can do that and stay in business.

Scottie was with us for a day or two before going back to Vassar and we have had a letter or two from her. Everything seems to be going well with her. She says she really felt like getting back to work.

I hope you are feeling better and I'll be glad to hear from you.

Sincerely,
Harold

October 3, 1939

TLS, 2pp. (PU)

Miss Frances Fitzgerald
Vassar College
Poughkeepsie, New York

Dear Scottie:

I am sorry not to have written you sooner about your story, but I have been very busy the last few days. I have read your story and two other readers have read it also and I am sorry to say that none of us is very enthusiastic about it.

I think you ought to do some more work on it before it is ready to offer. There is, for instance, a very confused paragraph on page five.

I think one trouble with the story is that you have told something that really happened. Such an incident rarely makes a good story as the writer is apt to be hampered by what really happened. The background is all right but you need to get some kind of a plot. I am sending the manuscript back to you, under separate cover. If you have any ideas for rewriting it, I'll be glad to see it again.

We were very glad to have your letter and we hope to see you soon.

Sincerely,
[Harold Ober]

October 3, 1939

TL (cc), 1p. (AO)

PLEASE ANSWER ABOUT TUITION MONEY STOP YOU HAVE NO IDEA HOW MUCH A HUNDRED DOLLARS MEANS NOW
      SCOTT FITZGERALD.

Wire to Ober 4 October 1939. Encino, Calif. (AO)

F. Scott Fitzgerald, Esq.
5521 Amestoy Avenue
Encino
Los Angeles, Cal.

Dear Scott:

I have your telegram asking about the tuition money. I am not wiring you because I wrote you yesterday saying that I would send half the amount to Vassar. You'll get the letter before a telegram would reach you. I have sent One Hundred and Twenty-five Dollars to the Comptroller at Vassar. As I told you, I haven't received the money and I may not for another month or two.

Sincerely,
[Harold Ober]

October 4, 1939

TL (cc), 1p. (AO)

October 7 1939

Mr. Harold Ober
40 E. 49th Street
New York City

Dear Harold:—

Thanks for your letter. Thanks for taking care of Scottie. And your saying that you had written me several letters and torn them up did something to clarify what I had begun to interpret as some sadistic desire to punish me. I sent the stories to Collier's for the simple reason that it seemed difficult to deal with someone who treats you with dead silence. Against silence you can do nothing but fret and wonder. Your disinclination to back me is, of course, your own business, but representing me without communication (such as returning a story to me without even an airmail stamp) is pretty close to saying you were through with me.

I communicated directly with Collier's and wrote a series of pieces for <u>Esquire</u> because we have to live and eat and nothing can interfere with that. Can't you regard this trouble as a question of a man who has had a bad break and leave out the moral problem as to whether or not, or how much it is his own fault? And if you think I can't write, read these stories. They brought just two hundred and fifty apiece from Esquire, because I couldn't wait to hear from you, because I had bank balances of five, ten and fifteen dollars.

Anyhow I have "lived dangerously" and I may quite possibly have to pay for it, but there are plenty of other people to tell me that and it doesn't seem as if it should be you.

I don't think there is any chance of fixing up that other story. It just isn't good.

Sincerely,
Scott

P.S.   Could you mail me back these stories? I have no copies. Don't you agree that they are worth more than $250.? One of them was offered to <u>Collier's</u> in desperation—the first Pat Hobby story but Littauer wired that it "wasn't a story".‡ Who's right?

5521 Amestoy Avenue
Encino, California

TLS, 1p. (AO)

F. Scott Fitzgerald, Esq.
5521 Amestoy Avenue
Encino
Los Angeles, California

Dear Scott:

I have just had a note from K. S. White§ of the New Yorker, wanting to know if there's a chance you would have something for

---

‡Probably "A Man in the Way," *Esquire*, February 1940.
§Mrs. E. B. White, formerly Katherine Angell.

them, either prose or verse. She says they would welcome anything
from you.

Sincerely yours,
[Harold Ober]

October 9, 1939

TL (cc), 1p. (AO)

October 11 1939

Mr. Harold Ober
40 East 49th Street
New York City

Dear Harold:

In reply to your letter of the 9th, what does the New Yorker pay
for prose pieces?

Sincerely yours,
Scott Fitzgerald

5521 Amestoy Ave.
Encino, California

TLS, 1p. (AO)

F. Scott Fitzgerald, Esq.
5521 Amestoy Avenue
Encino
Los Angeles, California

Dear Scott:

I am returning the five sketches you sent me. The one entitled
BETWEEN PLANES¶ seemed to me the most interesting. I'm not
surprised that Collier's didn't like the one you sent there. I don't
think the general public is very much interested in the work in
studios; at any rate, editors do not seem to think so.

The New Yorker's top price for fiction is fifteen cents a word for
the first 1200 words and eight cents a word thereafter. The things
they use in the back of the book bring somewhat less. You may
remember that they paid $50 for a piece you wrote called A BOOK

¶Published as "Three Hours Between Planes," *Esquire*, July 1941.

OF MY OWN and $30 for LINES FOR AN URN and $25 for
LAMP IN A WINDOW.

Sincerely,
Harold

October 17, 1939

TLS, 1p. (PU)

*Nearly all the Fitzgerald/Ober correspondence for 1940 is missing, but it
probably was not extensive. After their break in July–August 1939, Fitzgerald acted as his own agent in negotiating for a serial sale of* The Last
Tycoon. *The history of this novel can be pieced together from other correspondence.*

By October 1939 Fitzgerald had an outline and notes for The Last
Tycoon *and began the actual writing. Kenneth Littauer, editor of* Col-
lier's, *to whom Fitzgerald was trying to sell short stories, expressed interest
in the serial rights. Fitzgerald tried to use Maxwell Perkins as his unofficial
agent in negotiations with Littauer, and wired Perkins on 11 October 1939:*
PLEASE LUNCH IF YOU CAN WITH KENNETH LITTAUR OF
COLLIERS IN RELATION TO SERIAL OF WHICH HE HAS THE
OUTLINE. OBER TO BE ABSOLUTELY EXCLUDED FROM PRES-
ENT STATE OF NEGOTIATIONS. . . . On the 16th Perkins wrote a memo
to Charles Scribner stating that Collier's would be willing to pay up to
$30,000 for the serial if they accepted it on the basis of a 15,000-word
sample. Perkins expressed concern that Fitzgerald would want Scribners to
support him while he was writing the sample. On 20 October Fitzgerald
wrote to Perkins stating that* Collier's *was really prepared to pay only
$15,000, but that he couldn't live on that for four months. And on the same
day he wrote to Littauer:*

"Dear Kenneth:—

*"I was disappointed in our conversation the other day—I am no good on
long distance and should have had notes in my hand.*

*"I want to make plain how my proposition differs from yours. First there
is the question of the* total *payment; second, the* terms *of payment, which
would enable me to finish it in these straightened circumstances.*

*"In any case I shall probably attack the novel. I have about decided to
make a last liquidation of assets, put my wife in a public place, and my
daughter to work and concentrate on it—simply take a furnished room and
live on canned goods.*

*"But writing it under such conditions I should want to market it with
the chance of getting a higher price for it.*

*"It was to avoid doing all this, that I took you up on the idea of writing
it on installments. I too had figured on the same price per installment you*

had paid for a story, but I had no idea that you would want to pack more into an installment than your five thousand word maximum for a story. So the fifty thousand words at $2500. for each 5000 word installment would have come to $25,000. In addition, I had figured that a consecutive story is easier *rather than harder to write than the same number of words divided into short stories because the characters and settings are determined in advance, so my idea had been to ask you $20,000. for the whole job. But $15,000.—that would be much too marginal. It would be better to write the whole thing in poverty and freedom of movement with the finished product. Fifteen thousand would leave me more in debt than I am now.*

"On the question of the terms of payment, my proposition was to include the exact amount which you offer in your letter only I had divided it, so that the money would come in batches of $3000. every four weeks, or something like that.

"When we had our first phone conversation the fact that I did not have enough to start on, further complicated the matter; I have hoped that perhaps that's where Scribner's would come in. A telegram from Max told me he was going to see you again but I've heard nothing further.

"I hope that this will at least clear up any ambiguity. If the proposition is all off, I am very sorry. I regret now that I did not go on with the novel last April when I had some money, instead of floundering around with a lot of disassociated ideas that were half-heartedly attempted and did not really come to anything. I know you are really interested, and thank you for the trouble you have taken.

Ever Yours Gratefully

"P.S.   Whether the matter is dead or just dangling I still don't want Ober to have anything to do with the negotiation. For five years I feel he has been going around thinking of me as a lost soul, and conveying that impression to others. It makes me gloomy when I see his name on an envelope." (Scribners Archives, PU)

In November 1939 Fitzgerald submitted a 6,000-word opening of The Last Tycoon *to Littauer, who replied that it was not enough to base a decision on. Fitzgerald's reaction was to wire Perkins on 28 November to send the material to* The Saturday Evening Post: *I GUESS THERE ARE NO GREAT MAGAZINES EDITORS LEFT. The next day Perkins attempted to encourage Fitzgerald by offering a personal loan of $1,000. Apparently the* Post *expressed no interest, for on 29 November Fitzgerald wired Perkins to show the* Tycoon *material to Leland Hayward in the hope of setting up a deal for a studio to finance the writing of a picture based on the novel. Perkins tried, but Hayward did not take the bait.*

After this Fitzgerald made no further attempt to sell the serial rights, although at the time of his death he had completed five and a half chapters. The reason for Fitzgerald's loss of interest in the serial deal may be that the novel had grown as he wrote it so that he no longer regarded it as suitable for serialization in Collier's—*or perhaps he was waiting to find out what it would turn into. His original plan had called for a nine-chapter novel of 51,000 words, but the five and a half chapters he wrote totaled some 45,000 words. On 13 December 1940—seven days before his death—Fitzgerald wrote Perkins that he expected to finish the first draft "some time after the 15th of January."*

Fitzgerald supported himself in 1940 with the Pat Hobby stories and three movie jobs. He wrote "Cosmopolitan" (based on "Babylon Revisited") for Lester Cowan during April-June. He had two short assignments at 20th-Century Fox in August and September—"Brooklyn Bridge" (not made) and a script based on Emlyn Williams's play The Light of Heart *(produced as* Life Begins at Eight-thirty *in 1942 from Nunnally Johnson's script).*

Dear Harold:

As you see the Nazis are making an attempt to buy me up. Perhaps my future lies in pegged Kronen.

Scott

Pencil note at bottom of letter from King Features Syndicate (15 July 1940) asking about Scandinavian rights to "The End of Hate." (AO)

F. Scott Fitzgerald, Esq.*

Dear Scott:

I have sold a broadcast right on your story THE DANCE to the agency handling the Philip Morris program, for $100.

Sincerely yours,
[Harold Ober]

August 22, 1940

TL, 1p. (AO)

In November 1940 Fitzgerald had his first heart attack. He was working on The Last Tycoon. *On 20 December 1940 he suffered a second heart attack. He died suddenly the next day. He was buried on 27 December in Rockville, Maryland.*

---

*Pencil note in top margin, not in Ober's hand, reads: "HO took letter to Scarsdale to get address from Scottie."

Memo made by Harold Ober on being phoned of Scott's death #
by Sheila Graham

Hollywood 7730 until   2–05 in the morning
Santa Monica 53919   after 20 minutes before 3
after 10 (California time tomorrow)   for a short time
Secretary Frances Kroll Crestview 13704
                          Los Angeles

(Executors John Biggs + Max Perkins)
Scott Now at Pierce Bros Mortuary
              720 West Washington Boulevard
                          Los Angeles
There is $700 (about) that can be used
Monday the Secretary will know about Insurance
She has will and papers and rough draft of 2/3 of novel. Sheila G.
says Scott intended to rewrite the first part entirely—he wouldn't
want it seen as it is—

The will directs that [his] *the* funeral shall be at [the] lowest possible
expense. S. doesn't think he would like to be buried in California
because he really hated California. She thinks he would like to be
buried where his father is buried because he admired him.

Sheila G. wants to know whether [you are] *Scottie is* coming out—
doesn't think [you] *she* ought to come alone. She would come back
with [you] *her* if [you] *she* wants her to.

Sheila says the only relative Scott liked was Cousin Ceci. He liked
Zeldas mother [five words omitted by editors]†

Scott was talking about [you] *Scottie* a lot this afternoon. He had
never been so happy about [you] *her* as he was today He spoke of
how well [you were] *she was* doing at Vassar and said the one thing
he wanted [you] *her* to do was finish Vassar—

Two or three days ago Scott didnt feel very well and the doctor had
him in bed—but for the last few days he had been feeling well and
happy. Dr had told him not to do too much up and down stairs.
Sheila was with him this afternoon. *He had a kind of heart attack a*

Added in Anne Ober's hand in ink.
†These five words have also been opaqued out of the illustration.

month or two ago He was in very good spirits because he had been pleased with the writing he had done recently. He was talking about Scottie, got up from his chair and dropped dead. Sheila said she was sure he had no pain and that he didnt know there was anything the matter.

Sheila said the ms of the novel was all first draft and some of it was in a confused state—but some of it was beautifully done—some of the best writing he had ever done

Memo (pencil) 3pp. 21 December 1940.

Dear Harold:

Again, I am so deeply indebted to you, and so grateful for the kindness, and effort, that you have accorded to Scott and Scottie and myself. We have always wanted to be able to repay your courtesies which have meant so much to us; and somehow never could, and now we never can.

Though I dont know the story of the rupture between you and Scott I know that he was so used to being devoted to you that he couldn't really think of you in any other terms; and I know as grateful a heart as his never forgot the happiness *that you* have given Scottie and the sense of warmth and security that you have contributed to her life by your hospitality—both spiritual, and material.

I am heart-broken over Scott: he loved people and had deadicated so much of his life to the moral sustenance of many that I am sure that he must have left many friends. Many nights, he has worked on somebody elses manuscript, transposing a paragraph or giving a bit of advice *when he was too sick to take care of his own* He was as spiritually generous a soul as ever was; and gave as freely of his soul as he did of whatever hospitality a hard life left him to dispose

In retrospect it seems as if he was always planning happinesses for Scottie, and for me. Books to read—places to go. Life seemed so promisory always when he was around: and I always believed that he could take care of anything.

It seems so useless and purposeless that I wont be able to tell him about all this. Although we were not close any more, Scott was the best friend a person could have to me—

Maybe sometime you will be coming south. We would love to see you: or maybe something will someday take me to New York. In any case, my gratitude is always with you; as are my sincerest good wishes and my kindliest remembrances.

If I may, I will write some time—I would be sad to lose completely all contact with the world that we were once-upon-a-time so happy in.

Devotedly
Zelda

care Mrs A D. Sayre
322 Sayre St
Montgomery Ala

ALS, 4pp. n.d.—Anne Ober has dated this letter 24 December 1940. (AO)

Fitzgerald did the best job of indicating what Ober meant to him when he wrote Perkins on 19 December 1939: "When Harold withdrew from the questionable honor of being my banker, I felt completely numb financially and I suddenly wondered what money was and where it came from. There had always seemed a little more somewhere and now there wasn't."

Index